Contents

	Page
Preface and acknowledgement	iii
PART I INTRODUCTION	1
Aims and methods	3
Historical perspective	13
PART II PARKVIEW ESTATE	31
Parkview: Buildings and people	34
Old Borough residents and 'outsiders'	39
Resident perceptions of Parkview	41
Social interaction on Parkview	53
Kinship	53
Neighbours	55
Friends and workmates	67
The neighbourhood	69
Shopping	69
School	71
Work	76
Leisure	78
Residents and 'the council'	86
Parkview organisations and institutions	89
Parkview TA	89
Parkview Youth group	92
Eshag	95
Mothers' coffee mornings	100
Social Services facilities: Church Close Luncheon club and chiropody clinic	103
Parkview library	104
Ash Road nursery	104

Parkview sheltered housing unit   105

Summary   107
The process of urban renewal; from street turning to flatted estate   107

PART III 'THE COUNCIL'   119

Officers   121

The housing directorate; policies and organisation   122
Housing management; personnel, procedures and practice   127
Officers and Parkview residents   138
Housing management and other sections   139

Councillors   142

The elected member structure   142
Councillors and officers   144
The processes of decision making   147
Councillors and constituents   150

Summary   152
Conservatism and change   152

PART IV   LOCAL POLITICAL FORUMS   159

Introduction   161

Parkview TA   163

The formal charter   163
Committee politics   164
Committee work   172
Parkview TA and outside agencies   176
Parkview TA, an analysis   179

Parkview and the council: four case studies   184

Case i   The Steel's radio aerial   184
Case ii   Picket fencing and potatoes   186
Case iii Factions and feuds   189
Case iv   The policy making process; a community centre for the estate   191
Parkview and the council; an overview   195

Tenant participation in the Borough   200

Official policy and practice   200
The North Area Housing Board   204

The election process   205
Committee work   209

vi

Department of the Environment
Social Research Division
Housing Development Directorate

TENANTS AND TOWN HALL

C Lesley Andrews

London: Her Majesty's Stationery Office

© *Crown copyright 1979*
First published 1979

HER MAJESTY'S STATIONERY OFFICE

Government Bookshops

49 High Holborn, London WC1V 6HB
13a Castle Street, Edinburgh EH2 3AR
41 The Hayes, Cardiff CF1 1JW
Brazennose Street, Manchester M60 8AS
Southey House, Wine Street, Bristol BS1 2BQ
258 Broad Street Birmingham B1 2HE
80 Chichester Street, Belfast BT1 4JY

Government Publications are also available
through booksellers

ISBN 0 11 751383 0

Preface

About a third of the population of Great Britain now live in council housing. Many, particularly in the inner city areas, live in large, high-density estates. The original inhabitants of these estates were rehoused there from streets that were unfit or regarded as outmoded and were cleared away. These new estates were built with the idealism and high hopes that characterised the post-war decades. Their designers and the local authorities who commissioned them had visions of creating new, happy and healthy communities. There are many reasons why this optimism has turned sour over the last 10 or 15 years. Some of the housing built turned out to be quite unsuited to the needs of those living there. Money to match the designers' hopes with the level and style of management required was seldom available. Ancillary facilities sometimes never materialised, or if they did, proved less beneficial than expected.

This study is about a fairly typical estate of the post-war period in Inner London. It describes the lives of the people residing there. More importantly, the study attempts to throw light on the impact on tenants of the local authority's rôle as landlord and on the potential of new management strategies. There is no simple remedy to the problems outlined by the study. However, there are many Parkviews over the country, and ways should be tried to make them more congenial places in which to live.

The period of field work, 1974–5, coincided with a difficult time for the Borough's housing directorate. Borough offices were being restructured as part of the process of local government reorganisation, a new director of housing had just been appointed and severe economic cuts were being imposed by central government. The directorate continued to add to the housing stock but proposals to expand staff levels accordingly had to be substantially modified. The report needs to be assessed with this background in mind.

Parkview is not the real name of the estate and the setting is an anonymous Inner London Borough. The names of tenants, councillors and officers have all been changed. To help the reader, officers are distinguished by the use of colours for their names, eg Black, Brown, etc. In most cases residents chose their own fictitious names. Where the present tense is used in the text it refers only to the field work period.

In the inevitable time lag between completion of research and publication of findings, changes have occurred. Some in the Borough housing directorate may be related to the findings of the study. Nevertheless, it is clear from later research carried out within DOE that the basic issues raised by Parkview have still to be confronted and resolved.

Throughout the study I have drawn on the support of many people. First and foremost I depended on the residents of Parkview. Thanks to their ready acceptance my job was carried out among good personal friends and, very rarely, foes. I am especially indebted to residents on 'my balcony' and to members of the tenants' association committee. Thanks are due also to my research assistants, Wendy Healey and Don Entwhistle, officers and councillors of the Borough, and staff at the Social Research and other Divisions of DOE's Housing Development Directorate. Marie L'Estrange gave much time and effort to provide most of the photographic illustrations, figures and plans. Martin Funnell took the photographs for the survey ranking exercise and the historical photographs were provided by the local history section of the Borough library. Finally, I am indebted to many friends and colleagues for their help and encouragement in the field and in writing the manuscript for this book.

C. LESLEY ANDREWS
January 1979

Acknowledgement
The study reported here was mounted by the Housing Development Directorate in the Department of the Environment. The author was a Research Officer in the Directorate's Social Research Division. The Department's thanks are due to the anonymous Borough officers, staff and residents who allowed the author to live on the Parkview Estate for over a year and who gave a great deal of time and encouragement to the study, notwithstanding its sometimes critical stance. The views expressed in this report are those of the author and not necessarily those of the Department.

The participants' viewpoint   211

   i Tenants' representatives   211
   ii Councillors   213
   iii Officers   217
   iv Parkview residents   220

Parkview and the council; fragmented linkages   225

PART V   POSTSCRIPT   235

Parkview politics; August 1975 to December 1976   236

Parkview community hall   243

Commentary   254

Changes in housing management   256

PART VI   OPEN DOORS   261

People, place and policy   264

Policy considerations   271

Housing management functions   271
The organisation of housing management   272
Housing management roles   274
Staff training   275
Staffing requirements   275
Housing management and estate residents   276
Estate provision   276

APPENDICES   279

I   Selection and characteristics of Parkview sample households   281

II   Interview schedules   283

   1 Interviews with sample households   283
   2 Interviews with officers   286
   3 Interviews with councillors   287
   4 Interviews with resident representatives, AHB   288
   5 Interviews with committee members, TA   288
   6 Community hall—users survey   288
   7 Community hall—sample residents survey   291

III   Estate statistics   294

   AI Households with children by floor level   294
   AII Households with elderly persons by floor level   294

AIII Children and elderly persons per unit 295

AIV Households with no children under 13 295

AV Households with all adult residents 296

AVI Black or mixed marriage households by block type 296

AVII Black population by block type 297

AVIII Residence of black households prior to rehousing 297

AIX Applications for transfer by block 297

AX Length of residence in the Old Borough 298

AXI Place of residence prior to rehousing 298

AXII Length of residence on Parkview 298

AXIII Reasons for rehousing 298

AXIV Time lag between date of application and rehousing
by length of residence on the estate 299

AXV Time lag between date of application and rehousing
by reasons for rehousing 300

AXVI One parent families by block type 300

AXVII Non nuclear family households by block type 300

AXVIII Reasons for rehousing of households with preschool
children at or above the third floor 301

AXVIV Block by household size 302

IV   Conditions of tenancy for council dwellings in the Borough 303

V   Official letters to residents 307

VI   The work of the North Board 310

BIBLIOGRAPHY 319

INDEX 333

List of Illustrations

PLANS	Page
I Terrace street layout	15
II Terrace house layout	16
III Parkview estate layout	19
IV Y block maisonette layout	22
V Layout of fifth floor balcony, blue block	61
VI Proposed tower block development	97
VII Parkview community hall	244

FIGURES

I Parkview estate, isometric drawing | 21
II Respondents feelings to estate before and after residence | 43
III Ranking of blocks according to attractiveness | 47
IV Borough Housing Department prior to reorganisation | 124
V Borough Directorate of Housing: Proposed structure | 124
VI Borough Directorate of Housing: Estates management, development and administration sections, revised structure | 125
VII Borough Directorate of Housing: organisation of the Parkview management team | 128
VIII Number of potential participators by social categories expressed as a percentage of the total Parkview population | 221
IX Potential participators as a percentage of each social category | 222

TABLES

I Dwelling size by block type | 34
II Population breakdowns; Parkview, the Borough and the GLC area | 36
III Issues considered by the Parkview TA, 31 July 1974 to 31 July 1975 | 173
IV Issues considered by the Parkview TA according to committee leadership | 174
V Attendance at the North Area Housing Board during the research period | 210
VI Councillors attitudes to Area Housing Boards | 216
VII Officers attitudes to Area Housing Boards | 218
VIII Parkview community hall; programme of activities September 1976 | 245
IX Respondents reasons for not using the community hall | 251

ix

PLATES

after page 118

1 A community in locational terms . . .
2 Market Street at the turn of the century
3 Construction of the Y blocks
4, 5 '. . . small touches of a personalised exterior . . .'
6 The surrounding neighbourhood has a human scale
7 'Down the streets . . . everyone knew everyone else'
8 A play area that is little used
9 'The pram sheds . . . have become dumping grounds for unwanted rubbish'
10 Chestnut Road
11 Garden flats
12 Y blocks
13 Tower
14 Church Close
15 Sheltered housing
16 Ash Court
17 Looking towards A wing from the project flat
18 A personalised shopping situation
19 The view is much appreciated
20 For older residents the library serves as a kind of social centre
21, 22 The car deck playground
23, 24 The landscaped play area shares a border with the nursery
25 A hill overlooking the kickabout area
26 Supervised playgrounds at the park
27 Residents adjacent to the play area want it fenced and supervised
28 'Hanging around with mates'
29, 30 '. . . some equipment was quickly wrecked'
31 'putting the old community spirit back into the place'
32, 33 'the unattractiveness of the lobby'
34, 35 'from street turning to flatted estate'
36, 37 'a planned community'
38 'the library presents a solid brick facade to the estate'
39 Rubbish around one of the underground car parks
40 Mrs Glen showing the fungus growth in her garden flat
41 Mrs Montgomery and Mrs Field (left) talk with a councillor during the North Board tour
42 Fencing and potatoes. The garden in the foreground is the one which later sprouted an aerial
43 Parkview community hall
44 Parkview playgroup
45 The luncheon club in new premises
46 Luncheon club staff in the kitchen

Part 1

Introduction

Aims and methods

This study is part of a continuing research programme undertaken within the DOE by the Social Research Division. The programme is designed to assess the social implications of current and proposed government policies in public and private sector housing. Previous research experience and a heightened level of public debate on the subject suggested that more attention should be given to enhancing the quality of the environment provided by local authority high-density housing estates. It appeared that two factors which might be particularly significant in influencing the residents perception of estate living were the management service provided by the local authority and the leisure facilities available within the immediate locality. Accordingly, the brief for this project, as originally stated, comprised two main subjects, the first, to investigate the means of improving relations between the local authority and tenants, and the second, to report on the range of community services needed on or nearby council housing estates. The former aspect of the study was to include an assessment of the scope for involving tenants in the management of their housing estate, the latter a consideration of whether older children and teenagers have any special leisure time needs. Underlying the one was an official concern with the apparent problems facing local authority housing management services generally; underlying the other was a similar concern with the problem of vandalism. These two subjects were linked in a single brief because, on the one hand both imply that an estate and 'the community' are co-terminous, and on the other, community facilities such as a hall are frequently regarded as suitable for some form of tenant management. In the course of the study most attention came to be focused on gaining an understanding of the nature of the relationships between residents, council officers, elected members and the council organisation. No attention was given to vandalism as such since it was believed that behaviour which might be labelled deviant should be considered in a wider social context.

It was decided that the terms of the brief might best be met by an intensive study of one housing estate in the context of the surrounding neighbourhood and in relationship to the local authority departments concerned with the welfare of the estate and its residents. It was suggested that a case study of this type might provide a point of reference against which other housing schemes could be compared and understood. In addition, there was a recognition of the need to challenge the assumption that an estate constitutes something of a community of interest as well as a community defined simply by location.[1]

Expressions of community, other than that of geography, can be most readily discerned by a study of the nature and extent of the social relations between residents there. The complexity of these social networks and groups imposes fairly narrow limits on the size of the social field which can be studied. Another consideration was a concern to evaluate the brief mainly from the point of view of estate residents rather than the perspective of official policy makers and implementers. Finally, my own background in social anthropology meant that the Division felt able to consider a departure from the methods hitherto employed in policy-related research work.

After a preliminary survey of a range of estates in the London area, Parkview was chosen as the estate for study on a number of counts. Parkview was developed in four stages from the mid 1950s through to 1974. This meant that building type reflected changes in fashions in architecture in that time. It also meant that large numbers of residents moving in together as stages were completed have since experienced living on the estate for varying lengths of time. Other studies have suggested that building form and length of residence might be important variables in considering attitudes towards the estate.[2] Physically Parkview is clearly demarcated from the surrounding area and in locational terms at least might be said to comprise a community. (Plate 1) With 830 units spread over 19.5 acres it was considered at once a manageable size for the study and large enough to give findings useful in terms of the brief. Parkview has an average reputation; it is not considered a showpiece nor is it viewed as a 'problem' estate. This too was felt to be important if the findings were to be related to a broader context. Parkview already had some community facilities and a playground and community hall were scheduled to open in the course of the study.[3] Finally and most importantly, the local authority was prepared to host the study and co-operate in the research programme.

Work on the project commenced in May 1974 when two assistants[4] and I worked through records held at the directorate of housing, transferring to edge punch cards data on the household composition and previous housing history of each household resident on Parkview. This was my first experience of working in local authority offices and through our work there I began to build up contacts with the housing management team responsible for Parkview estate. The work also provided some useful insights into the family circumstances and general background of estate residents as well as into the administrative system in which the management team functioned.

On 24 June 1974 I took up residence in a one bedroomed maisonette in the blue block, one of three 11-storey Y-shaped blocks overlooking the park. The choice of flat was somewhat fortuitous since the availability of flats at the time was limited. Nevertheless, in retrospect the situation was ideal, close proximity to the main entrance afforded a view both of that and a large part of the estate beyond, while residence in the established part of the estate prevented an identification with residents in the new extensions and meant that I was able to

4

maintain my neutrality in the 'old' versus 'new' conflict which subsequently assumed an importance in estate politics.

The manner of approval of the project was not, however, so fortunate. The decision to host the project and allow my residence in a flat for the duration of field work was approved jointly by the director of housing and the chairman of the housing services committee. This procedure minimised delays but since the decision was quickly the subject of a Borough press release, the story was taken up by the local and to a lesser extent metropolitan press and radio so that the first that other elected members, officers and residents knew of the study was through the media. Not unnaturally this aroused some antagonism which might have been avoided had the initial approaches been handled differently and it was fortunate that on the estate any adverse reactions were shortlived.[5] It was intended that the field work period should extend over one year but in the event an extension of one month was sought and granted and field work ended on 31 July 1975 when I left the estate.

During this period field work progressed through a number of phases in the course of which various research methods were adopted. Lists of names and addresses had been compiled from files and during the first two months I attempted to contact a member of each household to introduce myself and explain the nature of the study. The explanation was given in terms of 'What sort of community facilities and services are needed on or nearby Parkview?' and 'How can we improve relations between Parkview residents and the council?', the latter especially evoked generally a ready response in complaints about delays over repairs, the poor state of the lifts, stairways and rubbish chutes, the alleged inefficiency of the resident caretakers, the general decline in the 'tone' of the estate, the influx of 'outsiders', the kids, the dogs or the neighbours, in short, whatever was of uppermost concern to individual residents. Often these introductory visits became social occasions; I was invited into many homes and began to build up important relationships. It was a time-consuming process; up to three visits were made in an effort to make contact and at that point a letter outlining the project was left. By the end of August this phase was virtually completed. At that time many residents were still unclear about the exact nature of the research but most were aware of the fact that Parkview was the focus for some kind of study. From the research point of view those first two months proved most worthwhile; personal contacts which had been made could be followed up informally at the market and shops, in the laundry or one of the local pubs and gradually I was able to form an impression of the residents' experience of the estate. This influenced considerably the kind of questionnaire later developed for use there.

From the outset I also had links with the committee of the Parkview Tenants' Association (TA) whose members approved my attendance at meetings in the rôle of researcher. Thereafter I attended all committee meetings and had a good deal of informal follow-up contact with individual committee members. In addition I was granted permission to attend meetings of the North Board since

Parkview was one of its constituent estates. This board is one of four area housing boards established by the local authority to facilitate the exchange of tenant, member and officer views on housing management issues. Subsequently this permission was withdrawn and in the latter part of the study I was able to attend only those meetings called for board elections and hence open to all residents.[6]

At the end of this phase, two research assistants were appointed to the project. A youth and community worker, Don Entwistle, was recruited specifically to work with young people on the estate and to make a study of their leisure time activities and needs. Don had previous experience in detached youth work in association with tenant-directed youth projects. His was an action research perspective; he responded to initiatives from a number of youngsters on the estate and actively assisted in the establishment of a youth group there. In addition, as a community worker he supported a group of residents in one of the two Parkview tower blocks. The initiative in this instance came from the project team in response to widespread complaints from residents in the tower blocks about the public areas of these buildings. Both of these group developments are documented in this report.[7] The second appointment, that of Wendy Healey, was made through the Institute of Education at the University of London. Her work was supervised by Professor Dennis Lawton of the Institute and was carried out in part fulfilment of the requirements for a Masters degree in Education. It was intended that Wendy would trace the link between the school and the home and so understand something of the nature of the influence of the school on the child. It was also intended that she should carry out research into the child's perception of the environment including such aspects as attitudes towards authority and notions of deviance. This programme was altered mainly in view of the wide variety and number of schools serving the estate and the consequent difficulty of evaluating the school careers of any large number of estate children. The study therefore concentrated on the three schools taking the largest number of students from the estate, Park primary school, and a boys' and girls' secondary school. In looking at these schools attention was given to the attitudes of parents, pupils and teachers and a special study was made of the place of community education in the curriculum. These findings were written up in a thesis[8] and some have been incorporated in the present study.[9]

During the initial phase and later, contacts were made by all members of the research team with officers in the area social services team, probation workers, the police, the education authority and local school staff, plus youth and community project leaders. Relationships were built up with senior housing officers and those more junior staff concerned with the day to day management of Parkview. Contacts were also made with some elected members and when other commitments allowed council committee meetings were attended. In all of these contacts our concern was to gain an insight into the outsiders view of the estate and its residents, never to obtain information on particular households.

In October a second circular was sent to all households. This again outlined the purpose of the study, introduced the work of Don and Wendy and explained to residents that a sample of 100 households was being selected for detailed interview sessions. The sample of households for interview comprised a random selection within stratified groups selected on the basis of household size, block type, length of residence and race from the 673 households for which information was then available on edge punch cards. The proportions were correct in regard to each of the four variables and within each block type the sample was fairly representative of the proportions of households by each of the other three variables. It was not possible to produce a sample which might be considered representative within a more detailed cross classification, nor was this considered necessary.[10] The interview schedule administered to sample households covered in some detail the characteristics of members of the household; the previous housing history of the household; the respondent's initial reaction to the estate and subsequent attitudes towards aspects of living there; the use made of facilities in the area; patterns of contact with kin, friends and neighbours; membership of various organizations; experience of council officers and elected members and desired changes especially in regard to estate management and the provision of community facilities.[11] A schedule was completed in the course of one or more interview sessions, each made by appointment and lasting generally two or three hours.[12] In some cases there was more than one respondent, general discussion outside the range of questions was encouraged and many sessions became social occasions over endless cups of tea (or something stronger) and freshly baked scones or cakes. Sometimes it was possible only to make rough notes at the time and the schedule was then filled in later. After the fieldwork period a coding frame was devised, the schedules were coded and a series of tables compiled by computer.[13] The information obtained is the basis for much of the discussion in Part II.

These semi-structured interviews were a necessary supplement to participant observation methods since it was soon evident that a form of social organization defined in terms of the estate was lacking. Moreover, these interviews validated my presence in a cross-section of Parkview households, and in the course of the interview and often afterwards during informal encounters, much useful information was obtained. However, a number of reservations about the quality of the findings should be noted. In relatively few cases did I know the respondent well enough to evaluate answers in the light of personal circumstances. In more traditional field work situations, relationships with respondents are much more likely to be ongoing ones, answers can be interpreted according to a wider contextual knowledge of the individual and inconsistencies or misconceptions can more readily be picked up and rectified.[14] At Parkview this was seldom possible. Further, a schedule involves the completion of a standard range of questions and gives equal weighting to answers from all respondents when in particular instances sections of the schedule may be virtually irrelevant. This objection is an obvious one and was partly counter-balanced in the present study by the taking of notes from interviews and incorporating them into field notes. Some of the issues put to residents were complex, especially those concerning possible changes in estate management. Inevitably, where there was an expression of real interest such sessions tended to become discussions and I found myself in the role of informant; this in itself undoubtedly affects the response. Finally, the interviews were very time-consuming. I do not know what approach would give better results; it may be that a situation like Parkview requires a longer field work period to obtain a more detailed knowledge of a greater number and range of households and so allow a more informed evaluation of responses to semi-formal questioning.

During some of these interviews I became aware of the existence of a number of problems faced by certain categories of residents. One of the most striking was the feeling of inadequacy and loneliness faced by some women at home. A small group of these women were encouraged to meet more or less regularly and informally at my flat and, from the discussions which took place, both they and myself learned a good deal about the nature of their shared experience. The work with this group is documented in this report.[15] I had hoped to set up other similar discussion groups but the time involved in doing so made this impossible.

Initially I had also hoped to collect some detailed information on the daily activity and visiting patterns of a range of respondents. In this way it would be possible to record in the form of a network analysis the patterns of social interaction between residents on Parkview and beyond. This was not followed up because the one section of the schedule which respondents seemed to be reticent about answering was that concerning the visiting of friends, relatives and neighbours. It may be that this was construed as an unnecessary intrusion or it may be that an admission of lack of family support and friends is regarded as symptomatic of social failure.[16]

Finally, throughout the field work period I attempted to sustain as many informal links with as many households as possible. Some followed the first introductions, others interviews and some developed from casual meetings. In this way I was able to visit informally many residents and was invited to parties, including a christening and confirmation party, 'family get-togethers,' Sunday lunch and tea, TA dances and other functions. These day-to-day activities and special occasions form the basis for my field notes and provide much of the stuff of the project report.

At the end of field work a letter was posted to every household thanking residents for their help and inviting a response from anyone who had not contributed to the study and yet would like to. At this point Don and Wendy left for other jobs. I spent most of the following three months interviewing all of those local authority officers whose jobs brought them into contact with Parkview residents. In addition, all members of the housing services and review committees and the North Board were approached for interview.

During the field work period and subsequently, various written reports have been prepared. The first of these was an interim report dated December 1974 for circulation within DOE and to a limited degree, the local authority. This outlined the proposed research and commented on findings to that date. In January 1976 a discussion paper was sent to all officers and councillors who had in some way assisted with the project and a specially prepared pamphlet was sent to every household on Parkview.[17] In the more recent reports provision was made for feedback. Informally, that from the estate was very positive. Three acknowledgements were received from officers, two from the area housing manager and the now-retired architect responsible for Parkview, incorporating criticism and comment. There was no response from individual councillors although I appeared before a review committee which considered my own and two other related reports.[18]

Some of the methodological issues encountered in the course of the research have been touched on already. Three others warrant further comment. First some account should be taken of the nature of the sponsorship of the research. Inevitably government sponsorship shaped both my rôle and the response of residents to me.[19] Undoubtedly there was some suspicion especially among those who encountered me only in the rôle of researcher. However, even then the rôle of 'official researcher' appeared to be modified by several factors. My continued presence on the estate meant that I was regarded as different from other officials who visited from outside. Indeed by some residents I came to be categorized as one of 'us' against 'them.' Thus, soon after my arrival one of my neighbours hastened to inform me that a newspaper reporter was 'snooping' about me; members of the TA faction with which I became identified assumed that my work would assist them in what they perceived as a running battle with the council bureaucracy and other residents approached me with stories about officialdom – 'here's another one for your book.' In addition my personal circumstances, a New Zealander with a classless accent, helped to ensure what was on the whole a very generous acceptance.[20]

A second and related issue is that of the rôle adopted by the researcher. Involvement in the field situation is necessary to gain acceptance and it is impossible to be a participant in a group without influencing it. The degree to which this involvement and influence can be controlled by the researcher varies considerably according to local circumstances and individual personalities. The researcher's rôle is in part self-defined, in part defined by others. It demands nurturing many relationships in a variety of contexts and taking part as neighbour, friend, mediator, interviewer and so on. At the same time participation may result in a confusion of rôles and a possible sense of betrayal if information given to the worker as friend is used as research material for a report. Many residents were aware of the ambiguities in my status and were curious about the 'techniques' I employed. 'Will you ever tell us what you *really* think about us?'. 'Drink up and have another – you're off duty now' were just two of the opening gambits in discussions about my rôle.

Involvement may also result in the exclusion of the worker from certain groups especially in a situation where there is a strong dichotomy of interests. In fact, estate politics as expressed through the TA would appear to be characterized by factionalism and to associate with one faction and to have friends among its members inevitably aroused suspicion or antipathy among the out group. Attempts at explaining the need for neutrality is most likely unacceptable to a group conceiving all outside their own faction as potential enemies. In the event Don became identified with one faction and I myself with another, and from this identification we were able to obtain a good deal of insight into 'our' parties. In the conflict which developed, however, we appeared to be treated as scapegoats by housing management staff concerned with the estate and by some councillors. The area manager reported himself 'perturbed' by the degree of involvement of members of the research team and further commented, 'I was under the impression that you would act merely as observers and interviewers. I think ... the setting up of an action group by Don Entwistle was divisive and caused an upheaval from which the tenants' association has not yet recovered.'[21] In these circumstances it became virtually impossible to talk to officers and councillors and continue to sustain credible relationships with those residents involved. Consequently, for the latter half of the field work contacts with officers and members were minimized and confined mainly to observing meetings between them and resident representatives. This stance should possibly have been adopted from the outset.

My identification with one faction on the Parkview TA affected also my coverage of the North Board. The representative from the estate was ousted from his position as chairman of the TA by 'my' group and later he gained support on the board for the view that I was acting as informer and recounting its business to the TA committee. The intensity of feeling aroused over this issue was considerable and I accepted without question the decision of the tenant representatives on the board and made no attempt to attend further meetings. This form of rôle-typing was difficult to control. Prior to the research period it seems that the TA committee had been fairly inactive. The commencement of the study coincided with the opening of an extension to the estate, the arrival of large numbers of new residents and the impending completion of a community hall. These factors in themselves drastically affected the estate's political situation but a good deal of the ensuing fracas was attributed directly to our presence. To the extent that Don supported a group of residents which came to be seen as a rival group to the TA committee our presence was a factor but I doubt that it was a causal one.

We thus faced a situation in which groups formed in opposition on the estate. The estate TA at times opposed the council representatives both elected and appointed. And within groups where we had acceptance there was a considerable awareness of the complexity of our rôles and most likely some reservations attached to us in most circumstances. This situation involved relatively few residents on the estate but in view of the focus of the study it was important for us to understand the nature of Parkview politicking. Generally we opted to document the perspective of residents at the possible expense of gaining a better insight into the official response.

Thirdly, within the research team itself, as a consequence of our different orientations, there was at times some tension between myself and Don. As a researcher I was concerned primarily to document the views and behaviour of Parkview residents as they related to the study; it was the intention that Don should undertake similar research with the estate's youngsters. As already indicated it was recognized that this should involve an active community work rôle; what was not appreciated was the extent to which the flexible and intuitive approach most appropriate to this work would present difficulties for the planning and carrying out of research. This problem has been encountered elsewhere and I do not know how it would best be resolved.[22] In the sum the label of official researcher proved not to be a serious handicap.

The rôle of researcher was, however, at times made difficult by the complexity of the local political situation and by the unacceptability of the 'outsider' stance traditionally adopted by anthropologists in the field. This problem of rôle definition was heightened by the multidisciplinary nature of the research team itself. I have attempted to come to terms with this dilemma in the writing up by acknowledging the rôles played by Don and myself where I have deemed this necessary.[23]

This introduction is followed by a short outline of the historical background to the estate's development. This is followed by three major sections, Parts II to IV; the first is a description of Parkview estate; the second is concerned to describe the officer and member structures involved in the management of the estate and the third comprises an account of the individuals and institutions linking Parkview and the council. This division expresses a model which regards Parkview and the council as two distinct social fields. The one is a complex social reality made up of all the social interactions in which Parkview residents engage, the other is a simpler social reality comprising only those interactions defined by a status as officer or councillor. Part IV describes the ways and the extent to which these two fields relate to and impinge upon one another. These relationships and interconnections can be seen in terms of linking institutions and individuals engaged in a rôle relationship as tenant, officer or councillor. The process of sustaining these relationships may be analysed in terms of the transactions and the exchanges of power and status which take place between those persons engaged in them. It is hoped that this arrangement of the material will facilitate an understanding of how the estate dweller sees the estate and the council and how he relates to both on the one hand; and on the other how councillors and officers see their own rôle in regard to Parkview and its residents. It is postulated that an understanding of these two perspectives, and particularly an understanding of any variance between them, is necessary to a consideration of the terms of the brief and especially to an assessment of the scope for improvements to the management of estates like Parkview. Part V comprises a postscript which describes developments from the end of field work to the time of writing, December 1976. The final section is concerned with the policy implications of the issues raised by the research.

Historical perspective

Until the mid 19th century the area comprising the old metropolitan borough,[24] though not far from central London, was still largely open country. It was an area of small farms, market gardens and a number of 'country' residences. One of the latter boasted 'standing for 2 or 3 carriages, stabling for 6 horses and appropriate officers, extensive gardens partly walled and clothed with the choicest fruit trees, pleasure gardens beautifully laid out and 3 enclosures of very productive meadow land.'[25] This rural aspect was transformed by the extension of the railway network through the area in the 1870s. The railway provided the impetus to a wave of speculative building. Between 1880 and 1914 the Old Borough assumed its present-day character of a primarily residential district with the construction of street upon street of two- and three-storey terrace houses. Skilled artisans, clerks and small shopkeepers, many of them attracted from central London, took up residence there. The effect on the population figures was dramatic. Prior to the building of the railway, the population of the borough was less than 15,000; by 1921 it had reached a peak of 158,000. Thereafter the population declined steadily as many of the younger middle income groups moved to newer suburbs. In 40 years, from 1921 to 1961, the population fell by over 40,000. The decline has continued in more recent years but the pattern has changed as younger people move back into the Old Borough often as owner occupiers.

Within the Old Borough there was some variation in the standard of housing though this was not marked by the extremes of poverty and wealth characteristically expressed in building form elsewhere. The largest early flatted developments were undertaken by several charitable trusts. For the rest, much of the area was built up in rows of terraced houses by property developers. According to another study most of these terraces of family dwellings were well constructed and 'The main impression ... was of decay and neglect of redeemable property rather than inherent defects!'[26] In part this neglect was a consequence of the housing stress to which the district has long been subject. Over the years many dwellings, often lacking modern amenities, came to be shared by two or more households. More recently this situation has changed again and whereas formerly most accommodation was rented there has been a marked trend towards owner occupation and the rejuvenation of some streets.

The first council owned housing was completed in 1925 and thereafter a number of small schemes were developed, several using the Old Borough's direct labour force. Most of these projects were interrupted by the war. With

13

the peace, the council again turned its attention to housing. 'The problem ... was complicated because of the lack of open space for development and the conditions of overcrowding generally as well as extensive war damage in the Old Borough. Suitable empty properties were requisitioned and reconditioned, sites throughout the Old Borough were developed for prefabricated bungalows and[27] plans were made for the erection of new flats.'

Parkview was the third major estate to be developed in the post-war period. Until then the area was one of terraces with between 20 and 30 small two-storey dwellings ranged on either side of a street (See Plan I). In total the area comprised approximately 450 residences, some in multi-occupation. Each dwelling was built to the same basic plan (See Plan II). Construction was brick, often locally fired and built in lime mortar. Roofs were in slate; structural timbers, softwood. The materials were basically simple and sound. However, most dwellings had little or no foundations other than footing courses and lacked damp proofing and timber preservation measures. Most of the dwellings relied on coal as a fuel for heating though in the early years of the century gas fitments began to replace the coal ranges and fireplaces and electricity was added during the 1920s. Ornamentation both externally and internally was often quite striking and to a high standard of workmanship. Externally moulded and carved stone window mullions, jambs and quoins were much in evidence. Front entrance doors were typically of four panels with glazed upper panels, many of stained glass leaded lights. Internally fibrous plaster work was used as decorative friezes and cornices. Joinery detail was also often carved or moulded. Most dwellings had a small garden in front and all excepting some of the commercial properties had a larger garden at the back. In this backyard the family might raise a few chickens or keep rabbits, budgies and pigeons.

Scattered throughout the area there were 4 public houses and some 41 commercial premises with accommodation over the shop. The shops ranged from a pawnbroker's, florist, furniture shop and shoe repairer to a cafe, tobacconist, off-licence and milkman. There were small backyard businesses like the wood merchant and the cartage contractor with stabling for the horses. A school fronted onto Market Street (Plate 2).

During the war the school and the area immediately behind it was bombed and there were small pockets of some 70 damaged properties in neighbouring streets. An official statement commented, 'bearing in mind the condition and age of the properties that remained the council decided that the cost of carrying out major works of reinstatement was not justified and that the land was now ripe for development as a new housing scheme.'[28]

The first flats on the estate were opened in 1957, the latest developments were occupied in 1974. Over that time plans changed according to the vagaries of architectural fashion, a desire to keep up to date with new technologies and the planning requirements of the various authorities. At different stages both the availability of land from the compulsory purchase order areas and the need for dwellings of a certain type imposed further constraints on the design.

Plan I. Terrace street layout.

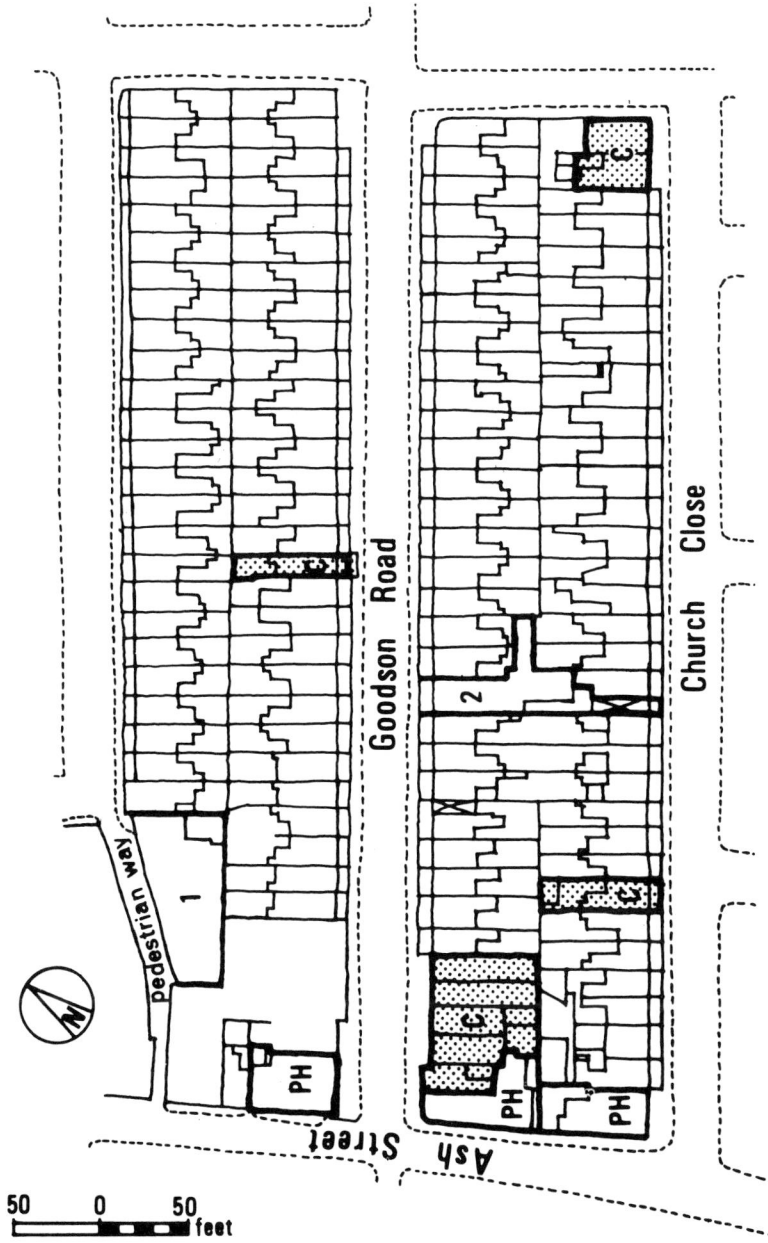

50 0 50
feet

C Commercial properties

1 Cartage contractors yard

2 Wood merchants yard

PH Public house

Plan II. Terrace house layout.

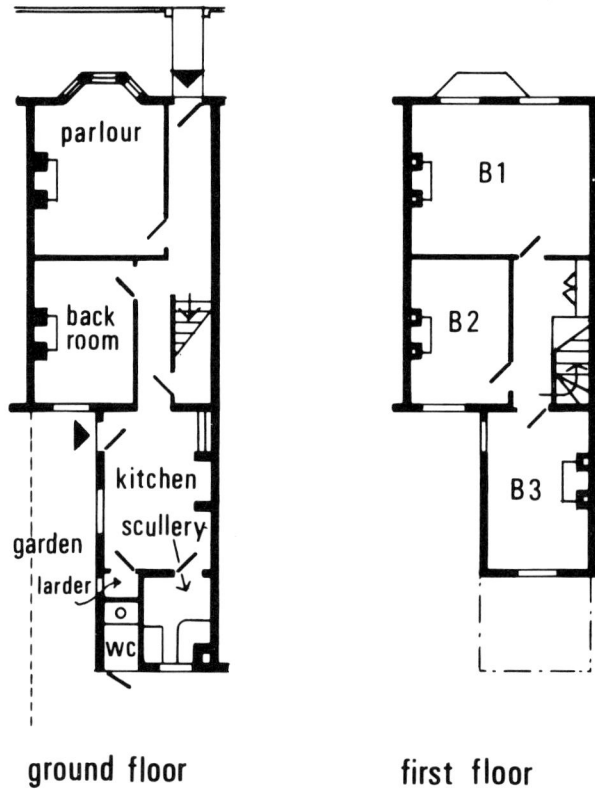

ground floor   first floor

0   5   10 feet

Finally, overall there was an attempt at each phase to improve upon the last. Somewhat unusually, the same project architect was engaged throughout. From interviews with him, and contemporary reports it is possible to sketch in the background to the estate's growth. During those early years, in the words of the architect, housing was 'very much a do-gooding exercise', and one in which the project team had a real sense of involvement. Their commitment was heightened by several factors. The council officers were less formally structured; architects had more contact with tenants and councillors, attended TA meetings and 'could get things done'. They were rewarded by the feeling that tenants appreciated their efforts. Moreover, this was a period when there was a widespread belief that architects could create a new world and in the process change for the better the old one they were replacing.[29]

Work commenced on the site in 1955. The first block fronts onto the market street from which it takes its name and contains seven lock-up shops with 2-storey maisonettes over them. At the same time Chestnut Road, a seven-storey balcony access block was built. This has nine 2-bedroom flats on the ground floor and fifty-four 3-bedroom maisonettes at the upper levels. The maisonettes are arranged so that the bedrooms are under the living room and kitchen. The official brochure stressed that within the flats, room size, aspects, amenities and fittings were to a good standard. All except the ground level flats have balconies opening from the living room and first bedroom. Two lifts provide access to the main decks. Every dwelling has an individual lock-up pram and bicycle shed in a basement storage area. External finishes were highly praised by the author of the official brochure.

The facing bricks are grey Leicester rustics and Lingfield multi-rustics. These have been skilfully used and blended so as to express the proportion and structure of the buildings.

The decorative treatment has received very careful consideration and bold colours have been extensively used externally. The balconies faced with glass panels and gaily painted railings present a pleasing effect.[30]

Two further blocks of a similar plan were built; in Goodson Road, bedsitters took up the ground floor level with three-bedroom maisonettes at the upper levels and in Ash Court bedsitter accommodation was provided at ground floor level and in an additional wing and the remainder comprised two-bedroom maisonettes and flats.

In 1957 plans were being drawn up for the next building phase. This comprised three 11-storey buildings, (Plate 3) based on Y shaped plans, to be sited along one boundary of the estate providing accommodation for a total of 258 households in a mix of bedsitter, one-, two- and three-bedroom units. It was noted that these blocks, 'advanced in design', would be 'the highest buildings yet [in the Old Borough] ..., and when completed will present an impressive landmark.'[31] Construction was in reinforced concrete and 'in order to harmonise with the existing development a large proportion of the external cladding will be in facing brickwork.' Other surfaces were painted and the blocks quickly became known as the blue, red and green blocks. Again each flat was provided with a balcony. Lift access, stairways and rubbish chutes take up the central core. The original plan incorporated pram storage sheds at ground level but later changes resulted in some storage sheds within the block and some in two specially built separate storage units. One block incorporates a branch library with an entrance opening onto the main roadway into the estate.[32]

At about this time trend setters in architecture were advocating high rise development as a way of achieving higher densities while at the same time releasing larger areas of open space. The Old Borough architect's office was convinced. Work on the next phase of two 17-storey blocks each of 68 flats, began in 1964. Construction is of concrete containing Portland stone fines, poured in situ and with a 'ribbed' finish. Four 2-and 3-bedroom units open onto each landing with, on the uppermost floor, four 1-bedroom units. Each block has two lifts and an access stairway and a waterborne waste disposal unit. is installed in every dwelling. There were tentative plans to use the base of the blocks for facilities such as a nursery but these were never realised. The official brochure issued on the completion of this stage stressed the advantage of building high.[33]

The estate that is taking shape on the site is planned to create as much open space within the perimeter as possible and, when all the tower blocks are complete, the intervening areas will be landscaped with variations in level and a degree of semi-mature trees transplanting (sic).

Experience has shown the need for the great care to be taken in the laying and positioning of paths through the landscaped areas to prevent damage and reduce the effects of the normal wear and tear. Everything will be done to overcome these problems and preserve the amenities of the estate.[34]

As part of the same extension Church Close, a five-storey block of 23 maisonettes and flats, was completed. This extension added 159 dwellings to the 407 already occupied.

Already the extent of Parkview reflected an altered concept of scale in the planning of such developments. Whereas up until the 1950s housing development projects of 200 or 300 dwellings had been the norm, projects of over 1000 were now considered acceptable.[35] Accordingly further extensions were planned to Parkview. In 1967 compulsory purchase orders were made on properties in adjoining streets; clearance was planned to make way for the new development. However, with the emergence of doubts about tower block developments,[36] ideas on the kind of design appropriate to the site changed. The final planning stage was consequently a lengthy one.

Initially proposals were for the building of three more 17-storey blocks and two 5-storey blocks. These would provide a further 290 dwellings. These plans were modified and in March 1968 the Housing Committee gave its approval to the construction of one 29-storey, one 7- and two 5-storey blocks. Later that same year these plans were 'revised' and 'in accordance with the council's new policy a fresh appraisal has been made'.[37] 'Revision' in this case involved scrapping all plans for tower block extensions and instead developing designs for a low rise high density scheme. The new plans comprised one 7-storey and ten 4-storey blocks of flats. The former was designed as a sheltered housing unit and included accommodation for staff. Within the latter it was intended that flats at ground floor level would be provided with gardens[38] and those at the upper levels with balconies. These plans too were modified; most units are maisonettes and the balconies were deleted. However, the aim of designing low rise high density housing was not altered. The 4-storey blocks (known as the 'garden flats') are of brick construction with two basic layouts. One type has three bedroom maisonettes at the ground level, one bedroom flats slotted in at the first floor level and two- and three-bedroom maisonettes above that. The

Plan III. Parkview estate layout.

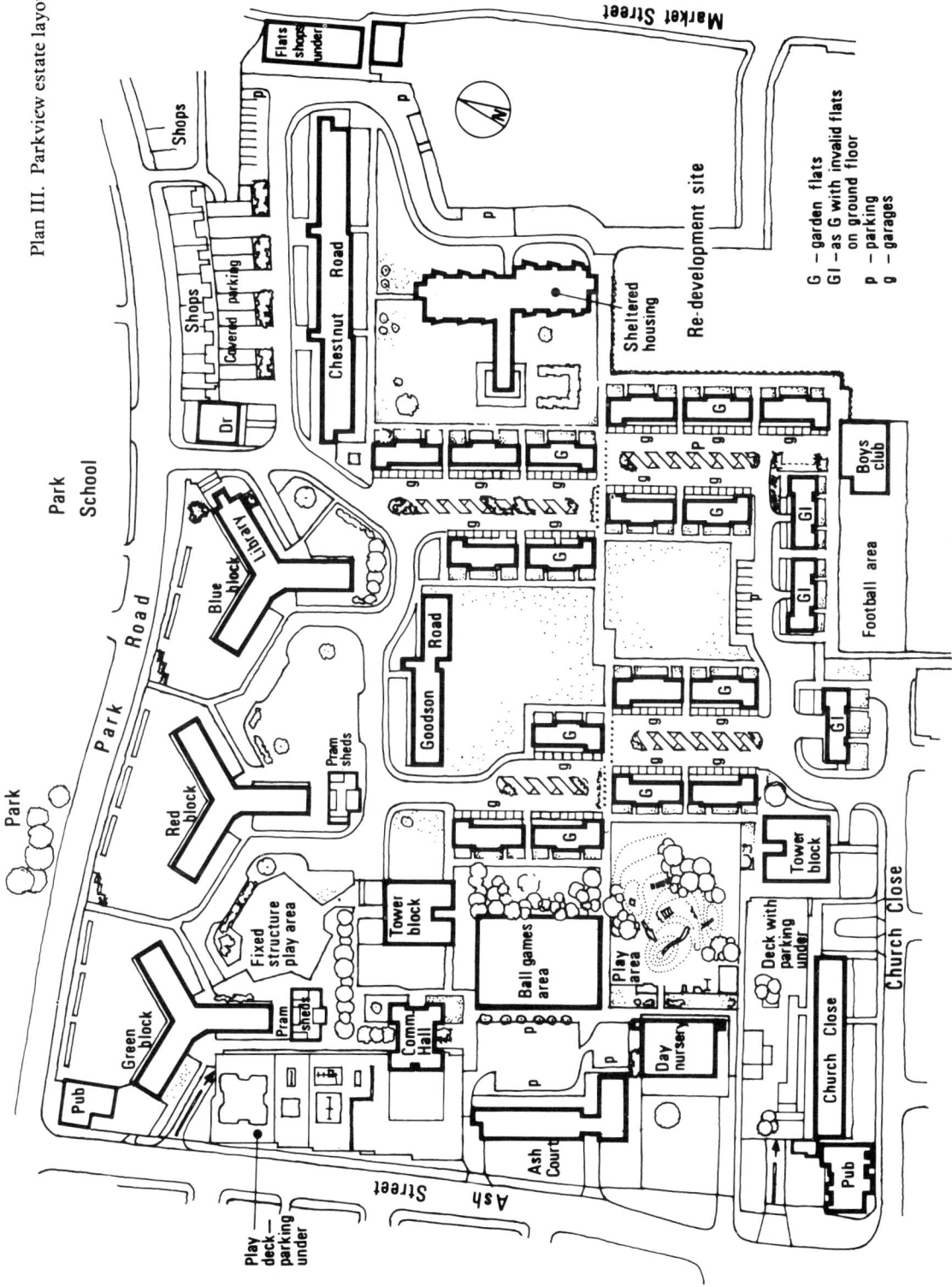

Park

Park Road

Park School

Shops

Shops

Covered parking

Dr

Chestnut Road

Blue block

Library

Red block

Pram sheds

Goodson Road

Green block

Pram shed

Fixed structure play area

Pub

Tower block

Comm. Hall

Ball games area

Play area

Day nursery

Ash Court

Ash Street

Play deck — parking under

Sheltered housing

Re-development site

Market Street

N

Boys club

Football area

G
G
G
G
G
G
G
G
G
GI
GI
GI
GI
GI

g
g
g
g
g
g
g
g
g
g
g
g

p
p
p
p
p
p
p

Flats shops under

Tower block

Deck with parking under

Church Close

Church Close

Pub

G – garden flats
GI – as G with invalid flats on ground floor
p – parking
g – garages

19

second type incorporates ground floor flats designed especially for disabled housewives.[39] Sheds and lock-up garages are an integral part of the design. 'The 4-storey blocks are arranged in an "intimate square" pattern with ... garages entered from a service road approach. All living rooms and principal bedrooms have the best possible aspect fronting grass and planted areas ...'[40] The architect's submission to committee noted that overall '... the new scheme and the layout takes into account the need for integration with the development so far.'[41]

This last phase of the estate does not simply reflect a different fashion in architecture. The style is also less confident, less assertive. The public image of architects was by now somewhat tarnished, beliefs in their social engineering rôle shaken.[42] There was no official opening of this stage and no official brochure marked the completion of the Parkview estate. Sweeping plans to extend Parkview the full length of Market Street were dropped. The development today comprises 830 units on a site covering nearly 20 acres. The busy street market forms one boundary, a main road and park another, while the remaining two boundaries overlook streets of terrace housing. (See Plan III and Figure I).

Many of the contrasts between the street dwellings and the typical estate dwelling are fairly obvious. Most Parkview dwellings open directly onto an accessway or landing. They have a balcony with a view. None have back gardens, few front gardens. The clutter formerly assigned to backyards has now to be contained in a shed that is unrelated to the dwelling. Car parking provision is of greater significance in the estate context and a variety of 'solutions' have been attempted. Ornamentation both within and outside the dwelling is minimal. Small touches of a personalised exterior to the individual dwelling are in evidence only in the garden flats extension (Plates 4 & 5). Inside the dwelling there is generally a high standard of comfort and amenity although in space terms the area available for family activities may be more circumscribed than in the terrace houses. (See Plan IV and cf Plan II).

Development of the dwellings was accompanied by the construction of other facilities. Two pubs were built as part of the estate and in replacement of older pubs on the site. It was also necessary to find alternative sites for an off-licence and doctor's surgery and these premises were designed in keeping with the first estate buildings adjoining an existing terrace of shops and presenting 'an attractive feature to the main entrance to the estate.'[43] Roads within the estate have not been adopted as public highways. It was intended that pedestrian walkways should connect all parts of the estate and that pedestrians should take precedence over vehicles. There are two semi-sunken car parks with accommodation for 155 cars. At the time of the latest development plans were drawn up for a two-storey stacked car park with space for 91 cars but these were later scrapped. Similarly at one time consideration was given to the building of play, health and adult training centres. Plans for a nursery, luncheon club and chiropody clinic were, however, realised. The original

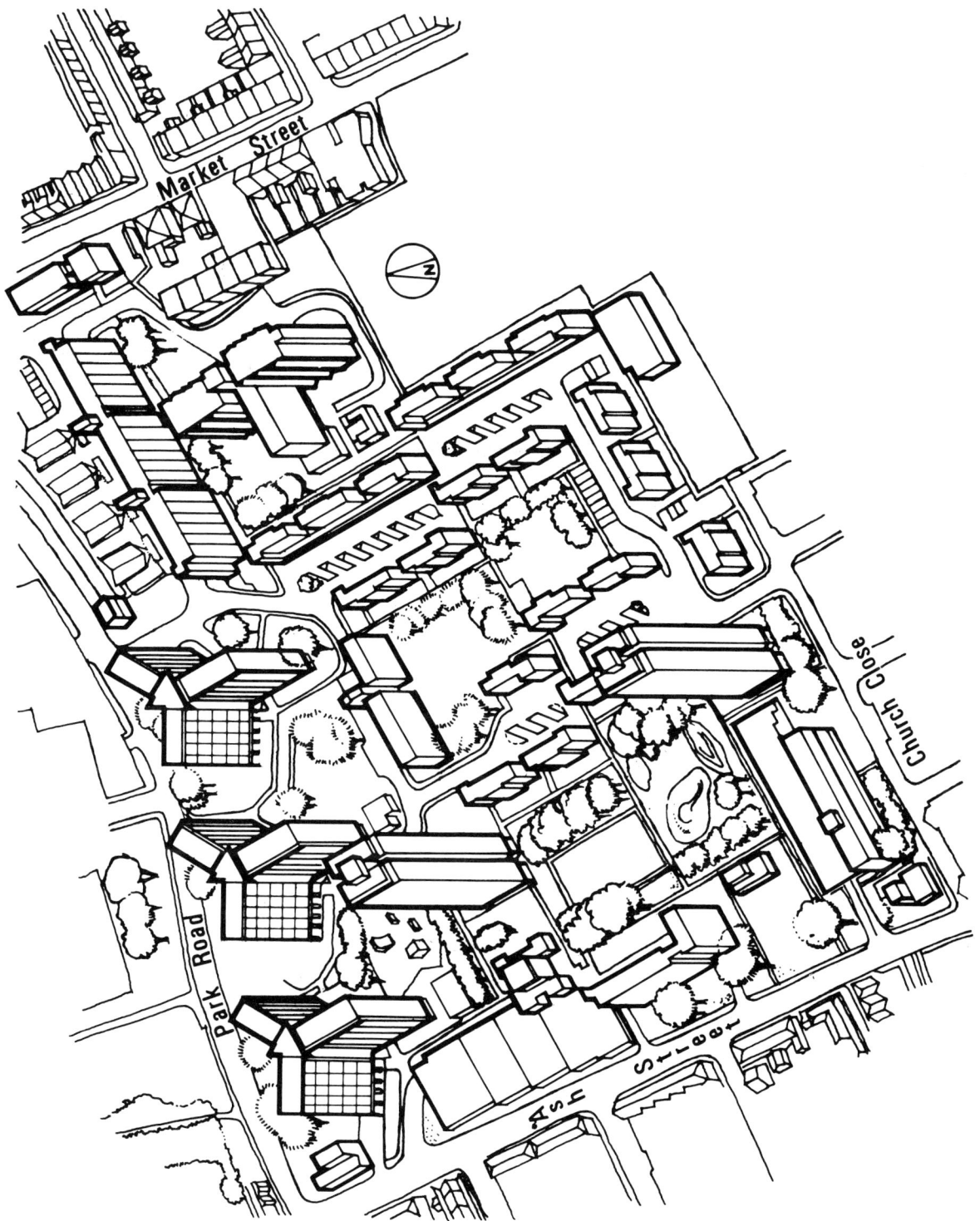

Figure I. Isometric projection prepared from an early plan of Parkview estate.

21

Plan IV. 'Y' block maisonette layout.

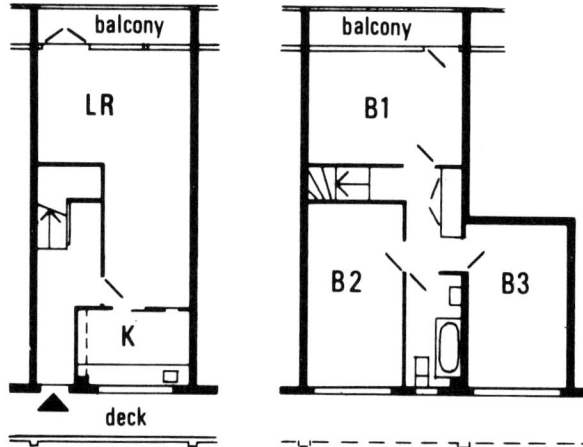

ground floor   first floor

0   5   10
          feet

concept included a community centre. This was shelved for a time but was later revived and has been constructed partly over the deck of one of the underground car parks. One of the earlier phases, incorporated a play area for small children with concrete sculptured play objects, a sand pit and a see saw. A cycle track, complete with model road signs and signals was developed on the deck of one of the car parks. Shortly afterwards this was replaced by another play area for small children. A third play area including a kickabout area, landscaped hills and fixed play equipment has been established adjacent to one of the new low rise blocks. The total area has been landscaped with formal rose beds and trees and lawns defined by low brick walls and fences. It is the kind of landscaping which suggests only 'visual uses and collective peripheral perambulation.'[44]

Throughout, it was the architect's aim to create a community, a new kind of neighbourhood. Today, while critical of some of the buildings, he feels he has been successful to the extent that Parkview estate has a real identity of its own. Another commentator made a more equivocal assessment of the efforts of the Old Borough architects in regard to new housing schemes as compared with the old streets. 'Two redeeming features of almost the whole neighbourhood are that the low two and three storey buildings (Plate 6), although dull, have human scale and most of the houses have gardens which add considerably to their enjoyment. It is considered unfortunate that so little attempt has been made to capture these advantages in the recent housing development.'[45]

Thus far the descriptions of the area and the development of the estate have drawn on the reports of outsiders. A somewhat different, and rather more colourful account emerges from the popular history recalled by present day residents many of whom had lived all their lives in streets demolished to make way for the estate or in others nearby. These residents can talk for hours about 'the good old days' before the war. It is difficult for people to say what made past decades seem good—most likely it is more a matter of feeling and memory—a sense of belonging and a liveliness which the stories of some of the older residents capture very well.[46]

Perhaps most important they consider that the Old Borough was a friendly place. Down the streets and along the avenues everyone knew everyone else. (Plate 7) Relatives lived nearby and often a word with the landlord was enough to get a tenancy handed on. The front door was always open, kids would be in and out and women would call on each other for 'a cuppa and a nag'. The layout of the neighbourhood did much to facilitate this form of casual interaction. From the front door of the house a few steps led down to the semi-private front garden. These steps were a favourite sitting out area and provided a good vantage point from which to view most of the dwellings in the typically short terrace. Back gardens provided further opportunities for casual encounters with neighbours on either side and with those adjoining at the back. Moreover, the opportunities for contact appear to have been taken up and the popular image of street friendliness seems to have had some substance in reality. Mrs Houlton, now a resident on the fifth floor of the blue block[47] previously lived at number 35 in the street shown in Plan 1. She recalls all the former neighbours in her own turning and has a considerable knowledge of people who lived at number 35 in the street shown in Plan I. She recalls all the former extending to family histories, occupations or personality characteristics.

From this and other accounts the area might be characterised by a richness of social networks. In contrast the houses might be poor and often lacked 'mod cons.' They might be overcrowded by modern standards. But a big bowl of whitewash was cheap and families took a pride in keeping the place clean. The tally man called weekly and payments on a suite of furniture amounted to 1/6d a week. Few people had much to come and go on but most got by with more or less regular visits to the pawn shop or with the aid of a loan from a neighbour known to be in the money lending business.

There was plenty of work locally. There was a brewery and a mineral water factory. The Marconi Company had a factory, there was the tin bashers where they made biscuit tins, laundries, engineering workshops, small contractors in the building trades, transport, the power station and the gas works. When the depression hit, one man with nine children remembered that he got 12/6d a week off the dole. His wife recalled taking a pillowslip to the convent where the nuns provided cakes and buns to those in need. During the war hundreds of women were employed nearby as part of the war effort. But even before the war women could find work if they wanted it. There was jobbing at the pie factory, work in posh houses, laundry to be taken in and polishing of 'big ladies' doorsteps at 2d a time.

Then there was the market. This has always been the centre of lots of activity, and a great place to shop for a bargain. On Saturdays the barrow boys stayed open until 10 pm and at Christmas they were on the streets until midnight. The atmosphere is recalled with great nostalgia. There were crowds of people milling around, costers shouting, lights up everywhere and perhaps the Salvation Army singing on the corner.[48] The price and quality of goods available is quoted at great length. Two loaves of bread cost 6d; one of the stores would fill a basin with cracked eggs for 6d; a fruiterer sold 'cut outs', (fruit with the bruises cut out), for 2d a bag. On Saturday nights late customers at the butchers could get a joint of beef, sausages and chops all for 2/6d. Down at the Co-op they would cook the joint for a 1d. Faggots and pease pudding for a family of four cost 9d. Eel pie was also cheap and popular family fare. Twelve pounds of potatoes cost 2d and bunches of carrots, onions, leeks and parsnips were sold in twopenn'orth lots as pot herbs for a family size stew.

There were hawkers as well. On Sundays the muffin man came around ringing his bell. The winkle man travelled on a bicycle and the catmeat man sold sticks of meat for the cat at 2d a stick. 'Tatie Jack' for years stood outside a couple of local pubs selling hot baked potatoes at a penny.

People organized their own entertainment then. Most pubs had pianos and regular sing songs. The barrow boys had Monday off and there was generally a good old knees up in the Cock—or if there was a score to settle there might be a fight outside. On New Year's Eve everyone came out onto the streets and family parties often became street parties with dancing and singing on the road. On holidays a treat for the kids might be a visit to the park with bread and dripping or a 2d bag of broken biscuits and a jug of cocoa. Some women organized street outings, most, in recollection at least, marked by hilarious incidents. The churches sometimes organized social activities and for a real night out there was the local cinema.

This remembered history is characterized by a feeling of intimacy with place and a richness of contact with people; there is a familiarity about it all. It was a place peopled by characters of whom apocryphal stories are told. The pair who turned a policeman upside down in a drain, the woman who flattened a male drinker in a pub . . . The scale is small. The incidents recounted are the stuff of oral traditions and folk song. The emphasis shifts somewhat in recollections of the history of the estate itself. Here no local characters or events stand out and residents speak more of physical surroundings or social standards.

Residents who moved into the first balcony access blocks and Y blocks claim that most people knew each other prior to moving to the estate since many came from requisitioned properties and most had ties with the immediate neighbourhood. They claim that residents took great pride in living on the estate;[49] the rose beds and trees were carefully tended, the general surroundings were pleasant and there was no problem with cleaning stairs and disciplining children. Some residents date what they regard as a decline in standards to the amalgamation of the boroughs in 1965; others to the opening of the newer extension. Whatever the date the rationale is the same. Allocations of flats drew residents from a wider area and the influx of 'outsiders' resulted in a lowering of social 'tone'.[50] The improved standards of the individual dwellings were still appreciated but in the wider context comparisons were made with a former place of residence; the streets were invested with a social meaning enhanced by nostalgic memories and for many the estate was found lacking. It is impossible from this perspective to assess the accuracy of these accounts. Nor is that important; popular beliefs have a validity of their own and colour perceptions of the present day reality.

It is, however, more feasible to document the changes which have taken place in the appearance of the estate and in the unplanned uses made of some of its parts. Inevitably there were minor changes to the design; for example doors at various levels had to be fitted to the rubbish chutes and cycle racks said to constitute a hazard to pedestrians were removed. For the rest, the sand pit did not last long as a children's play thing and this original play area (Plate 8) is now little used. The basements of two blocks regularly accumulate large quantities of rubbish and the storage sheds there are now virtually unusable. The pram sheds likewise have become (Plate 9) dumping grounds for unwanted rubbish and play spaces for youngsters seeking a hideout. One of the car parks was used for a brief period but both are now totally disused as car parks and few except children bent on adventurous play, go there.[51] Most of the original fencing enclosing the lawn, after 15 years of wear and tear, has been removed or is broken and bent. Other fences marking more private domains have been added. The routes of the established pathways may seem circuitous and a few well worn tracks have been beaten across some of the grass. Perhaps somewhat surprisingly, this is all very minor change and to the casual visitor, aside from some fairly unimaginative grafitti, there is little to be seen from the outside of the buildings which conveys the character of those who live within.

Notes

AIMS AND METHODS

1   There has been a considerable debate on the meaning of this term. See for example D B Clark, 'The Concept of Community: A Re-examination'; M Stacey, 'The Myth of Community Studies', *British Journal of Sociology*, Vol 20 No 2, 1969, pp 134–47; P Willmott, *The Evolution of a Community*, London, 1963; R Frankenberg, *Communities in Britain*, London, 1966.

2   See for example, P Willmott, 1963, especially p 111. This study suggests that the quality of neighbourly relations may be enhanced with time. By contrast an account of the way in which the same number (or fewer) contacts with neighbours may be sustained over time, is given in J F Wyatt, 'Residential stability in an inner-urban housing block: a restudy after 18 years' *Sociological Review*, Vol 24, No 3, NS, August 1976, p 566.

3   It was hoped to monitor in some detail the activities of user groups in the hall. In fact it was opened well behind schedule after the field work period. Some of the issues concerned with the hall are therefore dealt with in the main body of the text and the results of a short follow up study are incorporated in the postscript.

4   Sue Hewer and Tim Cotterill both at the time members of the SRD support staff. Later assistance was given by Sheila Dowling, Mahdu Patel, Cathy Holland and Nell Luetchford, all of SRD.

5   The press adopted as a story the 'government snooper, 1984' line or made play of the fact that my previous research experience had been in Papua, New Guinea–'from the leafy to the concrete jungle to study the habits of the natives etc'. Some quoted a statement of the chairman of the Tenants' Association to the effect that my residence prevented the rehousing of someone from the housing list. The chairman further claimed that 'the tenants' should have been consulted first. I was concerned that this type of publicity might adversely affect the research especially since some of the references to residents might be considered offensive. However, those relatively few residents who read or heard the reports were apparently impressed by the status supposedly conferred by media coverage and were not at all bothered by the content of the story; perhaps in itself a comment on the impact of mass media.

6   This is discussed in greater detail below. See p 10.

7   See below pp 92–94 and pp 95–100, 189–191.

8   'An examination of the school experience of children from a London housing estate with special reference to some social education elements in the curriculum,' Thesis submitted to the Institute of Education, London University, September 1975.

9   See below pp 71–76.

10   For example, the pattern of lengths of residence and household sizes in the sample of white households in tower blocks may not be representative of all white households in tower blocks.

11   The schedule is given in Appendix II.

12   Thirty-three schedules were completed in the course of one interview, 32 in two and eight in three or more.

13   Work on the coding frame was carried out by Betty Simpson of Cambridge. The computer work was carried out by Alan Strawbridge and Sharyn Davies of LUCS.

14   This problem has been noted by Oscar Lewis and he advocates the use of a series of intensive family based case studies to overcome it. See 'An anthropological approach to family studies', *American Journal of Sociology*, Vol 55, No 5, pp 468–75.

15   See below pp 100–103.

16   Other studies concentrating on patterns of social interaction do not appear to have been troubled by this.

17   The discussion paper was entitled 'A study of tenant/local authority relations and of community services on a high density estate ... '. the pamphlet, *Where we Live*. Neither purported to report any results from the study; the former was an attempt to put before the local authority in the form of a working paper some of the issues arising from the study; the latter outlined some resident views of Parkview and restated the background and brief for the project.

18   See below p 149.

19   In fact for most residents I was in some way associated with 'the council'; the distinction between central and local government systems was frequently not made by residents.

20   The official label did not pose a problem for the other two members of the team. Don was a youth and community worker engaged in that type of work on the estate and known at the same time to be assisting my research. His practical rôle was one readily acceptable to residents. Wendy worked mainly in the schools and again her presence there as a researcher was not unusual.

21   Black to self, 10 May 1976. Similar dilemmas were noted in one of the earliest in depth studies carried out in an urban Westernised setting. See William Foot Whyte, *Street Corner Society*, U. of Chicago Press, 2nd ed, 1955 especially the appendix 'On the evolution of Street Corner Society,' pp 279–358. Somewhat unusually in this instance the researcher was able to follow up and document something of the reactions of the participants to the publication of findings. Whyte's key respondent commented, 'The trouble is, Bill, you caught people with their hair down. It's a true picture, yes; but people feel it's a little too personal'. (p 347). Something of this kind of reaction is probably inevitable.

22   This problem has been encountered in the CDP teams, for example, see R Lees, 'The Action-Research Relationship', R Lees and G Smith (eds) *Action Research in Community Development*, London 1975, pp 59–66.

23   Similar dilemmas face anthropologists working in a variety of situation. An interesting discussion on which I have drawn is contained in P Kloos, 'Rôle Conflicts in Social Fieldwork', *Current Anthropology*, 1969, Vol 10, No 5, and in the commentaries following that article.

HISTORICAL PERSPECTIVE

24   The present borough comprises two former metropolitan boroughs formed on amalgamation in 1965. In this study I have adopted the convention of using the term Old Borough for the former metropolitan borough in which Parkview is situated and Borough for the two amalgamated boroughs.

25   *The Times*, 22 June 1815, cit Old Borough brochure on the opening of the Parkview estate 1957.

26   Most of this information has been drawn from an urban renewal study carried out in the Old Borough in 1963 by a private company on the invitation of the Minister of Housing and Local Government. I am indebted to the surveyor for the estate throughout its development for the sketch plans and for much of the detailed information about the redevelopment area. The project architect provided further comment.

27   Old Borough brochure issued on the opening of the first major post war housing scheme, 1956.

28   Old Borough brochure issued on the opening of the first blocks on the Parkview estate, 1957. According to the surveyor engaged on the original scheme, many of the properties would today be considered suitable for rehabilitation rather than demolition.

29   cf J Napper 'The Long Weekend', *Riba J*, November/December 1975, p 27; P Malpass, 'Professionalism and the rôle of architects in local authority housing', *Riba J*, June 1975, p 9.

30   Old Borough brochure, 1957.

31   ibid.

32   ibid.

33   This was a development which was fairly widespread at about this time. See Malpass, op cit, p 14.

34   Borough brochure issued on the opening of the extension to the estate, 1966.

35   Napper, op cit, p 28. This article also points out the implications of this change in scale for building technology and the design process.

36   Pawley has pointed to the complex nature of these doubts.

'In Britain reaction against high rise, although it culminated in public outrage at the progressive collapse of Ronan Point in 1968, came about for more complex reasons than concern for the welfare of small children playing in lift lobbies 100 ft in the air. Revelations of the real cost of building high ... and the exposure of the scandalous disparity in construction time between public and private contracts for identical buildings, led to an official volte face. The public sector was switched to high density, low rise developments ... This volte face coincided with the development of a more sophisticated set of architectural theories to replace the rather discredited and simplistic slogans of the '20s' and '30s'. Retreating from the uncompromising moral pronouncements of their peers, a later group of theorists seized upon the demonstrable truth that a relationship exists between context and behaviour and developed a kind of super functionalism based on scientific evidence ...' A Pawley, *Architecture versus Housing*, New York, 1971, p 85f.

37   Revised papers on the estate extension presented to the borough developments group committee, 4 November 1968 and the financial services group committee, 30 December 1968.

38   See below pp 186–8 for the controversy surrounding these gardens.

39   This is evident especially from the design of the kitchen. In fact in several households it is not the housewife who is the disabled member of the household. The architect intended that the detailing of each flat should be made in accord with the needs of particular clients. However, the allocation procedures were not adapted to allow for this.

40   Revised papers ... op cit.

41   ibid.

42   cf Malpass, p 11.

43   Old Borough brochure, 1957.

44   W Segal, 'Home Sweet Home?' *Riba J*, October 1973, p 480. Since the completion of fieldwork the hooped iron fencing has been removed.

45   Urban renewal study, 1963.

46   Of course not everyone would agree that the 'old days' were good, and residents stories are not necessarily historically accurate. A local history book gives a rather harsher view of life between the wars especially in the area known as 'The Avenues'. The account given here is based on that previously published in a booklet written especially for estate residents. I have retained the local slang expressions.

47   See below pp 60–65. The way in which a sense of identity may develop in a clearly defined locality like a street turning is discussed in Willmott, 1963, esp p 77.

48   The market started in the 1880s according to the Borough Libraries Archive Department, 'Notes on Street Markets of ... [the borough], February 1970. The market traders were apparently a fairly stable group with interconnections especially within 2 main groups. Many pitches have been occupied by the same trader for upwards of 30 years. More recently itinerant 'stranger' traders have taken up some of the stands.

49   This feeling may be compared with the architect's view that his efforts were 'appreciated' by the first residents. The surveyor also recalls that these first residents took a considerable pride both in their homes and in the amenities provided for Parkview as a whole.

50   This categorisation of the estate into old and new residents is a theme that is developed elsewhere, see below p 170. Newcomers had not, at the time of the fieldwork, developed strong views of their own about the estate beyond reacting against the old/new image.

51   These car parks have no doors and so offer car owners little security. There is also a problem of seepage through the deck causing damage to the paintwork of cars. At various times there have been proposals to make alternative uses of the buildings but none of the discussions have come to anything. One of the topics most frequently before the North Board is the provision of doors so that car parks can be brought into use. It is not clear what demand there would be even if some form of security was built in.

Part II

Parkview Estate

". . . the plans included spacious lawns with trees, shrubs and flower beds, and the scheme, with its bright and stimulating surroundings would bring happiness to the families who lived there."

(from a speech made on the occasion of the official opening of the first phase, reported in a local newspaper, 27 September 1957).

This section aims at understanding the social field bounded by the estate, and particularly the nature and extent of the social relations linking residents there. It will be evident that the estate boundaries, though clearly defined, are artificial; the lives of all residents extend outwards to the wider neighbourhood and forces within the latter, often reflecting events of metropolitan or national significance, impinge upon the estate. This complex reality, while not ignored in the context of the present study has inevitably been over-simplified to allow an analysis of the limited questions under consideration.

Part II draws throughout on basic data compiled for all households, the results of in depth interviews with 73 sample households and observations from field notes. I have adopted a convention of using the term 'residents' where data relates to the estate generally and 'respondents' where data relates only to the sample households. The section begins by outlining the general characteristics of Parkview and its residents, their previous housing history and overall reactions to the estate. A more detailed description of patterns of social interaction focuses on relatives, neighbours and friends. This includes inter-ethnic relations on the estate and a consideration of two particular age groups, the elderly and the very young. At this point the emphasis shifts beyond the estate to ties with the immediate locality and beyond, for shopping and other services, education, employment and leisure. This is followed by an account of residents' experience of official agencies. Finally, there is a description of the local authority services situated on Parkview, estate organizations and groups sponsored by the project. A concluding statement attempts to present an overview of the main themes which emerge from the section as a whole.

Parkview: Buildings and people

The estate as considered in this study has a total population of 2,154 persons, 614 children and young dependants and 1,540 adults. There is a total of 726 households on a site extending over 19.5 acres. However, in a consideration of overall densities the sheltered housing unit comprising 104 flats and 125 persons should be added. This gives an overall density of approximately 117 persons per acre.[1] The planned density for the estate was 136 persons per acre, or a total planned population of 2,652 persons.[2] The 73 sample households contain a total of 163 adults, 75 men and 88 women and 70 children and young dependants. Details of the way in which the sample households were selected and the manner in which they may be related to the estate generally are given in Appendix I. The physical and demographic characteristics of Parkview may be described in terms of the distribution of dwellings and households of various sizes and the composition, breakdown and distribution of the population according to age structure.

The distribution of dwelling size by block type is shown in Table I. All the bedsitter accommodation on the estate is contained in the balcony or Y blocks

TABLE I   Dwelling size by block type

Block type and completion dates	Bed-sitters	1 Bed-room	2 BR	3 BR	Total
Balcony* 1957–1966	31	0	39	102	172
Y blocks[1] 1959–1960	35	48	126	49	258
Tower 1966	0	8	96	32	136
Garden 1973–1974	0	34	67	59	160
Total	66	90	328	242	726

*Church close, Ash Court, Goodson Road, Chestnut Road, Market Street
[1] Red, Green and Blue

34

while one-bedroom accommodation is contained mainly in the Y or garden blocks. Two- and three-bedroom accommodation is more evenly distributed over the block types though with most of the former in the Y blocks and most of the latter in balcony blocks. It should be noted that Table I conceals differences within block types. Thus of the balcony blocks Church Close contains three-bedroom dwellings only and Ash Court comprises a mix of bed-sitters and two-bedroom units. The Y blocks though identical in appearance contain different proportions of unit size; the blue block has a predominance of one and three-bedroom units, the red and green of two-bedroom. The two-tower blocks are built to the same plan and the garden blocks though ranging from 8 to 24 dwellings have basically the same mix of unit size.

Fifteen percent of all units are built at ground level, 33% at the first and second floors, 24% at the third, fourth and fifth and 28% at the sixth floor or above. Bed-sitter accommodation tends to be situated at ground level, otherwise dwellings of all sizes are found at all floor levels.

The data for household size may be compared to information available for the wider neighbourhood covered by the area Social Services team. On the estate 18% of all households comprise one person and 21% two persons. These are lower percentages than those for the neighbourhood where corresponding figures are 30% and 32%. Conversely the estate has a much larger percentage of three- and four-person households, 47% as compared with 27%. Eleven percent of all neighbourhood households comprise five or more persons as compared with 14% on the estate. By contrast another council estate nearby contains an even smaller percentage of one person households (10%) and a much larger proportion (28%) of all households contain five or more persons.

The uneven distribution of units, and hence households, of different sizes, gives a particular character to the various blocks. Chestnut Road for example has no one person households while in Ash Court nearly 50% of all households are of this type. Church Close contains only households of three or more persons. There are in each of the red and green blocks only three households containing five or more persons while in the blue block there are 16 households in this category. (See Table A XVIV[3]).

The age breakdowns for Parkview estate are shown in relation to comparable figures for the Borough and the Greater London Council area in Table II.

This shows that the estate has a lower proportion of elderly dependants and a higher proportion of young dependants. Otherwise the figures for all three areas are fairly comparable.

Within Parkview, variations between blocks and block type is most striking in regard to population structure, particularly the densities of children and persons over the age of 60. The uneven distribution of these age categories is related to the incidence of various household types, particularly all adult households, dwelling sizes within a block and the period of occupation.

In regard to densities of children it can be seen from Table AIII that the density of pre-school children reaches a peak of one child to every 1.8

TABLE II Population breakdowns, Parkview, the Borough and the GLC area*

Age Categories	Parkview Number	%	the Borough† Number	%	GLC area† Number	%
0–5	183	9	14,910	8	648,090	9
6–8	143	7	7,090	4	331,105	4
9–12	158	7	8,430	5	403,820	5
13–16	122	6	7,970	4	370,880	5
17–19	92	4	7,675	4	299,065	4
20–29	332	15	36,615	20	1,118,930	16
30–39	242	11	21,865	12	871,085	12
40–49	241	11	20,490	11	930,470	12
50–59	274	13	23,850	13	962,720	13
60+	367	17	38,315	20	1,446,175	19
Totals	2,154	100	187,210	100	7,452,340	99

*In this table and all subsequent tables and text references percentages have been rounded to the nearest whole number.
†from the Office of Population Census and Surveys, Census 1971, England and Wales, County Report, Greater London, 1973, Part I. The base date for the Parkview data is 1 June 1974.

households in garden flats. The lowest density occurs in Ash Court with one pre-school child to every 16 households. Taking all children under 13 the highest density, in Church Close, is one child to 0.8 of every household, the lowest, Ash Court with one child to every eight households.[4]

Children tend to be concentrated, in relatively few households, and other figures than those above may therefore more accurately convey the character of individual blocks. Table AIV shows that over the whole estate 62% of all households contain no children under 13. As might be expected the absence of young children is most marked in the older established blocks; 69% of all households in balcony blocks are of this type, 76% of all Y blocks; whereas for the tower blocks and garden flats the percentage drops sharply to 57% and 39% respectively.

Over half (54%) of all households are adult households, ie with all residents aged 17 or over. This is higher than the comparable figure for the Borough of 47%. On Parkview, there is again a variation between block type. The range, as

36

shown in Table AV is from 32% in the most recently occupied garden flats to 71% in the Y blocks. Most all adult households are small; 33% comprise one person, 35% two persons, 24% three persons and 8% four or more persons.

For those households with children, floor level may be significant factor in their perception of the estate. Table AI shows that of the 132 households containing pre-school children over half are housed at ground level or on the first and second floors. Table AXVIII shows that those housed above that level tend to be in households with fewest options even in public sector housing. Twenty-one percent are housed at the third, fourth and fifth floors and the remaining 21% at or above the sixth floor. It is interesting to note that a higher proportion of households with children in the 5–13 age range are located at the ground floor. Otherwise the distribution of these age groups by floor level is similar to that for the under-fives.

In regard to old people there are 268 households containing one or more person aged 60 or over. As with children the ratio of such persons to households varies from one block to another. The highest density occurs in Ash Court with one elderly person to 0.9 of every household, the lowest in Church Close with one to every 7.6 households. Households containing elderly persons are housed at all levels. (See Tables AII and AIII).

It can thus be seen that the demography of Parkview estate is in some respects different from that of both the neighbourhood and the Borough. Parkview has fewer smaller households and the estate population is a slightly younger one. These differences reflect the availability of particular types of accommodation, the priorities accorded to categories of applicants on the waiting list and the characteristics of the population rehoused from slum clearance areas or wartime properties. Within Parkview the mix of units of varying sizes and the phasing of the estate's development combine to give the different blocks distinctive household type and age structure characteristics. And as will become apparent these differences may be accentuated further by two inter-related factors, the allocation process and the making of a reputation.

At this point two categories of households should be noted; the first comprises non-nuclear family type households, the second households where one or both spouses is a member of an ethnic minority group. Within the first category 62 or 19% of all households with children and young dependants are headed by one parent only. (See Table AXVI) This is the same as the figure for the Borough and very close to the area figure of 20%. It is much lower than that for other estates in the neighbourhood where the comparable figure for one parent families is 34%.[5] In addition 47 or 6% of all estate households comprise other forms of non-nuclear family type households. (See Table AXVII) Twenty-five such households are extended families of three generations with the children and grandchildren or children and parents of the tenants in residence. In all instances where grandchildren are part of this type of household their mother/father heads a one parent family. Other households may be categorized as follows: three include a relative other than the immediate family such as a niece or father's brother; eight comprise two or more siblings; three include an adult friend of the family and two incorporate married children. Another 32 households comprise unmarried sons/daughters aged over 35 and resident with both or more commonly one parent. In many cases all residents in such households are quite elderly.

There are 60 households where all residents are black or where one spouse is black. (See Tables AVI and AVII) This represents 8% of all households. The total black population is 228 persons or 11% of the estate population. These residents come from places as diverse as Ghana, Sierra Leone, India, South Africa, Mauritius, Nigeria, Grenada, Jamaica and other parts of the West Indies. Black households tend to be larger than white households 18 or 30% of all black households comprise 5 or more persons as compared with 12% of all white households.[6] The highest number of black residents on the estate are in the garden flats where they constitute 20% of the population. The lowest number of such residents are housed in the Y blocks where black families make up 5% of the population. In addition to these households another 21 comprise families drawn from other ethnic minority groups. These include Yugoslavs, Portuguese, Polish, Greek, Spanish, Italian and Hungarian families.[7]

It is of interest to note that in recent years there would appear to be a tendency to allocate units in one block type, the tower blocks, to those households which may be described as socially disadvantaged and/or have very little real choice in their housing situation. The tower blocks are characterized by relatively high child densities and the proportions both of households with no children under 13 and of all adult households are lower than for the overall estate. These blocks house the highest percentage of one parent families and non-nuclear family type households; they are second highest in the proportion of black families.[8] It is also significant that 14% of tower block households were rehoused on the grounds of homelessness. This may be compared with a figure of 4% for Parkview as a whole.

Old Borough residents and 'outsiders'

This then is something of the characteristics of the estate's households. Their previous housing history has now to be taken into account. Prior to re-housing on the estate 73% of the estate's households were resident in the Old Borough, 24% in the Borough and 3% were rehoused from outside these areas. Moreover, many residents have a long, often lifelong association with the Old Borough. Thirty-eight percent have lived in the Old Borough for 20 years or more and 22% for between 10 and 20 years. (See Tables AX and AXI) These residents with long associations with the Old Borough claim that in recent years flats on the estate have been allocated to 'outsiders', to people from the Borough and beyond, without ties in the locality and hence lacking identity with and feeling for the place. And indeed this assertion is to some extent reflected in the breakdown of the figures. Thus 77% of all residents in the earlier phases of the estate's development were rehoused from the Old Borough and 42% of them had been resident there for 20 years or more. In the most recently completed phase, the garden flats, 59% of allocations went to households from within the Old Borough, 24% of these resident there for periods of 20 years or more. As might be expected black families are least likely to have strong local ties with more than half rehoused from outside the Old Borough. (See Table AVIII). It is still very much a population drawn from the immediate locality; nevertheless the shifts are marked and in the popular perception probably more so than the figures would warrant.

Information on file detailing the reasons for rehousing are in some cases completely lacking and in others are incomplete. (See Table AXIII) Categories adopted for classification in the present context are therefore somewhat arbitrary. Medical grounds for example are often associated with generally poor conditions and overcrowding. These latter two categories combined probably account for most cases housed from the waiting list and comprise the largest single category (33% of all households). Redevelopment and slum clearance in the case of the earliest blocks also includes households moved out of properties requisitioned during the war and account for 22%. Some 18% of all households required smaller or larger units and presumably these would in the main be transfer cases. Homelessness accounts for a relatively small proportion (4%) of cases. Medical grounds, mutual exchanges and unknown factors account for the remaining 21%.

There would appear to be little change over time in the reasons for rehousing. The exception is homelessness which was recorded as a ground for rehousing mainly within the last three years. As applicants most Parkview residents (57%) were on the waiting list for less than three years. However, this figure is inflated somewhat since households rehoused from properties purchased compulsorily by the local authority are not applicants from the register and many of these would be included in this figure. Ten percent of households were on the waiting list for from 5 to 10 years and 7% were registered for periods longer than that. (See Table AXV) There appears to be little variation in the distribution of figures showing time lag between the date of application and the date of rehousing according to length of residence on the estate although among those housed in recent years long waits of over 10 years are less common than formerly. (See Table AXIV) Cases of overcrowding and poor conditions, that is households on the register, are more likely to experience a lengthy wait for their first offer. Households requiring a smaller or larger unit also often wait considerable periods though in many cases these households may be considered to be adequately housed. As might be predicted households allocated flats on the grounds of homelessness have the shortest wait and, perhaps unexpectedly, households where medical grounds appear to be an important factor may experience considerable delays.[9] For the estate population details of previous accommodation are not available. However, for the sample population 40% of all households were living in a self contained unfurnished flat and another 28% in non self contained unfurnished accommodation. Of the remainder 12% were resident in an unfurnished house, 9% in non self contained furnished accommodation, 3% in self contained furnished flats. All were in rented accommodation.[10]

Resident perceptions of Parkview

The way in which residents regard the estate may be discussed in terms of their initial response, subsequent evaluation and the opinion formed about specific features of living on Parkview.

Information on the initial reaction to the estate is available only for the sample households.[11] Most respondents (63%) accepted a flat on the estate as their first offer, 20% turned down one other offer before accepting accommodation on Parkview while relatively fewer had two or three offers. However, it should be noted that 18% of all respondents who accepted on their first offer claimed that they felt they had no alternative either because they were not aware of the local authority's preparedness to allow prospective tenants three 'reasonable' offers or because they feared that a subsequent offer might be even less attractive. Those residents in the sample who refused an offer did so mainly on the basis of their evaluation of the flat or its location. Reasons for acceptance were in order of preference, features of the flat, its location, family ties in the area and the estate itself. Once they have made the move residents tend to stay on the estate for long periods. (See Table AXII) 221 or 31% of all residents have been on the estate for 10 years or more and in the earlier development phases nearly half have been the sole occupant of the flat. Furthermore, of the 221 long established residents 134 have been resident in the Old Borough for 20 years or more and 100 have lived in council housing for the same period.

Movement out of the estate and natural turnover of tenancies may or may not reflect resident satisfaction and other factors need to be assessed as well. Transfers are not easy to arrange, nor are they encouraged, but the rate of such applications may give some indication of resident satisfaction and the general stability of the estate's population. The highest proportion of requests for transfers comes from tower block residents, just over one quarter of whom have applied to be moved. There is little difference in the rate of applications from the balcony and Y blocks (19% and 17% respectively) and as might be expected so shortly after occupation, there is an extremely low proportion of requests from the garden flats. (See Table AIX)

These figures may be indicative of a trend but it is also the case that transfer applications often disguise other problems not necessarily connected with an individual housing situation and many residents disenchanted with the estate, may for a variety of reasons still be disinclined to apply for a transfer. In order therefore to obtain a fuller understanding, respondents were asked for their reactions on taking up residence and for subsequent changes in their feelings towards their home and its environment. Other questions attempted to trace the reasons for any changes in attitude.

Overall most respondents (67%) said that compared to their former place of residence they prefer living on the estate. A small proportion of respondents (7%) have mixed feelings, acknowledging the better standards of comfort and amenity in their new housing but associating with their former residence a compensatory richness of social life which they consider to be lacking on the estate. This explanation was also the main one put forward by those (25%) who preferred their former residence over the estate.

This general assessment needs to be related to personal circumstance and experience. Younger respondents are much more likely to express a preference for the estate while middle aged and older respondents are more likely to prefer their former residence. Respondents housed most recently on Parkview are also more likely to prefer the estate whereas 28% of those housed in the earlier phases prefer their former residence and a further 23% have mixed feelings. These respondents were rehoused mainly from the immediate locality and they tend to view the old streets with considerable nostalgia. A fairly high percentage of respondents housed in the intermediate development phases continue to express a preference for their former place of residence. As might be expected those housed on grounds of overcrowding and generally poor conditions or for medical reasons tend to prefer the estate while 46% of those rehoused for slum clearance or redevelopment purposes prefer their old residence and another 11% express mixed feelings. Furthermore, while in relation to their previous dwelling respondents express a preference for the estate, comparisons between the estate and the terraced street as neighbourhoods tend to favour the latter. Thirty-seven percent regard the streets positively, 31% with mixed feelings and 25% make a negative comparison.[12] Most (59%) claim that a neighbourhood patterned on streets of terrace housing is qualitatively different from that comprising a flatted estate. Invariably the comparisons and sense of difference are expressed in terms of the social characteristics referred to already.

Whatever their evaluation of their housing experience, most respondents (74%) recall that they felt happy or pleased on first moving to the estate. The remainder claim that from the outset they disliked the estate or had mixed feelings about it. The views of nearly half of all respondents subsequently remained unchanged, 33% viewed their housing situation less favourably and 16% came to like it more.[13] The shifts in attitude are of interest. There is a tendency for those who originally expressed a more favourable view of the estate to subsequently adopt a less favourable one and those who expressed an unfavourable view or have mixed feelings come to like it more. Fifty percent of those originally adopting a more moderate opinion of 'pleased' remain unchanged in their assessment, 50% have become less favourably inclined. (see Figure II). Something of these shifts in attitudes can be documented; it is rather more difficult, without further information for a larger number of households, to attempt explanations.

Fig. II. Opinions on moving to and residing in Parkview.

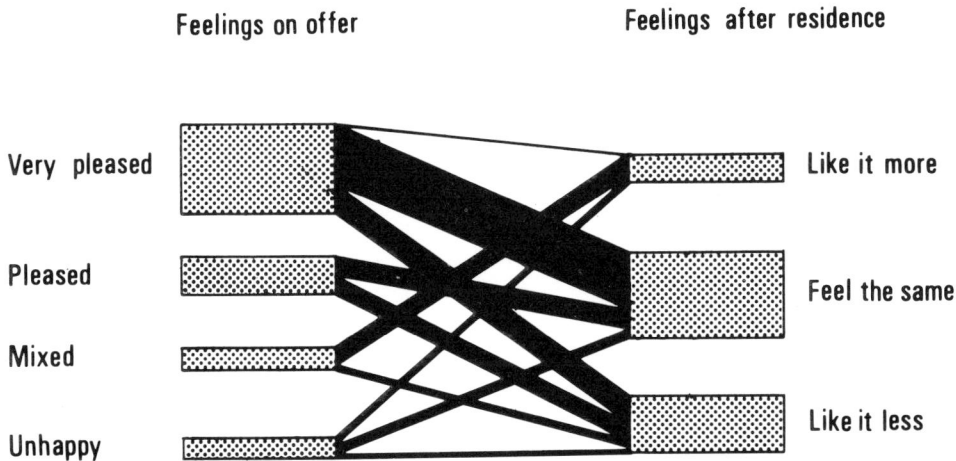

Feelings on offer

Very pleased

Pleased

Mixed

Unhappy

Feelings after residence

Like it more

Feel the same

Like it less

At the outset male respondents express least dislike and then tend to adopt a more negative view while more women initially express dislike or mixed feelings. Older respondents tend to remain unchanged in their feelings towards the estate or come to like it more, younger respondents are more likely to come to like it less. There is little variation in the reaction at the time of offer according to household type except that one-or two-person households are likely to have mixed feelings. Households with three or more persons and households with children are initially likely to feel pleased or happy and to later feel less positively about the estate. A higher proportion of black than white families express themselves happy on offer, but fewer remain unchanged in their outlook and the shift is more negative.

Former place of residence appears to have little effect in determining attitudes at the time of offer. However, in settling down it may be an important factor. Fewer residents rehoused from outside the Old Borough subsequently felt the same and more came to like the estate less. In regard to length of residence on the estate the most positive reactions relate to the latest development phase, the garden flats. There 75% of respondents expressed themselves happy on offer, 12% pleased, 10% had mixed feelings and only 5% expressed feelings of dislike. The most negative reactions on offer come apparently from respondents who moved into units which had previously been occupied. Subsequently the views of these respondents tended to remain unchanged or to become slightly more positive.

Block type does not seem to be a significant factor in shaping initial reactions. The exception, already noted, is provided by the garden flats. There is, however, some variations which may be related to building form, in later opinions. The highest proportion of respondents who came to feel more negatively (44%) are from the Y blocks. Initially there is little dissatisfaction expressed by tower block respondents, half remain unchanged in their views, 10% come to like their situation more and 40% like it less. Floor level apparently has little effect on the response at the time of offer. The most noticeable shift negatively occurs among respondents living on the first, second and third floors.

Tentatively, since few express extremely positive or negative views, it may be suggested that most respondents are moderately pleased with their overall housing situation. I am unable to suggest explanations for those differences which appear to be related to sex, race or block type. Those relating to floor level may be associated with higher densities of children and the possible nuisance caused to some residents by children's play. However, more detailed information would be needed before this possible explanation could be supported. Those most likely to sustain a favourable view of Parkview are older residents long familiar with the locality. Younger respondents, households with children and respondents formerly resident outside the Old Borough, are all likely to acknowledge with enthusiasm the marked improvement in their housing situation afforded by the move to the estate. Later they are likely to become more critical as any drawbacks attendant on the new situation become apparent, prospects for further improvement fade or the distance from 'home' assumes larger significance. At the time of the survey respondents in the garden flats, regardless of household type, continued to express themselves well pleased with their circumstances. It is not known at what point residents are likely to change their views and in this regard it would be of interest to follow up these respondents at say two-yearly intervals.

At the same time most respondents (67%) expressed no desire to move eleswhere on the estate and most (78%) felt that given their present economic and other personal circumstances Parkview offered a generally satisfactory environment. Of course this finding may simply reflect a realistic acceptance of the lack of alternative options open to most respondents. Even so in ideal terms with no constraints operative, most respondents have quite modest ambitions; 14% said that given a free choice they would opt to live on the estate, 26% would in such circumstances choose to live in the Old Borough and 25% mostly middle aged or elderly couples, would choose to live somewhere in the country or by the sea. Other choices, all in small numbers, were the Borough, other London boroughs, another city or overseas. For 66% of all respondents their ideal dwelling type in their chosen location would be a house with a garden.

This overall reaction of respondents to the estate needs to be supplemented by their experience of particular aspects of living there; the assessment of the individual dwelling, the dwelling in relation to neighbouring units, the estate outside the dwelling and the development of self image within the estate and beyond. Most respondents expressed themselves well pleased with their own flats. There was some criticism of features of design, a door hung so that it opened awkwardly, a lack of storage space, the size of particular rooms, the expense of operating the form of heating provided and so on, but these criticisms were considerably modified by two other factors; the contrast with previous housing conditions and a greater emphasis on features of the estate outside the dwelling, subject to stronger criticisms and for the most part considered beyond the control of the resident.

In relation to neighbouring units there was only one complaint of visual overlooking from the lower floors of one of the tower blocks into a nearby block of garden flats. More residents were aware of the loss of visual contact with people especially at the upper floor levels where the view was a roof or sky scape. 'You and the postman are the only people who have gone past today'. Another resident in one of the tower blocks commented that such buildings were not for his 'class of people', rather they should constitute luxury accommodation with porters on the door and 'middle class or upper class' residents. In his view the Y blocks with ' . . . doors opening onto balconies where you can see everyone are for the likes of us'. One resident in a garden flat praised the estate for its quietness. 'It's just like being in heaven; I sleep beautiful it's so quiet'. Perhaps not surprisingly this was an exceptional view and many more residents, particularly in this block type, complained of the lack of sound insulation and how, aware of the extent to which noise from neighbours and passers by intruded into their own privacy, they were conscious of the possible effect of their own behaviour on others.

Residents have a diverse range of views on the estate as a place to live, the appearance and relative ratings of various blocks and block types, the maintenance of the estate and the reputation of their estate in the context of the immediate locality.

' . . . nothing will make this place right. You walk home at night and it's like walking into an institution.'
'What we need is smaller estates'.
'This is a lovely estate. I'm very happy here'.
'It's not the place, it's the people . . . '.

When asked if they considered Parkview generally had any good features the most common response was the convenience of the individual flat. Approximately 30% of all respondents considered the estate had no good features and somewhat more felt it had no bad features. The consensus of opinion seemed to be that it was very much 'average' or 'just so so,' with little that seriously detracted and less to commend. Location of the estate was frequently mentioned as a good feature, the poor qualitative assessment attaching to the estate outside the dwelling most commonly as a bad feature. Predictably in regard to the latter most criticism was directed at the public areas of the estate and particularly the entrance lobbies, stairs and lifts. The lack of cleanliness, the public abuse of these areas and poor standards of caretaking were most common criticisms. Very few people (4%) were satisfied with the service in this respect. Most respondents attributed the general abuse of the public areas and the vandalism most evident there to children from within the estate. Fifteen percent considered that the blame attached to adults as well. Respondents generally felt that most improvement could be effected by better standards of caretaking and by design modifications to the buildings themselves. Otherwise the problem was felt to be a fairly intractable one; some advocated the punishment of offenders by caretakers or parents, others recommended the setting up of vigilante patrols or the institution of a system of fines imposed on parents while some 22% despaired of any remedy.

In order to get some appraisal of the ranking of block types on the estate respondents in the sample population were asked to rate blocks in terms of their attractiveness by reference to a serious of photographs. These are reproduced as Plates 10 to 16 together with a selection of the comments made by respondents. For the purpose of this exercise a photograph of the sheltered housing unit was included together with three photographs of blocks elsewhere incorporated within the single category of balcony blocks. (Plates 10, 14 and 16) The results have been weighted such that a first choice scored three points, second choice two points and third choice one point. The block selected as least attractive scored three minus points. The results are set out in Figure III.

It is clear that there is a large body of opinion in favour of the garden flats; a long way behind but still acceptable are the sheltered housing block, Church Close and the Y blocks. The tower blocks feature overwhelmingly in the negative assessment. In regard to reasons for choice it would seem that bricks are considered more attractive than concrete, an interesting shape is appreciated and a smaller scale is preferred. Perhaps most important are the general surroundings. The garden flats were popular as a first choice often because of their gardens; Church Close was liked because it is part of a pleasant view down to the church.

It also became clear from interviews and other discussions that visual attractiveness and other qualities are not entirely unconnected. Thus one resident in the garden blocks commented, 'Some snob value attaches to living in your type of block (the Y), our blocks are attractive and we all forget about the tower blocks, but who would feel proud to point to those and say they lived there?' (the older balcony access blocks). This assessment would appear to be based partly on the stereotyped 'council flats' image of the blocks so denigrated but probably also reflects another kind of evaluation. One block in particular has a high proportion of four and five-person households (just over 50%) and seems always to have housed a few 'problem' families. The block is situated in such a position that any disturbance there is very obvious. In these

Fig. III. Ranking of blocks according to attractiveness.*

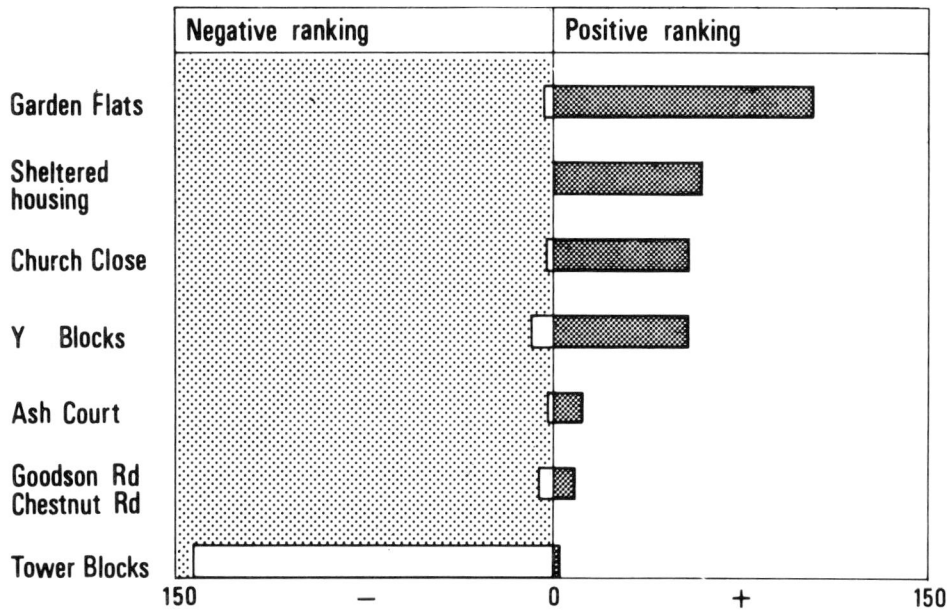

Negative ranking	Positive ranking

Garden Flats

Sheltered housing

Church Close

Y   Blocks

Ash Court

Goodson Rd
Chestnut Rd

Tower Blocks

150   —   0   +   150

* These figures are based on a response rate of 92% for the first choice and 77% for the last choice. For a variety of reasons some respondents were unable to complete this question, others declined, especially to make a second and third choice (recorded for 69% and 38% respectively), on the grounds that apart from first and last rankings any differentiation between the blocks was difficult or meaningless since they were all 'much of a muchness'.

circumstances the reputation of the minority easily attaches to the majority, however unjustly, and I heard the block disparagingly labelled as 'sin block'. The situation of a block may be quite an important factor in this colouring of reputation. Another small block with a higher proportion of four- and-five person households and high child densities has among its own residents often been the subject for complaints to the council about unruly behaviour especially among teenagers. It is however, on one boundary of the estate at some distance from other blocks, presents an attractive facade to the road and is generally well regarded by other residents.

Residents and outsiders also rank the estate in relation to others in the immediate locality. Familiarity with the area is important in this regard. For some residents their view is coloured with the nostalgia of time and they contrast their previous residence on other local authority estates unfavourably with their present housing situation. Thus a number of residents who formerly lived on one of the oldest estates in the Old Borough commented on what a 'lovely' estate it was, strictly managed and well cared for and friendly with people in and out for a cup of tea and in summer everyone sitting out along balconies bright with pots of geraniums. On another of these estates it was claimed that when one person had a party everyone joined in. In retrospect at least these first estates are described as sharing the richness of social relationships which in other contexts is reserved for street neighbourhoods. Now these same pre-war estates have a rather different image as 'problem' or 'dump' estates and former residents are quick to point out how they have changed in the interim and are now rated poorly in comparison with Parkview. This assessment would seem to be to some extent a reflection of the comparative modernity of the estate but other factors are also relevant. Thus a newer estate close by quickly acquired a mixed reputation on account of labelling as 'a league of nations', jerry built and generally undesirable as a place to live. In these negative assessments publicity through the local press is a factor influencing opinion. Another estate nearby which is generally highly rated as 'a beautiful estate' appears to have a high standard of caretaking and is said to be 'very quiet'. It is a relatively small estate with a fairly large proportion of all adult households. In this instance and to some extent in the less favourably rated estates opinion is shaped largely by contacts with friends or relatives resident there. The residents' image of their own estate in relation to the reputations acquired by other estates appears to be that Parkview is 'middling', a 'respectable' address, a good deal better than some even if not quite in the first rank.

I would like to live in [the estate] because you can play football in the green and you will not be late for school. and you can go to the play ground when you like to. And you are near to a library and some shops to make an an even better place you can paint it and clean the windows to make people keep it that way is to make Police live there.

One other dimension should be added to this resident view of the estate. Children too develop their own images and as part of Wendy's research children at Park Primary School were asked by their own teachers to write about what it is like to live on Parkview. Children who lived elsewhere were asked to state whether they would like to live there. The ages of these children range from six to ten. Their stories and drawings show a lively and perceptive eye for detail and a few are reproduced here to illustrate the vivid quality of their world view.

I like [the estate] Be cause there is a library and you dont have to walk a long way and You have got a park to Play in Flowers grow there too I would Just Put Some thing in the lift to stop them from Breaking the lift.

From these and other stories one theme that emerges is the possibility of trouble on the estate. The remedies suggested are at least original and included watchdogs, television and 'an electric charge through the roof' to stop boys from climbing on the library. One child commented that the caretakers were nice to talk to 'but they don't do much work'. Some children expressed fears of being trapped by fire or lift breakdowns and one commented that the estate would not be a pleasant place to live on account of excessive noise; from cars and lorries if one lived near the ground and 'from aeroplanes at the top'. Children who expressed a liking for moving to Parkview most often mentioned the close proximity to school and the existence of playgrounds on the estate. Suggested improvements to the estate included the cleaning and polishing of 'all the outsides of the flats until they shone', carpeted stairways, more trees and the provision of benches, a swimming pool, puppet shows and films. One pupil

I walk in my court it smells like dust bines it smells like rubies Just sometimes the birds cheep. All the trees in our court are dieing because people have knifes and cut the trees the grass is dirty And when I get in the lift it smells of wee and pooh from discusting stupid idiotic Boys I Just can't bear it Soon I will most probaly die of clostifobia if we had a chage to move we would. There is new flats going up but some all readed have writing on them and scribble when the sewers lorry comes to drain the sewers out when he gone it smells for a day. And sometimes in a big buidding it has a hole in it and the sewers water comes out all ove people. It has to be done ever month but it breaks again. The flowers were nice but they die because people play football and knock the flowers off.

claimed 'I would not like living in a small house with a big garden'. Another clearly outlined the difference between her previous residence and the estate.

We used to live in guest houses. We all had to live in one room. When we moved to Parkview I liked it because there were other children around. I had a room of my own. . . . Now we have a kitchen and Mummy cooks food for us.

This then is something of the general characteristics of the estate and its population and of the residents initial and overall response to living there. Discussion now turns to a consideration of the patterns and quality of social relationships in which residents engage.

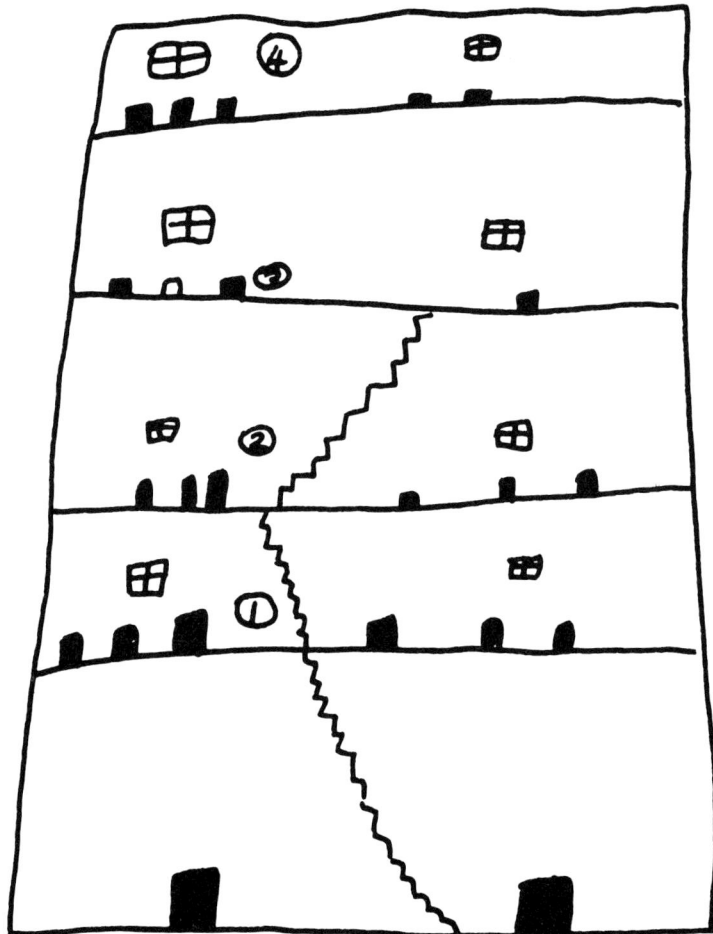

Social interaction on Parkview

Slightly more than half (53%) of all respondents claimed that in general their social life was unchanged by the move to the estate, 26% claimed that they experienced some deterioration in that regard as a result and 19% claimed some improvement. It will be shown that in the context of the estate 'unchanged' or 'improved social life' means close and frequent contact within a network defined mainly by kinship ties together with casual, involuntary contacts within a wider network defined by neighbourhood or locality ties. The discussion is ordered under the headings kinship, neighbours, friends and workmates.

Kinship

A metropolitan situation such as that of London presents kinship operationally in a very different light from that in rural or indeed many urban studies. When people live in separate independent units not related by kinship to their neighbours or others living close by; when their actions are free from daily oversight on the part of their kin; when their behaviour at work, and home or in recreation need not depend at all on kinship, people undertake social relations with their kin because they *are* kin, either from voluntary choice or because of their sense of obligation, and not because they are dealing with workmates or neighbours who happen also to be kin.[14]

Nevertheless, even in London, as Willmott and Young have shown in their study of Bethnal Green,[15] in some localities among particular socio-economic groups the sense of obligation may be very strong and personal choice may result in a pattern of social interaction that is almost entirely kinship based. It was to be expected, given the high proportion of residents with long and close ties with the Old Borough and the relatively homogeneous class structure of the estate, that many of its residents would also have relatives living nearby. However, it was somewhat surprising to find that 77% of all respondents claimed to have at least one relative resident locally, and only 18% had no relatives resident locally.[16] Just over half of those respondents with relatives locally were themselves middle aged, 21% were under 34 and 27% 60 or over. The middle age group is the one most likely to feel responsibilities towards both sons and daughters and ageing parents and to have the time to sustain relationships with them. Respondents with relatives resident locally are also more likely to have been resident on the estate for many years and to have been rehoused from the Old Borough.[17] Both factors are of course indicative of long family association with the area. Somewhat surprisingly 69% of black respondents have relatives living nearby although it should be added that black respondents without kin nearby tend to feel particularly isolated and vulnerable.[18] The largest single category of kin named was siblings (49%) followed by parents or parents in law (27%) other relatives (22%) and sons or daughters and their spouses (19%).

Twenty-five percent of respondents have kin resident on the estate. These were more often parents or parents in law, siblings and other relatives with fewer married sons or daughters. The large majority of respondents with kin ties on the estate have been rehoused from within the Old Borough (89%) and have long associations with the neighbourhood. The extent to which some families form an extended family network on the estate was in particular cases quite remarkable. Thus in Chestnut Road live three brothers and their wives, their sister, her husband and the widowed husband of another sister. This man also has his own sister resident in the sheltered housing unit and he regularly shops for her. Moreover, while he sees his brothers and sisters in law less often since his wife died, he still maintains more or less regular contact with her family. Two of these couples (a brother and sister and their spouses), have always lived close by, now have flats next door to each other and would like to be jointly allocated a house somewhere off the estate. In another block lives an elderly woman with her two unmarried daughters. She has two married children resident on the estate, one at a higher level in the same block and one, a daughter, visits daily. In addition another daughter works locally as a tea lady and every day in between breaks shops for her mother and sits with her for company. A middle aged couple in one of the garden flats have a married son resident in the same block as themselves and a second in another block. More commonly instances of relatives resident on the estate involve only two households. The Borough has no policy of favouring the rehousing of relatives in close proximity.[19] It would therefore seem most likely that the occurrence of kinship networks within the estate is an incidental effect of slum clearance programmes from areas with already established residential family groupings. Unless a policy is introduced to facilitate the allocation of tenancies to the kinsfolk of present residents it is also, given the tendency in recent years to draw tenants from a wider geographical area, a pattern that is likely to weaken.

One expression of kin ties is visiting patterns and something of this has already been indicated. It is of course virtually impossible to obtain accurate information on visiting and mutual support prior to the move to the estate.

However, other studies suggest that kinship ties are sustained after such a move[20] and on the estate existing patterns of visiting certainly suggest the social importance attached to kinship. This is particularly significant when set alongside the fact that friends and neighbours are seldom entertained in the home. Sixty-nine percent of those respondents whose parents live nearby claim to visit them at least once weekly. The corresponding figure for sons and daughters is 63% and for siblings 69%. Visiting, especially between kin of different generations, is often marked by various kinds of assistance as well as by sociability, thus a daughter who goes shopping for her mother every weekend, another who calls every day with a mid-day meal, a mother who fetches a granddaughter from school every day, a father who comes to Sunday lunch every week and so on.

Neighbours

A second important category of social contacts are those involving neighbours. Patterns of interaction between neighbours are here considered in terms of opinions about Parkview as a social environment and respondents assessments of ideal and experienced neighbourly behaviour. This is followed by some illustrative material on particular aspects of observed neighbour relations including conflict situations and the processes of interaction on my own balcony.

Forty percent of all respondents were of the opinion that others on the estate were the same sort of people as themselves. Almost as many (37%) felt that estate people were mixed and 18% felt other residents were different from themselves. Most commonly sameness was defined in terms of class or more general characteristics; 'working class', 'ordinary', 'average', or 'family' people. Difference was expressed in terms of status characteristics such as 'reserved', 'respectable' and 'rough' or, in a few cases, age.[21] These concepts are most clearly illustrated by a few comments from interview schedules.

'Some who move in here think they are a bit better than everybody else when in fact they all came out of slums'.

'. . . there are a few people who 'I love me'— think they run the estate—a bit toffee nosed'.

Another couple claimed that formerly they had a good deal in common with other residents. 'But now councils try to mix people up on the assumption that if you put the bad with the good it will make everyone alright—it doesn't work like that. You don't know who you've got living around you—the police are always here'. One man who cut himself off completely from the estate commented that he considered the estate a jungle and the caretakers useless. But the main fault was, he considered, with the tenants. 'They need to be educated. Most come from slum clearance and they've never got above that'.

Such comments were common among those who expressed views of difference or heterogeneity. However, rather fewer respondents (30%) were prepared to name any out groups. Those specified were, in order of frequency, 'coloureds', 'problem families', residents from outside the Old Borough and Irish families. It should be noted that direct questioning on group categorizations may not elicit a response and other evidence suggests that in terms of the processes of social interaction these understandings may be more important than the figures suggest. A few respondents expressed the view that black and white residents should not be housed on the same estates because the former have 'different ways'. Another claimed there was an allocation ratio of four to one in favour of 'coloureds'. 'We were given to understand that [two estates with an unfavourable reputation] would be given over to the coloureds and that they would move white families out. But they are taking over everywhere . . .' One resident claimed that the council, aware of the out group categorizations 'coloured' and 'non Old Borough' had taken the trouble to distribute households in these categories throughout Parkview. More common is the view of black residents as a group encroaching on and competing for housing considered to be the right of Old Borough residents. 'Granted they've got to live somewhere but it's just not on when our kids can't be housed by the council'. 'Our men fought in the war, my mother has seen two world wars; the likes of us gave up a lot for this country and to make a better life for our children. Now we can't get anything. They [black residents] get it all and they don't appreciate it.'[22]

One respondent claimed that most residents in her block were from the Old Borough and 'they don't want to know any one else'. Another, herself an Old Borough resident commented that while in her block few people knew each other initially, as Old Borough people they soon found themselves with people and places in common.

Some categorizations may be combined. One resident railing against Irish residents generally gave as an example a particular 'problem' family. '. . . he kicks the windows out when he's drunk and next day the council is down to put it back. If I break something I've got to pay for it and I wait months. She went on holiday with the kids and left him here and Welfare paid for it. Marvellous isn't it — you struggle for years and you don't get anywhere and people like that have it all handed to them'.

Those likely to feel estate residents are the same type of people as themselves are younger residents, households with children and recent arrivals on the estate. It is of interest to note that there appears to be little difference between black and white households in this regard and most black respondents said they felt other residents were in the same social situation as themselves. Middle aged and older residents, single person and two-person households and those with long periods of residence on the estate are more likely to incline to the view that residents are a mixed lot. The view of the established residents is generally linked to the opinion that formerly the estate did constitute a homogeneous social group but that in latter years it has declined as a wider range of behaviour has become apparently acceptable with an influx of other social groups. Those who categorize estate residents as different from themselves in whatever way are spread over all household types, lengths of residence and age groups.

Generally respondents who categorize estate people as the same or mixed tend to have a greater range of social contacts than those who express a sense of difference. In this context difference appears to imply social distancing and respondents expressing this view tend to have relatively few contacts on the estate. At the same time there are a few people who at once express a sense of affinity with estate residents and who yet claim to know nobody.

Respondents were asked to rate the neighbourly quality of estate residents generally. The qualities of a good neighbour stressed most were friendliness, helpfulness and a reserved manner. Friendliness and reserve were often mentioned together as attributes desired in a good neighbour; such a person should be friendly at least to the extent of 'passing the time of day' but not 'too friendly' in which case neighbours would be considered intrusive and interfering. 'People here are sociable. I mean you can't go round knocking on doors but they are friendly. Nobody on a council estate can afford to be snobby. We don't gossip though—we've never been one for that. You can't afford to get too close to people'. Other qualities in a good neighbour mentioned by fewer respondents were cleanliness and quietness. Forty-nine percent of all respondents said they felt that on Parkview people were good neighbours to each other, 16% felt that some were and others were not, 14% had a poor opinion of estate residents as neighbours and the remainder (20%) recorded a don't know response. Respondents were rather less critical in assessing their own neighbours. Thus, 67% assessed their neighbours as good, 17% as mixed and 5% as poor. The remainder said they could give no opinion. Those who rate estate residents highly are likely to know their own immediate neighbours and to have a wider range of contacts on the estate. Established residents are as likely as new arrivals to feel that other residents are good neighbours and middle aged and elderly residents are more likely to adopt an equivocal attitude. These responses are open to a number of interpretations. It may be that positive attitudes towards neighbours and a preparedness to initiate relationships are linked or it may be that favourable experiences with immediate neighbours forms the basis for an equally favourable assessment of neighbours in general. It would seem likely that the mixed feelings expressed by older residents are related to their ideal of the more intimate neighbourliness associated with the terrace street.

Nineteen percent of all respondents claim to know no other person on the estate. These respondents have a range of opinions on the neighbourly qualities of residents and such social isolation appears to have little relationship with place of residence prior to rehousing, length of residence on the estate, block type or floor level. There does however, appear to be an age factor; 71% of all respondents in this category are middle aged or elderly. This suggests that personality factors such as an inability to easily enter into casual relationships and physical factors like the immobility often associated with old age, might be important inhibiting conditions. At the same time 50% of respondents in the middle aged and elderly groups know their immediate neighbours and the middle aged group has relatively more contact than younger or elderly respondents with others on the estate as well. Contact with neighbours among the elderly tends to be concentrated in those parts of the estate where all residents are in that age group as in those blocks where all flats on the ground floor are bedsitters. In Ash Court for example, where the ground floor and one wing are given over to bedsitters there appears to be a good deal of contact between neighbours, in this instance facilitated by the activities of two quite elderly but particularly active and outgoing residents.[23]

Those respondents who both know their immediate neighbours and have other contacts on the estate tend to be either long standing residents or recent arrivals. This suggests that residents who moved in fairly considerable numbers at the time of completion of major phases in the development of the estate find it easier to make initial contacts with other residents all of whom are similarly placed in a new situation. This may be contrasted with the 'phase/stage hypothesis' tested in the Hyde Park estate study.

It envisages 3 phases in the development of contact amongst the residents in a particular area. In the initial phase contacts will be restricted by the unfamiliarity of the social environment and the uncertainty of new residents about their status in the community. Maximum levels of social contact will only be achieved after some years of residence, by which time roles are established and various integrating agencies like club membership and involvement in the affairs of young children will have been efective.[24]

Respondents whose former place of residence was the Borough are less likely to know their immediate neighbours, 45% as compared with 70% for the Old Borough, but in terms of all contacts on the estate there is little difference between the two. One possible explanation for this discrepancy is that Borough residents make contacts with others from their area but I have no evidence that this is in fact the case.

Families with children and extended family type households are more likely to know their immediate neighbours and to have other contacts on the estate when compared with one-or two-person households. The presence of children would appear to facilitate casual exchanges especially between women whose major rôle is that of mother. In this regard there is little variation in terms of ethnicity, floor level and block type. Y block and garden flat respondents have on average approximately 1.5 contacts with residents apart from their immediate neighbours, tower block and balcony access respondents slightly fewer. It should be noted, however, that such figures conceal a wide range of variations. In one of the garden flat blocks for example there is a good deal of casual contact between residents and a particularly high level of contact between a small group of households on the ground floor. As noted for the elderly, this pattern appears to be fostered by the presence of a few very outgoing and friendly housewives.[25] The home of one of these housewives was the venue for a new years party to which the whole block was invited. There is a fair amount of visiting between this and three other ground floor residences. This has not gone unnoticed among some of the residents in Chestnut Road which overlooks these flats. As one commented, 'It's like Coronation Street—they are always in and out of each others houses'. A resident on the upper balcony of this garden block commented that all residents there 'are pretty much the same age with kids and that helps in getting to know people'. She added that if her own children came home from school when she was out neighbours would take them in. At the other extreme a resident in a tower block commented that while the situation suited her because she was at work all day, she could go for three or four weeks without meeting anyone on her landing; she had never seen her next door neighbour and knew those opposite only by sight.

Most of those respondents who know their immediate neighbours and who have a fairly wide range of contacts on the estate claim that the move to the estate made no difference to their social life, 18% claimed their social life deteriorated and 27% claimed an improvement. Not surprisingly people who have no contacts with others on the estate for the most part claim their social life has remained unchanged or has deteriorated. Unfortunately I am unable to specify what factors lead respondents to categorize their situation as better or worse than that formerly enjoyed.

Respondents were asked if there was anybody they could call on if they needed assistance in the event of some difficulty such as illness in the family. Sixty-two percent said they would call on a neighbour, 20% relatives, 7% on a combination of friends, neighbours or relatives and 1% on caretakers. A few respondents (7%) claimed that there was nobody they could call on in an emergency.[26] These findings suggest firstly, that while some residents call on kin, a sense of mutual obligation in regard to assistance of this kind may well be modified by physical proximity since 77% of all respondents have relatives living locally. Twenty-five percent have relatives on the estate and it may well be that the more active of these are first called upon. Secondly, while 19% of all respondents claim to have no contacts with others on the estate, most even of these felt that in an emergency they could call on someone. 'Nobody ever offers or takes the initiative but they would help if you asked'. In these circumstances apparent social isolation may not necessarily preclude future contact.

Assistance from neighbours may in fact be of a very practical kind. One woman commented how when she herself was ill her neighbours offered her husband any help he needed. A resident in a block with a predominantly elderly population explained how she had been approached to replace a lightbulb or fetch a newspaper. Another woman spoke of how on the death of her husband she had received letters of sympathy from other residents on the balcony and several men had offered to do odd jobs for her. Some emergencies may involve widespread assistance. Thus when one flat was gutted by fire the TA organized a collection of money and furniture etc to help the victims. The response was very generous and one of the collectors claimed, 'These flats are very good like that. If ever there is any trouble people don't mind helping out'. Some assistance can be quite long term. An elderly couple living next door to an invalid and his aged parent for years cooked, shopped and generally cared for them both. Another elderly woman calls daily on an aged neighbour to check whether she is in need of anything. At the other extreme there are residents, particularly those elderly residents who feel themselves to be isolated, who fear that they could fall ill or die without anyone knowing or caring. Such fears are not without foundation; during my time on the estate a woman living alone in one of the garden flats died and was not found for a week. And there are crises in which the TA does not get involved. Sometime after I had left Parkview a young woman living alone with her two children died after a fall from the 7th floor of a Y block.[27] The TA made no attempt to get in touch with the family or offer assistance because in the words of the chairman, 'people are so funny . . .'.

There is clearly a wide range of opinion concerning both expected and experienced neighbourliness on the estate. Moreover it should be noted that even those who have a high opinion of the estate's neighbourliness still compare it unfavourably with their experience in the old streets of terrace housing. One woman who had received offers of help from her estate neighbours commented how at her mother's 'the door was always open and you could always go and knock for a cup of sugar. But imagine knocking here for a cup of sugar – if somebody wasn't used to the street way they would wonder'. Another said that when she visited her sick mother at her home in a nearby street the neighbours would offer to look after and feed the children if she had to go out. 'All that is lost on an estate'. The perceived difference in the quality of neighbourliness in the two settings appears to be connected with the feeling noted above that while friendliness is valued in a neighbour, 'over friendliness' is regarded as intrusive and possibly threatening to an individual's privacy. On Parkview the balance may be more difficult to sustain.

Here [on the estate] people get frightened of others being so close and think they will want things so they keep out altogether.

You don't want to be in and out of other people's houses. But it would be nice to offer hospitality from time to time and to call on help if you needed it. At [a nearby street and former place of residence] you could walk out onto the street and see somebody to talk to, old women took chairs out on the pavement and if you were ill a knock on the wall would bring someone in. You don't get that on estates.

People in terrace housing can afford to be friendly because they have a private world when they want it.

This then is how respondents speak of the overall pattern of interaction between themselves and other estate residents. Particular aspects of the observed behaviour, neighbour relations on a balcony, conflict between neighbours and ethnicity as a factor in social interation can be described in more detail at this point.

During my stay on the estate I was able to observe and take part in the social life of my balcony. I have no reason to believe that this balcony was in any way untypical; rather it would seem to be fairly similar to any other balcony in the Y blocks (Plate 18). The blue block in which I lived has at ground floor level a branch library which fronts on to the main roadway into the estate and major pedestrian pathways pass through it giving access to the green and red blocks and other parts of the estate. (See plan III) As on all Y block balconies 15 maisonettes open onto the access balcony with five 1-2—and 3-bedroom units opening onto each arm of the Y. Two lifts and a staircase open onto the central foyer area and there are two rubbish chutes, one on each side of the access area. My immediate neighbours were two families, the Thomas family with two young children and the Ewing family with four young children under seven. Other residents were an elderly widower Mr Ross and a Spanish woman Mrs

Plan V. Layout of Y block.

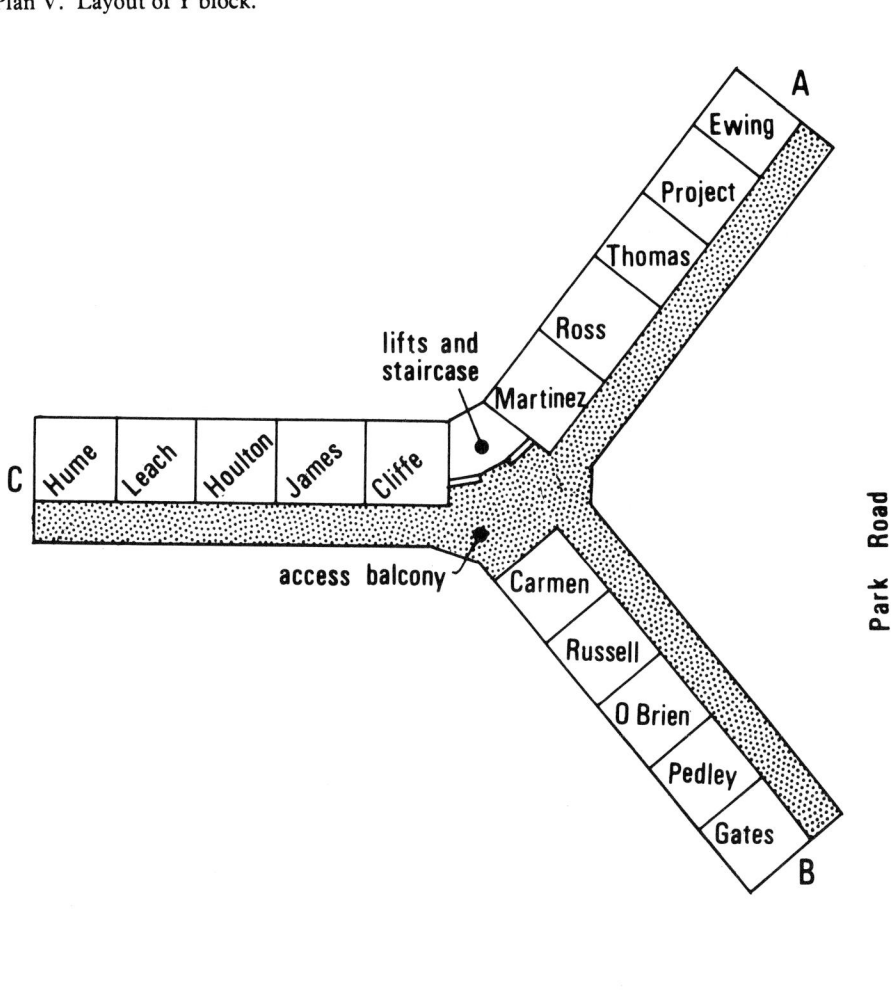

Martinez who lived with her school age son. The adjoining wing comprised two families, the Gates' with three teenagers and the O'Brien's with five children. The other residents, Mrs Pedley, Mrs Russell and Mrs Carmen were all widows living alone. The third arm of the Y has one-nuclear family type household, Mr and Mrs Houlton, her step sister and two grand children, an elderly couple Mr and Mrs Leach and three widows Mrs James, Mrs Cliffe and Mrs Hume. The arrangement of these households is given in Plan v.

Six households, Carmens, Leach, Hume, Cliffe, Ross and James moved into their flats in December 1959 or January 1960 when the building was first opened. Pedley and O'Briens moved in 1967, the Gates' the following year. The Houltons' took up residence in 1969, Martinez and Russell in 1970, the Thomases in 1971 and Ewing in 1972. Hume, Cliffe, Ross, Leach, Carmen, Gates, Pedley, James, Houlton and Russell all have long associations with the Old Borough. Hume, Cliffe and James were rehoused from the same requisitioned property. Houlton and Ross were formerly neighbours in the streets demolished to make way for the extensions to the estate while Leach and Pedley were formerly resident in the same council estate in another part of the Old Borough. There are thus many households who knew each other prior to taking up residence on the balcony, details of individual family ties and backgrounds were already familiar, residents could be placed and categorized. Other households have a shorter association with the Old Borough or were rehoused from elsewhere. During their time on the balcony the husbands of three women died while in two households teenage children have grown up and left to get married. My own observation of the contact between these households concerns mainly the wings marked A and B. This would be the case for any resident since these access ways overlook whereas visual contact between residents on C wing and those on A and B wings is possible only from the balconies of the maisonettes on the latter or from within the dwelling itself.

Overall there is very little visiting between residents. The closest ties were between two next door neighbours, the O'Brien household and Mrs Pedley. The latter visited Mrs O'Brien for 'a cuppa and a nag' but was careful not to intrude if Mr O'Brien was at home. Since the death of her husband Mrs Pedley had become very nervous of being alone in the flat at night and one of the O'Brien girls slept there each night. Both households are members of the same church and Mrs Pedley accompanied the girls to service. Mrs Pedley also visited Mr Ross especially on days when his sister called and she became a frequent visitor to my flat. This was one of very few instances of contact between wings; other residents tended to meet in the shared spaces while using the chutes or waiting for a lift. Apart from her balcony contacts Mrs Pedley had numerous social contacts on the estate and in the immediate locality. She was a great source of local gossip and a key link in the internal gossip networks of A and B wings. For other residents contact was much more casual and did not involve visiting. There was no other evidence of regular assistance or support and few instances of borrowing. Casual contact occurred outside the home. All residents know each other by sight if not by name,[28] and to 'pass the time of day'. As already pointed out for many this familiarity is coloured by shared associations with the area. Mr Ross spent a good deal of time standing on the access balcony watching the activity below and other residents from A wing together with Mrs Pedley would often join him for a chat especially on summer evenings. Similar exchanges took place between residents on B wing but there was little balcony interaction on C wing. In their different ways Mr Ross and Mrs Pedley played an important rôle in this interaction. She took an active rôle in seeking out anyone prepared to stop for a 'nag', he by standing outside his own flat for long periods invited passers-by to join him for the same reason. During the field work period Mrs Pedley left the estate and Mr Ross was transferred to a home for elderly people; these changes removed two of the main focuses for casual interaction on these balconies and with their departure the level of such contact dropped quite markedly. Otherwise residents might stop and have a chat in the market, at the laundry, supermarket or bingo. Mrs Martinez and Mrs Thomas often met when escorting their children to the same school.

The degree of involvement among neighbours was therefore fairly limited and there appeared to be a reluctance to become more involved. When Mrs Thomas was unable to collect her children from school on a few occasions she asked me to do it rather than Mrs Martinez. Mrs Cliffe offered to babysit anytime for the Thomases but she has never been taken up on the offer. And when on two occasions during the study period I invited all the women on the balcony to supper, they commented on how they never got together and for most it was the first time they had visited another flat on the balcony. This reluctance to get involved appears to be based partly on an unwillingness to be 'obliged' to anyone and partly on a desire to preserve the privacy of the home. Similar characteristics were noted for Green Leigh estate. There 'even where neighbours were willing to assist, people were apparently reluctant to depend on them too much or to confide in them too freely'.[29]

Some residents on the balcony have friends elsewhere on the estate. Mrs Carmen regularly visits and assists another widow in the green block. Mrs Ewing visits and goes shopping with a young mother resident in Chestnut Road. However, for most balcony residents kinsfolk were central to their social life and the most frequent visitors to their homes. Mrs Hume's married daughter, her husband and their baby often stay for a weekend. Mrs Thomas has several married sisters resident nearby and they and their families call from time to time. Other relatives periodically visit from Ireland and stay with the family. Both Mr and Mrs Houlton come from large families and they themselves have 15 children; their home is the centre for constant coming and going by sundry relatives. Prior to her illness Mrs James' mother called every day. Mrs Cliffe spends every Sunday with one of her married sons and her sister-in-law lives on the next balcony up. Mrs Pedley works locally together with several of her relatives. Mr Ross' sister visits weekly. For others kinsfolk live further afield and visits are less frequent if no less important. For Mrs Martinez Spanish speaking friends provide a substitute for kin.

Social activity on the balcony is family oriented and home centered. Neighbours for the most part share an experience of place and people but meetings between them are casual as the opportunity arises, seldom planned. This is not to say, however, that there is not a good deal of knowledge of the habits of the balcony dwellers, in some instances including a knowledge of what goes on inside the flat; this despite the fact that the informant may never have set foot within. Regular visitors to the balcony are recognized. Some few residents have a reputation for being very reserved, even too aloof. Others are thought to be too houseproud, or lacking in the quality altogether '. . . the bugs would move the furniture for her . . .' It is known that Mr Ross is mooching around on the balcony most afternoons, that Mr Leach goes down to the off-licence every evening for his Guinness, that Mrs Russell holds church meetings at her flat one evening every week. With the exception of the few who 'keep themselves to themselves' this observation of behaviour within the balcony extends to other parts of the block and to other blocks overlooked from the balcony. Comment on the wider situation is normally reserved for behaviour which might be judged deviant. A visit from the police, a 'punch up', a noisy party, the latest exploits in a fairly notorious 'problem' family may all be noticed in this way.

The observed behaviour on the balcony corresponds fairly closely to the patterns recounted by respondents and is similar to those described elsewhere.[30] In summary social life on the balcony is characterised by close contact with kin within the home and casual contact with neighbours outside it. Regarding the latter expressions of neighbourliness vary considerably. A few residents are always prepared to stop for a chat, others may not be spoken to for months on end. The opportunities for making involuntary contacts are anyway limited and may be further circumscribed by personality traits and individual schedules. Residents take a kind of pride in 'keeping themselves to themselves' and are careful not to intrude on the privacy of others. Visiting between neighbours is rare. Family visits by contrast occur frequently and are highly valued. Alongside the restrained and individualistic social world of the balcony there has to be set the curiosity which many residents have for what goes on within the homes of their neighbours. Parkview gossip is the subject for exchanges between neighbours, friends and kin. There is thus some individual expression of social approval and disapprobation and some individual judgments pass into informal gossip networks. Even here interest in the affairs of others should not be too marked or the informant is likely to be discounted as 'nosey'; 'news of the world' is the nickname attached to one such gossip. Further, gossip networks are casual and intermittent rather than linked and they do not provide the basis for group interaction; hence there is no mechanism for achieving a consensus of opinion and therefore no possibility of imposing effective social sanctions against or in favour of particular types of behaviour. The individuals reference group is only in part a neighbour oriented one. Moreover, links with neighbours are generally single stranded and lacking in intensity. This absence of cohesive group networks is important to an understanding of social dynamics of the estate and is a characteristic which has far reaching implications.

The more cohesive the group, that is, the more friendship ties there are within the group, and the more active the process of communication which goes on within the group, the greater will be the effect of the process of communication in producing uniformity of attitudes, opinions and behaviour, and the stronger will be the resulting group standard, as indicated by the degree of uniformity among members of the group and the amount of deviation from the group standard allowed in members.[31]

The converse would also appear to be true. This aspect of social interaction on the estate can be further developed in another context, that of conflict between residents, since it is then that any attempt to invoke sanctions in support of group norms would be most obvious. During the time of my residence on the balcony there was little evidence of any conflict. Nevertheless such conflict does from time to time arise and I was able to observe a few instances elsewhere on the estate. One incident involved two households on the same balcony and tensions came to a head when one husband assaulted the other. The police were called and subsequently the wife of the man who had been attacked came seeking my advice on whether they should take his assailant to court. Another incident involved the women of two households one in a flat under the other and concerned alleged noise nuisance caused by a sewing machine. In this case the protagonists attempted to involve another neighbour and member of the TA committee, Mrs Montgomery. The latter referred the two parties to the housing directorate and refused to be drawn in herself although when an abusive exchange turned into blows she did intervene and separate the women. In both cases no further action was taken. It is interesting to note that in these and other cases which came to my notice neighbours not directly concerned refuse to become involved beyond suggesting recourse to an outside agency, the police, the local authority or 'the welfare'. In many cases their advice is ignored anway. Exceptions would seem to be instances of noisy parties about which neighbours may complain either to the police or the housing directorate. There is seldom an attempt to effect a settlement directly between the parties. One of the few cases I heard of which did involve direct intervention concerned a resident whose sleep was disturbed at around midnight by boys playing football noisily on the green below. He went down and asked them to 'pack it in' and got 'a load of abuse'. He recognized one of the boys so went to the flat of his parents and knocked there. Again his request met with abuse and he was told to 'mind his own business'. In the absence of a tightly knit social fabric intervention of this kind is likely to be fairly uncommon and as here to meet with little result. The group consensus which might render internal settlements effective is lacking and for the most part there is a reluctance to do more than threaten to involve outside agencies.[32]

Finally, in this section on particular aspects of neighbour relations, consideration will be given to race as a factor in the process of social interaction. As already noted there appears to be little difference between black and white respondents both in the opinions they have of other estate people and in their experience of their neighbours. However, as with white residents, it would seem that interaction with neighbours is not as important as interaction with kinsmen and additionally for members of racial minority groups, others from the 'home' area. Since the association of migrant families with the Old Borough is relatively short this means that personal networks of kin and friends often extend across a much wider geographical area than those of white residents.

Surveys carried out by the Fair Housing Group suggest that on council estates there is a low level of inter racial tension.[33] From the present study it might be suggested rather that the level of latent tension may be quite high and that latency is ensured by the relative non involvement of most black residents in the social life of the estate and by their efforts to conciliate. At the same time as already noted some of the sample respondents specifically named 'coloureds' as an out group and in more casual conversation the attaching of derogatory labels to black residents is fairly common.[34] One incident may be cited in order to describe how open conflict may be expressed. A family from Bangladesh, Mr and Mrs Kassam and their two daughters reported how for some weeks they were troubled by youngsters aged about eight or nine hanging around their garden flat, calling out names, ringing the doorbell and occasionally throwing stones. Not unnaturally the family were upset, Mr Kassam approached his next door neighbour and the two men agreed that on the next occasion they would both go out and speak to the boys. When they did issue a caution one of the boys involved went home and returned with his elder brother and some of his friends. These young men knocked at the neighbour's door and in the ensuing affray Mr Kassam and his neighbour were injured. Both the police and an ambulance were called and the men were taken to hospital and later discharged. The police reported there was little they could do because neither party could identify his assailants. Later around the estate several small boys spoke to me of the identity of those allegedly involved. Certain aspects of this incident warrant further comment. It may be significant that the targets for attack were a Bangladesh family. There are few Asians on the estate and their cultural difference is highly visible. Moreover, it is doubtful if such behaviour would be directed at other minority groups; on the estate apart from Asians, all 'coloureds' are assumed to be West Indians, they are more numerous and the popular stereotype appears to be that they can and will retaliate and if necessary call on friends for assistance. Mr Kassam approached his English next door neighbour for assistance because the latter is 'a good man'. During the incident no other neighbours came out to investigate in spite of there being a good deal of noise. Finally, Mr Kassam explained to his friends and colleagues at work that he received his injuries as the result of some accident; he felt too ashamed of the truth for fear that people would assume that he lived in such a 'bad place'.

In concluding this section on relations between neighbours several general comments may be made. First, although a fairly high proportion of the estate's residents have a shared identity and long association with the Old Borough and to a lesser extent with each other, the level of interaction between them is relatively low and characteristically takes the form of casual or involuntary meetings. This may be accounted for by the tendency of some residents to see others as 'a mixed lot', by the high value set on a home-centred social life focused on the family to the exclusion of neighbours, by a reluctance to become involved in the affairs of others and by the contrasting perceptions which many residents have of neighbourliness on an estate as compared to a street of houses.[35] Secondly the opportunities for casual contact may be facilitated or constrained by factors like personal circumstance or the situation of the dwelling. Thus for elderly and less mobile residents close proximity to others and access to informal meeting places like an outdoor seat may increase the prospects for casual contact. Residents in the four blocks of garden flats facing inward in a square around the green have a high degree of visual contact with other households and therefore greater prospects for chance meetings. And in all ground level garden flats the provision of private gardens has resulted in some residents spending considerable periods of time in a semi public space in circumstances which allow for easy conversation with neighbours and other passers by. Such meetings are least likely to occur on the enclosed landings of the tower blocks where there is no surveillance of the public areas from the individual flats and no acceptable pretext for loitering.[36] Somewhere in between these two extremes are the balcony access blocks where residents leaning on the handrail and idly watching the activity below may well be joined by another neighbour prepared to pass the time of day.[37] At the same time it will be evident from the descriptions above that such factors as personality and the presence of one or two 'sociable' people on a balcony or in a small block can appreciably alter the quality of contact between other neighbours there excepting perhaps those who are very shy and reserved or those categorized as 'toffee nosed'. The overall pattern is a varied one, the underlying influences complex.

Friends and workmates

Thirty three per cent of respondents claim to have no friends nearby, 37% have three or more and the remainder have one or two friends locally.[38] Friendship networks outside the estate may provide a substitute for links with neighbours and kin or they may supplement these. In fact it would seem that those most socially outgoing on the estate tend also to have fairly extensive friendship links outside it. Thus 27% of respondents have four or more contacts on the estate and 45% of this sub-group have three or more friends nearby.

Those who have no contacts on the estate appear to fall into two categories. On the one hand are those respondents who choose to minimise their social contacts on Parkview itself but are able to sustain friendship links elsewhere. Thus 24% of those who know no neighbours have three or more friends nearby and 48% have one or two friends locally. On the other hand there are those respondents who are socially isolated both on the estate and in the immediate neighbourhood; 38% of those who know no neighbours claim to have no friends nearby either.

The highest proportion of those claiming to have no friends locally are residents in the balcony access and tower blocks. I am unable to explain the former but it is of interest that tower block respondents claim either to have no friendship links outside the estate (40%) or to have three or more (60%). I would suggest that this difference may be accounted for by the incidence of disadvantaged families in these blocks since these families tend to be socially isolated while the higher figure would be accounted for by those original residents rehoused from the immediate area and able to retain existing friendship ties after their move to the estate. Y block residents are most likely to have friends nearby and this undoubtedly reflects the local origin of much of the population of these blocks. For the same reason long established respondents are more likely than recent arrivals to have friends nearby. It should also be noted however, that as with lack of contact with neighbours, respondents claiming to have no friends nearby live in all block types and have lived in the area for varying lengths of time. For half of those with friends nearby contact took the form of casual encounters or planned meetings in places like a local pub. For half contact included home visiting; and in this case, especially in households with children, friends might be accorded the status and title of a fictional uncle or aunt. In most cases friendships formed at work were confined to that situation.

The neighbourhood

The interaction between the estate and the surrounding area can be described in terms of those functions which draw residents away from it; shopping and other services, education, work and leisure.

Shopping

One boundary of the estate fronts onto a busy shopping street with a full range of small shops, general stores, supermarkets and a regular street market. Not surprisingly 94% of all respondents shop there. Moreover, this shopping situation tends to be fairly personalized (Plate 19). Older residents bemoan the changes but it is still the case that users of the street stalls know particular traders and patronise them regularly while queues are often the venue for a casual chat about the weather or prices. Knowledge of the range of services and goods available in the main street may be limited by this concentration of custom; one long standing Old Borough resident who moved from an estate nearer the far end of Market Street commented how for some time after the move she felt herself in unfamiliar territory because previously she had never walked more than half way up the street. The market as a centre for chance meetings and general social activity extends to some extent to the busier shops and particularly to one of the supermarkets. There a few chairs are ranged along the front of the shop. They are always filled with those wanting a rest or an opportunity to gossip, the latter expectation invariably met as one familiar face or another comes through the checkout. Other residents have particular reasons for shopping elsewhere; a regular trip to a school in the Borough and familiarity with shops there or a need to shop from a work place. Nearly half of the respondents claimed that all of their shopping requirements were met in the main street. Thirty six per cent shop occasionally in neighbouring boroughs especially in the Borough where there are several major shopping centres and a good market which also has a West Indian trader group catering especially for the food requirements of migrant customers. Relatively few residents (14%) ever used the central London shopping area. Good public transport links by bus and underground connect the locality with other parts of London. More frequent use is made of the bus services both for local journeys to school, hospital and to visit friends or for longer journeys to work.

The extent to which this personalized locality can provide the individual with social supports of various kinds may best be illustrated by an account of a typical day in the life of a frail 78-year-old woman, Mrs Bateman. On the estate

Mrs Bateman is completely isolated, having no contact with neighbours, and over the years she claims to have lost all contact with her family. In the course of an interview Mrs Bateman described to me the pattern of her day and commented that for her every day was the same excepting Saturday and Sunday when the lack of luncheon club facilities and different pub hours prescribed a different routine. Subsequently I spent a day in her company and so documented something of the range and quality of the relationships she has built up in following her routine. Mrs Bateman gets up at about 8 am and potters about her bedsitter ground floor flat straightening out the covers which are spread over all manner of carefully hoarded papers and packets. For the rest she sits and watches the shadows on the wall and waits for her pensioner friend, Charlie, who, in return for some kind of payment, – 'Just between you and me I see 'es alright if you know what I mean', – calls each morning and stays until about 11 am, chatting, making Mrs Bateman a pot of tea and rolling a supply of cigarettes. Charlie has visited Mrs Bateman every day except Sundays over the past four months and has known her for about 18 months. Mrs Bateman's only other regular visitor is a home help who calls twice a week. She is said to be 'a big mouth' and is not liked. Mrs Bateman spoke of her sense of oppression in the flat; she feels that the ceiling is pressing down on her and 'you could die in this flat and nobody would know'. In fact Mrs Bateman spends most of her time away from the flat and at around noon prepares to go out. She has never mastered the double locking mechanism on the door and so on leaving or coming home she has to get assistance, usually from a caretaker. The latter know her and her movements and often stop to exchange a few words. She then walks a longer route than necessary to the luncheon club on the estate in order to buy particular sweets which she feels sure are sold only by one shop. At lunch she is greeted by the staff and some of the other club members but is regarded by the latter as 'a bit queer' and Mrs Bateman herself makes no attempt to join in the conversation. From the luncheon club Mrs Bateman goes to her local pub where she regularly occupies a bench to one side of the public bar. At lunch time the bar is fairly quiet, with a few other women, elderly men filling a leisurely hour, and market traders in for a quick pint. Most are regulars and several engage in a joking relationship with Mrs Bateman. At closing time Mrs Bateman walks to the end of the market to a small cafe attached to the public baths. There she is known by her given name to all three assistants. The atmosphere is friendly with semi-public exchanges between customers at the same and different tables and between customers and staff. On this occasion Mrs Bateman and myself were joined by two middle aged women, like others present known to her from both the pub and the cafe and like us waiting for the pub to reopen. They had obviously heard many stories concerning Mrs Bateman's past and had clearly filled in many similar afternoons in idle chatter. One of the male regulars gave Mrs Bateman a slice of bread and butter and according to our companions he sometimes shouts her a Guinness. At opening time Mrs Bateman returned to the pub to take up her accustomed place. She recognized everyone present but the bar was busier and she was left more or less to herself. There were no other women in the bar and men stood around in groups talking, at several tables there were groups of card players with a fringe of interested spectators and other customers sat reading the papers. At 8.30 pm Mrs Bateman declared it was time to go and we walked back to the estate. She goes into her flat, checks under the bed and in the cupboards and has a warm up by the fire for half an hour. She does not put the light on because people from the next block allegedly 'spy'. Then she goes to bed saying 'sod them all'.

I have quoted this account at some length because it raises a number of interesting points and illustrates well something of the quality of casual social interaction in the Old Borough. Mrs Bateman was until recently resident in the Borough and claims that whereas there she knew everybody and could fill in her day much more happily with regular visits to the cinema, when she moved to the estate she found it more difficult to cope. Nevertheless in many ways, even in an unfamiliar environment, she has coped extremely well. Mrs Bateman denies that she has any contact with or need for any welfare services although in fact she has a social worker and her move was arranged with the assistance of the then housing welfare section. However, apart from the luncheon club, Mrs Bateman has minimized her contact with official agencies and has built up a network of casual but regular contact with a pensioner from outside the estate, a local sweet shop proprietor and the customers and staff of a market pub and cafe. Mrs Bateman has defined her own routine but the fact that the Old Borough main street still has pubs and a cafe with this character allows and makes effective a personal network of this kind.

School

The relationship between the estate and local schools was considered to be one of the more significant neighbourhood links. All residents at some stage have contact with schools as pupils and most as parents as well. Education here will be discussed in terms of two aspects, parents aspirations for their children and the experience which both parents and children have of the school situation itself.

Fifty three per cent of the respondents had left school by the age of 14 and 71% by the age of 15. Half of the respondents felt they had no choice but to leave school at that stage. Slightly more than half had no further training on leaving school, some had on-the-job training and others had some form of further education or served a formal apprenticeship.

Respondents with school age children were questioned about their expectations for their education and job careers. For the most part parents want their children to achieve more than they had themselves in both fields. Thus, just over half wanted some form of tertiary education, about one third had no strong feelings claiming that school leaving was a matter for the children to decide and the remainder wanted their children to complete their secondary education. In only one instance did a parent express a desire for a child to follow the same career. Others either wanted skilled or professional jobs for their children or considered that job choice also was entirely a matter for the children. Parents recommend other types of jobs because of what they feel to be a lack of choice, promotion prospects, security or financial reward in their own jobs. And many parents simply said they would like something 'better' for their children.

The evidence from other studies on parents aspirations for the educational attainment of their children is somewhat contradictory. Bynner, for example, reports that most working class parents express high hopes for the education of their children and three quarters wanted them to get a non-manual job.[39] However, Willmott in his Dagenham study found that most parents on the estate were not educationally ambitious for their children and did not take a keen interest in their schooling.[40] My own figures are based on small numbers but informal talks with non sample households suggests that the attitudes of parents on the estate are closer to those described by Bynner. At the same time it would appear that parents form ideas on what is attainable for their children on the basis of ideal goals rather than from a knowledge of a child's progress gained through contact with the school and teachers. Perhaps it is not surprising that there is often a discrepancy between aspiration and achievement as the education career develops. Disappointments then and later in the job situation appear to be fatalistically accepted.[41]

The nature of this mismatch should become clearer in a discussion of the household's experience of the school. This begins with an outline of the school age population on the estate and the schools in the area. Then follows a brief description of the ethos of three schools, the nearest primary and two secondary schools. There is then a discussion of the attitudes of parents and children towards these schools and finally some attention is given to the community service aspect of work within the secondary schools.[42]

According to education welfare records the school age population of Parkview totals 403, 245 in primary education, 142 at the secondary level and 16 at special schools. The number of secondary students at grammar schools is very low, four boys and four girls. Within a radius of one mile of the estate there are nine secondary schools, two of which are girls selective and 26 primary schools. Within easy walking distance of the estate there is one full time nursery school and 10 primary schools, four with some nursery provision. The estate's school population, however, feeds into a much greater number of schools over a fairly wide geographical area. Pupils attend 56 different schools; 23 primary, 26 secondary and seven special. The list includes 12 Church of England and Roman Catholic schools. Four of the primary schools and three single sex secondary schools take the highest number of children from the estate; otherwise the numbers of estate children at any one school are very low. A corollary of this scatter of students is that with few exceptions friendship groups at school and on the estate tend not to be co-terminous especially after the student enters secondary school.

The nearest primary school is immediately over the road from the main entrance into the estate and takes appproximately 30% of the primary school children from it. Park school was timetabled to accept its first pupils at the same time as the first blocks on the estate were completed but the school was finished ahead of time and the reorganization of other schools in the area was brought forward so that it opened shortly before the estate. As a consequence some pupils from the first phase of Parkview had to enrol at other schools. Since Park school was regarded as the estate school this dispersal of pupils caused some resentment for a few years. Now however, the issue has been forgotten and parental choice largely determines which school a child attends.

Park school has infant and junior departments. Both comprise pleasing environments and are viewed favourably by parents. At the same time there is little contact on a day to day basis between parents and the school. Meetings called with parents for discussion purposes generally attract a poor attendance although on open days or for dramatic productions a turnout of parents from 70% of households may be achieved.

Secondary school placements are made on the basis of parental choice, the advice of the head teacher and the decision of the divisional officer for the education authority. Two single sex schools taking the highest numbers of students from the estate, each have rolls of around 1000 pupils. Both accept 20 students from the estate, scattered throughout all forms although from the entire estate school population there was, at the time of the survey, only one sixth former.

The boys school is organized along strict authoritarian lines by a headmaster who is opposed to committee and participatory democratic procedures on the grounds that decisions taken by himself in the light of his knowledge of staff and pupils are more efficient and effective. Corporal punishment is used whenever deemed necessary. Teachers there tend to see any problems in dealing with students at the school as due to 'poor environment' or 'home background'. All staff comments conveyed notions of the schools separateness from the backgrounds of the children rather than continuity with them. The school tended to be categorized either as a refuge or an exemplar. 'School takes the kids out of their environment for a while'. 'We hope that a bit of the school value system rubs off on the child'. Without exception every comment made by a student or parent from the estate concerning this school referred immediately to the 'discipline' there. In this context discipline meant the authoritarian form of organization and the use of the cane for punishment. Parents, other adults and students approved whole-heartedly of this strictness and considered it accounted for the increasing popularity of the school and its higher standards. 'It used to be a terrible place but now the kids are at least learning something'. The students agree.

I left another school to come here. There was too much freedom at my old school. I mean you could do what you liked. Usually nothing. When I came here they said "Get your hair cut", so I did. You like a bit of discipline. I mean you can't bunk off so easily from here. There you didn't ever need to go to school. Here they guard the flippin' place. You still bunk off of course but its harder. There's less of it.

The boys approved of the sense of structure, and, so long as it was used 'fairly' agreed with the use of physical punishment to maintain order. They also approved of the means employed to make truanting more difficult, (like locking the gates and having a caretaker on duty during breaks).

This viewpoint needs to be set in the context of the boys behaviour. All those spoken to at the school admitted to truanting more or less regularly. It would seem that while needing to play truant to maintain their image in the eyes of their friends, and while regarding school as largely time wasting, the boys still expect that truanting meets with disapproval. This ambivalence is reflected in the boys more general attitude to school. The purpose of schooling is to 'get you a good job' and to this end 'discipline is good for you'. 'Really school's like a job, because you have to be told what to do. So it helps you get a job'. The boys take the attitude 'we are quite prepared to work since it is in our own interests but we have to be made to'. If a boy works without being 'made to' he loses face with his peers. Status within the peer group is measured largely by the balance a boy achieves between evading the rules on the one hand and using the school instrumentally on the other. School is of great social significance, school interactions the prime concern; the content of what is taught in the classroom of secondary importance. These attitudes are similar to those described by Birksted in his study of a group of boys at a comprehensive in Brighton. ' . . . school is not a place to which life is oriented and which constitutes an organizational principle of life. School conveniently provides certain advantages; it fills in time, it is somewhere to be at . . . the boys see the purpose of school to be to get exams for jobs. If you need exams school is useful, if you don't school is useless.'[43]

The girls school projects an entirely different image to that of the boys. The physical surroundings are very pleasant when compared to the forbidding nature of the boys environment, the staff are totally opposed to corporal punishment and the school has an active school council where students discuss such matters as etiquette and uniforms. Parents views of the school tend to be less enthusiastic than those expressed about the boys, but the reaction is nevertheless favourable. 'A very nice school, they teach them how to behave there. They don't seem to learn anything at the other one.' The comparison is to a girls' school closer to the estate and taking 17 students from it. The image of the favoured school is one of acceptable social standards and some commitment to solid academic achievement in a caring environment.

In view of the subject of the main study, within the two secondary schools attention focused on the place given in the curriculum to social education. Community education in both schools, is seen as the most significant aspect of their social education programme.[44] According to official publications, through community service the pupils should acquire some knowledge of 'society's structure' and of its social provision for human welfare. In addition it is expected that those taking a community service option will 'gain in sympathy, understanding and the capacity to identify themselves imaginatively with others. They may also achieve a greater measure of self awareness.'[45]

Few boys took the community service option and they were the lower stream boys whom the school regarded as 'problems' and so were pleased to have gainfully employed for a few hours two afternoons a week. The work involved following up requests from a volunteer service agency and most commonly entailed doing odd jobs like gardening for a different elderly person each week. 'I'm helping the OAP's plus I'm getting off a lesson I don't like' was a typical attitude towards the option. On the other hand students who chose not to do community work did so because they wanted to pass exams and because they felt that community service was an activity not properly belonging to a school curriculum.

I come to school because I want to learn and get a decent job later. I do plenty of community when I'm at home. I work on Saturdays at the butchers delivering meat and I'm always helping old ladies carry their stuff. I help our neighbours too and I don't see why I should waste my time at school doing it.

More girls undertook community service as an alternative option to physical education and they were drawn from a wider ability range. At this school the emphasis was on the formation of a relationship between the pupils who visited in pairs and the elderly person whom they 'adopted' for the duration of the course. Any jobs done in the course of the visit were considered incidental to the social content.

At both schools those students taking community service commented that they enjoyed the visits and the work involved and found the option 'interesting'. Students often gained a good deal of personal satisfaction from feeling that their efforts were appreciated but the response was to an individual situation. There was no evidence that through community service students realised the broader benefits expected from their participation in the scheme. Few had any grasp of what the term 'pensioner' means, much less the structure of the society of which they are a part or the welfare services designed to meet their needs. The education study concludes that the links between school and community in all three schools are tenuous especially in the field of parental involvement. The policies of 'Education for the whole community' are often misunderstood in principle and have not been attained in practice. The main theme of the policy is continuity, for the pupil moving up through the system, in the use of school buildings for the community, and through the orientation of the school world with that of the outside world. The experience of the schools observed suggests not continuity but a rather disturbing discontinuity. Nor is there any evidence that either from the school situation or from the community service programmes, pupils experience that co-operative behaviour which might be posited as part of the social skills necessary to increase an individual's potential for social participation. At the same time it should be noted that at no time did any pupils express a desire to change any aspect of their schooling or of the world outside the school. They used avoiding tactics and 'bunked off' or did as they were told.[46] Furthermore, although the points of contact between the schools, their staff and parents were very few, none of the latter expressed any desire for change either.

These findings need to be viewed with some caution. The researcher concentrated on three schools; the estate feeds in to 56. Undoubtedly many of the students who evaluate school more in terms of passing exams in order to realise their occupational plans for the future, attend other schools. These will vary considerably in terms of their size, value orientation and contact with parents. And within the schools studied it seems likely that the range of attitudes among students may be understated. However, from observations around the estate it would seem that the study fairly portrays many of those who in the school situation would be evaluated as 'underachievers'. It is also clear both from these attitudes and from the small numbers of students in the upper forms at school that the high expectations which many parents have for the education and job futures of their children are unlikely to be realised. The way in which parents, students and teachers relate to the school would seem to be underpinned by sets of values at variance with each other.

Work

According to residents with a lifelong association with it, the Old Borough was known as 'the land of the painters and the chars' and something of this character can still be seen in the kind of work taken up by workers there today. Information in regard to work is available in some detail for those respondents in employment (51%) and in more general terms for all adults in the sample households. Most of the women work as cleaners, domestic helps, shop assistants or kitchen hands, fewer as clerks, secretaries or nurses. Men are employed predominantly in the trades as painters and decorators, electricians or plumbers, in generally small light industrial assembly plants or as drivers for transport firms. Few are employed as white collar workers. The characteristics of these jobs are related to the attitudes expressed by respondents towards their work. Thus, most workers felt they had some say over what they did at work and not many felt they were strictly supervised. This is largely accounted for by the nature of a work situation where workers basically work on their own or in relatively small teams; only five were themselves in a supervisory position. Most respondents had few job dislikes and in regard to job likes the highest proportion cited meeting people as a main attraction.

About half of the respondents had always been in the same type of work and slightly more than half had been in the same job for the past five years. Only one respondent was working more than 40 hours a week at the time of interview; the rest worked a straight 40 hour week or part time hours. Most respondents claimed they derived equal satisfaction from work and leisure. It is difficult to draw firm conclusions from these findings since the numbers are small and biased by the predominance of women respondents. Tentatively, it might be suggested that the estate's workforce is a fairly stable one employed in a relatively narrow range of occupations.

In the sample households there are a total of 163 adults. Sixty per cent of these were employed at the time of interview; 6%, half of them women were currently unemployed and seeking work; 13% were retired; 12% housewives; 4% students in full time tertiary education and information for the remaining 4% is lacking. Fifty one per cent of those in employment can be classified as skilled workers, 24% as partly skilled and 17% as unskilled. There were no adults in the professional and 3% in the intermediate category.[47] Most workers find employment locally; 29% work within the Old Borough, 11% in the Borough and 24% in neighbouring boroughs. Twenty two per cent travel further afield generally for more specialised jobs.

There were 88 women in the sample households, 51% in employment at the time of interview. The majority of women in the under 30, 35–40 and 40–60 age groups are in employment. As might be expected a relatively small proportion of women over the age of 60 are still working. Somewhat surprising is the relatively low figure for the 30–35 age group and I am unable to explain this.[48] It should be noted that employment for younger women is often part time, very local and with some possibility of arranging hours to suit family commitments. Thus, one young woman with two young school children escorts them to school and then takes a short bus ride to a nearby more well-to-do area where she does housework for two women resident in the same block of flats. After finishing work she returns to the estate via the market where she purchases any provisions necessary for the evening meal. Generally she has time to prepare this before going out again to collect the children from school. At home the children have their supper and are settled in front of the TV ready for bed by the time their father comes in from work. At that point his wife goes out for another hour or so to clean a dental surgery a few minutes walk from the estate. When the children are ill the housekeeping jobs can be missed for a few days, during the school holidays the children attend a school play project and if necessary they can accompany their mother to her evening job.

Both from this information about respondents and from a knowledge of other residents it would seem that most work is found locally, the men typically in skilled or partly skilled occupations, the women for the most part in unskilled jobs. There is little evidence of upward mobility through a career structure and job changes are more likely to be between companies offering the same type of work or less often, different forms of employment. At the time of field work there was relatively little job changing probably because of the depressed national economy and the possibility of unemployment. Generally the job situation affords some individual independence in organizing the job; thus drivers or tradesmen out on a job may call at home during the day for a quick 'cuppa', while women cleaners may be able to decide on the way in which their job is done. More restricted are those such as men working in a factory environment and women shop assistants. For them, as for some of the others, the presence of workmates is a compensatory feature.

Leisure

Other studies have pointed out the extent to which home and family absorb the leisure time of most working class families.[49] These are comfirmed by findings for Parkview where by far the most popular leisure activities mentioned by respondents were home based pursuits like watching television. Even minority interests like short story writing, painting, astronomy and short wave radio listening were all followed in the family home. Other preferred leisure activities were visiting relatives and friends, parks, cinema, pubs, bingo, sports activities, club activities and day trips, the latter generally cited only by those households with a young family and a car. The remainder of this section describes some leisure activities in greater detail and also outlines something of the range of other facilities in the area. Finally, attention is given to the extent to which there is a demand for further leisure facilities both on and off the estate. This section on adult leisure is followed by a similar account on the leisure activities and facilities for children and young people.

There are two pubs on the estate, another is situated near one boundary of the estate and there are others along Market Street. Fifty three per cent of all respondents claim not to make use of pubs, 18% go to a pub at least once weekly and the remainder less often than that. This is a higher rate of useage than that reported for Dagenham where it was found that among working class respondents, 63% never go to a pub, 15% sometimes but not in the past month and 22% had visited a pub within that time. In fact the figures for the estate may be understated since it is likely that the husbands of some of the wives interviewed visit pubs. The higher figures for the estate are probably accounted for by the much greater accessibility of a wide range of pubs each attracting custom on the basis of 'extras' offered; food, live entertainment or darts, and its general reputation. They are local pubs with familiar 'regulars'. Only two respondents used pubs outside the immediate locality and they were associated with work place and former residence.

A high proportion of respondents claim to make some use of parks in the area; 29% claim that on average they visit a park at least once a month, 37% less than that and only 28% of all respondents make no use of parks.[50] The most popular park is the local one which is separated from the estate only by a main road. It is a small park laid out with lawns, trees and shrubs and includes a children's supervised playground. It should also be noted that even among those who do not make use of this park, the view across it from the balconies of the Y blocks is much appreciated (Plate 20) and often pointed to as greatly enhancing the resident's enjoyment of living there. In addition most park users claim that they also visit other parks, mostly within the Old Borough.

The area is not well served by cinemas though there are several a short bus ride away. There is a small local theatre and some entertainment of various kinds including concerts and light opera take place in the Old Borough town hall. Twelve per cent of respondents are cinemagoers and 14% attend the theatre or concerts. In all cases attendance was irregular and most typically involved younger couples celebrating some special occasion by going to a show in the West End of London rather than patronage of the local theatre or nearby cinemas.

A more regular leisure activity for those who engage in it is bingo. There are several halls in the locality including the boys' club adjacent to the estate, where non commercial bingo is played for small stakes. There is also a commercial bingo in a converted cinema situated at the end of Market Street which has sessions several times a day seven days a week. Fifteen per cent of all respondents are bingo players, many of them playing several times a week. At the commercial bingo the evening sessions attract a mixed crowd of all ages and both sexes. Players tend to arrive from about 7 pm and join friends or acquaintances in groups of four or five often at the same table each time. Regular players recognize other regulars around. Between each game there is a short interval while the winners card is checked and there is a 'half time' of about 15 minutes. During these intervals there is a good deal of chatter, people order drinks from the bar or settle down with a tea or coffee and sweets. The social attractiveness of the game is proclaimed in the advertisements outside the hall. 'Meet your top rank friends in our top rank bar', etc and to some extent those claims are justified especially for some categories of people. Thus, one of my neighbours, a middle aged widow, regularly attended bingo partly because she feels it is one of the few places of entertainment where attendance without an escort is socially acceptable and once there she is sure of meeting acquaintances, the crowd generally is very friendly, the atmosphere warm and comfortable and it is a 'real night out'. Through her attendance at bingo over 13 years she claims to know many people from the estate. At the non-commercial bingo sessions like that in the boys' club, the sociability aspect is probably even more important since it is generally the same small crowd, predominantly made up of women, often sitting at the same table in the same company week after week. And of course as in all games the prospect of winning, whether a few groceries, £5 or £500, provides an extra excitement. According to another study 'Gambling is not really, for those people, an attempt to redress the balance of destiny, a small dream of escape, fame or fortune. . . . Gambling is an integral part of social life and leisure. Winning the pools is a remote mirage deep in the back of a working man's mind. Winning on horses or bingo just doesn't bring in enough money to make any difference. And when people do win, the money is fed straight back, to buy small comforts or gifts, into their ordinary lives'.[51] It might be suggested that gambling provides both a dream and a pastime but from the Parkview survey I am unable to comment on the validity of these viewpoints. I did, however, hear accounts of a few small wins and mainly they did seem to be used for gifts, especially for 'the children' or small luxuries.

As already mentioned there is a branch library on the estate in a ground floor wing of the blue block. Forty-four per cent of the households in the sample make no use of this facility, 37% of households contain at least one regular user, that is a visit on average once in three weeks, and the remainder use the library less frequently than that. For some, particularly older residents, the library (Plate 21) serves as a kind of social centre; they make use of the library as a reading room especially to peruse newspapers, have a quiet chat with other readers or simply watch the activity around them. On weeekdays this includes regular visits from classses of the local primary schools.

Most respondents (67%) do not belong to any kind of club or organization; 31% are members. This is a slightly higher rate of club membership than that recorded for Cosely where 27% of the survey respondents were members of a club, and considerably higher than Dagenham where the corresponding figure was 16%.[52] The difference might be explained by reference to the wide variety of organizations in the vicinity and offering to meet all manner of interests and leisure time needs in art, drama, music, sports and educational fields. At the same time few residents avail themselves of these facilities and club membership would appear to be restricted to a relatively few categories. Nearly half of all members belong to a social club, slightly fewer to church groups of one kind or another and a sprinkling to firms clubs, sports clubs, trade union or political organizations. Women are more likely to join than men and club membership attracts in fairly equal proportions those from all age groups. For some, membership of a club like that for the elderly sponsored by a nearby settlement involves regular attendance at weekly functions which may be a highlight in an otherwise fairly empty life. For others, membership may be scarcely activated at all. More than half of the clubs are situated locally.

At the time of the survey the last undeveloped area of Parkview was being landscaped as a children's play area and a community hall was under construction. Respondents were asked for their views on how they felt the public areas of the estate and the community hall should be used. Most respondents expressed a liking for the landscaped areas of the estate mainly because they felt these enhanced the overall appearance of the estate. Just over half would like to see these areas used more for recreation purposes either for children or for children and adults. (At present while there are few formal restrictions, in practice, playing on the grassed areas is forbidden by caretaking staff). The improvements suggested for these areas were generally fairly minor; more gardens, especially private gardens, and more seats. There was however, an overwhelming feeling in favour of the community hall; 93% of respondents felt there was a need for such a facility on the estate. They advocated its use to cater for all ages and for interests such as indoor sports, educational classes and bingo. General social activities were rated highly. The demand is thus to duplicate the activities already available in the area but within a more localised setting and thereby presumably attractive to a greater number of people. Respondents professed a range of opinion on how the centre should be managed; 37% favoured tenant management; 15% management by the council, 30% management jointly by tenants and council representatives and 3% opted for a paid manager.[53] The reasons given in favour of some form of outside control were a fear of 'fiddling' and consequent lack of trust in management by residents and a presumed need for some form of authority in dealing with 'stroppy' members.

Respondents made no demands for additional facilities for adults to be provided in the locality of the estate although in conversation with other residents occasional mention was made of the need for facilities such as tennis courts, a swimming pool or squash courts. There is in fact a swimming pool at the end of Market Street and the other demands would appear to be fairly much minority ones.

Within the estate and nearby there are various facilities catering for the leisure time needs of children and teenagers. This section begins with a description of these and then gives an account of the manner in which parents and other adults view these and other facilities which they consider are required. Finally the attitudes and activities of the young people themselves will be described.

When the study began there was on the estate only a small fixed structure playground designed for very young children as part of the landscaped surrounds to the Y blocks. Previously there had also been a kickabout area and a cycle track on the roof of one of the underground carparks; the former was lost in the building of the garden flats extension while the latter was abandoned and then fenced off as construction of the community hall progressed. However, in the course of the study two play areas were opened. One replacing the old cycle track was designed for very young children and comprises an enclosed plastic turf kickabout area, swings, (Plates 22 & 23) slides, climbing frames and a rocking horse. The second area incorporates a tarmac kickabout area (Plate 24) equipped with high wire mesh fencing and floodlights together with a landscaped fixed structure area including swings, slides, a shelter and climbing apparatus. The landscaped area is not in any way enclosed. These facilities are intended to cater for the needs of children up to the age of about 13, and, in the architect's view, provide the estate with play facilities which are 'as good as you'll get'. In addition there are communal grassed and planted areas around the estate but these are not intended for play and the caretakers may exercise their authority to forbid games there.

Other facilities are nearby. The estate shares a boundary with a boys' club. This is an activity oriented club catering for boys interested in football, boxing, table tennis, cycling and swimming. Cycling and boxing are particularly well supported; during the study period club members completed a cycle expedition to Paris and in boxing the club has a high reputation largely due to the active support it receives from Old Borough boxers. The club also produces a number of dramatic or musical productions each year. It has one full time youth leader, several part time leaders and a number of unpaid volunteer helpers.

Another type of play facility near the estate is a temporary adventure playground situated in a building site immediately beyond the park. The playground comprises a changing assortment of wooden towers and frames and two huts, one used to house animals which the younger children help to look after. The site has two part time play leaders and in addition employs as play assistants some of the regular attenders in the 15 to 16 age group. In the same locality is the park itself. (Plate 25) This includes football pitches and a supervised play area which incorporates a sand pit and paddling pool as well as the more standard play equipment.

The nearest club offering social activities for mixed groups is one organized by the Methodist Church in premises about ⅓ of a mile from Parkview. This club has a particularly strong membership in the 15–19 age group and is run to a large extent by the members with volunteer adult support.

Parents in the sample group with children in the 5 to 13 age range were asked where their children play and all respondents were asked for their views on the type of facilities which should be provided on or nearby the estate to cater for the needs of young people of all ages. According to their parents the space most commonly used for play by children is indoors or on landings and balconies. Then in order of frequency parents mentioned anywhere on the estate, the local park, off the estate generally, the children's play areas on the estate, and organized play facilities. There was relatively little difference in response according to floor level or block type. Regardless of floor level parents stressed that their children play mainly indoors although in regard to outdoor play there is a tendency for parents living at the third floor or below to say that their children play anywhere on the estate whereas parents resident at higher levels are more likely to specify the estate playgrounds. The parents of children resident in the garden flats are more likely than those from other blocks to say that their children play mostly indoors or along access ways. These findings need to be treated with some caution. No attempt was made to log the apportionment of time spent in various play activities in different locations.[54] It may be that mothers over-estimate the time spent by children indoors since that is when they are most aware of them. Furthermore it is not possible from the survey results to distinguish between responses for children in the 5 to 9 age group and those in the older bracket.

All respondents were asked about the adequacy of facilities in the area for youngsters. In regard to the 5–13 age group 18% were of the opinion that existing facilities were adequate, 37% felt more were needed both for sports and social activities, 11% recommended more in the former field and 20% in the latter. A small minority expressed the view that no facilities should be provided and 11% expressed no opinion. For the teenage group 27% recommended that no provision should be made. All respondents who were opposed to the provision of special facilities for one or both of these groups pointed to the paucity of provision in their own childhood and deplored the apparent laziness of parents and children in their unwillingness to travel to take advantage of existing facilities. The largest group of respondents (29%) who advocated facilities for the teenage group stressed the need for some form of social club, 4% wanted more sports facilities and 18% wanted more of both types of provision.[55] Most respondents had no opinion on whether such facilities should be exclusive to the estate or not. There was a tendency to favour making facilities for younger age groups exclusive and to make those for older groups open. Most respondents (67%) felt some form of supervision was necessary. The playgrounds on the estate were liked by most respondents (60%) but another 26% admitted to mixed feelings mainly on the grounds that the areas needed supervision.[56] Residents on the ground floor of the garden flats adjacent to the landscaped play area felt strongly that it should be fenced as well as supervised (Plate 26). Staff at the nursery which shares another boundary with the same area agree.[57] Respondents with young children resident in other parts of the estate claim that the designated playgrounds are too far away and that they want to be able to watch their children at play. Some suggested the use of portable play equipment for use on the green outside the homes of very young children so that supervision could be provided by parents. Informally a group of households in one of the garden blocks attempted this. They placed a paddling pool and rugs on the lawn for the children and later in the day some of the adults joined them in a game of rounders. This behaviour became the subject of a complaint to a caretaker and he ordered them off the grass. Another parent with a family of four boys enquired about letting a garage behind his home with the intention of turning it into a playroom where they could play table tennis and generally have a place of their own. He was discouraged from making a formal application.[58]

Most young people from the estate appear to make limited use of the facilities provided either on the estate or nearby. In part this would seem to be a reflection of the range of standards which parents attempt to impose on their children and in part a consequence of a range of choices exercised by the children themselves. There are some households like those described by Morris[59] where very young children are looked after by a slightly older sibling and spend most of their time outside the home being carted around from one place to another with a minimum of parental supervision and control. The older sibling from this type of household is often a 'hanger on' to the small informal friendship groups which meet about the estate. These groups comprise children ranging in age from about 10 to 14 or 15. They are informal groups of the type described by Downes rather than gangs. 'The norm ... is the fluid street corner clique, (Plate 27) averse to any form of structure and organization, but with persistence over time.'[60] Girls become attached to the group only in so far as they are acquainted with individual boys. These youngsters tended to spend a good deal of their leisure time outside the home and frequently expressed feelings of boredom.

I just walk around the flats with my friends at night. That's it mainly. I don't spend any time at clubs or anything. I don't do that sort of stuff. At night we hang around in a gang and we are always being told by the caretakers to move along because we are making so much noise or they've had complaints from people that we're doing things.

These informal groups moved around a few regular haunts - the sheds, a basement, a 'hut' on top of one of the Y blocks, the laundrette, the sweet shop. These children admitted to taking part in 'anti social' behaviour from time to time as a diversion from boredom and 'for laughs.' 'Well like when I was about 11 or 12 I used to hang around here a lot, you know, with a couple of kids. They see a little crack in a window and they go up to it and they smash it out completely.' It was some of these boys who formed the core of the youth group.[61]

Other young people on the estate claim not to have friends there. This may partly be a reflection of the extent to which friendship networks are fragmented especially on the move from primary to secondary school and on the distances the older children travel to school. It may also reflect an assessment of other estate youngsters. 'I don't mix with the children on [the Estate] because they are too tough or think they are tough.'[62] Other children are not allowed out to play with others on the estate because their parents adopt this view of other estate children. Often these are the children who are encouraged to take part in organized leisure activities away from Parkview as guides or scouts, at swimming, gymnastic or dancing lessons.

When the playgrounds on the estate were first opened they attracted children from the estate and others from neighbouring streets. In addition a teenage group from another estate attempted to make a bid for control of the landscaped area. They were opposed by groups from the estate and there were a few evenings when the police were called, weapons were confiscated and gangs warned off. Thereafter the playgrounds settled down, attracting some children and their parents during the day but proving also atractive especially at night to an older age group for whom they were not intended. For some months after opening these areas were not time studied and so the caretakers cleaned them as and when they could.[63] There was inadequate provision for maintenance checks in the early period of intensive use. Some equipment was quickly wrecked (Plate 28 and 29), a brick shelter was used as a fireplace and then partly taken to pieces, swings soon needed oiling and grassy areas were worn bare.

Many boys from the estate join the boys' club adjacent to it, often for short periods only. Their drift in and out reflects in part the changes in their own interests and those of their friends and in part is a withdrawal from a situation of alleged bullying and intimidation. This latter behaviour is ascribed particularly to a gang based in a street neighbouring the estate. Other facilities near Parkview attract few youngsters from there. The adventure playground attracted only two regulars from the estate and according to the leaders draws mostly on streets in the immediate vicinity. The church youth club leader could recall at no time having any support from estate teenagers. Other organised activities have already been mentioned in connection with parental supervision of leisure. Some organizations such as the army and navy cadets also attract some of the non home centred teenagers who otherwise eschew supervised leisure activity. As with the boys' club individual participation tends to be fairly shortlived.

For many of the teenage boys another area of interest is football. Some are regular attenders of particular club games; more are simply supporters and team allegiances along with current girl friends are the most popular subjects for spray painted wall slogans. After the age of 16 when most estate youngsters leave school and until they start 'going steady' the leisure time of teenage boys tends to be spent away from the estate in all male groups of 'mates'. Again, however, as with the younger age groups there is a considerable range of variation from this pattern.

Generally it seems that for most Parkview adults the greater part of leisure time is spent within the home. Outside the home, clubs, pubs and bingo attract custom often as much for the casual sociability afforded as for the activities engaged in. The demand for extra facilities on Parkview is predominantly for a more localised and probably more informal setting for the same activities. Two facilities which attract a fairly large number of users for other reasons are the park and the library. Younger children tend to play locally and relatively few are regular attenders at venues around Parkview. Play for children would appear to reflect in part the degree of parental supervision and control and in part the child's choice. Teenagers up until such time as they become wage earners also tend to spend a good deal of leisure 'hanging around with mates' on Parkview. Parents' demands for facilities for young people include more estate based provision and often a stipulation for supervision. Thus, leisure pursuits are locally based. For all ages there appears to be a dislike of institutionalised or organized activities with formal structures and ongoing commitments. Leisure activities outside the home are characterised by casual social contact in a semi-public setting.

Residents and 'the council'

Except where an approach involves a mundane 'neutral' matter, residents are generally reluctant to contact officials of all kinds. As might be expected this attitude is most marked in dealing with the police but it extends to all manner of situations where more personal issues are of central concern. One resident recounted how she had witnessed the smashing of a car and theft from other cars on the estate late one night. She did not call the police or offer assistance when they were finally alerted 'because I don't want to get involved and have to give my name and all that'. Another resident whose own experience of the NSPCC had been most beneficial spoke of a case of child neglect and abuse a few doors away but declined to report the case because her husband felt they had 'no business to interfere.' Other residents approached me seeking advice or practical help and often when referred to the appropriate agency, say Social Services, Education Welfare or Citizens' Advice, were clearly reluctant to take up the matter themselves and sometimes asked further if I would take it up on their behalf since obviously I 'must know about these things.' This attitude appears to be a compound of an unwillingness to become involved and a feeling of uncertainty in coping with a formal 'official' situation. The former attitude is illustrated by the fact that most respondents stated that if they saw something around the estate needing attention they would either ignore it or refer the matter to a caretaker, only 4% said they personally would intervene and 12% would refer to an official other than a caretaker.[64] Caretakers too, are of course officials but they are a personalised officialdom and this alters residents perceptions of them. Moreover while relatively few respondents (20%) admit to feeling unconfident in their contact with officials, virtually all have an experience of officials only when something goes wrong and then they feel themselves cast in the role of supplicant.

Respondents were asked about their experience of the Directorate of Housing. Sixty two per cent claimed to have had at least one contact in the past year. In most cases the contact was by phone or letter and related mainly to repairs with isolated cases of rent matters, transfers, or estate matters generally.[65] In their dealings with officers 30% of respondents felt they had been poorly treated. One respondent alleged that council officers make tenants feel 'the lowest of the low'. Another claimed that officers 'always make out it's a favour just to get your papers out. And they are always at pains to point out there are many worse off than you.' Another made a similar complaint, 'you feel as if they are doing you a favour in simply accepting a piece of paper from you' and added that 'in fact we employ them and pay for them by the rents we pay.' One respondent claimed that officers take the view that 'you haven't quite made the grade if you live in a council house' and commented that when she and her husband made enquiries about getting a mortgage through the council for a house purchase they were treated quite differently. All of these complaints concern the manner of treatment and for those who had an unfavourable experience in this regard that appeared to rankle more than any complaint about the effectiveness or efficiency of the service received. As regards the latter 26% of respondents expressed themselves well satisfied, others complained of the lack of response to letters or phone calls and the slowness of the repairs system. These assessments relate also to the impersonal nature of most contacts between tenants and council officers. Some residents know of a few senior housing management officers as names from letters, local newspaper reports or TA meetings. These officers are not, however, engaged in day to day management and the estate dweller contacting the officer to report a repair, request a transfer, or query a demand for payment of arrears is likely to be referred from one anonymous officer to another, from section to section by which time patience, confidence and the supply of small change for a telephone box have all been exhausted.

At the same time, in answer to a hypothetical question, 34% of respondents felt they could completely trust the officers to act in the best interests of the residents; 22% took the opposite view, claiming that no trust could be placed in the officers and the remainder took a more equivocal view.[66] Those whose assessment of officers was poor or mixed often hinted at some form of corruption, a suggestion that money could buy an allocation, or less seriously, 'it's not the points system, it's the pints system.' None of these stories can be substantiated but the feeling that there is some form of 'fiddling' is fairly widespread among this group and the belief itself, regardless of its foundation, clearly affects attitudes towards the officers.

Relatively few respondents, (11%) had had any contact with a councillor. In most instances contact was with a ward councillor but some respondents had built up some kind of personal link with another councillor, maybe through residence in another ward and these links might be reactivated after the move to the estate. Contacts with councillors mostly relate to transfer applications or other personal matters, rarely to repair or estate matters (although of course through the TA committee a councillor does receive a good deal of complaint about the latter.) Irrespective of whether they had had contact with a councillor 8% felt no trust could be placed in the elected members; 22% felt part trust; and 26% said they couldn't say. A further 26% declined to give an opinion on the basis that they had had no contact.[67] When compared with officers, councillors are more likely to be evaluated according to a respondent's conceptualisation of a role rather than according to personal experience and those who are known are likely to be subject to criticism. Thus respondents who do have some experience of councillors and are critical of them claim that 'its all political' and 'they are in it for what they can get.'

Relations between residents, officials and elected members impinge little on day to day living but when there is contact it is characterised by a perceived status difference. The resident is cast in the role of applicant for benefits of some kind or in the role of guilty party; the officer as dispenser or arbiter; the councillor as advocate or mediator. Residents do not experience governmental agencies as impersonal institutions carrying out reasoned policies. Moreover, in the context of the directorate of housing, this would be an unrealistic expectation; the experience of residents is not that of a caring, effective, professional relationship.[68] Nor do residents see themselves for what they are, an interest group which can exert pressure on these agencies. This is not surprising. Resident attempts at pressure group tactics have seldom been successful. Action taken by resident groups often displays an acceptance of a situation as defined by council or other outside agencies; group tactics are generally politically naive.

For most residents contacts with officers and councillors are intermittent rather than ongoing. For others, especially those engaged in TA committee work who are politically more aware, or those categorised as 'problem families' for one reason or another, contact is likely to be more intensive and relationships with individual officers and members may be developed. In these cases there is often an attempt to personalise the relationship. This personalisation is based however, not on reciprocity, but on personal motives imputed by the resident to the officer or councillor concerned and invoked in attempts to capitalise on the goodwill of those presumed to support resident objectives. Both officers and councillors tend to be evaluated according to a resident's assessment of their personal worth. Thus, even though an officer or councillor may be ineffective in securing a desired end, he will be excused and blame attached to 'the system' if he personally is felt to be 'genuine'. In this context 'genuine' means on 'our side,' 'trying to get what tenants want'. As a result of these attitudes and experience it would seem to be the case that so long as the officers and councillors give the estate residents what they want they may be regarded as acting honestly and impartially. When they fail to do so the commonest explanation is that someone with powerful connections and self interest opposed to the estate is wielding influence in the situation.[69] It is as if a feeling of assumed powerlessness in such a situation can be compensated for if the impersonality of the exchange can be altered.

Parkview Organizations and Institutions

Parkview contains various organizations and institutions which may be categorised according to the sponsoring body and their membership or client groups. The TA is an estate based organization sponsored by and for residents only. Eshag,[70] the Parkview Youth Group and the mothers' coffee mornings were established with the direct assistance of members of the project team for specific resident groups. The chiropody clinic, Church Close luncheon club, Parkview library, Ash Court Road nursery and the sheltered housing unit are all operated by externally based official agencies and cater for clients drawn from a wider area than Parkview estate itself. This definition of client groups according to Borough rather than estate needs is opposed by some residents who consider that the nursery, luncheon club and sheltered housing unit should cater primarily for Parkview. These organizations are discussed here in turn.

Parkview Tenants Association

The politics of the TA committee and the interrelationships between the committee and external agencies are considered in greater detail elsewhere.[71] This account is concerned to describe the work of the association in so far as it is directed more towards other estate residents.

Nearly two-thirds of all respondents (64%) were members of the TA at the time of interview. A further 12% had been members at some time in the past and 24% had never taken up membership. Proportionately the highest number of members is drawn from the 35–59 age group while most respondents who had never joined were in the younger age group. There appears to be little connection between length of residence and a preparedness to join and continue membership.[72]

In the course of fieldwork, 18 of the people who served on the TA committee in that time were interviewed. All were agreed that the work of the association incorporated two main tasks; organizing social activities for estate residents, and taking up on their behalf with the council, outstanding complaints. Six committee members held that the promotion of social activities on the estate should be the first priority. These and some of the others, all of whom attached more or less equal importance to both functions, considered that ideally tenants should be able to obtain satisfaction for grievances on an individual basis. The significance and range of social activities were variously described by committee members. One spoke of 'creating a community atmosphere'. A leading committee member expressed the hope that the TA would 'get people to take an interest in their own home', and 'encourage people to meet socially through the hall and outings with the aim of fostering good relations between all'. Another stressed the need to establish better liaison with the council and in so doing 'explode the myth of difficult officers'. Others were more specific and recommended competitions between sports teams, the issue of weekly newsletters, the fostering of mother and baby groups and old age pensioner clubs, camping trips for children, a scheme to adopt elderly residents as 'grandparents.'

The combination of activity, on the one hand taking up difficult problems with the council, and on the other promoting social activities on the estate would seem to accord with the views of most tenants. In the interviews with sample households respondents advocated a social welfare type work rôle together with a representative function in dealing with the council. Specific comments on the type of work respondents felt the TA should undertake reflected their knowledge of what has happened in the past. Most suggested taking up complaints and organizing outings or parties for the children. A few respondents, however, made other suggestions; campaigns to keep rents down; the building up of a cell type organization based on balcony representation; the establishment of an aid centre where residents could go to get shopping arranged for an elderly or sick neighbour, for legal advice and for information on welfare rights; a visiting service for all newcomers, the elderly and the lonely.

Committee members were also asked about the form of organizational structure they felt was appropriate for the TA. Ten members considered that there should be sub-committees working to a main committee and/or block representation with in one instance, a block committee as well. Sub-committees were at one time set up but after about a month the association reverted to working through a single committee.[73]

During the fieldwork period a good deal of committee time was in fact spent in taking up complaints not simply at an individual level but on an estate wide basis as well. Questions like lift breakdowns, rubbish collections, dampness in flats and the flooding of pathways affected many residents and were all taken up by the association. Attending to such complaints brought committee members into touch with at least some of the tenants concerned. For the first few months of fieldwork collections of monthly membership subscriptions were still being taken up in some blocks and there was also door to door selling for several raffles to raise funds for various Christmas functions. These activities were important ways of keeping committee members in touch with other residents. This more or less regular contact was lost when the subscription collections were abandoned for lack of volunteers, and thereafter contacts were sporadic and limited largely to the participants at functions, general meetings and, indirectly, the issue of occasional newsletters.

The most memorable of the social events in the estimation of the committee, and probably also in the eyes of many estate residents, was a gala held in

September 1974. Committee members canvassed shops in the area, old and new goods were collected from households, items for sale were made by a band of women supporters, games were organized, a set of stocks built, and a barbecue fitted up. Stalls were arranged around the green. Housing directorate officers assisted by providing sound equipment and a portable stage. There was bunting everywhere and a fancy dress parade added to the colour. The Mayor officiated at the opening, it was a fine day and a large crowd of several hundred people milled about the area in the course of the afternoon. The committee were elated by this success. Financially they had raised just over £300; and the response of residents was even more gratifying. There were comments of how 'grand' it was 'putting the old community spirit back into the place' (Plate 30). Other events organized in this period were two outings to a seaside resort, two dances, parties at Christmas for pensioners and children and an Easter bonnet parade. TA committee members also helped to organize a party on the estate to celebrate a local sporting event and assisted with outings for children organized during the school holidays through a nearby settlement.

In addition to this work the committee is also active in what may be termed a welfare function. Thus, they decided to collect money and furniture for a family whose flat was gutted by fire and made a small donation to an elderly person robbed of some pension money. More commonly, this type of work tends to be undertaken spontaneously, in between meetings, by individuals who have built up some kind of personal reputation through committee work. The fact that committee membership is characterized by a high turnover also means that approaches may be made to ex-committee members as well and for the most part they appear to respond. A block collection of money for the bereaved family of a former committee member, furnishing a flat for an elderly resident in the sheltered housing unit, pressing for a transfer for an invalid, settling a dispute between neighbours, and stocking with groceries the empty cupboard of a housebound pensioner were all matters taken up in this way.

It is difficult to assess the impact of these activities on residents as a whole. Most functions attract only a fraction of those eligible to attend. General meetings may be attended by up to 60 or 70 residents. An old time music hall for pensioners attracted about the same number. Dances attract mainly residents known personally to particular committee members, other committee members on estates in the locality and councillors. Sometimes the response is considered very disappointing. Seats in a coach may be sold to outsiders—friends and relatives of committee members—because of the lack of response from Parkview itself. Committee members deplore the fact, cite their own strenuous efforts to canvass all households and bemoan the apathy of tenants generally. And yet there are always those who claim to have heard nothing about a particular event and are disgruntled about paying membership fees to belong to an organization from which they get nothing. (This latter argument continued long after it had been decided to stop the collection of subscriptions.)

The notion that membership confers too few benefits may be related to suspicions over the handling of money and doubt as to the motivation of those involved. 'And of course now there are those new people—not been here longer than you some of them, think they own the place, want to run the place only because they want to run it if you get my meaning. That Mr.— going round "I'm the guv'nor". It would be alright if they were genuine but they're not—I can see through those types.' 'Did any of them ever ask the tenants? Who nominates members?' 'What are they doing? What happens to the money?' Those comments are typical. Committee members are aware of the criticism and sensitive to it. They feel resentment that tenants say they value social activities and when they are organized often withhold real support. In more despondent moods committee members often express doubts as to the worth of what they are doing; but then there will be some small 'victory' or the excitement of being busily engaged and wholly absorbed in some new project and they are sustained until the next attack.

Both in the range and number of activities sponsored the TA is unexceptional. In its social contacts with and benefits for members on the estate the committee concentrated on occasional, typically festive, functions. Its difficulties are typical of 'the group originating in voluntary agreement and in which the established order claims allegiance only by virtue of the satisfactions they derive from membership'.[74] For TA members satisfactions lie potentially in securing the redress of grievances and, more immediately, the prospect of joining in various activites. These latter would appear to be regarded as particularly important by both committee members and the association membership generally. Their importance is basically symbolic; the expression of a 'community feeling'; an apparently desirable social characteristic in which the estate is somehow felt to be lacking. The gala was considered an outstanding success because it was seen as evoking a community spirit reminiscent of former days. The party for the sports event, with its music and dancing on the green,[75] was compared to the street parties held at one time to mark significant national events and to celebrate the new year. Significantly, both events involved fairly large numbers of people in all manner of activities, preparing and placing decorations around the buildings, baking, setting up tables and stalls, assisting with selling or serving and so on. Yet, as noted, even these events have limited appeal and the 'community spirit' is contained within the event itself and quickly becomes a cause for nostalgia. As an organization the TA would seem to be unable to sustain ongoing personal networks of social contacts which might allow for the development of a Parkview identity expressed in social terms.

Parkview Youth group

Another organization which is to some extent modelled on the TA and aiming to perform its social/welfare function particularly through the involvement of the estate's young people, is the youth group. As already noted there are in the vicinity of Parkview a number of facilities catering for youngsters of all ages.[76] These attract small numbers of young people from the estate and then often only for short periods of time. When the fieldwork began there were few facilities and no organizations for youngsters on the estate itself. An attempt to remedy this lack stemmed from an approach I received late in October 1974 when one boy requested that a small group of youngsters be allowed to form a junior TA. They wanted to form their own committee and promote activities like discos and a coffee bar. They also had ideas, he said, of forming a band 'to entertain the old folk', and organizing a clean up campaign on the estate. It was decided that this demand should be met by Don, the youth and community worker at that time recently appointed as a research assistant to the project.

Early in November a small group of boys aged between about 9 and 14 started meeting in the project flat. They were soon joined by the sister of one and by Jane, a 17-year-old girl, resident in the flats for many years, well known to many of the youngsters from her work at the local sweet shop, and interested in working with them. This group formed a committee and elected three of the older boys, Tony, Kevin and Richard as chairman, secretary and treasurer respectively. Gradually the group grew until it attracted around 30 youngsters from all parts of the estate. Most were boys but a number of girls from about 12 to 14 years old attached themselves to the periphery of the group. Two of the leading members of the group, including the chairman, were black. Most youngsters did not attend regularly but there was a core group of about 10 or 12 young people, including the office holders and original members. These members were committed to the idea of a youth group and while individual enthusiasms waxed and waned and some members fell out with others from time to time, they were nevertheless, with Don's support, able to sustain the group over the next nine months. Special activities organized by the group attracted the casual attendance of many other youngsters on the estate.

Throughout the fieldwork period one of the difficulties faced by the group was the absence of a satisfactory meeting place. During the first two months weekly meetings were held in the project flat. When that became rather cramped Don obtained permission for the group to make use of the luncheon club premises. This was adequate for meetings but was not suitable and not readily available for other activites. Consequently, the committee pressed through the project and the TA committee for the use of storage rooms in the basement of one of two of the older blocks known to have such rooms. Negotiations with various council officers extended over several months and came to nothing when it was decided that such use would contravene fire regulations and moreover create a noise nuisance for residents overhead. Don then looked into the possibility of using part of one of the underground garages which the contractors for the community hall had walled off and provided with basic services but this was not followed up. Towards the end of March the youngsters decided that the old disused pram sheds offered potential for conversions into huts. A meeting was arranged with a senior housing management officer who commented that while he could see no objection he would have to look into the matter further. Approval was given and the boys went ahead. They purchased paint, started to knock down a partition wall between two sheds to make a larger 'room', fitted a padlock to the door and furnished what was now a hut with milk crates and an old settee. Originally the group had offered to clear all debris away from the area but this was not done and some of the rubbish was used to start fires in the sheds. The fire brigade had to be called twice. Youth group members claimed the fires were started by rival gangs. The fires and the general messiness of the area incurred adult criticism; the young people apparently lost interest and moved off elsewhere. At about this time (April 1975), the youth group apparently dropped the search for their own premises in favour of planning to share in the use of the new community hall.

From the outset there was an attempt, fostered by Don, to link the youth group to the TA committee and many of their activities were organized with TA help. Jane supported a link between the organizations and of the group was most familiar with the work and members of the TA committee since her mother had, until recently, been a committee member. At one of their first meetings the group proposed that Jane attend TA committee meetings as their representative. Accordingly, at a TA committee meeting in early November Jane described to those present how youngsters aged between 9 and 16 had 'nothing to do' on the estate. A group of these had got themselves together to form a youth group. They hoped to find a room for their activities and wanted to help generally by doing such things as shopping for pensioners. Committee members all agreed that more needed to be done for young people on Parkview and offered the group their support.

Over the Christmas period the TA organized parties for the youngsters and the youth group participated. The youth group, with some help from interested adults on the TA committee, organized a New Year's disco in the nearby boys' club. They also organized a sponsored walk. Both the walk and the disco raised money and the group was very pleased to find itself with a bank balance of over £70. During this time Jane attended a few more TA meetings but by the end of January she had left the estate and the formal link between the two committees was broken.

Soon afterwards it became apparent that members of the TA committee had misgivings about the youth group. Early in February, the then TA Secretary Mrs Montgomery called on me to say that she felt the youth committee should be a sub-committee of the TA and that youth funds should be incorporated in general TA funds. At the next TA meeting this was discussed further and it was decided to send a letter to the youth group inviting them to send a representative along to the following committee meeting. When Kevin and Tony attended a committee meeting in March it was impressed on them by the TA chairman Mrs Field that both groups were part of the estate and should work together. They would have to share the community hall and should try to work things out in a friendly fashion. She added, 'There is also a nagging feeling about the money situation. We should know what's being run on the estate under our noses. We would like to know how you feel about this'. Tony explained that the group intended to use the money raised by the sponsored walk to buy a billiard table for the hall. Another adult committee member stressed that in such organizations all funds should be in one account with sub-committees responsible to a main committee. The two youngsters were told to go back to their own committee and report back in due course. This they did. All youth group office holders were present and they declared that their committe had voted unanimously about 'the youth group joining up with the older group's money'. Their spokesman added that they intended making leaflets to put through the doors of pensioners flats to advise them of the assistance the youth group could give them. They hoped to collect waste paper for recycling and to revive the idea of a campaign to clear rubbish from Parkview. They also had plans for a football match. Mrs Field commented that all these intentions were 'marvellous' and the mood of the committee seemed to be that this productive channelling of youthful energies and the combined resources of the two groups augured well for the future of the estate.

Perhaps inevitably these high hopes were not fully met. Tony was the only youth group member to attend further TA committee meetings and he came twice. The three office holders did, however, attend the AGM and were introduced to the meeting. For the rest interest in formal TA business dropped. And not surprisingly there were more plans conceived than were put into action. The group did organize a disco, a rock concert, a football match and sponsored walk and they took part in a borough youth carnival. They published two editions of what was intended to be a regular newspaper, the Parkview Gazette. Thus they organized with some success activities for themselves and their peer group; they did not realize plans involving other age groups as well. The development of the youth group illustrates the difficulty faced by a small group forced in some measure to rely on another group for support and access to those resources necessary in carrying out its aims. In situations where one group consists of young people and the other adults, this reliance may also incorporate an inbuilt tension arising from a difference in values and accepted norms. In this case the main TA committee assumed a right to overall control and particularly to vet expenditure. The youth group on its part was, for whatever reason, unable to accomplish any of its wider welfare type aims.[77]

Eshag

Eshag a name formed by adding to the title of a block of flats the initials of Housing Action Group developed as a consequence of the team's decision to respond to complaints often expressed in the course of the introductory visits to residents of the 2 tower blocks on the estate. Residents grievances focused especially on the entrances to the blocks; the general unattractiveness of the lobby area; the glass doors which all too often lacked their glass panels; the biting cold of the wind while waiting for lifts which were frequently out of action and when in use were seldom clean from constant abuse. Similar complaints were voiced in all other blocks with lift access but in the tower blocks the complaints were expressed with a greater vehemence of feeling which did seem to be borne out by a fairly grim reality. The research team decided that an approach might be made to one of the blocks to see if residents there would be prepared to take part in a live planning exercise. An explanatory note was contained in the project's interim report.

On Parkview estate, where consideration is being given to handing control of a new community centre over to tenants, it would seem important to have available as much relevant background material as possible especially with regard to forms of organization. In this field a worthwhile experiment might be to involve interested tenants from one of the tower blocks in discussions on how the entrance to the blocks might be improved. This should include a prior assurance from the council that suggestions be seriously considered and where feasible experimented with.[78]

The block selected was the tower block nearest an estate boundary and hence more vulnerable to entry by outsiders and more exposed to high winds. Over a period of two weeks calls were made on most of the 68 households. The issues most commonly raised by residents were the state of the lifts, (Plates 31 & 32) lobby and landings, the rate of lift breakdowns, and the water-borne waste disposal system. These complaints contrasted with a high degree of satisfaction with the interior of the flats. As a result of these intitial visits Don sent a letter to all residents quoting the names and addresses of some residents and stating the various ideas they had put forward. At that stage these included a cabin for a porter who should be on duty full time, a playroom, a corner shop, workshop and laundrette. The letter invited residents to a meeting held on two consecutive evenings. Six residents attended the first meeting held on 26 November and proposals for a doctor's surgery and Social Services room were added to the ideas already put forward. Four more residents and others from the previous evening attended the second meeting. This meeting discarded the suggestions for a shop and workshop. Those present felt that the shop would not be a profitable proposition and hence premises would not attract a businessman while the workshop would degenerate into a clutter of messy tools and parts. Other ideas mooted were a public telephone booth, post box and the provision of better entrance areas.

At both meetings residents brought up other problems such as general maintenance and transfer applications. The researcher suggested that only improvements to the base of the block should be considered relevant to the group; other matters were more appropriately dealt with by the TA. This ruling was accepted. Don agreed to ask an architect from DOE to consider their proposals and arranged a meeting between the architect and the group. This meeting took place in early December and more residents attended for the first time. The architect considered that the scheme for a nursery, laundrette, doctor's surgery and Social Services room was feasible and undertook to make sketch plans. At this meeting the question of the waste disposal system was again raised and there were strong complaints about the inconvenient siting of the bins for larger rubbish. Some residents advocated looking into the possibility of alternatives to the water-borne system.

After this meeting residents themselves undertook to go around and talk to all other residents in the block, to inform them of what was happening and ask for comments. A questionnaire was left for completion by residents and there was a response rate of about 50%. Most respondents agreed with the proposals for developing the base but a suggestion that the waste disposal system should be removed was rejected for lack of any feasible and acceptable alternative. These results and the sketches were considered at the next meeting on 15 January. (See Plan VI). Those present decided that if the council would provide a nursery and laundrette, the group's first priorities, residents would undertake to manage them.

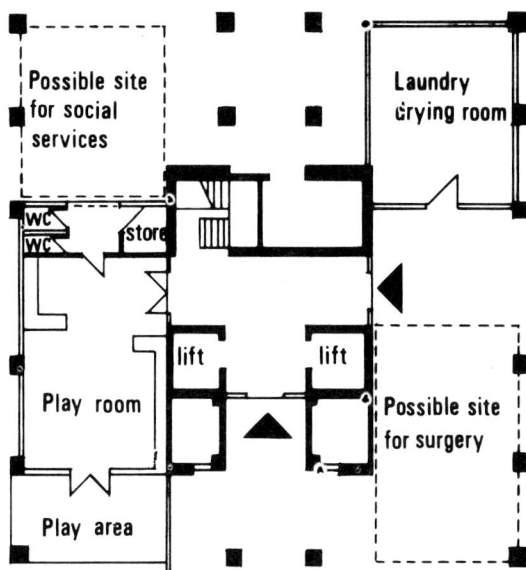

Church Close

In the course of this meeting the group wrote a letter to the Housing Manager expressing disatisfaction at the state of the lighting in the block. This was the first formal contact the group had had with the council and while drafting the letter members hit upon a name for themselves, Eshag. They also planned a meeting with councillors, to present the findings of their survey and the proposals for redevelopment of the base. A week prior to the meeting with councillors, the group met again to discuss strategies. An agenda was drawn up and it was arranged to serve tea and biscuits to all present. There was some discussion as to whether all residents should be invited to the meeting. This was an issue because in the experience of some members of the group, meetings with councillors tended to become general grouch sessions about outstanding repairs. It was decided that the meeting should be an open one but the invitations were not issued until the last possible moment.

This meeting took place on 29 January. Those present were the Vice Chairman of Housing, Councillor Harty, the three ward councillors and tenants, all except one of whom had attended previous group meetings. The agenda contained six items, '1. Lighting; 2. Building of a nursery/playroom; 3. Laundrette; 4. Possible rooms for Social Services and a doctor; 5. Better doors with less glass; 6. Installation of public phone and post box.' Harty as spokesman for the councillors in attendance dismissed outright items 2, 3 and 4 and promised to look into the others. The chairman Mrs Biddle asked why the group had been misled into thinking that their proposals would be considered. Don explained the team's position and the effort taken to keep the Director of Housing informed. Two of the councillors denied any knowledge of the proposals contained in the project's interim report.[79] Councillor Harty asked that the group send a letter to the estate TA outlining the aims and objects of the group. This they refused to do.

At the end of the meeting Councillor Harty issued an invitation to all present to go to a local pub. Some accepted. There one of the group, an ex TA committee member, Mrs Dee, launched into a bitter attack on those members of the TA committee who were also in the bar. The stage was set for open conflict between the two groups. Within Eshag the feeling after the meeting was one of resigned acceptance; a rebuff after all was what was expected and a different outcome would only be explained by reference to the power of the government department involved. The researcher was not to be blamed; he also had been misled. At the same time members felt they would be doing exactly as the council wanted by giving in and not meeting again. The external opposition was apparently intended to quash the group or subordinate it to the TA; in effect it served to strengthen their resolve to continue as an independent group.

The group met again in early February and reformulated their aims; they would now concentrate on minor improvements – adequate lighting, a directory of numbers in the lobby, repairs to the main doors and a more satisfactory rubbish service. At that time the group had not received a reply from Councillor Harty as a follow up to their meeting and it was decided to write again. Harty had in fact written to the Housing Manager and in due course the group received a reply from him. This indicated that all the matters queried were either in hand or being investigated. Not satisfied the group drafted a reply which concluded 'We have been very reasonable on all these points, but we feel the only course now left is to contact the media, and although we fully realize that this course of action could be very embarrassing and hurtful to the council in general, but no more than we have been'.[80]

At about this time 2 members of the group, both ex TA committee members, attended a meeting of the Federation of TA's of the borough and were there introduced to a senior officer of the council's Direct Labour Building Organization (DLBO). He accepted their invitation to talk to members of Eshag at a meeting on 26 March. Lloyd who arranged the introduction was also present at that meeting as the North Board representative from Parkview. The group concluded on the basis of the report of the DLBO representative, that their difficulties stemmed from the lack of co-ordination between the Directorate of Housing and the DLBO in the processing of works orders. It was therefore decided that representatives from both organizations should be invited to attend the next meeting. Both representatives accepted but the representative from Housing, did not attend.

Shortly after this meeting the most prominent members of Eshag were elected onto the main TA committee and Mrs Dee became chairman of the latter group. Eshag members continued to assert a separate identity but more and more the energies of its members were taken up in fighting with the 'old TA members'. At the time the fieldwork ended it seemed as if the TA committee was about to split although it seemed doubtful if Eshag members would withdraw into their own separate group again. Most of their immediate grievances had then been remedied and there was no prospect of reviving the original aims.

In the course of its development Eshag attracted 18 tenants representing 16 of the 68 households in the block. A representative from the second tower block was invited to attend the meeting with councillors. An open invitation to attend the meeting with the DLBO officer was extended to this block and two tenants responded. As noted above, Lloyd also attended on that occasion. Within the Eshag group there was a core of five regular attenders, all women. At the first few meetings residents often had only a casual knowledge of each other and no one person assumed a leadership role. Initiatives and suggestions tended to come from the researcher. In the later meetings the two most articulate members were those with experience of TA committee work, Mrs Biddle and Mrs Dee. However, all took part in discussions and all members of the group signed letters to officials and councillors. The regular attenders on their own initiative undertook to canvass other residents and so assured at least some feedback to the block as a whole.

Later, members commented how enthusiastic they had been in working out their proposals and how much they enjoyed the whole exercise. The social rewards in this instance were an outcome of working together on a particular project; the group cohered on the basis of agitation for improvements to the public extensions to their own homes. Undoubtedly there was a high degree of commitment among members to the original aims. Agitation on this basis promotes group solidarity. It also implies a confrontation with the agency best able to undertake remedial action. The opposition encountered by Eshag, both on the estate and external to it, reinforced the group's identity. Councillors and officers were provoked into adopting a stance of support for the established organisation, the Parkview TA. This implied that Eshag was considered to pose a threat and paradoxically increased its local importance. In fact the group developed over a relatively short time and it remained a fragile organization with no legitimacy apart from project support.

Something of the nature of both the strengths and the weaknesses of the group can be seen in the key confrontation with councillors. When the group was planning the meeting with councillors, members asked that the researcher act as spokesman. He refused and Mrs Biddle accepted the position of chairwoman for the evening. None of the members felt very confident about the meeting and their diffidence was reflected in the arrangement of people at the meeting place. The three male councillors ranged themselves with Mrs Biddle on one side of a table. Directly opposite were two other members with TA committee experience. All other members of the group and the woman councillor sat at the other end of the table. This reflected a division whereby those in authority faced the politicised tenant representatives while other members of the group, along with the female councillor were left to one side. The discussion group situation had hardly prepared Eshag members for this confrontation type situation. According to the researcher's account, most of the tenants present felt not only defeated but belittled by the manner of treatment and somewhat intimidated by the formality of the occasion. It would seem that the group's sociability and strength of identity found effective expression only in those situations confined to group members or including those outsiders, such as the DOE architect and the DLBO representative, prepared to meet the group on its own terms. The imposition of controls based on an assumed superior status as with the councillors, resulted in a publicly passive defence.

Mothers' coffee mornings

In the course of introductory visits on the estate I first became aware of the incidence of loneliness and mental illness among women when some of them invited me into their homes and what was intended as a brief explanation on my part became a long outpouring of pent up talk on theirs.[81] Some of these contacts were followed up with further visits or casual exchanges around the estate. My awareness of the problem was heightened by some of the indepth interviews with sample households. Since women at home comprise one of the three groups who spend the greater part of their time on the estate it was decided to organize a series of coffee mornings as informal discussion group situations. I hoped from them to understand more both of the nature of the difficulties experienced by some women and the type of action which might best suit their needs. Moreover, if those attending the project flat meetings felt they wanted to continue seeing each other informally there was the possibility that similar gatherings might be organized in the community hall. The proposal to hold meetings was put before the TA committee. Their approval was given and two women committee members, Mrs Montgomery and Mrs Field, attended sessions from time to time.

Initially an attempt was made to invite small groups of five or six women and to obtain a mix of those who were just lonely or simply lacking in self confidence together with those with more serious problems. In fact this proved difficult to arrange and background work to the sessions was more time consuming than expected; women would agree to come and then not turn up. On several occasions in the early stages nobody came. On a subsequent visit some would confess that while they would like to take part they had felt too nervous; others had forgotten in the flurry of some minor domestic crisis. In some cases it was necessary to pay three or four visits before women accepted the invitation to meet at my flat with a few other women for a chat over coffee. One woman had a fear of lifts and always used the stairs in her own block; with her it was a matter of phoning and arranging to meet her at the entrance of my block to accompany her in the lift. The easiest invitations to arrange were where two neighbours were known to each other and could be asked to come together. However, once women had been introduced to the group they all, with one exception,[82] came back; there was scarcely a trace of shyness in the constant chatter over a cup of coffee or tea and the atmosphere was always very friendly and relaxed.

Five coffee mornings were held over a period of as many months[83] and at the last session in the school holidays the women themselves made arrangements to hold a barbecue for their children at the new playground. This took place late in July and was voted a great success. In all, apart from the two TA committee members, 18 women attended these gatherings. Attendances for the various meetings were 5, 4, 12, 10 and 9. Most women attended the barbecue. Nine were known to me through indepth interviews, five through follow-ups to initial introductions and four came to the group with neighbours. There were two sets of next door neighbours, one set of three neighbours on the same landing of a tower block and one of three women in the same block previously known to each other only by sight. They came from all parts of the estate and from all block types. Five of the women belong to racial minority groups and three are married to men of a different culture. Four of the English women have their roots in the Old Borough. Most were known to me to have experienced some kind of difficulty in coping generally or in adjusting to life on the estate. For some it was a matter of feeling isolated and unable to make other personal contacts; four had a history of recent nervous breakdown, one a past record of mental instability, another was making a poor psychological adjustment to a physical disability and six had backgrounds of current marital problems or past broken marriages. Most were aged between about 25 and 40. In later sessions a few women who apparently coped admirably were introduced to the group. These included one middle aged woman who had told me and subsequently described to the group the agonies of shyness she suffered before attending a sewing class at one of the local schools. She is now firmly convinced of the value of such classes, feels that too many of the 'wrong' women attend, (ie, 'middle-class', women from a neighbouring borough), and offered to introduce anyone interested when term started again. Two older women of over 60 attended the last few mornings. Meetings began at around 10 am and lasted until about 12.30 pm when women had to dash off to meet children from school or prepare a meal for their husband.

The topics of conversation ranged widely. Women in the new flats spoke of problems caused by the dampness and others contributed stories of the difficulties they had experienced in dealing with the council. On one occasion a woman married to a Ghanainan spoke of the tensions which she felt arose from the differences in their cultural backgrounds. Another woman similarly placed described how she had come to terms with the situation. Both women admitted in the course of the conversation to having had nervous breakdowns. Others contributed comments about their own marriage experience or times when 'things get you down'. At another session a woman outlined how in her view a Pakistani family at the end of the balcony was being harrassed by members of a particular family on the same balcony. This turned into a general discussion and there was a good deal of comment from most women present. One of the TA committee women favoured calling in 'the welfare' and asking the council to take action against the disruptive family possibly by moving them elsewhere. Another woman objected that this only moved the problem: tenants had to sort things out for themselves. When faced with similar difficulties she had finally come to blows with her neighbour and thereafter there had been no trouble! She recommended that the Pakistani family fix a gate across the balcony since the flat was at the end of the balcony but then recollected that since the council had forced her to repaint a backyard fence she had painted with gay flowers they would hardly allow a gate. Of course nothing was solved or decided in this or other exchanges but there was a good deal of thought-provoking conversation as well as much general chatter.

It is difficult to assess the social significance of these gatherings for the participants. Several women from different parts of the estate immediately recognized each other from a queue in the post office on child allowance day or from the school gates but commented that prior to meeting at the flat had not known one another sufficiently to exchange greetings. The general feeling from the discussions seemed to be that it was pleasant to have a 'get together' on an informal basis and to appreciate that others shared your predicament. There was some support for activities like a sewing and knitting circle or cookery classes but there was also a strong feeling that meetings should remain informal and not be in anyway personally demanding. As one woman commented, 'If you ask people for something that means making a commitment—well, people like me can't make a commitment. I can come here and talk or not depending on how I feel.' From these meetings several women formed casual friendships. On the way home after coffee two neighbours from a tower block were invited into one of the garden flats and the women agreed that the children of two of them could play together and that all three should meet again. Two young West Indian women subsequently visited each others homes and one invited two other women her Yugoslav neighbour and a young English girl back for coffee. She found a great deal in common with the latter since both have backgrounds of marriage difficulties; they exchanged confidences and greatly enjoyed a long afternoon of non stop conversation. The two Asian women in the group kept up a casual acquaintance. A number of possible friendship networks were thus emerging by the end of the fieldwork period.

A second outcome was the extent to which women who had become fairly familiar with me in personal interviews and coffee mornings made further approaches of some kind. Five women came to me, sometimes on more than one occasion, ostensibly seeking advice on such matters as an immigration permit for a relative, an eviction notice, the transfer of a tenancy to adult sons and daughters, training schemes for the unemployed and the taking into custody of a teenage son on an assault charge. Two calls included requests to accompany those concerned to, in one instance an immigration appeals board and in the other, the local police station. I seldom felt able to give advice, nor did that seem required. Information, a contact with some local agency or access to a telephone might be helpful but mostly it was simply a sympathetic listener that was called for.

It is impossible to draw any firm conclusions from so few meetings with so small a number of women. Another project which carried out group work with lonely women on a housing estate in Bristol linked social stress to such factors as an unhappy childhood, a fluctuating income due to periods of unemployment, lack of contact with neighbours and ill-health within the family. The Bristol mothers like those at Parkview formed a small group which met informally in a members' home. There was no set programme of activity. 'The aim was that they should enjoy one another's company enough to be able to give each other a sense of support and so to establish confidence in human relations.'[84] In both projects the group did not survive the departure of the research teams although it does seem likely that at least some individual links continued to be expressed. Thus, on return visits to Parkview a woman would comment on whether or not she had seen others from the group and add that at least she felt there was someone she could call on if the need arose. Even so, on the basis of the two projects it can be concluded that on estates like Parkview there is a hidden need among certain categories of residents, like isolated women, for ongoing social support of various kinds.

Social Services facilities: Church Close luncheon club and the chiropody clinic.
The luncheon club and chiropody clinic are situated at ground level in Church Close. They are near one boundary of the estate and face outwards from it onto streets of terrace housing. Church Close luncheon club is a small one with a staff of three and able to cater for 32 pensioners. There is no provision for use

other than the serving of a midday meal and all users leave immediately afterwards when the club is closed again until the next day. However, some people do arrive early and read a newspaper or chat to other pensioners. Those making use of the service expressed their satisfaction with it and commented because it was a small club there was a friendly atmosphere and it was possible for those attending regularly to get to know one another. Approximately five of the users at the time of the study were drawn from the estate; the rest came from nearby streets. There was then a waiting list of about 50 names, some from the estate and some dating from 1973.[85]

These premises are rented from the Directorate of Housing by Social Services and although in use for relatively short periods the club room was not normally let to other organizations. However, it was made available, at no charge, for some meetings of the TA committee, general meetings of tenants called by that committee, Parkview youth group and Eshag. All groups experienced considerable difficulty in making a booking and in arranging to collect and return the keys.

The chiropody clinic is open for a few hours several days a week. Its existence was not generally known about on the estate, even to those who might be eligible to attend, and not surprisingly, it drew its clients from a much wider area than the estate.

Parkview library

The library takes up the ground floor of that wing of the blue block facing onto the main entrance into Parkview estate. It comprises one large room divided by stacks into several bays, some with small tables for reading. There is an attractively displayed children's section. Inter-loan services from other libraries are available but more specialist services like record lending are available only from the main Old Borough library. As a branch library Parkview attracts readers from an area wider than the estate.[86]

Ash Road nursery

The nursery, in terms of its location, is much more a part of the estate. The entrance to it is set back from one of the roadways into Parkview and the nursery itself faces inwards onto the estate. It shares boundaries with one of the estate playgrounds, an underground car park and the lawns of Ash Court a block occupied predominantly by pensioners.

This facility opened toward the end of 1974 long after completion and following lengthy delays apparently caused by protracted negotiations between Architect's Department and Social Services personnel about the finishes and design modifications to the building. The nursery has places for 60 children and by the end of April 1975, 49 had been filled, six by children from the estate. Children ranged in age from six weeks to five years. They were allocated places according to a Borough wide policy based on need. Hence most of the children were accepted as Priority 1 cases, namely, children at risk or children from one parent families. There is a staff of 11 caring for children up to one year old separately and thereafter in mixed age groups of up to 10 children. The matron expressed her concern to have around 10% 'uncomplicated' children but due to the pressure to accept priority cases this balance may be difficult to achieve.

Staff of the nursery feel that the building is badly sited. Access from the street is difficult and the orientation suggests a relationship with the estate which is practically non-existent. Ideally the matron feels that all places should go to children from the estate; in fact the proportion is low and staff are aware of the antagonism this has caused. It was not intended that the nursery should serve the estate only but its situation has contributed to a fairly widely held belief that it is 'our nursery'. And there is certainly resentment among young mothers at having a facility so close yet which for most of them is inaccessible. There is, moreover, at least one case of a one-parent family whose pre-school child already has a place in one of the Borough nurseries. This was conveniently located prior to the family's move to the estate but is no longer and a transfer has not been allowed.

Additionally, within the estate the orientation of the building is considered to be poor. One boundary of the nursery is formed by a playground and this has simply resulted in the nursery being used as an extension of it. The roof is attractive for climbing on as are the walls to the nursery garden. Some damage has been caused and staff members feel themselves to be in a vulnerable situation. As a result they successfully agitated for a high wire netting fence to be added to the walls around their own play area.

At the nursery staff attempt to involve parents as much as possible. A permanent jumble table is set up to attract mothers and staff suggest that parents might like to stay and help with the children. This is seldom taken up; in the matron's view parents may feel intimidated by the professional quality of the staff and most adopt the attitude, 'I bring my child to get rid of him/her for the day—it's your job to do the looking after'. This reluctance to get involved applies equally to parents resident on the estate.[87]

Parkview sheltered housing unit
The sheltered housing unit incorporates 74 double and 33 single self contained flats and three flats for resident staff within the one storey building. There is thus a potential population of 181 elderly residents. In October 1975 the population was 125, all in single person households except for 12 couples. Approximately 80% of the residents are women.

Since the opening of the unit in August 1974 the staff have experienced considerable administrative difficulties. The facility has been to some degree the responsibility of two directorates, Housing and Social Services. Staff allege that the lines of responsibility were never clearly worked out and that this has too often resulted in neither directorate accepting it even for such matters as the supply of stationery. Moreover, staff feel that their loyalties are divided. Other administrative policies have created rather longer term difficulties for the staff.

It was intended that a joint Housing/Social Services committee should consider allocations to the unit. This procedure was not adopted and instead Housing agreed to consider nominations put forward by Social Services. The area team consider they were largely ignored, unit staff consider that a significant number of referals from both sources should not have been made. A few residents have been too ill to cope with a flat even with the support services available. More were offered flats because they needed rehousing rather than because of any special need for sheltered accommodation. About 30 residents are considered to fall into this category and 12 of these cope perfectly well with full time employment. Naturally these residents tend to resent the caring element of the unit while staff for their part resent the waste of time and effort in dealing with residents who have no real need for their attention.

These apparent misallocations have done nothing to help the unit establish a reasonable relationship with the rest of the estate. Again it was widely believed that older residents on the estate would be given the option of transferring to the sheltered housing unit if their situation appeared to warrant it. In the event very few of the allocations went to estate residents and many of the newcomers were challenged as to how they got flats when the questioner's own aged parents, aunt or neighbour undoubtedly appeared to have a better case and had more-over lived a lifetime in the Old Borough. This antagonism was heightened by the provision, clearly visible from other parts of the estate, of a common room for the use of residents. The warden has attempted to persuade residents to extend an invitation to other Parkview dwellers but the residents resent the intrusion and have insisted that the activities organized there are exclusively for them.

This exclusiveness attracted wider attention. The question of whether the unit was part of the estate was raised at a North Board meeting and at various times members of the Parkview TA committee have made approaches to the warden or the tenants of the unit. These overtures came to nothing until June 1975 when the unit's committee agreed that one of their members might be co-opted onto the main estate committee. This has not, however, so far resulted in a sharing of resources or joint activities of any kind.

Unlike the nursery the sheltered housing block has no defined boundaries, and residents, particularly those on the lower floors, feel vulnerable and exposed; there have been complaints about the noise and the use of the grassy area outside the unit as children's play space. It is felt that the garden provided for residents, a small formal courtyard opening off from the common room, lacks privacy and, as a consequence it is seldom used. The response of residents has been to agitate for a fence to be put around the block.

Internally, according to staff, the building works very well in social terms. Initially there had been some misgivings about the height and the size but neither present any problems. Residents on the upper floors express considerable satisfaction with their housing situation and are said to appreciate especially the peace and quietness enjoyed. It is also considered that the number of residents is sufficiently high to reduce the level of gossiping and possible intrusion on personal privacy.[88]

Summary

The process of urban renewal: from street turning to flatted estate
On the basis of this study Parkview may be classified as an average estate set in a fairly old-established inner city neighbourhood. In this latter regard it is fortunately situated; many residents have a long association with the neighbourhood and strong loyalties to it. For some their homes were demolished to make way for the estate as part of the post-war drive to build physically improved environments which might also create better social communities. This ' ... merging of social reform in slum clearance ... attaches a meaning to particular streets and houses wider than their amenity or discomfit, or the memories they recall. The definition of a slum is also a definition of the people who live there. Their own attachment to the neighbourhood is reinforced by the insistence of authority that in moving they must change, not merely their surroundings, but the way they live'.[89] Parkview reflects a belief in the efficacy of this kind of social engineering through physical change.

Within the home the physical improvements and social benefits afforded by estate dwellings are almost without exception acknowledged by estate residents. Better amenities and improved space standards often enhanced family life.

Within the area, the development of the estate over a period of some 20 years resulted in a neighbourhood with a markedly altered physical aspect. A greater variety of building forms with homes opening on to landings, balcony access or pedestrian ways around a landscaped public area combined to provide a setting that is very different from streets of rows of small terrace houses with alleyways through to main roads. Corner shops, pubs, backyard businesses and public areas given over to a variety of uses have been replaced by a planned community (Plates 35 & 36) incorporating areas designated for play, parking, pedestrian access and so on.

A concomitant of this transformation would appear to be the attachment to the estate of a set of values which are different to those attaching to the street. It would seem that the designation slum and the connotation of social improvement given to clearance are accorded not simply by the authorities concerned in the programme but by those who make the move from street to estate. Parkview is judged by its residents in terms of its outward overall attractiveness and particularly the effectiveness of estate caretaking services. In this concern with appearances the hanging of washing on balconies, the storing of junk in any semi-public place and messy children's play is often regarded by residents as unacceptable behaviour. Terrace streets, by contrast, are more likely to be evaluated in terms of social characteristics and there backyards might harbour an assortment of ramshackle sheds, washing lines and miscellaneous clutter, all inappropriate in the new environment.

Furthermore these outward changes seem to be related to an altered social milieu as expressed through relations with neighbours. On Parkview interaction between neighbours may be characterized by casual friendliness and reserve. A minority of residents attempt to withdraw even from this form of contact and others feel themselves to be completely isolated. Another minority and one with a greater influence on the processes of interaction within a block or balcony are those residents who go out of their way to be friendly and are always ready to stop for a gossip. The majority are prepared to be friendly, only to the extent of 'passing the time of day' and otherwise place a positive value on 'keeping themselves to themselves'.[90]

Parkview residents contrast this pattern with the valued conventions of neighbourliness attributed to street life. It would seem that dispossession from the established street neighbourhoods threatened the whole structure of personal attachments and hence the sense of social security which they embodied. These attachments, for a variety of reasons, have not been readily re-established in the new setting.[91] According to respondents something of the quality of the old neighbourhoods attached at one time to the small pre-war estates and to a lesser extent the earliest phase at Parkview. The difference is associated with the amalgamation of the two boroughs and the development of the feeling that Parkview no longer comprises a population with shared associations and values. There is a tendency nowadays for residents to perceive the estate's population as a heterogeneous one when in terms of background, education, work experience and social circumstances it is still fairly homogeneous. This difference may also be related to phase in the family life cycle, the changing rôle of women and economic circumstances which often necessitated the acceptance of mutual obligations and support. The terrace streets represent a stable social world against which all subsequent changes can be measured. Moreover, its compass was small, the environs familiar and other inhabitants known in a variety of contexts. This may be an idealised and romantic view of a past social life but it is the one model within the experience of most residents to which Parkview can be compared.

The design of Parkview to some extent gives recognition to the importance of these aspects of neighbourhood. There is an attempt to create new forms for community life and substitutes for old meeting places. Community on the estate in planning terms finds institutionalised expression through the integration within the overall design of such features as a nursery, library, luncheon club and sheltered housing unit.[92] Certainly the location of these features in itself would seem to imply some kind of relationship with the estate and some members of user groups are drawn from it. In fact this kind of community planning has been variously regarded by residents. In the case of the nursery and sheltered housing unit some residents adopted a proprietorial attitude; they assumed that while the facilities were for the area generally residents would be given priority. There is no evidence that official assurances to this effect were given but it is clear that a set of expectations developed regarding right to use. Moreover the estate could in fact supply a large proportion of the user groups and given the concept of community apparently informing the design these attitudes were not unreasonable. In the case of the specialized services offered by the library, chiropody clinic and to a lesser extent the luncheon club, it is accepted that clients should be drawn from an area wider than Parkview. However, in all cases any apparent connection with Parkview is negated both in design and management terms. The luncheon club and clinic face outwards from the estate, the nursery is surrounded with a high fence and brick wall. The library (Plate 38) presents a solid brick facade to the estate and the sheltered housing unit has recently been set off by the planting of a belt of trees. In management terms there is no attempt to form a relationship with estate residents.

In terms of social organization the main attempt to develop an estate social life has been institutionalized in the form of the Parkview TA. This finds no equivalent in the street where social interaction was expressed more through interlocking gossip networks and ad hoc semi-formal groups organized around special events.[93] Perhaps not surprisingly, the TA has met with limited success in its attempt to realize its stated aim of the fostering of a community life defined in estate terms.

... The urban situation makes it difficult for a community association to find activities which have enough appeal to form the basis for contact on which communal-type relationships can grow. There are not many instances in any society where 'being social' is an activity which maintains itself on the strength of the satisfaction it itself brings. Rather, being sociable is a bonus the group enjoys as a consequence of successful co-operation on some activity other than the production of sociability as such. There are few activities which throw fellow residents together in necessary co-operation. The dominating contacts of the urban dweller are those of his family and work; family relationships are sealed off in the private home, and work relationships are characteristically between people who do not live in the same locality – and this is especially true of housing estates.[94]

Other groups on the estate, Eshag, the youth group and the coffee mornings had more limited aims, were less formally structured and owed much of their impetus to the presence of the research team. It is noteworthy that in the case of the coffee mornings many of the women were drawn from what might be regarded on the estate as outgroups and this would suggest that those categorized as such may be subject to additional social stresses.

Within the neighbourhood beyond the estate the changes for estate dwellers have not been as dramatic as in many slum clearance programmes. Some of the old shops, many of the pubs and the street market remained. Most of the residents are local people with shared experiences and a wealth of local ties. Moreover, in terms of social interaction the estate is not the most significant unit. Propinquity does not necessarily imply social intimacy. Parkview, although physically discrete is socially well integrated into that part of the Old

Borough which centres on Market Street. This integration is effected through home based networks encompassing close kin. The life style is a home centred family oriented one. Kin often live locally and provide the individual with his most meaningful social supports. Neighbours, friends, schoolmates and workmates are less important. Shopping and other services, leisure activities and to a lesser extent work and education are all locally based. The individual's social network thus crosses estate boundaries but is confined to a relatively small geographical area. Integration within this neighbourhood is effected through personal links with other individuals rather than through membership of various groups and hence a multiplicity of group loyalties and overlapping networks.[95] This is a social pattern which has probably been little altered by environmental changes. It is presently sustained for most residents by the presence of kin, the continuity of personnel around the market place and through a familiarity with old haunts.

In other respects too, the experience of the neighbourhood has probably been changed hardly at all by the new residential situation. The experience at school is for parents one of minimal involvement combined with high expectations for the educational attainments of their children. Such ideals are unlikely to be realized; most children leave school on reaching the minimum school leaving age after a career which often appears to give little scope for the development of initiative and the acceptance of personal responsibility. Education, except where regarded as of direct relevance to job prospects, may moreover, be regarded as of little consequence by the students themselves.

The experience of school may find a parallel in the work situation.[96] Few residents occupy supervisory positions and for most job satisfactions come from contact with other workmates. Leisure time activities complement this life style. Much leisure is spent in the home or in the company of friends at the pub or bingo hall. It is socially rather than activity based, informal rather than structured.

The unchanging nature of these wider experiences need to be kept in mind in assessing one other important change attendant on the move to the estate. For all residents estate living involves some form of rôle relationship with officers in the directorate of housing. In the street neighbourhoods 'management' was a simple matter of self-help within the individual dwelling supplemented by standard Borough services such as refuse collection. The new estate environment by contrast had a built-in need for outside management and this was effected by narrowly defining the rôle of the householder as tenant and allocating other functions to housing management officers, caretaking and maintenance staff, lift engineers and gardeners. The relationship between residents and white-collar officers is marked by a difference in assumed social status. This reflects the values of a wider society which implies that its more successful citizens help themselves without the benefits of such official intervention. The experience at home reinforces that of school and work; the individual is almost inevitably in receipt of benefits conferred by others. And as with school, the contact with housing officials may be minimal, the understanding of the system imperfect, the expectations unrealistic.

On Parkview, from one household to another, there is a considerable variation of circumstances. The overall pattern is one of an interplay of cultural continuity and change. Change is evident particularly through the altered social meaning attached to the living environment and in the associated relations with neighbours and officials. Continuity is most evident in the persistence of a family-oriented life style, in school and leisure patterns and in the subordinate social position occupied by residents in relation to the wider society beyond the estate.

Notes to Part II

1 Except where specifically stated, the sheltered housing unit has not been included in general estate statistics.

2 According to a submission to the DoE for finance for the children's playground, the number of planned child bedspaces (probably overstated) amounted to 1619. The planned adult population is therefore 1033. Thus 38% of child bedspaces are actually in use while the effective adult occupation is 161%. The overall occupancy rate is 85%. This is not exceptional in the Borough. According to a survey of 90.6% of the council owned stock 28.7% was in under occupation. Borough Housing Occupancy Survey, January 1972.

3 This and subsequent references to tables with the prefix A are to be found in Appendix III.

4 Other research has shown that 'The level of observed vandalism, vandalism in communal access areas, to lifts and to dwellings, was likely to be higher in buildings where there were more than 6 children aged between 6 and 16 per 10 dwellings, or where the total number of children of this age in the block exceeded 20'. Sheena Wilson, 'Vandalism on London Housing Estates', Home Office Research Studies Series, HMSO (forthcoming). From observations on Parkview it can be noted that Ash Court appeared to have a very low incidence of vandalism of this kind. Church Close had a reputation among the Borough lift engineers for frequent lift breakdowns due to vandalism but in other respects it would appear to differ little from other blocks on the estate.

5 It should be noted that the small area statistics for the Borough relate to families with children under 15 or unmarried children under 25 who are students; the figures for the estate relate to households with children and young dependants under 17.

6 There are no strictly comparable figures for the areas or the Borough. In the area 6% of all residents were born in the New Commonwealth and 13% of all children have New Commonwealth parents. The comparable figures for the Borough are 9% and 18%.

7 The Borough does not keep records on racial origins. The figures for black and other minority groups were recorded in the course of introductory visits on the estate. Both figures may therefore be understated.

8 They also have the highest rate of requests for transfer. See Table AIX.

9 This relates to the ordering of priorities and to the limited availability of the ground floor accommodation often required in such cases.

10 In some cases both for sample and other households the tenure under which property was occupied was not clear. Properties compulsorily purchased by the council for clearance programmes would be on file as council owned properties whereas prior to that they might have been in the privately rented or owner occupier sector.

11 Statistical tests of significance are not reported for the data relating to the sample households since, owing to the non-availability at the time of some files, these were not drawn from data comprising the total estate population.

12 This information is not available for 3% of respondents and in a few cases (4%) where there was no experience of the traditional type of neighbourhood, a response was deemed not applicable.

13 This may be compared with another study which found a much higher rate of continuing overall satisfaction. See Stevenson et al. *High Living; a study of family life in flats*, Melbourne, 1967, p 46 f.

14 R Firth, et al, *Families and their Relatives*, London, 1969, p 10.

15 *Family and Kinship in East London*, London, 1957.

16 In 4% of cases where for example families were overseas the question was deemed not applicable. In the interview the definition of 'local' was determined by the respondent. In most cases the place of residence referred to was in the Old Borough.

17 83% of those housed in the years 1957–62 have relatives locally, 93% of those in the years 1963–68, 54% in 1969–72 and 74% of those in the years 1973-75. I am unable to explain variation between the time periods. 84% of those rehoused from the Old Borough have relatives nearby as compared with 64% for the Borough.

18 I do not know whether for black respondents available kin are restricted to fewer categories, say a predominance of siblings. It may also be the case that interaction is valued as much for mutual services and support as for sociability expressed through family ties. More information is needed in this area.

19 Among some officers this may even be regarded with disfavour.

20 J & R Darke, *Suburban housing estates: social compostition and social characteristics*, CES Working paper No. 40, London, 1969, p 23.

21 This kind of categorization has been noted in other studies. See for eg Elias and Scotson, The *Established and the Outsiders*, London 1965; R. Wilson, *Difficult Housing Estates*, London 1973.

22 This invoking of war service to legitimize claims of what is now considered due is a subject which came up fairly frequently in conversation with middle aged or elderly residents. It is no doubt in part a reflection of the popular images of war and peace, with sacrifices in the one meriting just reward in the other. A letter in support of an application on file reads.

> ... They were signed on [the waiting list] seven years ago. I'd break my heart to see the Blacks getting lovely houses and making dirty slums out of them and my daughter whose father died through his wounds in the last war and my son who fought in Cyprus and yet the strangers who never raise a gun to help this country can come from the other ends of the earth and get places straight away. *Is that fair?* (Writer's emphasis).

23 Cf Bryant and Knowles who suggest that 'the relatively high level of contact achieved by established young/middle-aged families with young children are unlikely to be maintained as they become older. At that stage households may become more introvert and more selective regarding the frequency and nature of their associations with other members of the community'. 'Social Contacts on the Hyde Park Estate, Sheffield'. *Town Planning Review*, Vol. 45 No. 2, April 1974, p 210 f.

24 ibid, p 210.

25 The importance of key individuals in this regard hs been noted elsewhere. See for example Molly Harrington, 'Co-operation and Collusion in a Group of Young Housewives', *Sociological Review*, November 1964, pp 255–82. It should be noted however that I came across nothing resembling the cohesive social network of the group which she describes in her study.

26 This information is missing in 3% of cases.

27. The verdict returned by the coroner was an open one. There was speculation on the estate as to whether it was suicide and the ambivalent attitudes towards death by this means may account for the reaction.

28 It is interesting to note that residents who might be classed as reserved tend to be referred to by the use of their surname or their name may not be known at all. The original residents know each other by given names and Molly Pedley's sociability placed her in this category. Mrs Martinez was always referred to as 'the Spanish lady' and the housewife in the one 'problem' family on the balcony was nicknamed 'nutty Nora'.

29   Willmott and Young, p 142.

30   Ibid. It was noted in Bethnal Green that 'most people meet their acquaintances in the street, at the market, at the pubs or at work. They do not usually invite them into their own homes'. p 107. Similarly Goldthorpe and Lockwood found that among working class families visiting between neighbours was in the main discouraged. ' . . . home and family absorbed the individuals' time and interest'. 'Affluence and the British Class Structure'. *Sociological Review*, NS No. 9, March 1961, p 142.

31   L Festinger et al, *Social Pressures in Informal Groups*, London, 1963 ed, p 175.

32   cf T Morris, 'Delinquency and the Culture of the Criminal Area', in W G Carson and P Wiles, *Crime and Delinquency in Britain*, London 1971, p 88.

33   See for eg Nottingham Fair Housing Group report, September 1971; R Ward, report for the Manchester Fair Housing Group, January 1971.

34   The expression of prejudice is complex. J J Ray cites research which shows that people who acknowledge prejudiced attitudes may or may not behave in a discriminatory way toward other ethnic groups. The same is true of people who deny prejudiced attitudes. 'Do Authoritarians hold Authoritarian Attitudes?' *Human Relations,* Vol 29 No. 4, 1976, pp 307–325.

35   The accuracy of this latter perception may of course be challenged and most residents making the comparison are referring to a street neighbourhood known to them at a time when their own personal economic and family circumstances were rather different.

36   This kind of hypothesis is taken further by J Olivegren, 'Better socio-psychological climates for housing estates', *Ekistics, 245,* April 1976, pp 216–23. 'The lift, staircase and corridor in a multi-storey house often constitute sociologically a kind of nullity-zone, a no man's land to be fled as quickly as possible and where invitations to contacts are seldom welcome'. p 218.

37   It is my impression that the Y blocks are more conducive to casual contact in this regard and small groups of neighbours chatting were much more in evidence there than on the older style balcony access blocks. I cannot explain this difference beyond speculating that because the balconies on the older blocks are in a straight line broken up by a solid shaft housing the lift and stairwell residents feel more awkward and exposed there. The balcony rail in the Y blocks is also better for leaning on! Another study argues that homogeneity in terms of common background, similar interests and shared values is more important than propinquity in affecting the range and quality of neighbourhood relations. 'Although propinquity initiates many social relationships and maintains less intensive ones, such as "being neighbourly", it is not sufficient by itself to create intensive relationships. Friendship requires homogeneity.' From the Parkview material it will be apparent that the interplay of these two factors is complex and that others such as personality traits are important also. H J Gans, 'Planning and Social Life' *Journal of the American Institute of Planners,* vol 27, February 1961, p 135.

38   The information is lacking for 4% of all cases. As for assessing contact with kinsfolk, 'nearby' was defined by the respondent but from replies generally denoted within walking distance.

39   J Bynner, 'Deprived Parents', *New Society,* 21 February 1974, p 448 f.

40   Willmot, 1963, p 115 f.

41   cf Cotgrove and Parker cit D Downes, 'British Delinquents and American Subcultural theories', in Carson and Wiles, p 125.

42   As noted above the research programme included a study commissioned through the Institute of Education at London University and carried out by Wendy Healey. Except where

otherwise stated all material in this account draws on her thesis. As already noted the brief for this part of the research programme was altered in the light of local conditions. See above p 6.

43   I K Birksted, 'School Performance Viewed from the Boys'. *Sociological Review*, Vol 24, No. 1 New Series, February 1976, p 72 f.

44   Social educationalists make a distinction between social education and community service. 'The difference is seen as lying in the fact that in the latter the choice of how to develop the community and individuals within it is determined by the teacher–who either diagnoses social needs himself or accepts the diagnoses of the social agencies. In a true 'social education' situation the basis for taking a decision as to what to do is in the hands of the pupils who will have surveyed and familiarized themselves with their environment with a view to taking action which they feel to be necessary'. Healey, p 61.

45   DES, *Education survey 20: Community Service in Education,* HMSO, 1974, cit Healey, p 70 f.

46   Healey, p 231.

47   Information for the remainder is not known. These classifications were made according to the registrar general's classification.

48   The figures are under 25, 62% in employment; 25–30, 88%; 30–35, 33%; 35–40, 67%; 40–60, 63%; and over 60, 23%. A larger sample might equalize these numbers.

49   See for example J H Goldthorpe and D Lockwood, p 142; Willmott and Young, 1957.

50   Information is not available for 7% of all respondents.

51   P Harrison, 'The Gambling Class', *New Society,* 20 March 75, p 722. The filling in of football coupons did seem to be fairly popular among residents and there were several betting shops very close to the estate but I have no information on either of these aspects of gambling.

52   Willmott, 1963, p 85. The figure is for working class respondents. Doris Rich, 'Spare Time in the Black Country', in L Kuper (ed), *Living in Towns,* London, 1953, p 366.

53   The remainder had no opinion.

54   A detailed study of children's play has been carried out by the department. See *Children at Play,* Design Bulletin 27, HMSO, 1973.

55   11% expressed no opinion; 1% not known.

56   It should be noted that most interviews were conducted prior to the opening of the playgrounds; somewhat different responses might have been recorded had more parents actually experienced using the area with their children.

57   See below p 104 f.

58   cf R C Moore, 'Patterns of Activity in Time and Space: The ecology of a neighbourhood playground', in D Canter and T Lee (eds), *Psychology and the Built Environment,* Architectural Press, 1974, for an examination of the idea of an entire estate etc as a playground.

59   T Morris, 'Delinquency and the Culture of the Criminal Area', in Carson and Wiles, 1971, p 82 f.

60   D Downes, 'British Delinquents and American Subcultural Theories', *ibid,* p 116.

61   See below pp 92–95.

62   cf P Willmott, *Adolescent Boys of East London,* London, 1966, p 147, where he describes a general cult of toughness that is more a matter of folk law than of day to day behaviour.

63 For the purposes of working out bonus payments all work undertaken by the caretakers is subject to a time study. This was carried out but when I revisited the estate in September 1976 the area had apparently not been included in the work schedule of the caretaking staff and they claimed that the periodic clean-ups which were done were carried out from a sense of personal responsibility rather than official duty.

64 The breakdown was as follows; 20% said they would do nothing, 52% refer to a caretaker, 12% refer to 'the council', 11% don't know and 4% would attend to the matter personally.

65 The amount of contact may be understated. Respondents were asked if they had had any dealings with the housing department—this implied that the respondents took the initiative. They were not asked if 'the council' had contacted them say over arrears or a complaint of rowdy behaviour. Residents might be reluctant to admit to calls on these grounds and in most cases where the initiative came from an official, the resident would be cast in the rôle of a wrongdoer.

66 15% stated that officers could be partly trusted, 12% stated that some officers could be trusted and others not, 11% expressed no opinion and the information is lacking for 5% of cases.

67 The information is not available for 5% of cases.

68 See pp 121–141.

69 An analysis of a tendency to see political issues in terms of persons and partiality in connection with village politics is contained in P Loizos, *The Greek Gift; politics in a Cypriot Village*, London, 1975, especially p 200 f. I found similar sets of expectations and beliefs in a study of New Guinea businessmen and their relationship with officials in a government agency which was set up to promote their interests.

70 This name comes from the block initials and the designation Housing Action Group.

71 See below pp 163–183, 191–195.

72 Membership is generally claimed by tenants who have at some time paid membership fees. For much of the study no collections were made so membership was not current.

73 The developments on the committee and the reasons for this change are dealt with more fully in Part IV.

74 N Dennis 'Changes in Function and Leadership Renewal', *Sociological Review*, NS, 9, March 1961, p 71.

75 On this occasion too streets in the neighbourhood put up bunting and organized parties. The local newspaper ran features on these and some of the estate celebrations.

76 See above p 81 f.

77 Of course it may be that these objects were put forward simply with a view to pleasing adults. The fact that some adult committee members and one of the caretakers claimed that the suggestion for the various projects came from them would seem to support this view. However, my impression was that the youth group members were also quite genuine. Unfortunately, I do not have sufficient knowledge of youth group members to be able to comment further.

78. Interim report, September 1974. Copies of this report were sent to the Director of Housing, the Chairman and Vice Chairman of the Housing Services Committee and the three ward councillors.

The action project was undertaken by my research assistant Don Entwistle. The account which follows is based on Don's report 'Research into the process of tenant action'. I helped with some of the preliminary work but thereafter had little direct involvement and did not attend any meetings. Moreover this would have been impossible; once the TA committee regarded Eshag as a rival group Don became identified with 'them' and I became identified with the Field group. Explanations about the stance of team members as researchers were probably not accepted since the rôle of a researcher and the expression of personal commitments are easily confused.

This account of Eshag and the earlier account of the TA focus on the activities of the group as they relate to resident support groups and in the case of the TA, the estate generally. The relationship of both groups to outside agencies is dealt with more fully in Part IV. The division is somewhat arbitrary and in real terms, meaningless. In principle, however, the distinction is important: participation can be viewed in terms of the establishment of additional and more meaningful links between the two fields of social interaction, the estate and the council. This section concerns the estate. Part IV is concerned with understanding the nature of the existing linkages between the two.

79   In fact the proposal had been raised in discussions between members of the research team and the director of housing. He had agreed to consider favourably some proposals. The two researchers considered whether councillors should also be involved in similar discussions. This would give them time to assess the issues before facing a possible confrontation with tenants. Arguments against discussions were that councillors would in such situations act as social monitors, dampening down action they considered unacceptable and encouraging that which they felt was worthwhile. It was felt that such a strategy would discredit tenant action. On those grounds we decided against prior briefings of the councillors and none of those invited broached the subject or requested information either from team members or the director of housing. In retrospect it seems to me that the dilemma is a very real one and the issues raised are important. I still do not know what would have been the 'best' course of action in the circumstances.

80   Eshag to the Housing Manager, 27 February 1975.

81   I do not use the term mental illness in any clinical sense. In this context it is the reference of the women themselves to mental ill health that is considered significant. Other research suggests that there may be a higher incidence of mental ill-health among this section of the population. See for eg G W Brown et al, 'Social class and psychiatric disturbance among women in an urban population' *Sociology*, Vol 9, No 2, May 75.

The Social Services team for the area commented on the relatively high level of referrals from the estate on the grounds of mental ill health. These would not of course all be women. I am unable to comment on the scale of the problem: the group was in no way representative and my awareness of the existence of a problem was an incidental finding of the research.

82   The exception was a seriously disturbed woman who stayed only a short time and whose somewhat dishevelled appearance and withdrawn demeanour may have caused some temporary upset. The woman herself claimed afterwards that the drugs she was then taking had a hallucinatory effect upon her.

83   11 March, 9 April, 18 June, 2 July, 15 July.

84   R. Wilson, *Difficult Housing Estates*, London, 1963, p 129.

85   After the completion of field work the clinic was closed and the luncheon club moved to the estate community hall, see below p 320. Figures relate to December 1974.

86   See above p 80.

87   Most of the information given here was obtained from an interview with the matron, 29 April 1975. All figures relate to that date.

88   Most of the information given here was obtained from an interview with the warden, 22 October 1975 and figures refer to that date.

89   P Marris, *Loss and Change*, London, 1974, p 56 f.

90   cf G D Mitchell et al, *Neighbourhood and Community*, Liverpool, 1974, esp. p 70.

91   cf op cit, p 57.

92   This expression is most explicit in the provision of a community hall. See below pp 243–253.

93   At the time of writing, October 1976, a good deal of activity in streets and estates in the area was being generated in plans and fund raising activities for the occasion of the royal jubilee celebrations.

94   Dennis, p 79.

95   The importance of this mechanism in other social contexts is fully explored in M Stacey et al, *Power, Persistence and Change, a second study of Banbury*, London, 1975.

96   The significance of these parallels in relation to rôle definition has been pointed to in another study ' ... the boss takes the place of the schoolmaster as the unreasonable overdemanding figure of alien authority whom to deceive or defy is a mark of cleverness and success'. T Morris, in Carson and Wiles, 1971, p 86.

1 A community in locational terms . . .

2 Market Street at the turn of the century

3 Construction of the Y blocks

4

4, 5 '... small touches of a personalised exterior ...'

6 The surrounding neighbourhood has a human scale

7 'Down the streets ... everyone knew everyone else'

8 A play area that is little used

9 'The pram sheds . . . have become dumping grounds for unwanted rubbish'

10 Chestnut Road

11 Garden flats

12 Y blocks

13 Church Close

14 Tower

15 Sheltered housing

16 Ash Court

17 Looking towards A wing from the project flat

18 A personalised shopping situation

19 For older residents the library serves as a kind of social centre

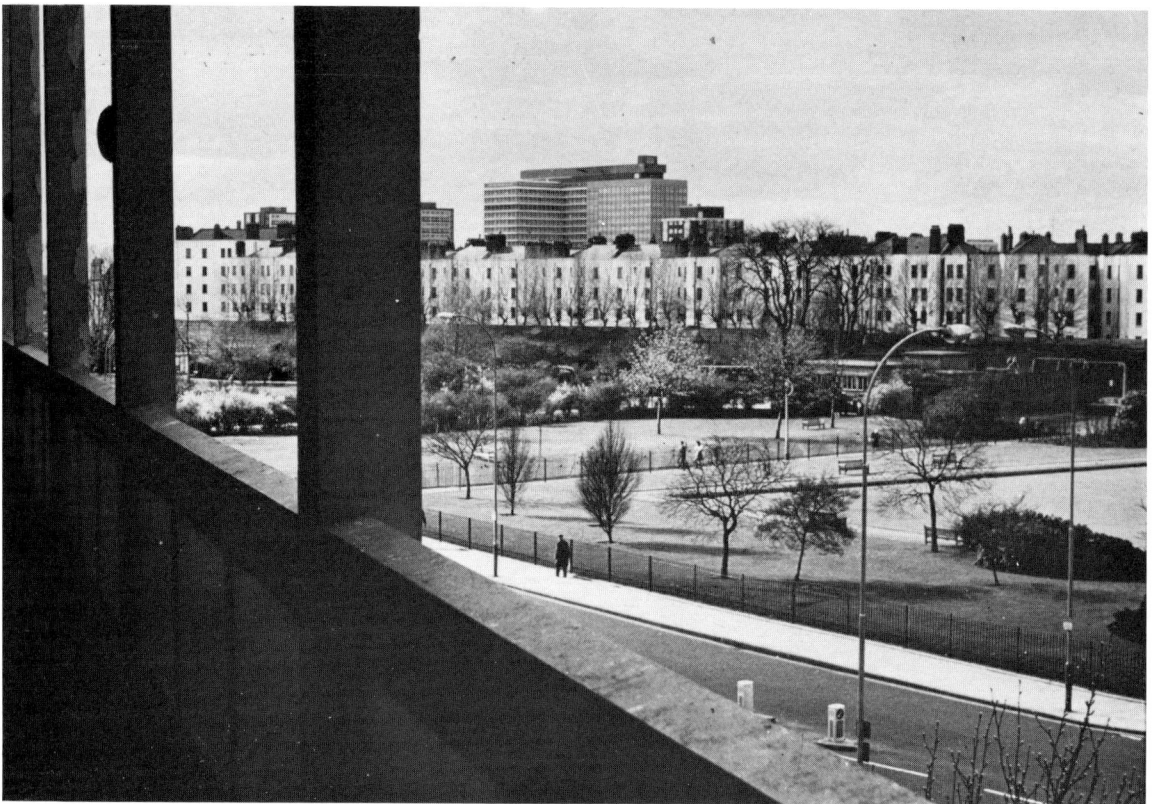

20 The view is much appreciated

21 The car deck playground

22 The car deck playground

23 The landscaped play area shares a border with the nursery

24 The landscaped play area shares a border with the nursery

25 A hill overlooking the kickabout area

26 Supervised playgrounds at the park

27 Residents adjacent to the play area want it fenced and supervised

28 'Hanging around with mates'

29 '. . . some equipment was quickly wrecked'

30 '. . . some equipment was quickly wrecked'

31 'putting the old community spirit back into the place'

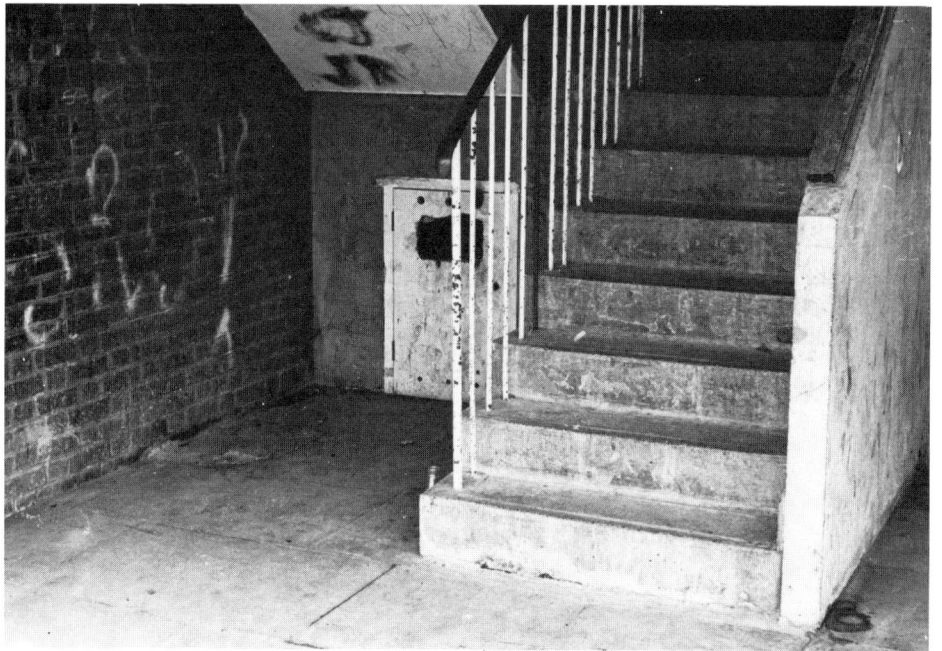

32, 33 'the unattractiveness of the lobby'

34, 35 'from street turning to flatted estate' ▶

36

37

38 'the library presents a solid brick facade to the estate'

◁ 36, 37 'a planned community'

39 Rubbish around one of the underground car parks

40 Mrs Glen showing the fungus growth in her garden flat

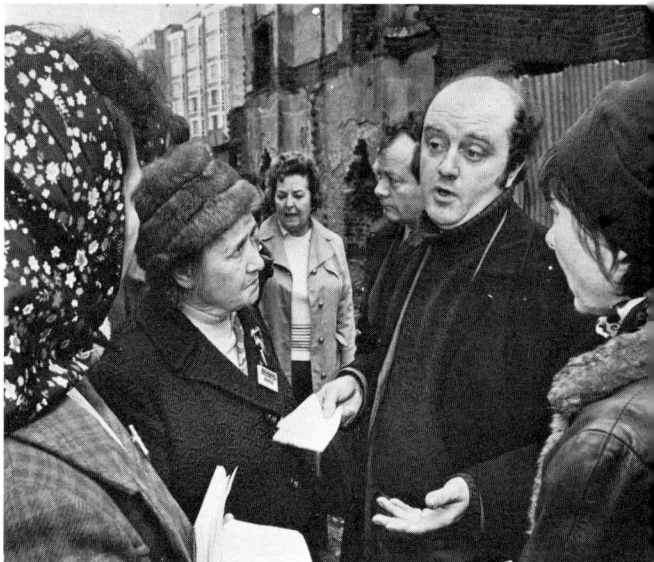

41 Mrs Montgomery and Mrs Field (left) talk with a councillor during the North Board tour

42 Fencing and potatoes. The garden in the foreground is the one which later sprouted an aerial ▶

43 Parkview community hall

42

43

44 Parkview playgroup

45 The luncheon club in new premises

46 Luncheon club staff in the kitchen

Part III

'The Council'

Officers

Local authorities in Great Britain have the undoubted benefit of a professionalized housing management service which is unrivalled throughout the world, and has been frequently envied by housing experts in other countries: nevertheless it can be contended that it frequently takes a course of action which is administratively convenient and economical, without assessing whether this is really what tenants would prefer.

> D Fox, 'Tenant Participation—a new task for housing management?' unpublished paper, DOE, December 1973.

Housing manager: 'enjoyed' evictions

Old Borough housing manager White confided last week that he used to enjoy evicting rent defaulters. . . . 'It was lovely, and quite frankly I enjoyed it. At the time when it came to the crunch we could evict them and the old London County Council had to take them . . . Now if we sling them out, the worst that can happen is that they get somewhere better to live.'

> from a local newspaper report, 18 April 1975.

This section describes the officer and elected member organizations labelled by estate dwellers, 'the Council'. The focus within this field is on the housing management sections of the Housing Directorate, the three housing committees served by the directorate and other sections and directorates where the work impinges on housing management and on the estate. It should be noted that while much of the information used in Part II draws on close observation over the study period, that available for the council draws more extensively on formal reports and interviews. However, it was possible to observe officers and councillors at meetings and some four weeks were spent in the management office while working through files.

The account which follows has been ordered according to two main subjects, the one concerning the officer group, the other the elected members. In the first an introductory section is followed by a description of the policies and form of organization developed within the directorate, the personnel and practices involved in day to day management, the attitudes of officers towards Parkview and the relationships developed between housing and other directorates. Under the second heading there is a consideration of the organizational framework and work roles established for councillors. Part III concludes with a summary and attempts also to link some of the main themes both from this and Part II.

The Borough Housing Directorate is faced with problems of housing stress not unlike those of many inner London boroughs. However, in comparison with some areas the public housing sector constitutes a relatively low proportion of the Borough total. In 1975 the council housing stock comprised some 14,000 dwellings, 2775 of them acquired properties. This represented less than 15% of the Borough's total housing stock. Approximately 90% of the dwellings in public ownership comprised flatted developments, mainly in small estates, with only four of over 500 dwellings each.

Prior to the upgrading of housing to the status of a directorate the Borough's housing stock was managed by a department under the control of the Director of Administration. According to the then Chairman of Housing the re-organization of the department was opposed by three other parties; the Borough architect, engineer and treasurer all feared that areas within their competence, housing design, repairs and mortgages would be incorporated in a new directorate aiming at a comprehensive housing service. These inter-departmental struggles are reflected in the scope of the reconstituted directorate's operations.

Associated with this upgrading was a move to new premises. Until September 1974 housing offices were located in several old and somewhat cramped premises in a main thoroughfare of the Borough. These were, however, easily accessible from most parts of the Borough by both bus and underground train connections. The new premises comprise a converted warehouse in closer proximity to the main administrative services of the council but less conveniently located for clients relying on public transport systems. The new building is approximately $3\frac{1}{2}$ miles from Parkview.

As part of the attempt to project a different image these offices have been called the Borough Community Housing Centre. Here housing aid and lettings are on the first floor, housing management on the second, housing administration and the offices of the director and his assistant on the fourth. All offices are open plan with, on the first and second floors, a public lobby area separate from the offices. The housing aid/lettings lobby has special facilities designed for interview situations; the housing management lobby, one counter for the payment of rent, another for enquiries and a general waiting area.

The housing directorate; policies and organization
The upgrading of the department to the status of a directorate involved also the reclassification of the most senior position in the organization. In January 1974 Brown, an applicant from outside the existing organization took up the position of Director of Housing. He was concerned to promote a more dynamic approach to the whole problem of housing stress in the borough. Some months after taking up his appointment Brown was quoted as saying 'Housing has tended to become staid in the past, ... it has been stuck in the mud and hasn't moved on with the times. We need motivation and we intend to get it going in [the Borough]'.[1] Within the public sector Brown was committed to developing a style of tenant oriented housing management. 'We want to involve tenants a lot more. We want to familiarize these people with the council and let them have their say in the way their flats are run.'[2] There was to be a strong emphasis on effecting change to make the Borough a trend setter in the housing world and to project a new modern image.

122

The first official statement of these aims came early in 1974 when Brown submitted to the Housing Services Committee his proposed objectives for the directorate and an organizational structure designed to facilitate their implementation.

... the prime objectives of the directorate will be:

a. to co-ordinate all spheres of the Council's housing activities so that their priorities are determined and controlled;

b. to establish a "positive" housing service whereby all types of housing need can be considered and alternative solutions to people's housing difficulties can be explored;

c. to achieve an amelioration to the problems of the Borough's housing stress by tackling the unsatisfactory conditions at source, rather than perpetuating them; and an attempt to improve housing and home environment, in addition to the provision of modern amenities;

d. to seek a clear understanding of what people want from the housing which can be provided, and to secure its management along these lines;

e. to maximise the use of the Council's existing housing resources, and to initiate consideration and action towards its expansion and improvement;

f. to promote professional and attitudinal training of its staff so that its service can be efficient, expert and consumer orientated.[3]

The new director criticized the existing organization for what he termed its negative orientation towards clients, its fragmentation, its lack of research capacity, its over-specialization and duplication of management functions and its inability to recruit and retain professionally qualified staff.[4] Brown stated that acceptance of his objectives assumed Council's preparedness '... to change that emphasis of its housing service, so that it is *comprehensive* ie the total housing function in the private and public sectors can be controlled and co-ordinated, and it is *positive* ie the directorate sets out to discover how it could provide the greatest contribution to housing needs, instead of merely considering those who apply for assistance.'[5] (Brown's emphasis).

This then was the general intent of policy. In organizational terms Brown proposed establishing administrative units responsible for specific localities.

To identify the staff with the public they serve, involves the creation of area teams. Separate teams for Council and private sector tenants will be formed based upon four corresponding areas (coinciding with the social services areas), which will deal with most of their requirements direct. These teams will work from the directorate's central offices, but will spend a major time (sic) on site, and will be supplemented by special ad hoc offices for HAA's and estates. Particular emphasis will be laid on the co-ordination of the public and private sector teams.

It was estimated that these plans involved increasing the staffing level of the directorate from 170 officers to 246, the latter figure including 25 trainees. The old and proposed organisational charts are reproduced in outline in Figures IV and V. It can be seen from these charts that apart from the establishment of area teams the main changes are the setting up of a section under the Housing Co-ordinator, and the abolition of the housing welfare, rent collecting and home

FIGURE IV   Borough Housing Department prior to reorganisation

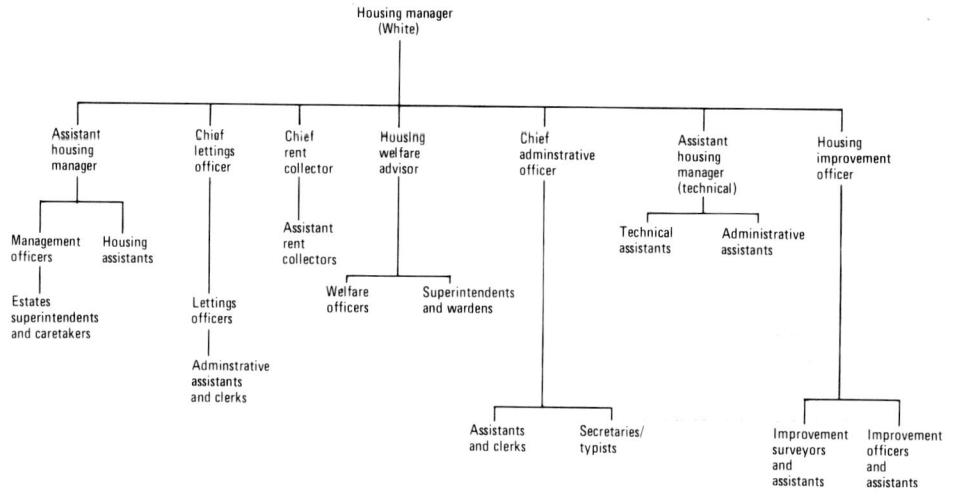

FIGURE IV   Borough Housing Department prior to reorganisation

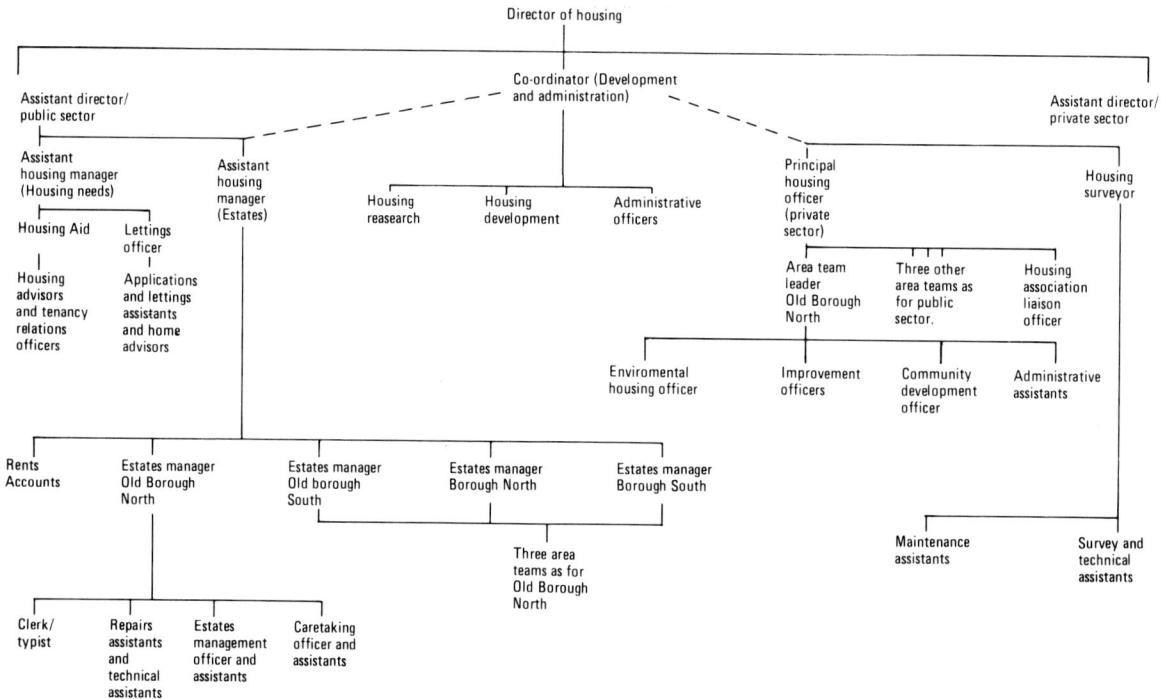

FIGURE V   Borough Directorate of Housing: Proposed structure

improvement sections. At the time Brown stressed the urgency of his need to obtain approval to the plans. In fact, although approval in principle was shortly granted, approval in detail was withheld for almost a year. Meantime the proposed re-organization went through numerous changes. (See Figure VI). It is worthwhile examining in more detail the nature of some of the constraints experienced by Brown.

FIGURE VI Borough Directorate of Housing: Estates management, development and administration sections, revised structure

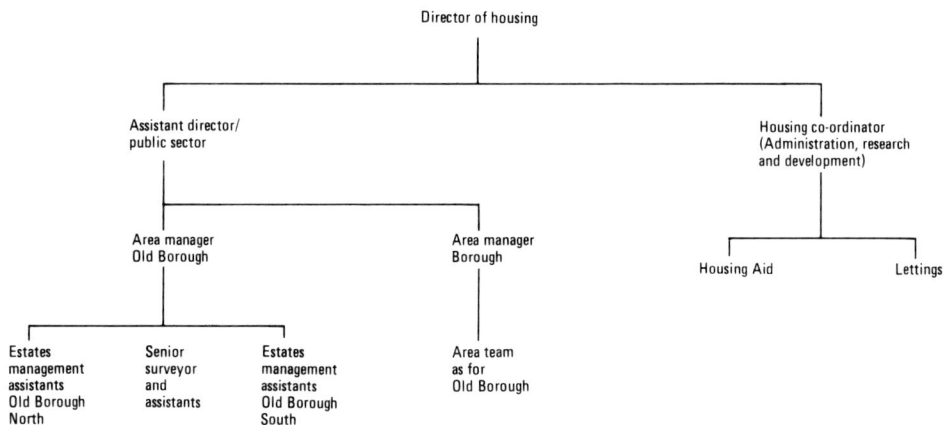

As noted above the plans were first put forward in March 1974. It was soon apparent that the overall expansion of council staff would have to be curtailed in view of cutbacks in spending necessitated by national government policies. The various directorates found themselves competing for staff allocations. Within each directorate it became necessary to argue job classifications, phase expansion. These cutbacks were seriously detrimental to the proposed reforms of the housing directorate. Over the next three years the housing stock was to increase by 30%. Estates management staff increased by only 8%. Brown's plans depended on the appointment of new staff in such numbers and with sufficient skills as would allow a more intensive management approach sensitive to local needs. Lack of staff necessitated deferring the establishment of the four area teams in both the public and private sectors. The area based team concept was key to Brown's proposals and now it survived only in a truncated form: throughout the study there were two teams, one for each of the former metropolitan boroughs, though within each there was a development of the area concept at a more junior level than intended.

These factors were largely externally defined and their import for the directorate, though containing was clear. Other constraints within the directorate were rather more diffuse and undercover. A new director is inevitably faced with a heritage of promises and obligations which his predecessor has not been able to fulfil. In the case of the directorate, the former housing manager had at all stages been a contender for the position of director. The appointment of an outsider constituted a potential threat. In fact the new director, Brown, refused to acknowledge any obligations to the established staff. Moreover, he considered that the existing approach to management in the department was based on an authoritarian and paternalistic management philosophy. Brown made it clear that he was firmly opposed to this orientation. At the same time senior staff members remained in powerful positions and were able to mobilize sentiment against Brown and employ delaying tactics to subvert his new policies. In the early days, according to Brown's personal assistant, any initiatives involving the housing management section met with non-co-operation or stone-walling. Indeed at that stage, judging from comment among the former housing managers supporters it seems likely that the legitimacy of Brown's entitlement to the position of director was not accepted in housing management and there was some feeling that if things were made difficult enough he might leave.

Brown thus faced two inter-related problems; how to implement his goals and, as a prerequisite to the solution of this problem, how to eliminate the resistance of staff to his plans. It has been suggested with reference to another context, that the new manager of an organization has two major tactics open to him; ' . . . the technique of informal solidarity and/or the technique of impersonal routinisation or other changes in the formal organization.' The first requires ' . . . a greater consensus of ends and sentiments between management and workers than exists . . . It is difficult to maintain to say nothing of creating, informal solidarity in pursuit of ends which are differentially valued by group members.' Further the successor would require ' . . . knowledge of the informal networks and the private sentiments they transmit if he were to manipulate them successfully. But because he has little inkling of the subtle arrangements and understandings comprising the informal structure, they are inaccessible for his purposes.'[6]

For obvious reasons, Brown did not try this tactic with officers in housing management, though he did endeavour to build up informal solidarity within housing aid a newly established section with younger professionally qualified staff whose ideas were closer to his own. In response to the situation in housing management Brown drastically attenuated the management function, instituted formalised controls and made use of what may be termed strategic replacements, appointments of a personal nature calculated to enhance the manager's own power base. The latter are especially important for an incoming manager since they set up a new informal group that potentially may conform to his needs, support his status and through the network so formed, can guarantee that the meaning or spirit of his orders will be communicated. Brown chose to recruit strategic replacements for key positions outside housing management itself, the assistant director (private sector), the housing co-ordinator and the housing aid service manager. Initially he hoped that White might be persuaded to retire immediately he was eligible to do so. This possibility was ruled out by White himself and he continued as assistant director for the public sector.[7] Consequently Brown chose to develop the resources of the private sector and of housing aid and to remove from White's competence two of the sections previously scheduled as under his control. Thus lettings and housing aid were both placed under the housing co-ordinator and he assumed the responsibility for briefing the architects for new housing projects.[8] (cf Figures v and vi). Apart from downgrading housing management in this manner Brown relied upon instituting formal communication flows through a bureaucratic organization.

The working through of these tactics caused a good deal of discontent among officers in post prior to Brown's appointment and especially among long-serving officers. There were complaints that the staff were not consulted about the changes, officers resented the appointment of new, often younger staff to senior positions on the basis of paper qualifications and housing management staff felt bitterly that they were being neglected. Throughout the study period it was very evident that the succession of proposed changes, the process of regrading and reclassifying positions, the making of new appointments and the personal uncertainty all this entailed for many officers resulted in a fairly high degree of disgruntlement within the management section.

Brown justified his strategy not simply as a response to the realities of the political situation pertaining in housing management but by reference to the composition and nature of the Borough's housing stock. In this view housing stress in the private sector warranted both the building up of services designed to meet need there and the creation of an important rôle for a housing co-ordinator.

Housing management; personnel, procedures and practice
The Housing Community Centre offers any member of the public the chance to have an 'over the back fence' talk about their housing problems with experienced council officials.

(from a local newspaper report 13 September 1974)
A chance to obtain training in housing . . .
Only those with intense social motivation and who care deeply about people should apply.
(from a Borough advertisement for housing management trainees in the national press, 7 August 1975).

Some understanding of the manner in which the Borough's housing stock is managed may be achieved by describing, on the one hand, the management tasks assigned by Brown, and on the other, the formal management organization of, and duties undertaken by, the area team responsible for

127

Parkview. This understanding may then be widened by discussing the extent to which this ideal is modified by the background, attitudes and practice which staff bring to the management function. According to Brown, the directorate should assume responsibility for the 'management of estates including rent collection, accounting and arrears, advice on 'fair rents', specification of repairs, programmed maintenance and minor improvements, establishment of priorities for DLBO and direct control of private contractors on minor works, promotion of tenant participation by Area Housing Boards and individual estate associations'. Specifically the area teams should have ' . . . control of tenants' welfare, exchanges and recommendations for transfer, caretaking, outdoor rent collecting, the control and recovery of rent arrears and specification of repairs but excluding the functions of giro and office rent payments and rent accounting. Close liaison with the Area Housing Boards and associated tenants' associations will be required, involving a gradual movement towards a degree of tenants control over the management of their estate'. In order to achieve these aims Brown stressed the need for the directorate to develop its own research team. In addition, 'There will also be an outstanding need to install a comprehensive training programme, so that not only can the council generate its own professional and technical staff, but existing staff can be kept up to the date with modern techniques, practices and attitudes'.[9]

FIGURE VII   Borough Directorate of Housing: organisation of the Parkview management team

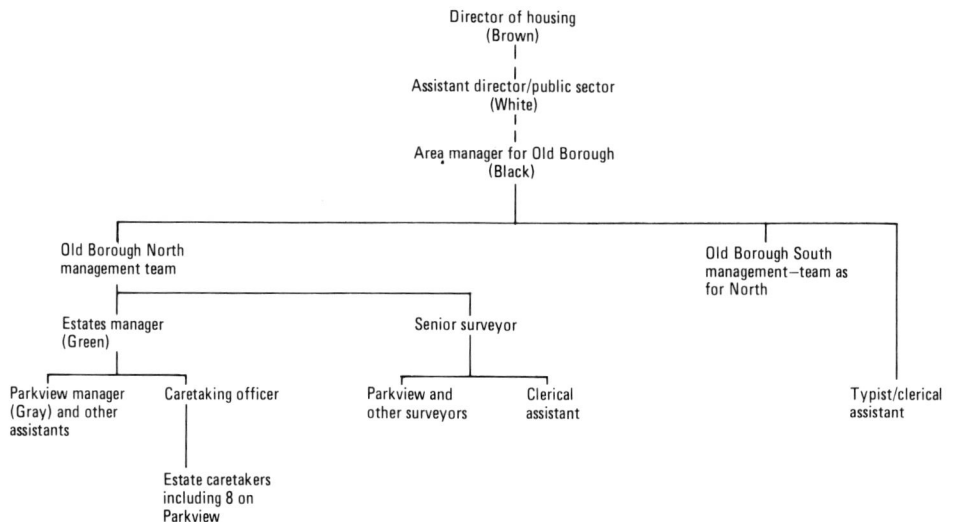

128

The form of organization devised for the management team is outlined in Figure VII.[10] Brown, as director, has overall responsibility for the development of policy options, policy implementation and general administration. He has weekly meetings with the assistant directors but otherwise relies on informal contacts with officers. Brown professes a dislike for working to rule and prides himself on an ability to cut through 'red tape' or ignore 'correct' procedures when necessary. Such instances may involve direct contact with more junior staff. He cited one example where on being criticized for delays over conversion works he intervened personally and demanded an explanation from the surveyors concerned. When told they awaited an order of simple drawing equipment he told them 'to bloody well walk down the road and buy some'.

Assistant director White is Brown's deputy, has general responsibility for the public sector and control of the two area teams, one of them under Black. He has weekly meetings with the two area managers and monthly meetings with all officers at the estates manager and more senior levels. Both Brown and White on occasion attend tenants' association meetings.

Black, as area manager for the Old Borough has direct responsibility for two office based area teams comprising approximately 30 management and technical staff and approximately 40 estate based caretakers and wardens. His brief includes all aspects of management; rents, especially arrears; repairs; maintenance; tenant welfare; tenant participation; liaison with other divisions within the directorate and with other directorates. Black claims that his aim is to care for the property in his area in such a manner as to ensure that it improves over time, rather than, as so often with council housing, declines. Black has most contact with senior members of his team, Green, the Estates Manager for the Old Borough North, and the senior surveyor, and with more junior members if they have a particularly difficult case. He regularly attends meetings of the North Board and meets with tenants' associations and their committee members on request. As estates manager for the Old Borough North Green has direct control over the officer responsible for the Parkview estate. However, like Black he deals mainly with general cases not the specific concern of any estate management assistant or with difficult cases referred to him by junior officers. Green assumes responsibility for cases of rent arrears where court action is intended; he approves the serving of a notice to quit and supervises the preparation of notes for submission to the borough solicitor. If an action is taken to court he is required to appear. He may liaise with Social Services and Education Welfare officers on these and other problem cases. On occasion Green attends the North Board meetings with Black and he assists Black in dealing with tenants' association affairs on constituent estates. Internally he has contact with the senior surveyor and his staff over repairs and with the lettings officer in regard to transfers.

Green's assistant for the Parkview estate is Gray.[11] As management assistant he is responsible for day-to-day management matters and for dealing with tenants both in the office and on the estate. The duties involved include relatively straightforward matters like visiting and making welfare reports on applications for a transfer; administering claims for redecoration payments[12], car parking; answering general queries from tenants and manning the counter for the collection of rents at the housing office for one week in every three months;[13] and attending to what may be termed difficult or problem cases; the handling of arrears and dealing with complaints about individual tenants.

Gray responds to complaints about tenants by visiting the complainant and possibly talking with the estate caretakers in an attempt to establish the legitimacy of the complaint. He then reports to Green or if the matter is very serious, Black, and subsequently visits the tenant concerned. The usual procedure he adopts is to explain that the action complained of constitutes a breach of the tenancy agreement signed by all tenants. Gray claims that this warning is often sufficient to induce conformity. In cases where it is not further action will be threatened and this may include legal action. (In fact no cases for misdemeanours where there are not also rent arrears, have yet resulted in a successful court action). Alternatively it may be suggested to the tenants that they accept a voluntary transfer to a different type of property. Gray commented that this merely moved rather than solved the problem.

The procedure adopted for arrears cases is prescribed by the use of a series of standard forms. When an account is shown by the computerized accounting system to be two weeks in arrears a letter advising the tenant of the fact is automatically sent by the rents accounts section. Thereafter the case becomes the responsibility of the estates management assistant. Where the arrears persist a second more threatening letter is sent.

Unless the whole of this debt is discharged immediately and rent paid regularly each week, in accordance with the Council's Conditions of Tenancy, I shall have no alternative but to serve you with a Notice to Quit the premises you occupy.

At this stage the management assistant tries to make a personal visit to the household concerned. He may also send 2 of these letters and then if the warning is still ignored will send by recorded delivery a formal notice to quit over the signature of the director. This form gives not less than one month's notice to 'quit and deliver up ... the possession of all the above–named premises held by you ...'. According to Gray this letter is sent with due consideration to the circumstances noted on file and if, for instance, the tenant was a pensioner he would visit instead. After the expiry of the date specified in the notice to quit a further letter is sent to the tenant. This notes that the expiry date has been ignored and that the account is still seriously in arrears.

Proceedings for possession will be instituted through the Borough Solicitor unless a substantial payment is made on or before Friday,–and thereafter regular weekly payments made in accordance with the Council's Conditions of Tenancy plus an agreed sum off the balance of the debt out-standing.

The letter is signed by Black and the period allowed is normally two weeks. Gray commented that even those tenants who ignored the notice to quit, responded to this letter.

130

From the time of serving the notice the management assistant is required to keep a weekly rent arrears record. In cases where the letter advising of court proceedings does not produce a reduction in the arrears the assistant visits and makes out a report preparatory to handing the case, through his senior officer, to the borough solicitor. This report details information on the rent for the dwelling/garage/shed, water and general rates, electricity and/or gas payments at occupancy date and currently and the extent of arrears. It also includes information on the occupation of the tenant, name of employer, place of employment, household composition and household income. In court the directorate may seek to obtain a court order for the current rent plus an amount to reduce that outstanding or they may seek an order for immediate possession by eviction.[14] The procedure is lengthy and each case involves housing management and the borough solicitor's department in a considerable amount of work. This effectively limits the number of cases that can be handled at any one time. It should be noted that where the standard letters have no apparent impact the arrears increase over a period of many months and by the time prosecution is pending may be very high indeed. Gray was unable to estimate the number of arrears cases he was handling at the time of interview[15] but he considers their follow up his main problem and attending to them takes up the greater part of his time.

The caretaking officer for the Old Borough North has general supervisory control over all estate caretakers there. This involves compiling time sheets, calculating and authorising bonus payments and ordering stores as necessary. Daily inspections are carried out on estates in the area. There are, on the Parkview estate eight resident caretakers working on a four on and four off basis from 8.00 am to 9.00 pm. Their duties are to sweep and clear rubbish from roads, footpaths and lawns on the estate, and to check and clear bin rooms every day. There is also a daily check of the lift alarm system and daily cleaning of lift interiors. Once these duties have been completed the caretakers are engaged in a supervisory patrol capacity. On a weekly basis they are required to sweep car parks, pram sheds, basements, landings and staircases and in addition staircases are mopped once a month. Caretakers may also accept and hand on tenants' requests for repairs and they are expected to assist in emergencies. They may report tenants to the housing management section for an infringement of the tenancy agreement.

The senior surveyor for the Old Borough North, is the technical equivalent of Green, and as such is responsible for the day to day and programmed maintenance[16] of council property in that area. This includes handling repairs and improvements to acquired properties and general upkeep of all dwellings on a change of tenancy. In most jobs the DLBO act as contractors to the directorate but in some cases of lift maintenance and in a few specialist fields like rising damp or special roofing the surveyors may deal directly with private contractors.

The Parkview surveyor, has responsibility on the technical side of housing management for the same area as Gray.[17] His duties include the inspection of properties in need of repair or redecoration, the issue of orders for repairs and maintenance and the examination of works in progress and on completion of the jobs. He prepares specifications for works to vacant property and measures internal and external decoration works for bonus payments. He attempts to expedite urgent matters and deals with general enquiries. In site work the surveyors liaise with the foreman. The estates surveyor has no control over DLBO.

Under the normal procedure the Parkview surveyor receives a request for an order from the clerical assistant. He inspects the property and makes out a works order. This is passed back to the clerk for entry onto a card system and is then sent to the DLBO for execution. The DLBO foreman works out the bonus for the job and then issues an operative in the appropriate trade with a works order. The surveyors are notified on completion of a job and this is recorded on the card system. On the Parkview estate in response to agitation from residents and councillors the system was modified when a small DLBO team comprising a foreman, carpenter and plumber[18] was based on the site. The Parkview surveyor took job orders direct to the site foreman, the latter had bonus payments calculated at the depot, arranged for materials and then allocated tasks to workmen on the estate.

The Parkview area clerical assistant works directly to the Parkview surveyor. She handles all phone enquiries and requests for repairs. If the matter is one of some urgency ie a burst water pipe, an electrical fault, a serious roof leak, a gas leak, a blocked toilet or manhole, the clerk can, on the authorization of the senior surveyor, phone the works depot immediately and confirm the order with a written authorization. Other jobs requiring no complex specifications may be ordered directly by the clerical assistant. All others needing an inspection are referred to the Parkview surveyor. The clerical assistant administers the card recording system of job orders and completions and arranges the paper work for payment after inspection and approval by the estates surveyor and the senior surveyor.

A number of general statements can be made at this point. It is difficult to relate the day to day concerns of the area team officers to the broad objectives for the directorate as defined by Brown. On the other hand, in the absence of any statement on how to realize those goals[19] the team does undertake some of the management functions specified by Brown. Exceptions are the institution of a planned maintenance programme and the exercise of control over the priorities worked to by the DLBO, control over lettings and recommendations for transfers and exchanges. In addition there is no evidence of any mechanism to facilitate overall co-ordination and in particular there is no evidence of formal links between public and private sector area teams. There have been no staff training schemes within housing management and, indeed, there are no general staff meetings in this section.[20] Brown was critical of the over-specialization of functions within the old housing department but the effects of

132

circumscribing the responsibility of housing management and the nature of the work itself are to concentrate the energies of field staff on a relatively few tasks undertaken according to standard bureaucratically defined procedures. This is somewhat ironic in view of Brown's avowed dislike of bureaucratic constraints. Finally, the form of organization suggests a pattern of scheduled communication, typically comprising the issue of instructions, in a downward flow from superior officers to subordinates. These formal channels of communication may, of course, be modified by unscheduled communication between peers.

This then is the formal nature of the housing management section. Its actual working may be further modified by the background, training and attitudes which officers bring to their particular duties and which inevitably colours their response to the work.

Most of the officers in housing management have been trained for their jobs only through practical experience in the section. Brown has professional qualifications in housing management and Black has environmental health and administrative qualifications but they are exceptions on the housing management side. White has a record of a lifetime in local government. Green worked previously in the treasurers and repairs department and when the latter position was abolished on re-organization he applied, in January 1975, for a transfer to housing management. Similarly, Gray has a background in insurance and rent collecting and he transferred to management on re-organization in late 1974. Of the technical staff, the senior surveyor has experience as a clerk of works and the Parkview surveyor as a plumber and general foreman. Six of the 15 team officers interviewed, including four of the caretakers, have a background of experience with one of the armed services.

White claims that under the present set-up housing managers have nothing to manage; with a points system to determine allocations; statutory provisions for the homeless and no evictions,[21] management can be equated with administering a machine. Basically Black agreed. He commented that his own personal involvement in policy had declined markedly and with that there had been a loss of job satisfaction—whereas previously he sat on working parties as White's representative he now had no involvement in future planning, no say in lettings or exchanges[22] and felt himself left with rents and property maintenance. At the same time Black stressed that his policy-making rôle should be strictly delimited; the function of housing managers is to carry out policy once it has been formulated and he claimed to adhere to this dictum.

The general attitude towards management developed by the two estate managers, Black for the Old Borough and his counterpart for the Borough are at variance and represent two fairly typical stances in the housing management world. They are best exemplified by the orientation reflected in the papers each submitted to a committee which was considering proposed changes to the tenancy agreement. The existing agreement was fairly typical of many council tenancy agreements. Under this agreement the tenant undertook not to contravene 14 prohibitions and to meet 21 specific obligations. There were an additional 10 general conditions. Black commented that 'experience in the enforcement of the existing Conditions of Tenancy has brought to light the fact that they are probably read by few tenants and are for the most part almost impossible to enforce.' Moreover, in trying to cover all possible contingencies '... the more important Conditions such as those concerned with rent arrears, proper occupation and disorderly conduct, tend to become submerged in a host of more trifling prohibitions, and any attempt to highlight any particular items leads to a diminution of the others.' Black advocated the adoption of a very simple and short statement of basic conditions on that basis. The Borough manager argued the case for the retention of the existing conditions of tenancy. He denied that the agreement was paternalistic or authoritarian and claimed rather that it reflected the caring concern of the established authority for the welfare of tenants. The conditions afforded residents a sense of security. They were designed to uphold a minimum standard of behaviour and protect the council's valuable assets. The Borough manager allowed that while some minor amendments were desirable

There is a need in some instances for positive measures in order to restrain. If this is accepted then it follows that the local authority needs to adopt a very firm line with a minority element who are not being deprived or disadvantaged, but who are able to vandalise property, defy reasonable regulations and make life a living hell for their neighbours.[23]

Thus on the one hand there is the stance of the 'practical' man, prepared to adjust attitudes and responses according to changing conditions. This is an ad hoc approach to management and it is one which seems not to be imbued with any ideological imperatives. On the other hand there is the commitment and conviction which come from the moral stance adopted by the Borough manager.[24] Clearly the attitudes of the two team managers must affect the work of their subordinates. The differences between them are well known to all staff members and affects the degree of contact between the two teams. The Parkview team is firmly placed within the ad hoc model.

At the more junior level staff tend to be drawn either from rents as in the case of Gray or from the former housing welfare section. It is at this level, and particularly among ex-rent collectors, that there appears to be least job satisfaction. Visits for most transfer applications are felt to be futile because few will be arranged and in any event the management assistant has to hand the case over to another section, lettings, for further consideration and action. The arrears problem is felt to be of such enormous proportions as to be overwhelming and unbeatable. Junior staff especially attempt to simplify the problem by resort to a 'pay up or else' approach. Officers are expected to investigate the personal circumstances of the client but these then seem not to be related to any subsequent course of action. The incidence of 'difficult' families is small but management assistants find that the demands on their time may be considerable, the personal relationship so involved are often uneasy, and there is seldom a straightforward 'solution'. Perhaps not surprisingly, unless some immediate action is necessary, there is a tendency to ignore such cases. One ex-rent collector commented that he got most satisfaction out of his one afternoon a week spent doing outdoor rent collections from pensioners because he returned to the office afterwards with a sense of having achieved something positive; those visited have been known for many years and in some cases a visit involves other small services like shopping, the contact is welcomed by the tenant and the assistant feels he has something to show for the afternoon's work.[25] At the same time, while they deplored the lack of potential in their own jobs, ex-rent collector assistants saw no merit in the case work approach favoured by ex-welfare assistants; indeed the latter were disparagingly labelled 'soft soapers'.

The technical staff have a more limited brief and are able more easily to evaluate their own effectiveness. They are also able to attribute failures in the repairs/maintenance programme to their contractor, the DLBO.

Overall, the housing management section may be characterized as bureaucratically organized with an emphasis on work according to set rules and regulations. It does not, however, appear to be an efficient bureaucracy since there are few inbuilt controls and no regular mechanism for monitoring action. Thus particular assistants may not always act according to the prescribed procedures for dealing with arrears cases and this may go unnoticed.[26] Hence, the outward dependency on standard forms conceals a reality that is often disorganized and confused. At the same time the existence of an ideal of form filling procedures inhibits the expression of individual initiative. Officers are not encouraged to accept responsibility for working outside the established framework, and most lack the personal skills necessary for this. As already noted the section has very few staff members with any special training orientated towards the development of expertise in housing management.[27] Some officers, like the Borough manager appear to interpret the rules according to a personal ideology, more adopt what seems to be Black's pragmatic approach. A few like Green express a genuine concern to come to terms with the problems encountered in the work and admit to being at a loss for an 'answer'.[28] For all there is an uncertainty and insecurity that is ill-concealed by the apparent certainty and inflexibility of the organization itself and the dogma to which it clings. This ambiguity is a compound of the attenuation of functions and the lack of professionalism directed towards them. (The two factors are not of course unrelated). The status of the section is low, both within the housing directorate and in relation to other directorates. It has been an easy target for attack. A report released during the period of my own study criticized 'The authoritarian paternalism practised in the Directorate of Housing towards tenants' and claimed there was a 'resulting dependency and impotence of the tenants.'[29] Perhaps not surprisingly the section has become defensive and tends to over-react to such comment.

The work of housing management is thus defined by the political weighting within the directorate and the council structure as a whole; approaches to work are then modified by the norms, framework and communication patterns of the section and by the attitudes of the various officers towards the tasks which they perform. It remains to describe how some of these tasks are in fact carried out when the officer is faced with a client.

Towards the end of the field work period, in the course of a morning from 10 am to 12.40 pm I accompanied Gray on visits to eight tenants on the Parkview estate.[30] Three residents were not at home and visiting slips were left. These ask the tenant to advise the officer 'of a day and time during normal business hours, when it will be convenient for a visit to be made giving, if possible, at least three days notice.'[31] In the five cases where contact was made the visits lasted between 10 and 15 minutes. All excepting one of the contact cases concerned routine matters. The exception was a tenant with a long history of causing annoyance to neighbours. In that case Gray requested that I did not accompany him because he did not wish to embarrass me. Visits for the purposes of arrears were excluded from the round for the same reason.

The visits made comprised one case of a request for permission to house an additional occupant and four requests for transfers. One of the transfer applications followed a query from a ward councillor and concerned a woman confined to a wheelchair and resident in a tower block. A second transfer applicant claimed to have supplied medical evidence in support of a transfer a year ago but the absence of any records on file meant that another certificate had to be obtained. The third applicant also requested a transfer on medical grounds and was likewise asked for a doctor's certificate. The final request for a transfer came from a young woman who simply disliked the flat and estate and wanted a house with a garden. She was told that she had little chance of a transfer and was advised to try for an exchange. In fact this applicant has virtually no chance of a transfer and there is little likelihood of two of the other three requests being met. In these cases the families are resident on the 10th and 16th floors of a tower block and the wives, neither of whom work on account of having young families, claim to suffer from depression brought on by the situation of the flat. According to the lettings officer handling applications this type of claim is accorded very low priority.[32]

During these visits Gray was clearly anxious to please but possibly owing to the constraints imposed on individual initiative by the set procedures he was also very cautious. It was difficult for him to effectively follow up the visits or to give any firm indication of the likely outcome. The interview situation was characterized by a confusion of rôles.[33] The invidious position in which the assistant is placed is not helped by the lack of opportunity to develop communication skills. In all cases Gray simply introduced himself as a representative from the borough and those visited were not told his name nor that of his section.[34] One tenant introduced him to another member of her household as 'the man from the welfare' and it is easy to see how such misconceptions arise and are perpetuated. The forms which were the basis of the interviews had been partially completed from information on file and only supplementary information was required. The rationale of the procedure and the likely outcome was not clearly explained and given the circumstances of the residents it seems likely that all were left with the impression that their case was being attended to and that some action was being taken on their behalf. In fact apart from the application for an additional resident and the transfer of the tenant in a wheelchair, Gray's visit probably augurs no change in the tenants' circumstances.

Gray returned to the office and in the afternoon attended to the filing and referral of the forms to the appropriate officers for action or noting. At that time he had 17 more applications for transfer pending visits and approximately 12 such applications are received each week. During the previous week Gray had sent out 85 letters concerning arrears for the period 29 May to 28 July. The letters were to tenants at all stages of the procedure adopted in handling such cases. The remainder of the afternoon was spent in attending to phone calls and visits to the office from tenants in receipt of these letters.

Clearly no claims can be made for general statements based on these limited observations. However, Gray is not untypical of estate management assistants in the section office and the procedures he adopts are those formally approved and used throughout housing management. Gray has not been offered housing management training to add to his experience in rent collecting. His contact with tenants is limited by the official hours of work and the directorate's rigid adherence to form-filling. Interviews were very brief and no consideration was given to other possible ways of coping with the problem. Thus the explanation of the two women suffering from depression was accepted without question although to my knowledge there were in both cases complicating factors, in one incipient marital breakdown and in the other a combination of financial and marital difficulties. In the handling of arrears, the lack of personal and professional resources is, especially given the sheer volume of the work, even more serious. Any welfare orientation is scorned by officers like Gray and the simplest expedient is to resort to the sending of standard forms for presumed standard cases. This means that by the time individual cases begin to be handled on an individual and more personalized basis the problem is of such proportions as to constitute an enormous psychological and financial burden for the tenant and an unmanageable problem for the manager.

In order to assess the extent to which officers themselves envisaged or desired a way out of this apparent impasse, team members interviewed were asked if they would like to see any change in their own job description or in the work of the directorate generally. White and Black advocated expanding the functions of management to reincorporate lettings and housing aid and to include direct control over labour for the carrying out of repairs. Black also pressed for more consultation with officers at the area management level on development and planning issues. For day to day management Black considers that the ideal would be a team of say 10 management assistants each responsible for a small area. In addition each team should have a specialist for arrears; once it was known that X was the rent arrears officer tenants would not like the neighbours to see X knocking on their door. Black also wanted more and better administrative support services and a superintending caretaking officer. However, he commented that it would be difficult to effect much improvement in the overall management service on account of the very mixed abilities of the staff presently available to him. Green claimed that the council took on too much and that some matters, like disagreements between neighbours, should be left for tenants to sort out among themselves. His assistant Gray advocated an increase in staff to allow for closer involvement with a smaller area. The technical staff supported greater control by housing over a direct labour force and the Parkview surveyor suggested the establishment of area offices to facilitate contact between officers and tenants. Four of the caretakers came up with a number of practical suggestions; the reintroduction of small repairs as part of their duties; improved communication between caretaking and office staff; more effective backing from council when caretakers report tenants for misdemeanours; the incorporation of playground supervision in caretaking duties; the employment of a night caretaker; a more equitable division of the work areas on the estate; and the encouragement of a caretaker rôle in tenants' association affairs. The changes suggested relate to scope of work, forms of organization and administration or level of staffing, few are very radical; there was little reference to altered methods of working, none to training schemes or communication networks within the directorate and beyond.

Officers and Parkview residents

Black claimed to adopt an objective stance in his dealings with the residents of Parkview estate. 'We might go along to meetings and work with groups but let's face it we have a professional detachment which means all that is left behind when we go home at night and that's what they can't understand.' In fact in this context professional detachment probably means more a sense of non involvement and an assumed knowledge of policies supposed to accord with the best interests of the residents.

Undoubtedly the attitudes of staff towards the estate and its residents colours their perceptions and may affect their response to working there. In the course of interviews members of the management team were asked to describe the reputation attaching to the Parkview estate in relation to other estates in the borough. Of the eight office based staff members, six considered the estate 'about average', 'middling', 'half way down the league table' and two accorded the estate a slightly higher ranking than 'average'. These ratings were apparently based on the popularity of the estate as evidenced by requests for transfers, and rates of refusal of offers and on the incidence of 'problem families' and arrears cases. It is of interest to note that the caretakers, the officers with the closest day to day contact with Parkview, took a rather more favourable view of it. They said that it was 'very good', especially taking into account its size and one went so far as to claim 'It's like a palace compared to most estates'. The caretakers' evaluation was based on the ease of control and a relative lack of 'trouble'.

Housing management and other sections

There has already been some indication of the kind of contact housing management has with other sections and other directorates—and this will be outlined in more detail at this point. From time to time and at various levels management officers may have contact with all other sections within the housing directorate; with the borough solicitor's office; the engineers department; the directorate of social services; the Greater London Council; contracting and insurance firms; gas and electricity boards and sundry other organizations. At the most senior levels of director and assistant director these contacts may be of a formal nature through the directors board and other corporate committees. Brown considers that for the most part these are a waste of time; they tend to have the negative effect of reducing the directive element and delay decision making when what is needed in housing is quick action.

At the more junior levels contact with other sections and directorates is on an ad hoc basis in regard to particular cases and problems. Most are characterized by tensions which reflect differences in perceptions of an ostensibly shared interest. Within the directorate relations between management, lettings and housing aid are admitted to be often strained. An instance of how this situation can arise was cited by the housing aid manager. In one month housing aid heard by chance that housing management had 25 cases of arrears pending possession orders. Housing aid staff took immediate action to get the proceedings stopped; a response resented by management because arrears cases were not felt to be matters concerning housing aid anyway. They justified their reaction on the grounds that continuing with the legal processes would incur incalculable social costs and prohibitive economic costs simply in terms of the bed and breakfast accommodation which might be required. One of the families affected was a family of 10 with a current weekly rent of £10. They were visited by representatives from both housing aid and housing management and it was found that no rent rebate had been applied for. The housing aid officer filled in the appropriate form and asked his housing management colleague to explain the workings of the scheme. This he was unable to do. Such incidents are not calculated to foster good working relationships.

Relations between housing and other directorates most commonly involve the DLBO, the architects' department and social services. The link with the DLBO is particularly fraught. Repairs are often a sensitive issue; delays mean housing officials have to cope with irate tenants and on occasions councillors. Responsibility for the proper maintenance of the dwellings is DLBO's, control of the workforce lies with the borough engineer. DLBO operatives work to a bonus system[35] and this is open to abuse. Thus, cases brought to the attention of housing management staff have included isolated instances where jobs recorded as completed appear not to have been attended to. In such cases management staff take the brunt of resident criticism and yet are themselves in a position to do no more than complete another job order form. A rather different explanation was given in a Borough report which noted that

The Housing Directorate does not know the basis on which the DLBO establishes its programme of work and there are no regular meetings between the two directorates to agree one. Consequently the Housing Directorate does not know when maintenance and repair work will be attended to. Neither do they have an effective information retrieval system to check delays on specific orders. This results in their being unable to inform residents of progress or advise the DLBO that a tenant has had an unreasonable delay.[36]

The counter argument was put forward by the controller of the DLBO. He claimed that his organization which employs 250 operatives and 57 administrative and support staff completed a total of 33,000 jobs in the previous year. 90% of all jobs are completed within 21 working days of receipt of the order. The controller admits that it is possible that some jobs are signed for when they have not been done but a random check of at least 10% of all jobs is undertaken to check the abuse and a man caught is immediately dismissed. Otherwise all jobs are carried out if the orders are placed and if the work is not done it is because the orders have not been handed on by the housing surveyors. The competence of the housing surveyors was questioned and some of the aspersion cast on the DLBO by dissatisfied clients was blamed on the alleged inept management of that section. Examples cited by the controller were cases where it was alleged that tenants had received promises that a workman would call to carry out a job at a particular time. Quite apart from this not being a function of housing staff, the officers concerned then neglected to inform the DLBO that such promises had been made anyway. The outcome was a predictably irate tenant. The controller noted that it was intended to set up area teams on the Parkview model and it was hoped that this would further improve the service to tenants.[37] It is impossible to comment on the merits of these claims. The problem is a common one and has been noted elsewhere.[38] What is significant in the present context is the division of responsibility and the lack of formal links or informal co-operation between those jointly involved in providing a particular service to tenants.

Some of the more senior officers on occasion have dealings with architects. The housing management reaction is typified by Black's categorization of architects as drawing board specialists with no knowledge of how the council system works; people full of 'fancy' ideas for pretty plans but with little practical 'know how' and less political expertise. A more ambivalent attitude has developed in regard to social services. On the whole the relationship has not been very good. The leader of the social services area team commented on and objected to the fact that Black, her colleague in seniority, invariably refers her to one of his more junior officers. For some officers like Green this increased contact has modified his views. From regarding social services officers as 'a load of old busy bodies' he has now come to regard them as having a useful function.

Some few officers, generally ex-housing welfare officers, develop informal contacts with the area social services team. Others tend to wait until they have a serious arrears case or a problem family for referral to social service for assistance. The latter tend to resent being called in so late and are not anyway prepared simply to pick up arrears cases. Here too there are no formal or regular links and it is very much up to individual officers to initiate and sustain contacts.[39]

It seems likely that these difficulties in communication are largely attributable to the differences of ideology within the various departments. It was noted above that the housing management section is lacking in professionally qualified staff. Many of the counterparts of management officers in other sections and directorates are so qualified. There are tensions inherent in the inter-relationships between bureaucrats and professionals even when the latter are themselves working within a bureaucratic structure. Rather than base his decision on rules and directives the professional attempts to consider each case on its merits and acts according to his evaluation of the problem.[40] Both social workers and architects adopt this strategy, accept the responsibility entailed and generally take unkindly to 'unprofessional' incursions into their respective domains. The DLBO has in its employ 'expert' tradesmen and through the political power of the borough engineer is able to maintain its closed administrative system. Housing management has little option but to officially take recourse in formal procedures and regulations and respond to the crises of the moment on an ad hoc basis.[41]

Councillors

The other part of 'the council' comprises the elected member committee structure. In recent years, with the exception of one term, council committees have been characterised by large Labour Party majorities. In the 1965 elections Labour won a comfortable majority of 52 seats. The situation was reversed in 1968 when Labour held only six seats against a Conservative majority of 54. Labour recovered at the following elections in 1971 when the Conservatives were reduced to a minority of two. At the 1974 elections Labour held 48 seats, the Conservatives 10 and the Liberal Party two seats. This was the composition of the council for the duration of the study.

The account which follows focuses on a number of subjects; the organisation and terms of reference of the various housing committees; the role relationship developed between councillors and officers; the processes of decision making and the constituency role of the elected member.

The elected member structure

In the present context the relevant committees are those served by the Directorate of Housing; the Housing Services Committee, the Housing Utilisation Review Committee and the Housing Provision Review Committee. The Housing Services Committee has as its terms of reference

1. To consider all the housing requirements and needs of the Borough and to prepare strategic proposals for meeting in the long term those requirements and needs and the manner of implementing them (for this purpose letting policies with reference to points scheme shall be included in this item.)
2. To consider and prepare proposals for General Improvement Areas (after consultation with the Development Services Committee), and area housing renewal or replacement.[42]

Under its delegated powers the committee has the authority

1. To carry out surveys and research from time to time in connection with the Committee's delegated powers.
2. To act as housing authority within the terms of the Housing Acts and to consider the future of clearance areas and to make proposals relating to the carrying out of programmed improvements; to make improvement grants and give assistance to Housing Associations and to determine the policy relating to categories of applicants for loans for the acquisition of property, to implement General Improvement Areas, and schemes for area housing renewal or replacement, and to consult with Social Services Committee on the provision made for homeless families.
3. To enforce the provisions of the Housing Acts relating to unfitness, houses in multiple occupation; the abatement of overcrowding.

4. To manage the Council's Housing Stock and to implement letting allocation, to consider amenities on housing estates and to consider reports from Area Housing Boards.

5. To prepare and consider all schemes for new local authority housing.

As part of the re–organization process review committees were established to work to main committees. Housing has two each with particular powers delegated to it. The subjects covered by the Housing Provision Review Committee are council house building; acquisition of properties; house purchase advances; programmed improvements; council house modernisation and rehabilitation; improvement and special grants; temporary accommodation; sheltered accommodation; co-ordination with housing associations and hostels for single homeless people. The Housing Utilisation Review Committee encompasses lettings; rent rebates; rent control; management; maintenance; rent allowances; housing inspections and tenancy relations. Both review committees are charged with considering proposals and making recommendations to increase the effectiveness of the council's provision of these services. The delegated powers of Housing Utilisation are threefold.

1. To examine whether all the relevant services (as shown within the Corporate Plan) are effectively provided, and to authorise analysis of activities.

2. To bring to the attention of the Chief Executive matters concerning the efficient utilisation of resources.

3. To consider and resolve where necessary any complaints or representations from members of the public on the activities in the Corporate Plan covered by this Review Sub–Committee.

Thus, broadly the two review committees cover property and management issues respectively. The rationale for their establishment was that work should be referred to them from the main committee for in depth assessment and report back to it. For this purpose the review committees meet on a six weekly cycle that is slightly in advance of the Housing Services cycle. In this way it was hoped that the review committee would at once take some of the more detailed work from the Housing Services Committee and contribute to it in a way that enabled policy decision making on a more carefully considered basis. An additional, and in the view of Brown, a major reason for setting up the review committees was an attempt to involve back benchers in council work in a more meaningful way.

The standing orders for those committees provide for the delegation of certain powers and functions to the officers. These powers relate to the fulfilment of various statutory requirements and to the implementation of established policies. In addition, general standing orders allow for the chairman, or in his absence, the vice chairman, to take action in the name of a committee in relation to its delegated powers as follows:–

i. where such action can conveniently be taken and is required to enable executive action on matters of a routine character to be implemented between the ordinary meetings of the Committee, . . . or

ii. where the committee . . . have expressly authorised a decision to be made either particularly or generally in relation to a Part II power [ie powers exercised for and on behalf of and in the name of the Council but subject to the Scheme of Delegation].

There are constraints on the exercise of these powers such that the vice chairman should be advised, the Director of Operations should be informed and should report to the next ordinary meeting of the appropriate committee, and an officer should not act on instructions issued in this manner except in emergency or extreme urgency unless written authority has first been received. A total of 20 councillors serve on the three housing committees. All members of the Housing Services Committee also serve on one of the review committees. However for 8 review committee members, housing utilisation or provision are minor committees unrelated to their major committee interest. The party breakdown of membership is one Liberal, three Conservative and 16 Labour.

Councillors and officers

In the course of fieldwork 24 councillors were formally interviewed[43] and although most currently served on at least one housing committee it should be kept in mind that their experience of the officer group does not necessarily relate most directly to the housing directorate. Questions asked of councillors included the type of level of contact with officers and their understanding of the councillor/officer role relationship. For all councillors their contacts with officers fall into two main categories, those made as representative of a ward or ward resident and those made as committee member. Some councillors devote more of their time and energy to fulfilling the first role, others to the second. Few made the distinction in describing their contacts with the officer group. Both types of approach may involve letters, phone calls or personal visits to council offices.

All councillors claim that they feel able to approach officers at any level in the hierarchy. Three commented that in practice they always made approaches at director level because of feeling that they themselves do not know which officer is the most appropriate contact. On the other hand, two councillors claimed that it was in fact almost impossible to get to see a director; they are away on conferences, or working "flexitime" or have secretaries who effectively screen them from councillors. Ten councillors claim to have most contact with specific officers who have become known to them personally. Those named were at the level of section head, such as the lettings officer or the area manager for the Old Borough. One councillor made a distinction between his role as a chairman and that of a backbencher; in the former capacity he first approaches his director and then goes to any officer who might have the answer; in the latter he normally deals with the middle range of officers cited. Another councillor attempted to identify particular officers appropriate to specific issues but like those who make a practice of dealing with directors admitted some difficulty in understanding the structure and hence the allocation of tasks within it. According to this councillor this problem is one which has increased since the introduction of corporate planning. The significance of such knowledge for this aspect of councillor work is suggested by the member who, claiming to know the way round the bureaucratic system, takes great pride in being able to go directly to the officer concerned and insist on action. This approach is deemed to be effective at the cost of other cases taken up by councillors less familiar with the system because officers allegedly take the view that certain councillors 'make a noise' and therefore have to be attended to; otherwise members intervention is said to be resented and ignored wherever possible.

More formal and ongoing councillor/officer relationships are those concerned with committee work and policy matters. All councillors agreed that ideally their own role was that of policy maker with officers acting as advisers and policy implementers.

... members make policy decisions on the basis of all relevant information from officers and the latter then implement them ...
... officers should give back up advice on policy with alternative strategies objectively assessed and implement policy once decided ...

Minor variations on this ideal model are supported by two respondents.

... members throw up problems and officers find a way of overcoming them, or members might say 'This is where we are at, this is what we want to achieve, how do we get there? Once a policy is going, officers may throw up further problems–policy making is a two-way process ... officers are professionals and its up to councillors to take their advice and query where necessary ...

The ideal relationship is thus one of clearly defined and separate responsibilities with possibly some allowance for shared functions. Ten councillors consider that in practice the ideal is realized: others, typically younger Labour backbenchers are more critical. They express the view that officers take on a policy making function by pushing very hard for their own preferred option, omitting facts from reports or acting as effective policy makers without reference to committee. One councillor commented how he had often congratulated officers on an unfailing ability to come up with precisely three alternative courses of action for every issue. 'One alternative is persuasively argued to convince one and all that everything is beautiful, the second is clearly second best and the third is an absolute outsider which nobody is expected to take seriously.' This presumption of an officer imput in policy making is resented and was described as a trend to be resisted by those councillors who commented on it. 'Officers form a middle class bureaucracy and as such run the country'. 'Officers become directors and as good as ministerial advisers–taking the view that all councillors are idiots so let's humour them. They see themselves as experts and councillors who don't listen are fools.' Some councillors related the alleged abuse of power by the officers to the increasing complexity and volume of work placed before all committees. Moreover, while the various chairmen of committees are generally well briefed, backbenchers are less so and some feel a lack of expert knowledge on which to counter arguments of the officers and base decisions. Councillor Mackie as chairman of housing did not feel this was a drawback. In his view it is the function of the chairman to probe; 'other councillors may be thick and they may ask daft but embarrassing questions. These two factors mean that officers can't really get away with partial reports.'

This was not a view shared by other councillors. One commented that agendas are ' . . . so hefty that a lot of effort is required to come to grips with most of the material. Directors and chairmen work out basic agreements anyway. So in committee we are likely to spend half an hour deciding whether gates should be fitted to some estate and two minutes formalizing the spending of £1½ million because members can grapple with the little things and can't cope with the bigger issues.'[44] This councillor added that there was not enough time to go into reports and agendas and order priorities in a meaningful way. An opposition backbencher, aware of the importance of the informal processes of decison making, commented how the problem of coping with complex issues was heightened by an access to background information limited only to the formal reports presented at committee meetings.

Other councillors spoke of the informal decison making process specifically with reference to the close working and social relationships developed between some directors and chairmen of committees. That in housing between Brown and Councillor Mackie was deemed to be particularly close and was viewed equivocally by some housing committee members. The co-operation implied in a genuine partnership was lauded, the tendency to express that through the use of delegated powers under chairman's action, deplored. In fact the balance is difficult to strike.

Leaders need authority . . . since without authority leaders cannot carry out their functions. But the delegation of authority in a democratic group is never a mandate for any leader to employ authority without the eventual approval of the group. Where responsibility for action is not subject to critical examination, a democratic organisation no longer exists. Nevertheless some freedom of action is almost always imperative lest leadership become a sterile and unimaginative position making for red tape and unending delays[45].

As perceived by councillors, then, there is an ideal rôle relationship between members and officers in the council. This ideal may or may not be realized in practice according to the extent to which personalities, political pressures, volume of work and the influence of the officers intrude. Before assessing these factors, and in order to understand more of the member view of the officers' part in compromising the ideal, it is necessary first to examine the latter's experience of councillors.

At the level of director Brown accepts the popular notion and claims to have deliberately fostered with his leading councillors the closest relationship that has ever been built up within the Borough, 'and possibly within the country.' These relationships comprise largely informal links and are expressed most strongly outside the formal structure. The intention has been to develop in both officer and member groups a politically committed leadership based on shared goals. This leadership function does not, however, extend to lower levels in the officer hierarchy. Brown regards his own and the assistant director level as the 'thinking levels' and in housing management he considers this function is fulfilled only by himself. 'Policy is not a matter for the officers generally – they are not the thinkers.' His subordinates appear to accept this dictum.

White has had contact with councillors in the Borough over a much longer period and has defined his relationships rather more in terms of formal committee functions and responses to problem cases. In policy matters he claims almost always to have got his own way. Most of the problem cases concern outstanding repairs and maintenance, transfer or general welfare problems and for the most part these are now referred to Black. He in turn may seek background information or action from his subordinates and particularly in the Old Borough team, Green and the senior surveyor. Other initiatives may come from councillors as a result of their work with TA's. Black claims that invariably he undertakes to look into a case and added that in fact things do get 'pushed' when taken up by a councillor – 'but then its like that everywhere.' He pointed to the difference in approach between Labour and opposition members; the former always promise to personally attend to a matter while the latter, with one exception, refrain from making promises and refer the matter to the appropriate officer for action. A few team members commented that many councillor approaches were unnecessary since all that was required was a simple explanation to the tenant concerned. There were, however, no overt expressions of resentment against councillors; incursions might be bothersome but they were for the most part manageable.

As might be expected there is some agreement and some divergence of views about officer and member rôles according to the standpoint of the two groups. There is more agreement in regard to the handling of individual cases. In these matters councillors on the whole make contact with middle range officers and these claim to be at once accessible and responsive to them. Few junior officers have had any direct dealings with councillors and this would appear to run counter to the claims of those councillors who consider they have contacts at 'all levels' of the hierarchy. And while it may well be the case, there is, contrary to councillor beliefs, no clear evidence that officers ignore or resent their initiatives. There is a more marked difference in perception in policy matters where councillors assume a general officer input while Brown categorically limits the advisory function to himself and a few subordinates. Junior officers themselves deny any role in policy making.

The processes of decison making

Something of the way in which policy decisions are taken has been discussed already in considering the content of the role relationship between the two groups. The actual process of decision-making can be described here. It is difficult to comment in any detail, having regard to the emphasis of the study, on this function, whether formal or informal in both the housing committees and the directorate. No attempt was made to uncover those 'private political manoeuvres which lie behind every public decison.'[46] Nevertheless a few statements can be made about the manner of policy making and the locus of responsibility for it. Councillor Mackie acknowledges that the executive powers delegated to him while considerable are not clearly defined and freely admits that he and Brown have been able to make extensive use of the mechanism. Certainly, these two men appear to have established a close working relationship based on mutual understanding and respect and perhaps most importantly, political bargaining, the extent of which is not evident simply from the number of agenda items marked 'chairman's action.' It is a system of concessions for gains and of compromise made possible by the considerable power held by each and the need to maintain some kind of balance. There are often no written records of the 'deal.' A minor instance of this process is the setting up of the Parkview project itself. This was ostensibly agreed to by the chairman and director and announced as a fait accompli at the next housing committee meeting. In fact the proposal had most support from Brown and in order to secure Councillor Mackie's approval he conceded some small gain to the latter in another field. Later when a short extension to the study period was required it was arranged, on Brown's insistence, informally and with nothing in writing. However, perhaps because bargains have often been struck on an informal basis in an 'unofficial' way there have been notable occasions when Brown and Councillor Mackie appear to have acted in complete opposition to each other. Thus Councillor Mackie as Chairman of Housing commissioned the architect's department to carry out a survey on a housing estate in terms of such a brief as clearly impinged on housing management and without incorporating housing in the overseeing of the survey work or initially, the evaluation of the findings. In the event the report was controversial and somewhat colourful versions were given extensive coverage in the local press. The chief executive wrote an official reply from the council. Councillor Mackie also wrote a reply of his own apparently without reference to any officer. Such an action might be held potentially to jeopardize the legitimacy of the official stance should the two responses conflict. A tendency to rely on informal mechanisms may moreover, on occasion contribute to communication breakdowns. Towards the end of the fieldwork period consideration was being given to a community work type replacement for the Parkview project. Discussions were held with officers and tenants and the ward councillors were informed.[47] Councillor Mackie learnt of the development by chance and his immediate reaction was to threaten to stop the scheme. These are minor incidents (there were many rumours and stories of much more significant episodes) but they serve to illustrate something of the tensions inherent in a rôle relationship which goes beyond the bounds imposed by the formal rôle definition. In such a situation there may be considerable gains when the main parties are in agreement but disagreement becomes difficult to resolve or contain.

Councillor Mackie claims that prior to Brown's appointment there was no policy; the value of the new director is that he brings ideas to an ideologically bankrupt directorate. Certainly it is true of the council, as of most large organizations, that policy may come to be equated with past precedents modified mainly according to outside decrees, in this instance, to statutorily defined obligations. Under such a system it is the handling of difficult precedent creating case which gradually defines the range of policy options open to the officers. At this level it is often quite low ranking officers who effectively wield considerable power. Policy in Councillor Mackie's sense is the introduction of innovation while in fact the inbuilt conservatism of an organization like the directorate is scarcely conducive to the acceptance of radical change.

Even from so limited an account it seems that the simple categorization of officers as policy advisors and executors and councillors as policy makers and constituency representatives is no more than a convenient and politically acceptable labelling device for what is rather more complex reality. This is supported by more detailed research elsewhere. Hampton accounts in part for the dilemma facing councillors by describing their dual function in terms of the different roles appropriate for each and suggesting that many members fail to make the distinction.

... In their role as executive members of committees, the councillors should be concerned with debating the broad choices open to the corporation; they should also examine critically the criteria upon which the officers recommend one course of action rather than another, there is no need for them to choose the colour of the curtains at a children's home, and it is often positively harmful for them to interfere with the professional decisions of social workers. In their role as representatives of their *individual* constituents, however, the councillors must be able to question authority, and to obtain information from the relevant department. When those two roles are confused there is a danger that neither is fulfilled: a mass of detail on an agenda may cloud the policy decisions that need to be taken, without providing the greater openness in local administration that is needed in the interests of democratic control.[48]

Malpass is particularly concerned with understanding the member rôle in the policy function and claims that the expert advice necessarily sought is often not easily challenged. He describes a meeting of a housing committee in Newcastle where

... there were very little discussion by the councillors of the reports presented by the various officers. The purpose of the meeting appeared to be to provide the officers with an opportunity of informing the members of what they were going to do: the councillors function was to formally approve the 'advice' of the officers which was not advice but statements of intent .. . .[49]

The appraisal of expert advice in itself requires some expert knowledge. Heclo claims this is 'a stern and perhaps unrealistic challenge to the unpaid part time amateur.'[50]

In the Borough housing directorate this kind of problem has been recognized and in part at least, the setting up of the review committees was designed to increase member awareness of policy issues. To date the agendas of the Housing Utilisation Review Committee have concerned such matters as conditions of tenancy, the operation of the repairs service, caretaking and tenant participation. It is probably too soon to assess their success as learning situations for both members and officers. One meeting attended in the course of the research did not, however, seem very promising in this regard. This meeting was called to consider two reports on tenant participation, all compiled by outside researchers, of whom I was one. It was apparent that few of those present had read the papers before the committee, most of the discussion centred on an issue, tenant control, quite outside the scope of any of the research findings, there was no questioning of the researchers present, and the level of debate was singularly uninformed.

Some councillors in the Borough touched on aspects of the dilemmas which they face in their replies to a question asking if they felt the need for any changes in the committee part of their work. A few stressed the need for greater co-operation and co-ordination between committees and between officers and members. One criticised the power of the chief executive as adviser to the leader of the council and as convenor of the directors' board on the grounds that both mechanisms had the effect of minimizing member awareness of officer conflict and the lack of consensus in professional judgements. Another stressed the need for more and better information and secretarial services to councillors.

There were mixed feelings about the review committee structure. Four councillors claimed that the review committees ensured that members were better informed about policy issues but five were critical of their operation or opposed to their existence. It was alleged that they functioned only as talking shops or as 'mini committees' to main committees rather than as review committees. Another councillor considered that the main committee should be concerned with future policy; the review committees with the critical monitoring of established practice.

For the rest three councillors consider that the present system is working well and that no changes are required. Others were critical of the length of committee agendas or of the emphasis on procedural matters. One member suggested that agendas should be ordered in terms of the importance of items, another that agendas be distributed in sections throughout the period prior to a meeting. Six councillors expressed the opinion that the scope of the work undertaken by main and review committees was so wide as to be unmanageable. (On the other hand, a member of housing provision claimed that once set up it was a matter of searching very hard in order to fill an agenda to keep that particular committee in existence.) Many councillors claimed that if constituency work and other interests[51] were added to their committee work load they simply had insufficient time to devote careful attention to major issues. Thus, where they acknowledge a problem in adequately coping with council duties, councillors for the most part stress the volume of work involved and imply that if the scope or amount of the work placed before them was more restricted they would have the time and resources to effectively deliberate upon it. In fact, as already noted, it is probably more the nature and complexity of the work which diminishes the decision making functions of member groups and increases the power of senior officers and chairmen.

Councillors and constituents

The constituency aspect of the councillor role may be described briefly with reference to the Parkview ward. There are three ward councillors, all members of the majority party. None live in the ward though two live very close to its boundaries and short distances from the estate. One, Councillor Williams, is deputy leader of the council, the other two, Councillor Mrs Ewing and Councillor Mitchell, serve on Social Services and Housing respectively. Councillor Mrs Ewing and Councillor Williams are both employed in local government, the latter as a corporate planner, Councillor Mitchell is a sales representative. All three are young, under 35, and all have served on the council since the elections of 1971.

In their work on Parkview all three members adopt a policy of contact with constituents on the estate either through TA or North Board representatives or in response to calls for assistance from residents. Some of the latter will also be referred on by TA or North Board representatives. Apart from electioneering they make no attemps to initiate contacts.[52] This limits the number of contacts the councillors have and affords them a view of constituency needs that is expressed in terms of individual crises. As already noted most Parkview residents have little knowledge of their ward representatives and few have any experience of direct contact. Hampton has documented the extent to which the response to crises approach gives the councillor a distorted view of the priorities accorded to various issues by members of the public.[53] Young outlines the difficulties faced by the councillor concerned to remedy this partial view.

The member is not given any *structural* support for his representative role in understanding and articulating the *total* needs of the geographical area which has elected him. Appointed only to committees which have a borough or city wide focus, he is unable to monitor the cumulative effects of council policies and their delivery on the area he represents. His whole representative role is treated as illegitimate. However good a grassroots worker he may be he is reduced to the status of a medicine man who spends his time sorting out *individual* problems, *and,* by incantations and blustering, gives the impression that he is pursuing collective ends.[54]

Thus added to the complexities of the policy making function, the councillor has to grapple with a representative constituency function which is confounded by the discontinuities between local government structure and ideology.[55] The demands on the time and resources of the part time member are formidable, and it is difficult to see how under the present circumstances, the Parkview councillors could more meaningfully define their rôle as Parkview's elected representatives to the Borough council.

Summary

Conservatism and change

Generally, this overview of 'the council' inclines to a negative position. Within the management section the concepts of housing management range from the 'caring' and 'moralistic' to the expedient and opportune. This split in itself reflects the state of flux in which the subject of housing management finds itself. A stance of moral arbiter upheld by the potential enforcement of powerful and socially approved sanctions is no longer widely acceptable. At the same time there is little to replace this once coherent ideology beyond resort to a practice founded on opportunism. In the Borough office apart from the continued development of the area board system of tenant participation, there was, after 18 months, little evidence that Brown's stated policy objectives had fired a 'new and dynamic' approach to housing management in the field. Indeed, many of the criticisms directed by Brown at the White administration could with some justification be applied to his own. The reasons for the failure, in spite of sincere intentions, to attain the desired goals, are many and complex.

As already noted, a number of constraints effectively limited the scope and content of reforms undertaken within the directorate. Some, like the cuts in spending were externally imposed. Others, like the political situation facing Brown were a predictable consequence of introducing a new style of management input into an established organization with its own set of entrenched interests. These constraints were probably heightened by Brown's own coping strategy. Thus in removing future planning and lettings advice from the competence of housing management he denied the section an interest in what might be termed the more positive and creative aspects of management. This left the section with administrative matters and the handling of difficult management problems, particularly arrears control. And the fulfilment of even this limited brief relied, at least ostensibly, on the use of standard formal procedures. A more flexible innovatory approach was not encouraged and there were no staff training programmes or professional supports for any officers who might be prepared to take new initiatives. The limitation of job description contributed to the lack of officer commitment and a low level of job satisfaction. The section had become insular and defensive and lacked any positive ongoing links with other sections and directorates. All of these factors combined to negate the impetus for change originating from the director's office.

For their part, the councillors appear to continue to accept a traditional representative rôle in the constituency and hold to the ideal of conducting council business through committees served by officers acting in an advisory capacity. Formal committee work may involve deliberations and decision making on complex and important issues. The accepted modes may not any longer be altogether appropriate for the business of the local authority and this may explain the apparent shift in the weighting of power in favour of the officer group at director level and committee chairmen and directors working in informal alliance.

Relationships between the officer and member groups may be characterized by exchanges of services, status and power. The complexities of the organization are seen in the multiplicity of points at which it fragments. Thus there may be splits between directorates, between the chief executive and the directors, a particular director and his subordinates, within peer groups as between the two area teams or between ex-rent collector and ex-welfare housing management assistants, between bureaucrats and professionals, officers and clients, between officers and councillors, opposition and Labour party councillors and within the latter group, between the Borough and the Old Borough, the right and the left, the members from the '74 elections and those from '71, the young and the old. The group allegiances inherent in these categorizations will be differentially expressed according to the situation. Within the housing management section, the Old Borough team expresses a certain rivalry through a joking relationship with the second team. Both might combine under pressure from say housing aid or lettings and when the directorate as a whole was under attack from the architects report on one of their estates, Brown, Black and the lettings officer submerged their differences and presented a united front to their opposers. The same process could be described for the member group. This combining of groups according to situations at once allows and is an expression of the manipulation and use of such mechanisms as scapegoating which overall maintains some kind of balance.

There appears to be little demand, either from the officer or member group, to change work roles and form of organization and so alter the nature of this balance. However, this resistance to change needs to be set in the context of the recent upheaval caused by the amalgamation of the boroughs, the introduction of corporate planning and the process of re-organization.

In regard to Parkview residents both officers and councillors have a fairly similar experience. Senior officers attend board and resident group meetings and at these are likely to meet the more politically active of estate residents. More junior officers have contact with residents generally as applicants for some kind of benefit or as wrongdoers. Councillors also have contact with the political activists and with other residents generally in response to some kind of crisis.[56] Both officers and councillors inevitably base their view of Parkview on these contacts. The view is undoubtedly a limited one and it is questionable how much credence should be given to claims to know what the tenants want when the background knowledge informing such judgements has such a partial basis.

On the basis of the findings of Part II it would seem that officers and members underestimate the persistence and social significance of personal attachments and loyalties to the neighbourhood. Certainly there is no explicit acknowledgement of these factors in policy terms. At the same time they overestimate the extent to which shared loyalties and community interests exist and can be expressed within the estate context through the promotion of estate based organizations such as the TA. The extent to which this view is unrealistic is shown more clearly in Part IV. 'Community concerns' tend to be expressed by residents in terms of complaints about the appearance of the estate, the lack of cleanliness, the loss of 'social tone' and in these matters the council seems unable to satisfy resident demands. For the rest, resident interests are more individualistic and family oriented.

From the estate, for most residents, the view of the council is similarly limited. The opening of the Community Housing Centre has done little to alter resident perceptions. Many have a long experience of a rôle relationship with the housing management section which has narrowly defined their status as council tenant in terms of a restrictive tenancy agreement. This definition in itself reflects differences in the social status of the parties involved. And the general experience of officialdom has been such as to inhibit and minimize resident initiated contacts.

The findings on both the estate and the council point to the strength of the forces for continuity and conservatism. Brown's reforms need to be expressed in changed relationships. Such social change is bound to produce tensions, conflicts of interest need to be allowed for and a long time scale for the assimilation of the reforms acknowledged.

Notes Part III

1   Local newspaper report on the opening of the Community Housing Centre, 13 September 1974.

2   ibid.

3   The Directorate of Housing, report March 1974.

4   ibid.

5   ibid. Brown's emphasis.

6   A W Gouldner, 'The Problem of Succession and Bureaucracy', in Gouldner (ed) *Studies in Leadership*, New York, 1950, p 653 f.

7   White resigned towards the end of 1976. One of Brown's own appointees, the housing co-ordinator was moved to fill the position of assistant director for the public sector. The vacancy for the position of housing co-ordinator was left unfilled. I do not know what the effect of this change has been.

8   There is some evidence that the move to give the co-ordinator a wide ranging brief had, for Brown, the unexpected side effect of promoting a somewhat unlikely alliance between White and his counterpart in the private sector both of whom became concerned to protect their domains against further incursions.

9   Directorate of Housing, report, March 1974. Apart from the specific directive to promote tenant control these statements are little different from the standard management functions laid down by Macey and Baker, *Housing Management*, 2nd ed, London, 1973, cf pp 325–6 and 460–62.

10   Most of the data which follows was obtained in the course of interviews conducted shortly after the completion of fieldwork with all members of the area team. Interviews with caretakers, two of whom refused to take part in the study, were carried out on the estate by Don Entwistle. It should be noted that this was a time when housing management and the DLBO were particularly sensitive following the release of a report critical of them both and compiled by the borough architect's department with reference to another estate. Black agreed to my interviewing staff on condition that I check with him on matters of fact so as to avoid further misrepresentation. Moreover, several officers in the Borough team told me they had been instructed not to speak with me and if I approached them they were 'to tell me nothing'. Some officers expressed an interest in the study and suggested meeting outside the office. I doubt if these attitudes adversely affected my work; by this stage I had anyway a fair amount of contact with members of the area team and I was concerned only to obtain a formal statement of their work. It should also be stated that most officers claimed to have no written job description; those given in the text therefore reflect the officer's understanding of his job. An outline of the interview schedule appears in Appendix ii.

11   Gray's area includes streets on two boundaries of the estate. These contain some acquired properties but no other estate developments. The total number of dwellings in his care is approximately 1000.

12   The borough operated a scheme of contributing to the cost of redecoration where tenants undertook the work themselves. The scheme was being phased out during the study period.

13   In addition Gray was on relief for another week.

14   Reduction of the debt can be obtained under the Attachments of Earnings Orders Act 1971. The somewhat confused legal situation in regard to evictions in the public sector is discussed by D Yates, 'Evicting Council House Tenants'. *New Law Journal,* September 4 1975, pp 873–6.

15   However, see below p 155. At the time I interviewed Brown, (14 November 1975) he claimed there were 600 cases of arrears in excess of £300.

16   At that stage it was proposed to institute a system of regular planned maintenance but economic restrictions delayed implementation.

17   At the time of interview the Parkview surveyor was classed as a technical assistant but he was an applicant for an assistant surveyors position and it was intended to appoint two technical assistants to each team surveyor.

18   The foreman was able to call on any other tradesman he required. When the backlog of work on Parkview had been cleared the area covered by the team was extended to include two neighbouring estates nearby.

19   After the completion of fieldwork Brown did make proposals for an alternative form of estate management on a new estate nearing completion. The scheme proposed the appointment of a resident management assistant responsible for the supervision of part time cleaners, routine estate management, reporting of repairs, standby for emergencies and giving advice to a TA. Brown hoped that this form of management would be a step towards a scheme incorporating fuller tenant participation. The proposals were rejected in council in view of threatened strike action by the caretakers union.

20   There is a staff training programme in Housing Aid. In addition the directorate has a programme of recruiting housing management trainees. They learn by practical experience in the various sections and by attending day release courses for certificated study programmes.

An attempt was made to improve communication within the directorate by the issue of a regular newsletter but this had lapsed at the time of interviewing the staff member responsible.

21   White was referring to the fact that in eviction cases the local authority is now obliged by law to rehouse the tenants. He considers this has greatly reduced the effectiveness of any sanctions which the directorate can invoke to secure 'acceptable' behaviour.

22   Some attempt was made to reduce this grievance when, towards the end of the fieldwork period each of the two area managers were allotted a small number of allocations for which they could nominate particular tenants.

23   Submissions by the area manager to the Housing Utilization Review Committee, 17 June 1975. The old and proposed conditions of tenancy are set out in Appendix IV. The Area Housing Boards were consulted on this issue. Three out of four elected to retain the existing tenancy conditions, thus supporting the Borough Manager.

24   Damer writes about the ideology of housing managers in his study and postulates that the ethic of 'control, orderliness, cleanliness, and supervision' is inspired by the Public Health Acts of the latter half of the 19th Century. See S Damer, 'Wine Alley: the Sociology of a Reputation', paper to the British Sociological Association, Leeds, 1972, especially p 12.

25   The difficulty of adjustment for rent collectors has been noted elsewhere. 'The assistants who had previously been seen to do "a good days' work" (by collecting rent, balancing cash, banking and ordering repairs) were faced with seemingly intangible housing management duties which did not immediately show reward for work effort expended.' However, the change with planning and retraining can result in 'most unlikely "rent collector" becoming interested in wider aspects of housing management.' See I J Walker, 'Housing Management: old concepts revised.' *Housing Monthly,* July 1975, p 20 f.

26 This type of omission is of course difficult to prove. It was brought to my notice by one of the housing management staff and does lend support to the claims of several Parkview residents who protested to me that they had received notices to quit without any prior warning.

27 Since the time of the study seven new professionally qualified staff members have been appointed.

28 This attitude may be compared with the confident assertiveness described by Jon G Davies in *The Evangelistic Bureaucrat*, London, 1972.

29 Department of the Borough Architect, [An Estate] Interim Report, March 1975. The sections of Housing attacked here include lettings as well as management.

30 Permission to do this was reluctantly given after Brown had issued instructions to housing management staff that all officers were to co-operate with the study. I decided not to press for further work observing officers particularly since I had already seen many of them at work in other situations.

31 I myself received a visiting slip after I had notified the office, as I was formally required to do, of the fact that my parents were visiting and staying with me for several months. When I subsequently phoned Gray he said the visit was to check what arrangements I had made for their accommodation.

32 The order is, clearance; homelessness; redevelopment; major works; normal transfers ie, larger or smaller units; GLC nominations to the borough; transfer on medical grounds ie medical grounds like the wheelchair case rather than 'nerves' or 'depression'; housing list applications.

33 This may be contrasted with the attitudes described by Damer and Madigan, 'The Housing Investigator', *New Society*, 25 July 1974, p 226 f. At the same time Gray spoke approvingly of the manner and demeanour of the tenant who disliked the estate. The home was clearly well cared for and the family were considered ideal tenants. Gray commented that he wished he could 'do something' for her. It seems inevitable that in this type of work the visiting officer reflects the value judgements of those 'respectable' and 'successful' sections of society with which he himself identifies and this stance undoubtedly affects his response to particular cases.

34 Since the completion of fieldwork Brown has issued instructions that all staff members should give their names to members of the public with whom they are dealing.

35 'The bonus system is of the type known as "incentive bonus" and works in its simplest form in the following manner. A job has a known time element which is the job target time. The operative carries out the task and provided he does it in less than the time target he is paid a percentage (66⅔) of value of the time saved.' Report of the controller of the DLBO to the Housing Utilisation Review Committee, 5 June 1975.

36 Department of the Borough Architect, [An Estate] Interim Report, March 1975.

37 Controllers report, op cit.

38 K Thurby and Ann Richardson, 'Organizational Problems in Housing Maintenance,' *Housing Review*, May—June 1972, pp 81–84.

39 At one time there were proposals for regular sessions to exchange information and co-ordinate efforts but no meetings took place during the fieldwork.

40 This conflict is discussed by Malpass, 1975, especially p 12.

41 For examples of this see Part IV.

42 Standing orders, 1974. Unless otherwise stated all subsequent reference to committee terms of reference and to the powers of chairman and officers, are taken from the standing orders.

43 For a breakdown of councillors interviewed see Table VI below p 216. An outline of the interview schedule appears at Appendix II, p 287.

44 Cf Parkinson's '. . . Law of Triviality. Briefly stated, it means that the time spent on any item of the agenda will be in inverse proportion to the sum involved.' Parkinson then describes a committee meeting where an item for an atomic reactor takes $2\frac{1}{2}$ minutes of committee time, that for a bicycle shed 45 minutes, while an item on refreshments supplied at meetings of the joint welfare committee takes $1\frac{1}{4}$ hours and the item is deferred for further information and submission to the next meeting. C N Parkinson, *Parkinson's Law*, London, 1958, p 69 ff.

45 B Kutner, 'Elements and Problems of Democratic Leadership', in Gouldner (ed) p 460.

46 P Marris and M Rein, *Dilemmas of Social Reform*, London, second ed, 1972 p 24 f. The writers add, 'People will talk more freely of past struggles than those in which they are at the moment engaged, and an outside observer risks degenerating into a gossip monger if he tries too insistently to unravel the personal conflicts of those round him.'

47 For an account of the setting up of the project see below pp 304–311.

48 W Hampton, *Democracy and Community*, Oxford, 1970, p 286. Hampton's emphasis.

49 Malpass, 1975, p 26.

50 cit Malpass, 1975, p 27.

51 Almost without exception the councillors interviewed are involved in a multifarious range of other activities from party political organizations to school boards, sports bodies, local charities and various community organizations.

52 It should be noted that with the opening of the community hall the ward councillors instituted a fortnightly surgery.

53 See Hampton, chapter 8, esp p 207 ff.

54. R S Young, *The Politics of Change in Local Government*, Local Government Research Unit, Occasional Paper No 6, 1975 reprint, p 9.

55 See *ibid*, p 8.

56 Role relationships between officers, councillors and residents are dealt with more fully in Part IV.

Part IV

Local Political Forums

Introduction

Part IV describes the links between the two social fields, Parkview and the council, outlined in Parts II and III. Some links are effected through institutions, the Parkview TA and the North Board, others through less formal resident groups like those involving the tower block and garden flats and some through individual initiatives from residents, officers or councillors. Part IV gives an account of these different kinds of linkages and the nature of the relationships set up through them.

The organizations and events described concern relatively few people. Nevertheless an understanding of them is central to part of the project's brief; to assess the means for improving relations between local authority landlords and their tenants. This is a subject which in recent years, has gained considerable attention. To this end central government has increased its involvement in local government housing management. Within the Department of the Environment an advisory group on housing services has been set up and a professional advisor on housing management has been appointed. This interest stems from a recognition of the need to re-examine present housing management methods and functions in view of an increasing number of apparently intractable problems faced by many authorities throughout the country. Vandalism, rent arrears, estates which are difficult to let[1] even in areas of acute housing shortage – these are issues frequently mentioned.

Thus far, both at the central and local government level some form of tenant participation in management has been most commonly advocated as a means not only of securing an improved housing management service but also of reducing the severity of problems like vandalism, which are often regarded as symptomatic of a wider social malaise. Perhaps not surprisingly, tenant participation has become the topic of widespread interest. Housing managers' conferences on the subject have been well received and reported[2]. 'Labour's Programme for Britain 1976' suggests various ways in which residents might be enabled to more effectively participate in the management of their own homes. The report of a government working party on housing co-operatives recommended the establishment of management co-operatives and other schemes to promote resident involvement[3]. The government circular issued following this report encouraged local authorities to experiment and commented that 'Where conditions are not suitable for co-operatives, tenants should nevertheless be involved through consultation and participation in the running of their homes'[4]. At the time of writing the department is producing a handbook for local authority guidance entitled 'Getting Tenants Involved'[5]. To its advocates the meaning of participation ranges from a preparedness to take resident views into account to resident control.[6] The arguments for and against find vigorous exponents among councillors, officers and other outsiders. And like the general move to improve housing management, attempts to promote tenant participation find very practical justifications, albeit often overlaid with an ideological imperative, grassroots democracy[7].

As might be expected, the response to these initiatives has been varied. Most tenant participation schemes were set up in Labour controlled London boroughs following the 1971 elections[8]. By 1975 when a national survey was conducted, 85% of the London boroughs and 41% of all housing authorities had instituted some form of tenant participation[9]. The housing schemes documented by this survey range from informal consultative practices to more formal systems of committees.

The Borough has developed its own formal scheme of tenant participation based on four area housing boards. In addition, as already noted, the director, Brown is committed to change in the Borough through the introduction of a new and improved management style. In the context of the Parkview study it is posited that the formal participation scheme cannot be considered in isolation. Rather it needs to be seen in relation to other forms of contact between officers, councillors and residents. Furthermore, the case for tenant participation has to be critically assessed not only with reference to the interests of administrators but also having regard to the situation of the estate and those resident there. Finally, in determining the scope for other means of improving relations between residents and the local authority something of the range and nature of existing links needs to be understood. This emphasis reflects the belief that the residents' past and present experience of the council is particularly important in shaping the response to any proposed reforms.

This section begins with an account of the Parkview TA, the one established estate based organization which has as part of its aims the representation of resident views to the council. This is followed by four case studies each concerned to describe how contacts between Parkview and the officer and elected member groups can be established for particular purposes. The Borough tenant participation scheme is the subject of the next section while a concluding section attempts to analyse the significance of these existing linkages between Parkview and the council.

Parkview TA

The most important organization linking estate residents with the council is the Parkview TA[10]. This section outlines the constitutional basis of the organization, the nature of committee politics and activity and then traces the relationships which the committee has developed with agencies external to the estate. A concluding section attempts to analyse some of the material relating to the TA.

The formal charter

Throughout most of its history the Parkview TA appears to have functioned without reference to a written constitution. According to members with long experience of committee work the first committees were constituted under the terms of a document held by the council. These members also claim not to have seen the document and have little knowledge of its import. In August 1973 the council sent the then secretary a copy of a model TA constitution. This document was presumably accepted though never formally ratified and by June 1974 nobody on the estate had a copy. The present constitution was drawn up by Mrs Field, for a time Chairman of the TA and was based in part on a document supplied by Black, the Old Borough area manager, and in part on a model constitution developed by the Association of London Housing Estates (ALHE). The council document was undated and appears to have been taken with little alteration from a standard housing management manual.[11] The council constitution has as its objectives 'to foster good fellowship and good citizenship among all people on the estate'. This can be compared to the objectives of the ALHE constitution which are to provide facilities for members of the general public in order to improve the condition of life for those persons making use of them and also to associate with the local authority, voluntary organizations and residents of the estate in an 'effort to advance education and provide facilities for training and recreation, and social, moral and intellectual development, and to further health, and to foster a community spirit for the advancement of these and other charitable objects'. The Parkview TA constitution adds to the council objectives a provision 'to take up complaints on behalf of tenants when all other channels have failed'.[12]

Generally good fellowship would seem to imply notions of increasing friendliness and neighbourliness. The committee appears to attempt to meet this objective through arranging special events like outings for children and Christmas parties for pensioners. It is not clear how the second objective, the promotion of good citizenship, might be defined nor has this been considered by the committee. The third objective is quite specific and might be held to oblige the committee to take up complaints whether or not they approved of them or considered them justifiable. It is in the course of attempts to meet this last objective that committee members have most contact with councillors and officers.

Committee politics

During its eight year existence, although the constitution provides for annual elections, the TA has only once in that time held elections for committee membership. Instead places on the committee have been filled by co-options. Moreover elections in themselves may be of little significance. Committee members tend to be self selecting and the process of selection owes more to personal interest often stimulated by links with existing members than to the formal mechanics of canvassing, nominations and voting.

Once formed committees may be characterized by in-fighting and the emergence of factions; resignations or withdrawals and the reforming of alliances. The shifts in individual loyalties to a particular leader or group are impelled by a complex range of factors. Committee developments and group allegiances are outlined here to illustrate something of the nature of Parkview politics.

During the field work period 25 people, 11 men and 14 women, worked on the committee.[13] Attendance at meetings varied from 4 to 14 with an average of nine members per meeting. The various committees met fairly regularly; in the period July 1974 to July of the following year there were 22 committee meetings. Most took place at fortnightly intervals.

The first committee meeting in that period was held on 31 July. At that time the association functioned under the chairmanship of Lloyd, for many years a leading figure in estate politics and a foundation member of the North Board. It quickly became apparent that the committee was in a state of crisis. The situation was engendered by a conflict centred on the chair and expressed in personality clashes between Lloyd and other committee members. Underlying factors in this conflict appeared to be personality clashes, the lack of committee activity, the form of committee organization whereby it was alleged that all power and responsibility for decision making was vested in and jealously guarded by the office bearers, and the incipient disagreement between committee members from the old and new part of the estate. At that meeting Lloyd proffered his resignation on the grounds that after 20 years of fighting for tenants he was accused of doing nothing. Davidson, a recently co-opted member from the garden flats proposed a motion of confidence in all the officers; Lloyd was persuaded to continue as chairman. Simpson as secretary and Mrs Lloyd as treasurer remained unchallenged. The same meeting accepted a scheme put forward by Mrs Field for the establishment of sub-committees to deal with social entertainment, youth affairs, TA finance, resident complaints and the production of a newsletter. These moves seemed at once to promise a reconciliation and the prospect of overcoming a major source of discontent by reducing the influence of the main officers. However, this harmony was shortlived. A special meeting was called and from that and the subsequent meeting, I was excluded. Reports from those present indicated that personal conflicts found expression in a dispute over the handling of funds from the estate's gala. A motion of censure was proposed against them by Lessor. Mrs Biddle moved a vote of no confidence in Lloyd and suggested disbanding and reforming the committee. A vote was never taken; Lloyd immediately tabled his resignation and was followed by his wife and two other committee members.

Despite the resignations the committee decided that, in order not to disrupt their plans for Christmas activities, no elections should be called until the new year. The committee carried on with Mandle as a 'caretaker chairman', Simpson as secretary and a new member, Franklin, as treasurer. Mandle was acceptable to all members but a retiring personality and a lack of experience in leadership rôles combined to make him no more than a token chairman. And although Lloyd was removed from the committee his influence was still felt. At the first meeting under Mandle, Davidson tabled a draft letter of thanks to Lloyd and his wife. This was accepted without demur. Lessor proposed that all committee members should attend the forthcoming area board elections and give their support to Lloyd. Simpson objected that voting was a matter for individuals and Mrs Field suggested that it might not be advisable to have as representative someone who was not in a position to report back to the committee. Throughout the period of the Mandle committee some members, especially those from the garden flats under the emerging leadership of Mrs Field, considered that Lloyd remained a dominant figure in committee politics, able to manipulate committee affairs both through his influence with council officers and his personal ties with other committee members, especially Simpson and Lessor. This belief in Lloyd's continued access to power, whether justified or not, resulted in a build up of resentment against him within a group forming around Mrs Field. Rumours of collusion were rife and working relationships on the committee were constantly under threat. Meetings of the committee, without clear direction from the chair, merely provided the opportunity for discussion and the confusion of rôles added to the underlying dissension. During a meeting on 22 January Lloyd called at the meeting room on the grounds that he was the only person acceptable to Social Services as responsible for the keys. Various committee members raised matters of business with him, Mandle vacated the chair for him and Lessor proposed that Lloyd be invited to rejoin the committee. The motion was lost.

In between that meeting and the next Davidson, Lessor, Mandle and Simpson tendered their resignations. Nevertheless Mandle and Simpson attended the meeting on 5th February and Lloyd also was present. He said that he had received an urgent call from officers of the housing directorate and that while he disliked the duty he was acting as North Board representative under instructions to dissolve the committee and make arrangements for the election of a new committee. Mrs Field objected and countered Lloyd's claim by quoting a letter from Black. It was dated 4th February and stated, 'I would be grateful if you would contact the secretary or chairman and suggest a general meeting of tenants to elect a new committee or confirm a membership of the existing committee as soon as possible'. Mrs Field said she considered there was an existing committee; Black would be informed and there was no need for a dissolution. The spate of resignations left a rump committee comprising Mrs Field, Mrs Montgomery and her husband, Mrs Glenn and Franklin. Mrs Field was elected chairman, Mrs Montgomery secretary and Franklin continued in post as treasurer.

The period of the Field committee was possibly somewhat confusing to outsiders. The committee drew members only from the garden flats. Previous committees had attempted to maintain more or less regular contact with all blocks on the estate by collecting subscriptions. The depleted resources of the committee made this very difficult and collections were discontinued. In spite of newsletters some residents concluded that the TA itself had collapsed. The situation was complicated by the activities of Eshag, an action group in one of the tower blocks. This latter group was supported by an assistant attached to the project and attracted some of the people who had resigned from the TA.[14] Both the council and the Field committee saw the action group as competing with the TA. The council was concerned to minimize the apparent conflict on the estate and particularly to legitimize a single representative committee which would then accept management responsibility for the Parkview community hall, a facility then nearing completion.[15] At the same time Councillor Mackie as chairman of housing intervened and instructed Black to have no dealing either with the TA or Eshag committees.

In response to pressures from both the officer and member group the Field committee spent some time writing a new constitution in preparation for the holding of the first elections of the estate TA. Arrangements for this election including the hiring of a school hall and the printing of letters were made with council assistance. And in view of the background of disputes Councillor Mackie chaired the meeting which was held on 30 April 1975. Black also was present but Councillor Mackie pointed out that his presence was certainly unofficial. Prior to the calling of nominations, on the instigation of the Lloyd group, Councillor Mackie agreed to a departure from the provisions of the draft constitution whereby the committee should elect its own officers and instead allowed the election of officers directly from the floor. The chairman elected was Mrs Dee, a former committee member who had resigned from the Mandle committee on the grounds that more should be done for older residents on the estate. Since then Mrs dee had played a prominent rôle in Eshag. Other officers were Mrs Field as vice chairman, Mrs Montgomery, secretary, and Franklin, treasurer. Franklin was the only man elected to the committee; other men with committee experience, including Lloyd, refused nomination.

Basically this new committee comprised two groups; the supporters of Mrs Field, all drawn from the garden flats, and the supporters of Mrs Dee, all residents of the one tower block. The former group had previous TA committee experience; the latter an identity through their action group experience. In addition there were two quasi-independents; Mrs James, Lloyd's daughter, a member of earlier committees and the only representative from the oldest part of the estate, and Mrs Hunt, a resident in the garden flats who, while a co-opted member of the Field rump committee, disassociated herself from both groups. The committee immediately split into two sections along the lines described. Discontent again focused on the chair and there were bitter personality clashes. Underlying factors were the Field group's concern with remedying defects in the garden flats and their resentment at the continuing and separate existence of Eshag. However, counter allegations from that group were that the Field group effectively functioned as the TA, acted independently and withheld communications to the secretary from the main body of the committee.

This committee never worked smoothly. In July the conflicts resulted in an open rift when a meeting cancelled by Mrs Dee went ahead at the insistence of Mrs Field. This meeting was held at the project flat and inevitably some blame attached to myself. The Field group then boycotted a meeting attended by the Dee group. The next full committee meeting, the last of the research period broke up in bickering about the previous two faction meetings, the alleged incompetence of the secretary, the still unresolved question of the constitution and committee business generally.

It will be clear from this outline that once a committee has been formed, the pattern of relationships between members becomes an important factor in understanding TA politics. These inter-relationships can be traced by considering the process of recruitment and the nature of the ties which link or divide individuals and groups. As already suggested members may be seen as clustered around several leading figures. The Lloyd group comprised Mrs Lloyd, their daughter Mrs James, Lessor, Mr and Mrs Simpson, Mrs Dee, Mrs Biddle and Mrs Paul. All were residents of the older parts of the estate and as committee members were enlisted by Lloyd. Most of the older blocks were represented by one or other of these committee members and part of their work, the collection of subscriptions, ensured some contact with many residents. In this group, Lloyd was the only surviving member of an even earlier committee which, according to disillusioned former TA members, collapsed for want of a meeting place. Mrs Field was recruited to the committee by Lloyd on account of her experience with the South Area Board. Other members from the garden flats, Davidson, Mrs Glenn, Franklin, Mrs and Mrs Montgomery were drawn into the committee following action taken by garden flat residents to secure private gardens for ground floor dwellings.[16] Alternative leaders to Lloyd, Mrs Dee and Mrs Field emerged from these groups. Other members were persuaded to join the committee by existing members with whom they had some link already. Thus next door or near neighbours of Mrs Glenn, Davidson and Mrs

Montgomery all for a time served on the committee. Mrs Hunt was known personally to several committee members. Simpson invited another resident of his block to join the committee. Mandle and Lessor are known to each other through residence in the same block, Mrs Biddle and Mrs Dee persuaded three members of Eshag to work also on the TA committee. None of the members recruited in this way as neighbours or friends ever assumed a prominent rôle in the committee. Most resigned or simply stopped attending after a few meetings. Some may be more forcibly excluded. One woman who expressed an interest in working on the committee for elderly residents on the estate was co-opted as a potentially useful member of the Field committee. Subsequently she was identified with the Lloyd group and was simply ignored and squeezed out of an effective membership rôle.

The groups which survive these processes cannot, however, be considered stable since over time allegiances may show remarkable shifts. Thus, Lessor, apparently a member of the Lloyd group was active in securing his defeat and later proposed that he rejoin the committee. Simpson at times acted with, at times against Lloyd. Mrs Dee and Mrs Biddle survived identification with the Lloyd group to lead a grouping based on links with residents in their own block and united in opposition to the Field/Montgomery alliance.

Within the committee most attention centres on the leaders or potential leaders. Some have had experience of political party committee work or trade union experience, others have no prior committee experience. Lloyd had been active in various political parties and has had long involvement in trade union affairs. Mrs Field has had a lifetime of active work in the Labour Party movement. Mrs Dee is a clerical officer in the civil service and has little active involvement in political affairs or committee work outside Parkview. A complete newcomer to committee work and professing to hold no strong political views Mrs Montgomery quickly assumed a leadership rôle by virtue of her strong personality and energy in organising activities. Her stance forced other committee members to support or oppose her and she was a powerful person before she took office in the Field committee. Others ostensibly in leadership positions, Mandle, Simpson, Mrs Lloyd and Franklin, in fact acted as supporters to one of the main leaders.

Outside the committee there are informal groups which impinge on it. Ex-committee members may continue to express some interest in TA affairs and may turn up at general meetings or social gatherings. Other residents with some knowledge of the leaders may be opposed to joining the committee because they dislike the personnel involved. Both sets of residents tend to be fairly critical of the committee; the former incline to open criticism, the latter more generally to rumour and gossip. More important are groups of neighbours, friends and relatives, sometimes from outside the estate, clustered around particular committee members. These groups may be mobilised for help at functions like a jumble sale or children's party, or for support by attendance at an estate dance. They may also serve as informal political forums; committee affairs, the assumed plotting between members, the in-fighting at meetings are all the subjects of avid discussion and comment and undoubtedly these informal debates affect the responses of individual committee members. Often these groups are simply the members own household but they may be much larger as in the case of Mrs Montgomery. Her husband, even when no longer a committee member, continued to show an interest and discussed matters at length with her and her two teenage children frequently expressed an opinion about the problems and personalities involved. Mrs Montgomery also has close friendship links with three other committee members, Mrs Field, Mrs Glenn and Mrs Noakes, and her mother, married sister and three married brothers, although not resident on the estate, are very close to her, visit frequently and actively assist at any TA function. Mrs Montgomery works for a few hours each morning and her children are basically independent so she has the time and energy to devote herself to local estate politicking and TA affairs generally. It is not easy to trace the influence of these member support groups back to the individual response at committee meetings. They are nevertheless of considerable importance.

When formal committee meetings do take place they are seldom well ordered affairs. Although an agenda may have been drawn up before a meeting it is often not followed. Occasionally there was no reading of minutes of a previous meeting. Members often did not speak through the chair but informally across the table. Sometimes there were two or more discussions going on simultaneously. Discussion flitted from subject to subject and there were frequent asides and irrelevancies. There was sometimes long discussion on one topic and then the committee would move onto another item without any apparent decision or agreement being reached. Formal motions put to the vote were rare. Matters were seldom considered in a cool detached manner; frequently strong feelings flared and there were open rows at the committee table even when outsiders such as Black were present.[17] One consequence of this was that issues might not be dealt with solely on their merits; rather support is given or withheld according to the current state of feuding and individual loyalty to particular factions. This is accentuated by the tendency of members to impute motives, generally of a sinister kind, to apparently quite simple proposals, because the proposer is considered to be in an opposition group.[18]

The reasons for the emergence of factionalism within the committee appear to be complex. Conceivably, factions could reflect ideological differences since members come both from the right and the left. However, there is seldom any expression of political viewpoints in committee and the TA does appear to justify its claim to be non party political. Nevertheless these differences could assume importance at any time and the reaction might produce very sharp divisions.[19] A more straightforward cause of dissension was member orientation to committee work. Some members considered that work for the estate's pensioners should be accorded top priority, others children, some felt complaints against the council should take precedence, others social activities on Parkview. Certain members strongly identified with a specific interest and became notorious for their attempts to further this regardless of its relevance to the business in hand.

A more basic reason for conflict as voiced by members themselves was that determined by place of residence on the estate. Residents in older blocks often regard the newer extension as a separate entity and the categorization 'old' and 'new' estate is common. In these circumstances newcomers in the garden flats who are prepared to take an active part in an estate wide organization may be resented. The following quote from one of my neighbours concerning the collection of jumble illustrates this point as well as voicing the suspicion which often attaches to TA committee workers.

"It's not genuine, if you know what I mean. Now those shops selling clothes for old people, they're alright,–they are run by ladies and there's no nonsense if you get my meaning. They won't take a penny off and that's as it should be. And who's that down there in the corner house with a notice in the window? Runs the estate she does and she hasn't been here more than five minutes."

This feeling is heightened by a belief popular among older residents that the newer flats were allocated predominantly to outsiders–to people from outside the Old Borough and to 'coloureds'. Many of these long established residents now have sons and daughters recently married or of marriageable age and with little prospect of finding decent accommodation in their home locality. Parents often express resentment in those terms. Moreover 'outsiders' are felt not to have the same loyalty to the Old Borough and their presence to contribute to the general decline of standards on the estate. In fact in recent years a greater proportion of allocations have gone to outsiders but overall the estate remains a local one. The committee members reflect this kind of antagonism even though all stress that they are prepared to work for the benefit of the whole estate. Lloyd commented at the time of his defeat that he had been warned that if he joined the newcomers they would 'stab him in the back' and since then he claims to have been approached by a number of established residents to form a separate committee.

This old/new categorization has another aspect. There are inevitably differences in interests among residents of an esate which has been developed in phases. The residents in the garden flats were faced with a new situation. Most wanted to make some form of contact with neighbours and many were affected by major defects which caused severe dampness in the flats. The layout of the blocks to some degree facilitated sociability among neighbours and the dampness provided a common cause against the council. Residents in the older blocks on the other hand had more settled social relationships with neighbours and their complaints with the council were much more likely to be of concern to an individual household or of a general kind such as recurring lift breakdown, and viewed after years of acceptance with a kind of hopeless despair. The phased building developments of the estate meant that the TA committee had perforce to contain two groups at different stages of TA development.[20]

Another factor may be the imbalance of sexes on the committee. The Lloyd committee was a male-dominated committee, the Mandle caretaker committee had approximately equal numbers of men and women and the Field and Dee committees were predominantly female. Franklin continued as treasurer on both of those committees but his involvement at committee meetings was always minimal. This factor is seldom made explicit but it would seem to be the case that for members there is an ideal committee of men and women working together with men appropriately in decision making rôles and women in work support rôles. When the short-lived scheme to establish sub-committees was instituted, the finance and complaints committees each comprised three men and one woman. The entertainments committee in contrast had women members only and others on the committee commented that the work of that sub-committee was anyway 'women's work'. The men on the committee have generally had experience only of male dominated work situations and organizations and they tend to have a dismissive attitude towards the ability of women to organize themselves and deal with the all male organization of the housing directorate. Commentators pointed to the difficulties of the Dee and Field committees by saying that what was needed was 'a good strong man'.

The exception to the pattern outlined here was the Field committee which conducted its business in an orderly fashion and was not rift by in-fighting. Partly this was due to Mrs Field's experience of conducting meetings, partly deference for her age. Perhaps more importantly, the committee was a small one party group where all members shared and identified with the problems tackled in committee meetings. Even so the appearance of unanimity is likely to be short-lived; new interests, goals or members, all may result in the emergence of splits and conflicts.

In both types of committee, the faction model or the one party model, the process of decision making and implementation is a complex one. Decisions may be based on discussions held between meetings with support groups and/or other committee members. These ongoing discussions might be quite intensive. In the Field and Dee committees for example, relations between Mrs Field, Mrs Montgomery and Mrs Glenn were particularly close and involved almost daily visiting between them. Inevitably committee business was a major topic of conversation. These exchanges might also affect the way in which committee decisions were implemented; certainly decisions agreed to in committee might be selectively applied by those designated to implement them. Under the Lloyd committee, Simpson as secretary, was instructed to write a list of grievances to the director of housing. He disagreed with this form of action on the basis that officers more directly involved were by-passed and so he chose to ignore the issue and the matter was forgotten. The Mandle committee decided not to buy children's presents for their Christmas party. Mrs Montgomery disapproved of the decision and in between meetings took it upon herself to purchase them. The Field committee voted to negotiate with Eshag and instructed Mrs Montgomery to write a letter to Mrs Dee as their main spokesman. In subsequent discussion with her informal support group, including in this instance another committee member, Mrs Glenn, she reconsidered and the letter was not sent. Even unanimous decisions may be overturned. The Mandle committee agreed to give pensioners on the estate a Christmas gift of a voucher redeemable at a local butcher's shop. Action was taken to effect this decision but the scheme was still dropped. The same committee was in full agreement in naming new counter signatories for the TA account. However, in between that meeting and the next, one of the counter signatories was dropped from the list given to the bank, apparently without reason. On this occasion those responsible, when criticized, admitted to having acted wrongly. Members might also initiate actions and then present the committee with a fait accompli. Davidson produced a newsletter for the committee without any prior consultation with other members. Unwitting ward councillors may accept an invitation from a committee member to attend a committee meeting only to find that the invitation had no committee backing and was a personal political ploy. Some of these actions represented marked shifts in policy or committed the TA to considerable expenditure; others were simply embarrassing. Those responsible might be reprimanded in committee but nevertheless felt strong enough to act independently outside it and indeed were often sustained against committee attack by the sympathy of a personal group of supporters.

Committee work

This then is something of the overall context of TA committee affairs on the estate. As part of the research detailed notes were taken of all committee meetings. From these notes it is possible to separate out and categorize issues and so give some account of the range and nature of the business undertaken by the various committees in that time.

Table III shows a breakdown of all issues considered by the various committees. Items are counted each time they occur so that an item like dampness in the garden flats which came up at meeting after meeting would be counted as many times. This was done to give some indication of the importance attached by the committee to the different categories. These gross figures also give some idea of the time which the committee devoted to various aspects of its business. The most frequently recorded items concern the day to day administration of the committee. Some of these matter, like the preparation of a newsletter or arranging for keys to the meeting place might involve quite lengthy discussions. Other committee business concerns mainly social activities for the estate or the handling of complaints. The planning and organization of social affairs form a large part of committee activity. Each event entails a good deal of detailed work to decide and allocate tasks, arrange purchases etc and the greater part of a meeting may well be devoted to this. The increased figures for November and December are accounted for by the spate of Christmas activity organized on the estate. The small number of individual complaints is accounted for by the fact that all committees have had a policy of taking up

TABLE III Issues considered by the Parkview TA 31 July 1974 to 31 July 1975

Issues before committee	\<- Date of committee meeting -\> 31/7	25/9	9/10	23/10	6/11	20/11	4/12	22/1	5/2	12/2	19/2	5/3	19/3	2/4	16/4	22/5	5/6	12/6	18/6	3/7	17/7	31/7	Totals
Minor defects, individual cases/complaints	1					1									3								5
Serious defects complaints estate provision*	5		1			2	1	1	4		1	4	1	4	9	1	3	2	8	1	1		49
Social events/fundraising																							
i Planning	1	8	4	4	3	2				1		1				1							25
ii Minor details		1	2	4	7	10	12	4				7	1	1									49
Welfare, estate provision*	1				1							2	1	1	1	1	1		1	1	2	1	14
Committee business*																							
i Day to Day running	3	4	2	2		1		9	7	10	3			1	2	2	1	1		6	2		56
ii Conduct		2	2	2		2	2	3															13
Consultation								1							2			1					4
Relationships with other bodies			1	1	1			1					3		1	1				3	4	2	18
Parkview community hall							1	5		2		1		5	1				1	1	1	1	19
Totals	11	15	12	13	12	18	16	24	11	13	4	15	6	12	19	6	5	4	10	12	10	4	252

*Notes: Complaints and estate provision incorporate only physical aspects of the estate in contrast with welfare and estate provision a category comprising socially supportive items such as compiling a list of old age pensioners and appointing a community worker to the estate. Day to day running of committee business includes items such as the printing and distribution of newsletters and the collection of subscriptions. Conduct denotes criticism of the manner in which committee meetings are held.

complaints only when the usual channels open to residents have failed or when grounds for complaint are considered justifiable by a committee member and not taken up at all by a resident, usually on the grounds of infirmity. The figures for complaints of all kinds are understated to the extent that a series of particular or general complaints may be incorporated in a single action by the committee. Thus the Field committee compiled a list of 200 repairs outstanding on the estate. This list has been counted as one complaint. Items for consultation were the Borough road plan, the GLC transport proposals for London, neighbourhood council documents and proposals to alter the council

TABLE IV Issues considered by the Parkview TA according to committee leadership

	Committee Leadership			
Issues before committee*	Lloyd 31/7	Mandle 25/9– 5/2	Field 12/2– 16/4	Dee 22/5– 31/7
Minor defects, individual cases/complaints	1	1	3	
Serious defects, complaints, estate provision	5	10	19	15
Social events/fundraising i Planning	1	21	1	2
ii Minor details		33	11	5
Welfare, estate provision	1	4	3	6
Committee business i Day to day running	3	25	17	11
ii Conduct		12		1
Consultation		1	2	1
Relationships with other bodies		8	4	6
Parkview community hall		6	9	4
Totals	11	121	69	51

*See notes to Table III

174

tenancy agreement. Only the latter demanded a response and was taken up at any length in committee.

Table IV shows the same categorization of items considered by the different committees. It is interesting to note that the changes in leadership appear to have relatively little effect on the work carried out and the variations in figures can for the most part be accounted for by factors independent of the committees themselves. Thus, as already noted, the Mandle committee's stress on social activities relates to the TA tradition of sponsoring Christmas activities for estate residents. These activities under the Mandle committee and planning for the election under the Field committee largely account for the concentration on administrative matters. The focus on criticism in the Mandle period related to the emergence of factions within and outside the committee. Discussions concerning the hall were very much determined by the stage of the building and council initiatives. The Field committee did, however, take on more complaints than either the Mandle or Dee committees and this reflected the concern of members to remedy outstanding repairs generally and particularly the defects in the garden flats.

The extent to which committee work is effective is more difficult to assess. Little comment about the social activities organised by the committee is necessary at this point since these events have been described elsewhere.[21] It can be noted, however, that most of these meet with success partly because members can mobilise their support groups in the preparation stages and on the day of the event others can usually be 'roped in' to help. This form of organisation is highly informal and to the outside observer appears chaotic but on the committee's terms it does work. And in part these events are successful because there are few constraints outside the control of the members; the committee can organise its own dance, gala, jumble sale or outing with a minimum of dependence on outside resources. Perhaps because of this control and the fairly popular nature of the events themselves, the committee tends to be over-ambitious and considers all manner of schemes. Some, like the idea of producing a booklet for the estate, a garden competition and a pantomime for the children, never eventuate.

Other aspects of the committee's work by their nature involve recourse to outside agencies. This is especially true of complaints to the council. In dealing with these the committee may be blocked by constraints beyond its control, by its own internal weaknesses or by a combination of external and internal factors. Some complaints come up with great regularity presumably because they are not dealt with in a satisfactory manner. Thus, items like car parking, cleaning and caretaking, the waterborne waste disposal unit, lift breakdowns, bins and rubbish collection are referred to the council on numerous occasions over the years. Some understanding of the reasons for this apparent failure to meet resident demands can be obtained from an account of the relations between the committee and those on whom they depend for the satisfaction of grievances, general assistance and advice.

Parkview TA and outside agencies

Foremost in importance among those agencies with which the committee has contact is the housing management section. The way in which this contact is established and developed varies from one committee to another. Under the Mandle committee official communications with officers were relatively few and informal links with Black were apparently maintained by Lloyd and Simpson. This resulted in a good deal of dissatisfaction since it was felt that Lloyd was manipulating committee affairs from behind the scenes. The Field committee concentrated rather more on trying to establish formal lines of contact with council officers. Meetings were arranged with the committee as a committee rather than on a semi-personal basis and letters were preferred to phone calls. The same policy was continued under the Dee committee but Mrs Dee claimed that it worked to her disadvantage and alleged that letters to Mrs Montgomery were responded to by the Field group in informal sessions prior to the formal meetings of the full committee. The charges were virtually impossible to prove or disprove but it is noteworthy that dealings with officers become a cause of dissension.

On occasion officers may take the initiative in approaching the committee. Most frequently these overtures came from Black and in meetings with the committee he adopted a firmly directive rôle. Other officers may be instructed to contact the committee over specific issues and they were more likely to be conciliatory in their approach. Whatever the approach the outcome is similar in that officers tend to act in conformity with their own views regardless of opinions expressed in committee.[22] As a consequence officers do not have an advisory function nor is there any attempt to use them in that manner.

The way in which resident initiated contacts with officers may be regarded is clearly evident in regard to common recurring resident complaints like the car parking and rubbish collections mentioned above. Initially the council may respond and have a blitz on illegal car parking or the inspection of the caretakers' work and repairs may be carried out on the waste disposal system. Agitation dies down until the next time the problem is brought to the TA's attention. Some items are simply not followed up either by officers or committee members. At a meeting of the Lloyd committee on 31 July for example it was reported that at a meeting involving Lloyd, Simpson, Davidson and Black the latter had agreed to the planting of hedges and trees around the sheltered housing unit. This was apparently forgotten and later in the same year there was some agitation from residents for a fence. Again nothing happened. Other requests meet with a refusal of one kind or another. Thus, the committee had on a number of occasions requested that the estate be provided with rubbish bins on the grassy areas and especially on the playground. In a letter to the secretary Black refused to accede to the request on the grounds that 'It has been found that if litter bins are provided these become collecting points for unwanted rubbish and have proved to be more of a nuisance than an amenity.' This Gilbertian type explanation is accepted, at least until, with a change of personnel on the committee, the question of rubbish bins is raised again. Other complaints are favourably acknowledged by the housing management section and works orders may be issued but the work can still be delayed for considerable periods for a variety of reasons including many outside the control of housing management. For instance, the question of fitting gates to the estate and the underground garages (Plate 38) have been under action for several years. This type of delay appears to have the effect of reducing the credibility of communications within the council structure and between the council's housing management team, the TA and tenants generally.

Other outside agencies are available to fulfil a wider resource function but most are used only to a limited extent. Thus when the Field committee was considering taking a Section 99[23] action against the council a representative from the ALHE was called upon for advice. Both this representative and other visitors she was able to introduce to the committee provided new information and offered practical support. Committee members expressed the view that they benefited a great deal from these sessions but the contact appears to have been lost. Committee membership changed, Mrs Dee identified the ALHE representative with the Field group, there were differences within that committee as to the emphasis which should be placed on the Section 99 action and the action itself finally lapsed.

Other agencies open to the committee are not used; instead committee members show a preference for using personal links. For instance, the Field committee decided they would like an opinion on the constitution they had drawn up for the TA and instead of referring the document to the local Legal Advice Centre they opted to ask the opinion of a legally qualified councillor known to them. Ward councillors and others known to the committee may be used as sources of information but this is limited by the stated reluctance of councillors to get embroiled in TA affairs. The resource network utilized by the committee is therefore a personalized, ad hoc one of restricted extent.[24]

Another agency which the committee might use for information and support is the North Board. The Lloyd committee had an obvious link with the Board through Lloyd himself and he automatically took cases up at board meetings. After his resignation from the TA committee some members felt themselves to be in opposition to Lloyd and his intervention as North Board representative in attempting to dissolve the committee marked a low point. Thereafter the TA committee made no attempt to use the board as a means of communicating grievances or requests to the council. They preferred to make the contact directly and the Field committee considered that the North Board was anyway no more than an ineffectual 'talking shop'.

Finally the committee may make use of contacts with the elected member group on the council. Most often these contacts are responses to committee requests and most involve ward councillors, other coucillors with whom individual committee members have links or those like Councillor Mackie, deemed to have an interest in resident concerns by virtue of his position as chairman of housing. Generally councillor support is' enlisted either to give extra force to resident grievances or to give enhanced status and importance to an estate event.

In many instances where outsiders are brought in it is the case that officers, councillors and other outsiders may all in their various ways be involved. It is the interactions set up in such cases that are of particular interest here. One example will suffice. During the research period the most serious issue taken up by the committee especially under the chairmanship of Mrs Field, was the question of remedying defects in the garden flats. Many were minor faults of the type to be expected in any new building. Others were more serious. In both instances residents and the TA had dealings with the contractors workmen and surveyor, the council on-site clerk of works, surveyors from the architect's department, surveyors from the housing directorate, housing management personnel, officers and workmen from the DLBO and councillors. Not surprisingly, residents were confused by this multiplicity of contacts and there were conflicting reports on what was to be done, by whom and when. In the event little appeared to get done at all and with the onset of winter many flats proved to be exceedingly damp, carpets and curtains were soaked and fungus growth on ceilings was common. (Plate 39). In the middle of March 1975 when feeling was running very high the Field committee organized a petition protesting about the damp. Copies were sent to the Director of Housing, the Chairman of Housing and the Public Health Inspector. A short time later on 20 March, the committee learned by chance that members of the North Board would be visiting the estate (Plate 40). The committee were irate that they had not been automatically advised of the visit and contacted the Chairman of the North Board. He professed ignorance of the committee's continuing existence, reluctantly agreed to meet with a few committee members and stressed that the visit was to look at playground equipment. The party would certainly have no time to look at damp flats. On the day of the visit, 22 March, the committee organized a demonstration by some of the petitioners and ensured publicity by inviting a reporter and photographer from one of the local newspapers. Within a few days two of the ward councillors called on Mrs Montogomery and agreed that communication between the council and the TA was unsatisfactory. One of them, Councillor Williams, suggested that a new procedure should be instituted. If a letter from the TA to the council was not acknowledged within a week one of the ward councillors was to be informed; if after three weeks the association had received no notification of the action taken in response to a query, the ward councillor was to be advised and would then take action on behalf of the committee. Mrs Montgomery informed Black of the procedure in a letter dated 27 March. As a result of the agitation a general meeting was held on the estate and those present were assured by officers and councillors that all complaints would be dealt with forthwith.

The Housing Services Committee considered the petition at its meeting on 9 April. There was some discussion prior to the consideration of the petition when one councillor took exception to the wording of it.[25] Nevertheless the petition was favourably received and as a result, Councillor Mackie announced the setting up of an emergency procedure to clear all outstanding repairs on the estate as quickly as possible. At its meeting on 22 May the TA committee noted that very little work had been done and in response to a follow up query from Councillor Mackie committee members compiled a list of 200 outstanding repairs. Meantime the Field committee had taken up the problem with the ALHE and had arranged meetings with an independent public health inspector and a solicitor with a view to taking out a Section 99 action against the council. The necessary inspections and reports were made and the initial letter serving notice on the council that proceedings would be instituted was sent. By early June a DLBO workforce was on the estate attending to a backlog of repairs and in the garden flats some remedial work had been carried out on an experimental basis in some badly affected flats. When I left the estate a short time later, it was high summer, the dampness was no longer in evidence, and the Section 99 action had been dropped.

I have outlined this example at some length because I feel it provides an apt illustration of many features of the TA committee, its work, and its relationships with councillors and council officers. At the time of the petition and demonstration the enthusiasm of the committee was high and related events, the response of officers at the general tenants meeting and councillors at the Housing Committee, were considered as victories. However, the momentum was not sustained. Assurances of action were accepted implicitly. There were no follow up newspaper reports and suggestions made during discussions with the solicitor that the minister and local member of parliament might be lobbied were not taken up. Similarly, the procedure suggested by Councillor Williams was not monitored by either of the parties involved. Mrs Montgomery was throughout very active on behalf of tenants yet also saw no contradiction in having informal talks with councillors and officers when she effectively briefed them on action contemplated by the committee. After such occasions Mrs Montgomery would claim that X or Y was 'really shook' by the revelation. It can be doubted if such was the case and indeed there was little cause; the Section 99 action was dropped because the two residents who were felt to have the best case were too uncertain of the implications and expressed a desire to withdraw. It would seem that the initial impetus is easily lost and once a constraint is imposed alternative channels are not explored. Thus even in dealing with a case which all parties would acknowledge to be well founded, the committee may still be unable to secure from officers and councillors remedies which residents would term satisfactory.

Parkview TA, an analysis

The existence of a TA on Parkview can be seen in part as a response to official overtures since it is council policy to foster TA's and part of Black's duties is to encourage their development. This support can be seen as one aspect of an overall policy to promote better consultation with tenants in order to develop an improved housing management service. There would also appear to be the assumption that TA's are 'a good thing' in that they may bring a sense of community into the artificially created neighbourhood of a council housing estate. The official objective to some degree accords with resident objectives and in part the continued functioning of the TA reflects the preparedness of at least some residents to actively promote an estate organization through participation on the TA committee.

It will already be clear that the working of the organization owes little to the formal charter which is its legitimizing base. This analysis therefore attempts to explain further the informal mechanisms; the recruitment of members to the committee and the nature of the political processes within the committee. References to other research findings attempt to set this case study in a broader perspective.

The numbers of residents attracted to TA committee work in the relatively short time scale of the research project were small and this makes it difficult to generalize about their characteristics. Reporting on the findings of a number of studies, York asserts that one consistent factor is that a higher proportion of men than women are members of voluntary associations and that this is particularly so of working class organizations. In all social classes men are particularly prominent up to the age of forty but thereafter women participate more. As might be expected men take part more in clubs and occupational associations while women tend to predominate in cultural and civic associations and community centres. Women members of whatever age or class, attend meetings more frequently than men.[26]

On the Parkview TA committee membership has been predominantly comprised of women. In the Lloyd and Mandle committees the main office holders were men and membership comprised approximately equal numbers of men and women. In the Field and Dee committees and the tower block group, women assumed the prominent positions and numerically were in a majority. However, there is some evidence that a more equal balance is considered desirable by residents and that the position of chairman is felt to be more appropriately filled by a man. Evidence from other studies in regard to age is less consistent and may be related to factors such as the age structure of the population. There is a general trend for the rate of participation to be low among young adults, thereafter rising to a peak in the forties and then declining. However, one study showed no difference in the proportion of younger and middle aged women and a lesser fall off after sixty.[27] Another study showed a difference in age according to type of organization.[28] On Parkview there is a greater age range among the women, from early thirties through to the seventies. This is accounted for by the fact that active participants include mothers with pre-school children, older working women with fewer family demands on their time and one woman of over seventy. With one exception the men have all been middle aged.[29]

As noted elsewhere and as might be expected the estate is socially fairly homogeneous. Nevertheless estate residents identify sub-groups which appear to have economic factors and status considerations as their basis. There are a small number of families with workers in the professional or intermediate job categories. There are a number of one parent families and families where there is a history of ill health or unemployment and consequently frequent dependence on Social Security benefits. Finally, there are approximately 81 households in various racial minority groups. Only one committee member has been drawn from any of these categories.[30]

Some researchers have suggested that participation in committee activity may be a function of social isolation.[31] There is no clear evidence that committee members tend to be socially isolated; indeed as noted some committee members are able to mobilize quite large personal support groups, often from outside the estate. However, other committee members have commented that prior to taking an interest in committee work their ties with other estate residents were very few.

Parkview politics may be characterized by the formation of unstable factions. It is difficult to account for the intensity of feeling that fuels the feuding. Undoubtedly there are personality clashes. More significantly the TA committee tends to be viewed by the leaders and some other members as an arena in which individuals and groups win or lose. Opposition groups are often described as 'getting the knives out' or 'stirring' in response to which counter groups will not be 'beaten' and 'go on fighting'. It is a model of ins and outs rather than a model of compromise and working to a consensus of opinion.

Possible explanations can be posited on the basis of the present and other findings drawn from similar studies of committee politics. First, the Parkview model of opposing groups is in direct contrast to the ideal of committee unanimity found in other studies. Secondly, mechanisms found elsewhere which moderate or contain such conflicts as do arise appear to be relatively ineffectual in the Parkview committee. Both factors are of course related.

Most committees from time to time consider issues which are contentious and in their deliberation potentially divisive. But alongside this may be set the ideal of preserving at least the appearance of harmony and agreement to work towards goals felt to be for the common good. Thus Barnes in his study of committees in a Norwegian parish noted that a common feature of the decision making process was a trial vote to establish which view had most support. There was then a confirming unanimous vote and only this would be recorded in the minutes. He raises the question of why the achievement of formally unanimous decisions should be considered so important.

People living and working together inevitably have conflicting interests but in general they have also a common interest in the maintenance of existing social relations. Individual goals must be attained through socially approved processes, and as far as possible the illusion must be maintained that each individual is acting only in the best interests of the community. As far as possible, that is, the group must appear united, not only vis a vis other similar groups, but also to itself. Voting is a method of reaching decisions in which divergence of interest is openly recognized, and in which the multiplicities of divergence are forced into the Procrustean categories of Yes and No. Significantly, voting is rare in simple societies and in small groups of modern societies. Membership in a collectivity implies accepting a share in the collective responsibility for the group's actions as well as a share in the decision to act in a certain way.[32]

Nevertheless, of course, conflicts may still occur. Frankenberg describes committees in a small Welsh village where membership did not consist of isolated individuals but of groups linked by kinship or other ties. Members of these groups tended to vote together, and in the event of a dispute, resign together. The dispute might thus be resolved in the committee by resignation or less dramatically by the non-attendance of dissident members but the arguments generally continued in the village and sometimes reappeared in later committees.[33] In such instances, however, conflict can be defused by the operation of mechanisms built into the social structure of the committee.

First, a scapegoat mechanism may be provided by the use of outsiders in nominally important positions. In the Welsh committees 'strangers' were elected to such key positions as chairman. This provided a scapegoat and allowed local people to maintain ongoing multiplex social relations on a tolerable basis. A different type of scapegoat mechanism may be allowed by a confusion of rôles and an absence of committee rules. Wheeldon describes how this works in voluntary association committees among Cape Coloureds.

Executive members of associations who have to make decisions which they know will not be universally popular tend to be deliberately vague both about the matter at issue, and the decisions taken ... committee decisions are long and often difficult to follow; a vote is seldom taken, it is frequently almost impossible to ascertain, at the meeting, what decision has in fact been reached (though this may be interpreted afterwards in private); minutes may be obscure or non existent; members frequently absent themselves from meetings which they fear will be acrimonious ... In such situations there is continual confusion about who has been invited to attend a particular meeting; what time the meeting is to be held; when it is to be held; what is on the agenda; whether an agenda was sent out at all, or in time; whether those who attend are merely representatives or observers; whether they have the right to vote; or whether their views are binding on the association from which they came. Committees are also frequently perfectly willing to abandon, reinterpret or reverse their own earlier decisions. The effect of this obscurity is to expand the range of choices open to the committee as a whole, and to individuals and factions in it. Conflicts are not allowed to emerge explicitly, and differences of opinion may then be publicly interpreted as 'mistakes' or 'misunderstandings'.[34]

Secondly, the existence of cross-cutting ties between members has a further modifying effect. In the Norwegian experience, for example, a man is a member of a household, hamlet, ward and parish and may belong to a missionary working party, a bull owning co-operative or a fishermen's association. At different times and in different places membership of one or other of these groups is relevant in defining what he does and in what manner he expresses his personal loyalties.[35] It has been claimed that the existence of cross-cutting ties of this kind prevents the intensification of hostilities within and between groups.

Overlapping conflicts that recurrently regroup the community into opposing factions along different lines prevent its division into two antagonistic camps that come to take opposite stands on virtually every issue as a matter of principle. The likely results of such a split into two antagonistic camps would be that grievances become cumulative and reinforce each other, hostilities grow more and more intense, and there is increasing social pressure to the effect that any means is justified to vanquish the enemy, which is the very orientation that is incompatible with the survival of democratic institutions. Cross pressures, finally, lessen partisan involvement, incline individuals to arbitrate controversies, and make conflicts generally less severe.[36]

All mechanisms may be invoked singly or together in varying circumstances at different times in the same committee.

In various ways each of these studies documents an ideal of unanimity in committee politics. The reality is at variance with that norm and, in order to approach the ideal consensus model, mechanisms have been developed to reduce conflicts within the committee organization to a tolerable level. Many of the traits outlined here are present in the Parkview TA but the extent to which they are used to reduce the level of conflict would appear to be limited. There is, for example, a confusion of rôles and rules in committee procedure but this is not to my knowledge used to explain 'mistakes'. Scapegoats are provided by 'opposition' committee leaders or ex-leaders and their supporters, and by outsiders such as officers and councillors. These scapegoats may be useful in explaining the apparent weakness of the committee to non-active resident supporters; they do not appear to reduce tensions within the committee. Finally, while on most committees members acknowledged no ties apart from committee membership there would appear to be some potential for the restructuring and realignment of groups on the basis of, say, place of residence (the older parts of the estate and the garden flats), 'philosophies' (the varying emphases which might be given to welfare and social work as opposed to the representation of resident grievances), identification with Old Borough residents as opposed to outsiders and the definition of male and female rôles. In fact these regroupings seldom occurred and appeared to little modify personal responses to specific situations. The explanation may be that in contrast to the Norwegian committee, the Parkview groupings have no significance for personal relations outside the committee arena. Parkview conflicts are so openly expressed because there is less need to validate an ideal of unanimity.[37] Unlike the other situations described Parkview residents do not sustain ongoing and intensive social relations with each other on a day to day basis. As already indicated the estate does not constitute a socially cohesive neighbourhood and egocentric networks extending beyond its boundaries are more central to the social life of most residents including those most concerned about estate affairs and involved through membership of the Parkview TA committee. In these circumstances leaders have no real power base on the estate. Furthermore, they have few benefits to confer on potential supporters and what rewards they can offer are attainable from elsewhere. The result is a weak organization, lacking roots within the estate and divided within itself.

Parkview and the council: four case studies

What follows is an attempt to outline in more detail something of the nature of the relationship between residents on Parkview, officers of the housing management section of the directorate of housing, and in two instances, councillors. For this purpose I have selected what may be termed case studies, each providing a different context and illustrating different aspects of the interconnections between the various participants. The first, the case of the Steel's radio aerial, looks at the response of officers to what they would regard as an individual problem case; case ii describes how an informal pressure group developed among residents concerned to take over gardens for themselves; the third illustrates the officer and member response to conflict within and between groups on the estate; and case iv outlines the negotiations between the TA and the council prior to the handing over to the committee of management responsibility for a new community hall.

Case i   The Steel's radio aerial
The Steel family have a ground floor maisonette in one of the garden flats. Steel is Jamaican, his wife English and they have three young children. One of Steel's hobbies is radio listening, he has an impressive array of equipment for short wave reception and especially enjoys tuning in to stations in the West Indies. Somewhat dissatisfied with reception on the estate, Steel purchased an outdoor aerial. At that point the family asked for my reassurance and explained that they did not intend asking the council for permission to fix the aerial to the building because they expected to meet with a refusal; instead they would act, plead ignorance and then perhaps begin to negotiate. On 21 January, a few days after the aerial had been put up I was stopped by several caretakers, 'Looking for a place to hang your washing out luv?' 'Terrible isn't it', 'What do they want that for, they've got a TV aerial'. One caretaker declared Steel's action 'malicious damage to council property. He's gone straight through the wall with that, wait till the guv'nor see's it'. In fact the first official response was not until 20 February when Gray, the Parkview manager called and asked that the aerial be removed. Steel's response was to write to the director of housing, Brown.

I am just writing this letter of explanation concerning an aerial that I have erected just above my sitting room window. First may I say that the aerial in question is not a TV aerial but in fact it is an aerial for receiving radio.
I would also like to add that at the time I was constructing this piece of apparatus I was in full

view of porters on the estate and at no time at all did any one of them say that I was breaking any contract between myself and the council.

I would also like to add that I'm prepared to remove the equipment and make good the damage to the wall, which I must say is very minor and can be put right with 2 wall plugs.

I would also be grateful if you would be kind enough to grant me permission to install this piece of equipment on the roof, where it is inconspicuous.

I would now like to explain the reason that this aerial is so important to me, I am at present a part time student at [a technical correspondence school] in Berkshire where I'm taking a course in radio and electronics with a hope of eventually bettering myself and family and this aerial is of considerable importance to my studies. Once again I apologise for any trouble I may have caused but I hope that I have satisfied you with my intentions.[38]

Receipt of this letter was acknowledged with a note that it was being handled by Gray's superior Green. A few weeks later Steel's received a notice to quit the flat by 14 April. No reason for the notice was given and Steel alleged that they had received no prior warning. On enquiry they were advised that the threatened action was on account of arrears of rent. Steel claimed that the arrears were caused by the council's failure to notify them of an adjustment to their rent rebate.[39]

On 21 March they received from Black a reply to their earlier letter:

... I regret I am unable to grant consent for the aerial which you have fixed to the structure of the block to remain. Whilst I appreciate your difficulties I cannot consider granting permission for the installation of such an aerial as this is against council policy.

Would you please therefore remove the aerial and make good any damage caused to the fabric of the building.

A few weeks later the Steel's were visited by Gray who confirmed that the aerial would have to come down. He also admitted that the matter had been taken up because of a written complaint. Mrs Steel commented to me that she suspected that the report was made by a particular council employee. He was, she alleged, prejudiced against blacks. Perusal of the file shows that Mrs Steel was correct in her accusation of this employee though I cannot comment on his motivation. Steel considered that Gray was critical of a council tenant having a lot of expensive radio equipment.

On 25 April they received a second letter from Black, this time setting out three complaints against the family; arrears of rent, failure to remove the aerial and encouraging their children to flout a caretaker's order not to ride bicycles around the green. The letter threatened that the matter would be handed over to the Borough Solicitor if the causes for complaint were not removed by 28 April. Mrs Steel visited the housing directorate officers the following Monday and was ushered before Black. He told her to forget the charge about the children, accepted her assurance that the aerial had been removed and gave her until Friday to clear the arrears of £50.[40]

After this Steel ordered an aerial which could be fixed to a pole in the garden. He considered that this did not contravene regulations since he could not be charged with damaging the structure of a council building. Some months later the garden suddenly sprouted a radio aerial.

In December on a return visit to the estate I noticed that the aerial had been removed. Mrs Steel explained that they had been visited by Black and told to remove the aerial or face eviction. Black further advised them to apply for a transfer to a property where it would be possible to have an aerial. He gave no reasons for the injunction and they complied.

Throughout this series of incidents Mrs Steel was convinced they were being 'got at'. She had most direct meetings with officers, at times when faced with threats of eviction she got very upset, and her behaviour was probably regarded as aggressive. Steel interpreted the events as yet another instance of the strange inhumanity he considers to be characteristic of English society. By the officers involved in the case the family were no doubt seen as troublesome tenants.

Case ii   Picket fencing and potatoes[41]

Residents allocated ground floor maisonettes in the garden flats found that a main pathway ran in front of their home about 12 ft from the front door. A short path connected each front door to the main pathway and on either side there was a small plot of ground, on one side overlooked by the kitchen window and on the other by the living room. Residents claim that it was not made clear at the time of the offer whether or not these areas were part of their tenancy but they assumed that in fact their private boundary extended to the footpath. They considered this assumption was reasonable; the path provided a natural demarcation line, the areas were not planted, and without some form of control over them residents felt their privacy was invaded by curious youngsters peering through ground level windows and themselves threatened by cyclists cutting corners in careering round the blocks.

In February 1974, residents from the first block to be occupied wrote to the council asking that consideration be given to fencing the garden plots. They received a reply from White, the assistant director, later that month.

... I am afraid I cannot deal with the land fronting your premises in isolation. The gardens are part of the general landscaping of the Estate and the Council would be faced with the possible task of fencing all similar patches of land around other blocks, which would be quite impracticable. I regret, therefore, that I cannot accede to your request and must also point out that these gardens are not part of your tenancy and will be maintained as are other grass areas by the Council's Parks Department.

Nevertheless garden development continued. In mid May when the field study was being planned, I accompanied Black on a visit to the estate and he made notes of residents with gardens. He claimed that a warning had already been given and that further action would have to be taken. Accordingly a number of residents received the following letter.

It has come to my notice that you have fenced off a part of the grass area in front of your flat and are using the same as an individual garden. This land is not included in your tenancy and those verges are part of the landscaping of the estate. I must therefore ask you to remove the fence and make good the grass. The estate caretakers have been instructed to inform me should you ignore this letter.[42]

At this point residents with an interest in the gardens started meeting among themselves and with the ward councillors. Other councillors also became involved and Lloyd and another prominent tenant representative on the North Board, Mrs Ruble, took an interest in the case. As a result Councillor Williams wrote to White to clarify a number of points and Mrs Montgomery who lived in one of the garden flats, organized a petition. Councillor Williams phrased his query in general terms and claimed the issue.

... concerns a tenant's understanding of what is in his tenancy agreement and what is not, or to be more particular, in this case whether they can take action on something that is not specified in the tenancy agreement. I was told by certain of the relevant tenants that they believed that the gardens came as part of the ground floor flat tenancies. However, when they enquired about this at the Estates Office which was on the site when the flats were first tenanted, they say they were given no definitive answer on this point and thereafter decided to go ahead with the laying out of their own gardens. It is not a matter of excusing what the tenants have done, rather a question of whether the advice they were given at the estate office was sufficiently clear and definitive ...

In both instances the replies were not encouraging. Councillor Williams was informed that tenants seek advice from all manner of people on site and such information might not be correct. 'The areas in front of the flats were intended as shrub beds to eventually provide a degree of privacy, though the Parks Department now consider that they should have been grassed and shrubbed as you suggest, to discourage the sort of annexation that has taken place'.[43] Mrs Montgomery was advised that tenants had not been granted permission to make gardens. (Plate 41)

We are faced with the prospect of all sorts of fencing being erected, some of it very unsightly, and some people have been growing large vegetables (sic) on this land. During its early days every estate is liable to be untidy and messy particularly when further building is going on, but the situation is not helped by tenants taking the law into their own hands and deliberately contravening their Conditions of Tenancy.[44]

However, this letter did add that Black would be prepared to meet with tenant representatives for further discussions. In fact that was hardly necessary; at the same time as these letters were written, Black briefed the Director of Housing for a general meeting called with all tenants on the estate. 'I am prepared to climb down and let them have the gardens but I have to go through the motions of meeting their reps and have written accordingly.'

Some three weeks later an official letter to a councillor stated that tenants would be allowed to cultivate and fence gardens. There was a rider '... I have requested the tenants association to try and keep these in some sort of order'. On the estate 'order' was interpreted as meaning the standardization of fencing and this was believed to be a condition of the approval. There appears to have been no official instruction to this effect although Mrs Field told me that she understood a special meeting of the council had decided that all fences should be the same. Accordingly, Davidson purchased timber and with TA approval built a fence as a model for everybody else to follow. Some residents/by that time had already made different types of fencing—Montgomery's had a white picket fence, another resident a light hoop iron fence painted green. These were changed to rail fences all painted white. The opinion of some residents was that uniformity enhanced the appearance of the blocks. Davidson commented that all the fences should be the same so that the whole block would look 'nice.' Others resented the loss of individuality and in one block, at that time inconspicuous beside the corrugated iron fence which surrounded the playground, residents made different types of fences, two painted brown, three fixed gates as well and the fourth planted a hedge.

At that stage the growing of vegetables was still not allowed. Only two residents both West Indians, had planted vegetables. One was Steel. He felt it was perfectly reasonable to plant vegetables in front of the kitchen and flowers in front of the living room. Residents continued to believe that vegetable growing was 'illegal' but official objections were no longer maintained.

There is a sequel to this case. In April 1975 during a special meeting of tenants at which officers and councillors were present one resident asked for permission to fix a front gate to her garden in order to make it a safe playing area for her small children. White refused saying that the council could not permit structures of any kind on council property; 'the next thing we know people will be asking to put up a shed!' He added that since she had decided to have children it was her responsibility to look after them. As noted above, other residents had already fitted gates and shortly afterwards Councillor Mackie called privately on the questioner and told her to 'go ahead'.

While talking to people on the estate about the case it became clear that all residents felt the idea of private gardens was a good one. Inevitably because there had been a policy of having all open space tended by the Parks Department, some ground floor flats were allocated to people with little or no interest in gardening and some upper flats to keen gardeners.[45] This was reflected in the varying amount of care lavished on the gardens. By the end of the fieldwork period most were carefully planted, (See Plates 4 and 41) but some few remained unfenced and unkempt. Subsequently, most officers in housing management gradually accepted the fact of tenant involvement in this way. Indeed the practice has gained official approval. Fencing, paid for by the council, has since my departure from the estate, been placed so as to provide gardens for the occupants of bedsitters in one of the older blocks.[46] Other officers remained opposed. One from the parks section of Leisure and Recreation considered there would be a waning of interest and with changes of tenancy an unsightly patchwork effect would develop. He further claimed that parks labourers would resent being told to take over at that stage. Councillors and others showing visitors around point to the gardens with pride and one resident went so far as to say 'they've made the place beautiful, its like being in the country luv'.

The development of Eshag as an estate based community group has been discussed elsewhere[47] and this account is concerned only to outline the conflicts which the group aroused and particularly the reactions of outside parties to it.

In September 1974 a general progress report on the author's overall project was sent to Brown, Councillor Mackie, Councillor Harty and the three ward councillors. This report included comments on the need for experimentation into the forms of organization which might be appropriate for tenant involvement in management and suggested the establishment of a group based on one of the tower blocks. As a follow-up to expressions of dissatisfaction with the living environment provided by the tower blocks, it was proposed that my assistant Don would see if there was any preparedness among residents to join a group set up to discuss what might be done, and then seek to implement plans should any be decided upon. The report stressed the need for assurances from the council that such proposals would be favourably received. At this point and subsequently informal discussions were held with Brown and he gave assurances of good intent.

During the last two weeks in November residents in one of the tower blocks were contacted and general support obtained for the setting up of a discussion group on how to improve the base of the block. Thereafter a series of meetings were held, most attended by six or seven residents. In total 17 residents from the block attended at least one meeting and throughout the group attempted to report back to all 68 households by letter, questionnaires and door to door canvassing. The group decided its priorities after a few meetings and called on an architect to draw up plans for altering the base of the block so as to incorporate a nursery and laundry facility.

Towards the end of January the group was ready to put proposals to the council and decided to do so by inviting councillors to a meeting. Those invited were Councillor Harty as vice chairman of housing and the three ward councillors. Councillor Harty assumed the rôle of spokesman for the councillors and without allowing for discussion of items on the agenda, immediately dismissed outright the plans for altering the block. The reason given was lack of funds. It was agreed that requests regarding minor faults and outstanding repairs would be looked into. At this point, not surprisingly, members of the group felt that they had been misled into thinking that some genuine consideration would be given to their proposals and Don explained what assurances had been given. It was clear that none of the councillors present appreciated the signficance of the iterim report; nor had they had any discussion with Brown. Councillor Harty closed the meeting by asking the group to report to the TA. This they refused to do.

On 6 February Don and myself met with Councillor Mackie and Councillor Harty in an attempt to explain the situation more fully. Councillor Mackie claimed that the whole scheme was totally impracticable. Perhaps more importantly, he added that if the group was successful there would be all manner of other groups springing up. He considered that would be undesirable; all activity on the estate should be channelled through one organization. Councillor Harty considered it significant that the group had refused to report to the TA. During this meeting Concillor Mackie instructed Black to have no dealings with tenants on the estate. A short time later a similar meeting was held between myself, Don and Black. He appeared to be unperturbed either by developments on the estate or by the chairman's instructions but he too commented that only a single estate organization would work.

These meetings did little to assuage the fears of councillors and others interested in estate politics because Eshag continued to meet. They corresponded with and received replies from White in connection with outstanding complaints and on 26 March met with a senior officer from the DLBO. Lloyd attended this meeting as North Board representative and the group invited representatives from the other tower block including ex TA committee member Lessor to join them. The same officer attended a second meeting to which Black also had been invited. He initially accepted but in the event did not attend. The group considered they were achieving small piece-meal successes in remedying defects and determined to continue. These developments were viewed by the Field faction as the coalescence of disaffected ex TA groupings around the leadership of Lloyd. The Field faction saw the Eshag faction as direct competition; rivals seeking acknowledgement of a legitimacy of status before the council. Eshag members saw themselves as pursuing matters which were peculiar to the tower blocks. They viewed the development of the group as a natural outgrowth of the planning exercise and themselves as in no way constituting a threat to the TA. There were no open encounters between the two parties but accusations and counter accusations were made by both sides and individuals met with councillors to explain their version of the situation. Outsiders apart from councillors became involved. Mrs Ruble complained bitterly that what had taken 10 years of her life to build up was now being destroyed. Councillors made similar allegations against the project and the affair was discussed by the North Board.

At a committee meeting on 2 April the Field group raised the question of Mrs Dee's eligibility as Eshag spokesman to attend meetings of the Borough's Federation of TAs. Mrs Field advised writing to the Federation along the lines that Mrs Dee had no claim to be a representative of any recognized group; Eshag was a few people resident in the block and concerned about the waste disposal system, it was a breakaway group and members had been told by councillors that all complaints must go through the TA. A week later the Housing Services Committee met and Councillor Mackie commented in the course of a debate that there had been many problems among the tenants of Parkview and that there was still a good deal of tension. There had, he said, been 'ghastly carryings on' and there had been 'breakaway groups' (sic) but there was only one recognized group, the TA, in existence. Councillor Harty stressed that the only people the committee could properly deal with were the officers of the association.

After the TA elections, as has already been noted, Eshag and the rump TA committee combined in a single committee. In fact this committee comprised two main factions and there was no sign of the feud abating. Eshag members felt they had an interest in continuing as a separate group as long as they had outstanding grievances. Accordingly they continued to meet, sent letters to the council under the group name and received replies in due course. Predictably, this encountered opposition from the Field group. Eshag members countered with the argument that the Field faction continued to function as the effective TA committee. Meetings were characterized by bitter discussions in exchanges which tended to be seen as power struggles between protagonists. On 21 June Mrs Field reported that Councillor Mackie had phoned to say that hence-forth all requests for repairs should go through the TA. This was conveyed to the next meeting where it was accepted by the one group as a clear validation of their position and rejected by the other as an attempt to deprecate their success. At the time the field work ended it was clear that this conflict would not easily be resolved; the breakup of the committee seemed imminent.

Case iv   The policy making process; a community centre for the estate.
The three case studies outlined so far have all concerned what may be termed dispute cases. The present case, although it includes disagreements, is somewhat different and describes the rôles and actions of officers, councillors and TA committee members in their attempt to work out the terms on which the new community hall might be transferred to residents. It is thus concerned with the processes of consultation, negotiation and decision making rather than with dispute settlement.

The architect's intention throughout the planning of the Parkview estate was to create a community and his design incorporated, as a focus for community activity, a centre for the use of estate residents. The original scheme was shelved, however, when plans incorporating a neighbourhood community centre were drawn up for the redevelopment of the nearby shopping centre of the Old Borough. Later, largely in response to pressures on the ward councillors by Lloyd and Mrs Ruble, the Parkview proposals were revived and the Lloyd committee gave its approval to plans for a centre at a meeting in June 1973. When field work commenced it was expected that the community hall would be completed during 1975.

In September, while construction work was still going on, I visited the hall with a TA committee member. Basically the centre is a multi-purpose one, with a main hall to seat approximately 150 persons, two smaller rooms, one designed with a bar/servery facility, the other intended for committee meetings, and an office, store and toilet facilities. The main room is one and a half storeys in height and the two smaller rooms overlook that from the upper level. On this visit a recurring controversy first became apparent; throughout the building stage members of the Lloyd committee claimed that the centre as built was quite different from the plans to which they gave approval. There is no evidence of any changes and it appears that the committee misread the plans. The split level effect and the height of the auditorium were not appreciated and actual dimensions of the building were considered to be smaller than those agreed to originally.[48] This issue came up periodically but more attention focused on two other issues, the furnishing of the hall and the terms of the proposed transfer of management responsibility to tenants.

Towards the end of the year, an interior decorator from the borough architect's department, called at the project flat to discuss the question of finishing touches to the hall. She had not been instructed to consult with tenants; I suggested that it would certainly be advisable to do so. The committee met that evening and I reported that they could shortly expect an approach from a council officer in connection with deciding the furnishing of the hall. The effect was unexpectedly dramatic. One member commented '. . . now you tell us some council official is coming to tell us what colours to paint our bloody hall'. Another claimed that if tenants were not given the hall on their own terms they would tear the place apart brick by brick. The furore turned out to be somewhat premature and was defused by the confusion of subsequent events.

A few days later the job architect called to say that the interior decorator had been given the job to keep her occupied and that consultation with tenants should not be done directly by architects but through housing management staff. Thereafter the committee heard all manner of conflicting reports on the source and amount of money available and on the use which could be made of it. Lloyd reported that there was a grant of £2575 but it was already committed since his committee had decided to spend it on office furniture and kitchen fitments and equipment. In mid-May the interior decorator again contacted me and said that she had been reallocated the task of furnishing the hall. She was referred to the committee and invited to a meeting on 22 May. The committee held lengthy discussions on the type and quantity of furniture needed and raised several practical questions. The officer reported that the sum of £3000 was available for spending on the hall and that she was there to advise them. She was unable to say whether the committee would be allowed to use the money on second hand furniture, or on equipment rather than furnishings, but agreed that items like a microphone and speakers would be appropriate, promised to investigate queries further, obtain firm quotations and report back. A week later Mrs Montgomery reported that Black had requested a meeting with the committee to discuss the furnishing of the hall. He expressed surprise that another official approach had already been made, claimed that the funds available amounted to £2500 and that spending would be allowed only on hard furniture. Black attended the committee meeting of 5 June. There were further lengthy discussions in the course of which Black accepted orders for curtains and crockery as well as for standard items of furniture like tables and chairs. Black stressed that they did not have to make a firm decision at that meeting;

his intention was to give the purchasing officer some idea of what was wanted and he could then arrange a meeting between the purchasing officer and the committee so that they could finalize details like colours and quantities. This was agreed to. In the event no such meeting took place. The choice of curtain material, paint for woodwork surfaces and floor tiles was made by the interior decorator. Black ordered all the other items through the purchasing officer. Furthermore it would seem that Black decided that expenditure should be confined to furniture and fittings on the basis that if the committee purchased equipment out of their own funds they would appreciate it more and take better care of its maintenance. In due course the committee accepted delivery as items came to hand. In some cases the specifications were quite different from those decided upon in committee.[49] The committee was given no record of orders placed or of costs of purchases.

A second major issue which involved the committee in negotiations with both officers and councillors was the working out of the terms under which the TA might assume management responsibility for the hall. When the matter first came up for serious consideration in January 1975, it was apparent that committee members found the question a confusing one. Accordingly I sent to all committee members a letter outlining some of the issues and accompanied by preliminary findings from the research on user demand for the hall. This letter was never considered officially by the committee although members spoke about it among themselves and one member reported my involvement to Black.[50] He took the view that the estate hall should follow the precedents set by similar facilities in the Borough, viz, that it should be handed over to tenants for a nominal rental and the tenants should then 'be left to get on with it'.[51] Black subsequently arranged a meeting in his office with members of the Mandle committee together with Lloyd as North Board representative. Mrs Field later reported that she felt the arrangements had been decided upon prior to the meeting and that the committee was simply acting as a 'rubber stamp'. From this meeting it emerged that the rent would be fixed by the council and the TA would be responsible for repairs, maintenance and cleaning. Details of the terms of the transfer were not considered and the meeting developed into an argument on the use of the hall.[52]

At about the same time I had informal discussions with Brown and raised the question of an official policy regarding the management of community facilities. He was at the time unaware that Black had made any arrangements with Parkview residents. Shortly afterwards the project team had a meeting with Councillor Mackie and Councillor Harty. They too disclaimed any knowledge of Black's negotiations with the residents, instructed him to restrain from further dealings and signified their own intention to intervene.

The situation for the committee was complicated by the fact that among the councillors there was a lobby which was pressing for the hall to be a broadly based community facility rather than a centre exclusive to the estate. Committee members were worried by this development and determined to fight for an estate club. They had a supporter in Black on this issue. He claimed that the original brief was for a Parkview hall and the architects' notes would support this view. He opposed changing the user group on the grounds that the residents understood the hall would be exclusively for their use and if it was not they would have no means of controlling who came onto the estate.

This was the position when Councillor Mackie instructed Mrs Field to call a meeting of her committee to discuss with Councillor Harty, the ward councillors and himself the whole question of the hall. Mrs Field requested that Black also be invited but Councillor Mackie refused. The committee met with the councillors on 13 February. The meeting opened with allegations from members that Lloyd was still a powerful force in negotiations over the hall despite the fact that he had resigned from the committee. The councillors made some attempt to clarify the situation and Councillor Mackie denied that Lloyd's attempt to dissolve the committee had been officially sanctioned. There was then a lengthy discussion on the need to call an AGM and have elections so that the legitimacy of the committee would be established. Some committee members claimed that it would be unfair to expect a newly elected committee to cope with the hall and proposed postponing elections until after its opening. The councillors pressed for an early AGM.

Discussion then turned to the status of the hall. Councillor Mackie claimed that it was a hall which must be made available for public lettings. Mrs Montgomery argued that it was a club room and commented '... I think that if tenants are told it's not for Parkview this will cause the biggest stink'. Councillor Mackie added that they would need to consider the question of rent and implied that unless the hall was widely used they would not be able to afford it. Under questioning he said 'It will be high. An economic rent and management will devolve on you and you do what you want. You must use it for revenue raising functions'. This statement led to further arguments from residents which Councillor Mackie countered by saying that the hall was 'built out of revenue, out of ratepayers' money and all have some rights to it'. Pressed still further Councillor Mackie said they would need to think in terms of a rent of £50 or £60 a week. Other possibilities, including a 50/50 agreement between the TA and the council, and the setting up of a hall management committee, were mentioned but not considered, in the course of discussion. Councillor Mackie reiterated his statement on the need for a general meeting to put the question before all tenants. He said that one of the councillors would arrange a booking for a nearby hall, the council would print and distribute letters and he himself would take the chair. Councillor Harty suggested that the agenda for the meeting should include a report from the present committee, an election of officers and a discussion on the hall. Councillor Mackie said that the hall should be discussed first so that people knew quite clearly what they were voting for. He promised to obtain all the relevant facts and report back prior to the general meeting. On this basis the committee consented to the calling of a general meeting.

After the councillors had left the committee agreed that the aim of Councillor Mackie and Councillor Harty had been to frighten them. There was some talk on the range of tactics now open to the committee. Montgomery suggested that one way would be to say to the council 'OK, we don't want it, you look after it'. Mrs Montgomery and Mrs Glenn said that if Lloyd was elected they would resign. Mrs Field said that very likely they could take over the hall and simply pay what they felt they could afford to pay; she considered it unlikely that the council could or would do anything if payments were in fact only token.

Shortly before the elections Councillor Mackie indicated to Mrs Montgomery that the hall would be let to the committee at an economic rental rebated to what they could afford to pay. As noted above, the elections were held and Councillor Mackie took the chair. He gave a few facts and made assurances about the hall but there was no discussion of the issue prior to the elections. Following the elections, during its first few months, the Dee committee paid little attention to the management issue. Other questions took up the committee's time, delays in the last stages of the building of the hall were innumerable and the committee itself was rift by division. Even when work on the hall was completed it took months to arrange an adequate insurance cover and the opening was delayed longer than necessary. At this stage committee members expressed the view that officers were a party to the delays because they were opposed to handing the hall over to a divided committee. However, in an interview, Councillor Mackie made it clear that the council did not want to manage the hall themselves; he intended meeting the committee and 'offering' them the management on a six-month trial basis. Shortly afterwards that meeting took place. Mrs Dee handed Councillor Mackie a letter in which she said that because of divisions on the committee she did not feel she could accept responsibility for the hall. She suggested it be run as a public hall on a market letting basis. She then threatened to walk out from the meeting but was persuaded by Councillor Mackie to remain. Other committee members asked if they could discuss the hall. Councillor Mackie's reply was unequivocal. 'There's nothing to discuss; it's yours'. The keys were handed over on 3 October.[53]

Parkview and the council; an overview
It will be apparent, both from these case studies and the account of the TA, that most encounters between residents and officers, residents and councillors and residents and mixed groups of officers and councillors take place in confrontation-type situations. This is so even when as at a general meeting some councillors may choose to identify themselves with tenants by sitting in the body of the hall. And even where the interaction takes the form of an attempt to negotiate an agreement the controls on the discussion and the outcome are always determined by the response of the officer or councillor in attendance. Moreover, in any one situation, groups like the TA committee or individual households like the Steel's may have contact with a considerable number of persons all adopting somewhat different rôles. Here an attempt is made to

describe some of the attitudes which shape the rôles played out in meetings between residents, officers and councillors.

The rôle of the resident in dealings with officialdom is typically minimal and clearly circumscribed. This is partly a consequence of a subordination which is a compound of perceived and actual powerlessness and a lower social status. Residents tend to be uncertain about the rôles and powers of officers and councillors. There is no clear understanding of the domains appropriate to either group. The functions of officers in different departments and of officers and councillors appear to overlap. This might possibly have the advantage of allowing tenants some scope for manoeuvre to their own advantage but in fact, given the apparent lack of communication between officers within the same and different departments and between officers and councillors, the result appears to be the duplication of effort with attendant frustrations for tenants. The negotiations over the hall provide a striking example.

Uncertainty in dealing with officialdom, for resident activists, may well be accentuated by a lack of credibility which they see attaching to their own position as a result of outside action. TA members may be told a series of contradictory statements in regard to say the opening of the hall or the expected completion date for remedial work in flats affected by the dampness. This information may be received from a variety of sources and then passed on to other residents either in response to queries or spontaneously. The fact that the information may turn out to be wrong or misleading is hardly the fault of the member but undoubtedly reflects badly on his status as broker for the estate in dealing with the council. In addition, officers and councillors frequently promise specific courses of action, which, for whatever reason, are not followed through. Black signified his intention to call a meeting of the committee and the purchasing officer so that details for the furnishing of the hall could be finalised. Councillor Williams proposed monitoring the response of officers to TA representations. In the event both Black and Councillor Williams failed to carry out their intentions.

Perhaps not surprisingly, the resident reaction to encounters with representatives of both the officer and councillor groups may be one of hostility. Most often this hostility is expressed outside the encounter itself. The Steels were sure of themselves and their rights in discussion with me and spoke of taking legal advice; in the face of threatened sanctions from officers Mrs Steel broke down and they quickly complied. Now they talk of exposing the handling of the case by taking the story to a local newspaper when they have been rehoused. TA committee members both in meetings and privately brashly assert how they will take a 'hard line' with officers and councillors; after meetings it is asserted that there was little alternative to agreement and plans for the next confrontation are gone over with a renewed determination to hold out for desired ends. Hostility in this context may, however, be lessened according to the tenants' evaluation of personal worth—a councillor or officer who is considered to be genuinely concerned about tenants will be exempted from unfavourable comment even if his or her actions are seen not to be effective.

As noted, residents involved in committee work may well share these hostile feelings but their expression is likely to be tempered by other considerations. Committee members often have contact with other residents in regard to complaints about the council. In dealing with such complaints the committee member generally has little relevant knowledge on which to draw, limited access to sources of information, and no command over resources. The committee member therefore acts as an intermediary and refers the complaint to an officer or councillor. He or she may also attempt to exert pressure on behalf of the complainant. Over time part of the status of a committee member will be seen to derive from an ability to gain access to a system external to the estate and at least on occasion to thereby appear to contribute to a 'successful' remedy. Success is not always, however, obtained and for the committee member the officer and councillor are at once reference points and scapegoats. It is difficult to measure how much status (or odium) attaches to this form of identification but that there is this aspect to TA work is tacitly acknowledged by such statements from committee members as 'He's only in it for the glory'. Status by association may at once confer prestige and lay the subject open to criticism. As Lloyd commented 'They all think we get something out of it. They say "And what do you get?". I always say "Nothing, not a penny", and their reply is "Well, you must be a mug then"'. Often such comments may be linked to suspicions residents entertain about committee members. Residents expressed the view to me that the best articles were 'kept back' at jumble sales, and 'it's not the points system you know, it's the pints system'. Disbelief that the motives of committee members might be altruistic, resentment at the slightest indication to the contrary, jealousy at 'perks' like invitations to a mayoral function, all combined to make the task of the committee member, especially the leaders, very difficult. In some cases the dilemmas so caused might be heightened by a perception of the council altered through committee experience. Simpson, for example, acknowledged that he felt more sympathetic towards officers and claimed that one of the main functions of the TA was to dispel the myth of council officers as tyrants.

Officers and councillors tend to adopt a similarly ambivalent stance in their relations with tenants. Black claims to value the work of the TA, in particular the sponsoring of social activities for residents. However, it is clear that a single unified estate organization dealing with non-controversial matters is the ideal model and the logical outcome of a policy of supporting TA's may not be acceptable. Strong pressure group organizations, political awareness and the emergence of factions, conflict over deeply felt issues, all these are unacceptable. Talk of a campaign against rent increases was deeply regretted by Black and put down to the influence of unrepresentative militants. On numerous occasions Black pointed to a TA on another estate in the Old Borough as a model for the Parkview TA to emulate. In fact this committee is relatively moribund on account of former splits and now functions mainly as an organizer of bingo evenings and as a booking agency for private lettings of a community hall.

In dealings with both resident groups and individuals some officers are concerned to maintain a certain social distance and to project an authoritative image. When the acknowledgement of a change in their own stance might be construed as 'losing face' officers refuse publicly to admit to such changes. Thus, privately in an interview, Black accepted that gardens might be fenced in a variety of ways and gardeners would be allowed to grow whatever they liked; he was not prepared to make a public statement to that effect.

The rôle of the estate based officer, the caretaker, should be considered in this context. Caretakers may act as reporters of tenant misdemeanours. They are, moreover, encouraged in this rôle. In his letter to tenants about the gardens, White noted that the caretakers had been asked to report on tenants who persisted in planting private gardens. At the same time caretakers may be neighbours or friends. Potentially they are in a situation of considerable rôle conflict and most caretakers attempt to minimize this by identifying closely with their employers and refusing to get involved in estate politics. Several of the caretakers commented to me how regrettable it was that the TA committee had heard about the visit of the North Board to the estate and ridiculed the demonstration in support of the petition. Other caretakers feel that they should be involved. The caretaker resident in the block requested and was granted permission to take part in the Eshag but when councillors intervened he was instructed to withdraw. Such actions serve to minimize rôle conflicts and identify the caretakers with the officer rather than the resident group.

Councillors also adopt an equivocal rôle. On occasion they will take up cases on behalf of tenants in opposition to officers. A striking instance of this is Councillor Mackie's visit to a resident to advise her that it would be in order to fix a gate to her garden after a senior officer had ordered the contrary. This kind of incident is discussed among the more aware residents and variously interpreted. In this instance several raised questions with me as to why the chairman of housing did not discountenance policies with which he did not agree and instruct officers accordingly. Residents asked whether the chairman of housing was 'above' the assistant director of housing or vice versa and interpreted the private deal as evidence of collusion; officers it was alleged grant councillors favours from time to time and in return councillors 'cover up' for their officers in public. Councillor Mackie's action may also be seen as reflecting something of the ambivalence which councillors display in responding to tenants. On the one hand they express a concern not to get involved in estate affairs and on the other they spend a great deal of time attending to quite minor matters and in doing so, often affect the direction of local political developments to a marked degree. Councillor Mackie, for example, spent much time in meetings with committee leaders and the committee itself in discussing arrangements for the hall, the election of a committee and the terms under which that committee might accept responsibility for the hall. His influence on development by virtue of this intervention was quite considerable.

Councillor intervention, like that of officers, is frequently designed to minimize conflicts among estate residents. This was most explicit in the response to Eshag. Councillors viewed the development as a threat to the existing TA and the possible proliferation of groups on the estate as undesirable. They attempted to subvert the group and incorporate it within a single officially recognized organization. Housing management officers followed councillor instructions in declining to attend meetings but they responded to written submissions in the usual way and officers in other departments in fact legitimized the status of the group by accepting invitations to meetings and responding to complaints.

Councillors, and to a lesser extent officers, may also attempt to personalize their relationship with residents by making personal visits to committee leaders, adjourning after meetings to a local pub or accepting invitations to estate functions, private parties and so on. This may be an effective means of increasing rapport but it may also lead to a confused understanding of private and public actions, and, with the rapid changes in leadership on the committee, to charges of bias and favouritism. This kind of involvement may be related to the councillors' concept of constituency work. Councillors see contact with TA's as fulfilling a large part of their constituency obligations on council estates and they assess the reactions of estate residents through what they regard as the effective filter of the TA committee. At the same time committee members attach a great deal of importance to their ability to call on ward councillors or the chairman or vice chairman of housing.

Finally, both councillors and officers filter and respond to approaches from TA committee members, and other residents often according to considerations quite apart from those of the immediate situation—a forthcoming debate in council chamber, or a personality clash in the area team for example. Furthermore, under the present set-up the maintenance of existing officer and member rôles depends on keeping the system under which they operate a closed one with access to it for tenants limited to those points of entry allowing mediation by the officer or councillor concerned. At the same time the officer attempts to make his mediation appear as open as possible because dealing with tenants provides him with his raison d'être and given the present policy of the housing directorate considerable importance may be placed on the 'successful' management of the estate TA. For the councillor, proof to the resident that he has more powerful points of personal intervention via the officer hierarchy may be viewed as sound politics. Perhaps not surprisingly both officer and councillor intervention, whether on behalf of the TA or individuals, tends to be viewed by tenants with considerable scepticism. Officers and councillors tend to be evaluated according to whether they are considered to be sincere in their motivation in assisting tenants rather than according to their apparent ability to get things done. For the rest officers are held to 'have things on' councillors and vice versa and the two groups together tend to be seen as constituting a more or less corrupt system which presents an impenetrable façade to the estate dweller.

Tenant participation in the Borough

This section begins by outlining the background to the Borough tenant participation scheme and the practice established in four years of operation. The North Board is then described with particular emphasis on recruitment to the board, the functioning of the board at formal meetings, and the views of participants and residents on the present and potential scope of board work. The North Board is then assessed in more general terms and set in the wider context of Part IV.

Official policy and practice
The first attempt to consult with tenants in local authority housing in the Borough came during the Conservative administration of 1968–71. The four area boards set up under this scheme did not include direct tenant representation but representatives from tenant organizations could meet with the boards to put forward their viewpoint. These boards were reconstituted by the incoming Labour ruling party following an election promise to include tenant representation on the boards. Accordingly at its meeting of 19 January 1972 the Housing Services Committee had before it a joint report from the Director of Operations, the Borough Treasurer and Director of Financial Services, and the Housing Manager White, on the reconstitution of the area boards. Their report suggested that the boards be established as sub-committees of the housing committee with the following terms of reference:

Part I
For recommendation to the Housing Committee:
Within the geographical limits from time to time established and subject to the authority delegated by the Council to the Housing Manager to consider matters of management and maintenance relating to the dwellings under the control of the Housing Committee and welfare of tenants thereof except:–
i. the allocation of tenancies and operation of the waiting lists:
ii. rent policy.

Part II
Delegated to the Housing Board:
To authorise the Housing Manager to incur expenditure within the sum set aside for this purpose for the Housing Board in the Committee's authorised annual revenue estimates being expenditure for the improvement and maintenance of the general amenity of Housing Estates.

The report recommended that the geographical boundaries of the boards remain unchanged; the four areas were clearly defined by major roads; they contained a fairly equal distribution of council property and the organization of housing management and maintenance services corresponded with the board areas.

The officers put forward four alternative means to secure tenant representation to the boards.

a.   To co-opt named tenants who might be known to the Council or
b.   To encourage the formation and growth of more individual Tenants' Associations for other estates or
c.   To promote a general Tenants' Association for the Borough as a whole or
d.   To promote Tenants' Associations which would be geographically co-terminous (sic) with the area boards. Thus on the present structure there would be 4 such Tenants' Associations.

They further commented that—

If the last alternative were to be preferred, we think the constitutions could be framed in such a way so as to ensure proper representation from all Council owned estates and acquired properties in each of the areas of the boards. The Housing Manager advises, however, that recently a number of Estates Associations have become very active and new ones have been established. Accordingly the establishment of 4 area associations appears not to be so practicable and it might be better to build upon the estate based Associations.

The officers noted that whichever solution was adopted the housing management officers within the new directorate would need to take a positive and active rôle in fostering associations. Suggested functions were the drafting of appropriate constitutions, assistance with meetings and general publicity and promotion. Thus 'active encouragement might be given by the administration but nevertheless one would hope that the Tenants' Associations themselves would develop a life and spirit of their own'. As regards the wider membership of the boards, the report pointed out that if their status was that of a subcommittee then two thirds of the members would need to be drawn from the local authority.[54]

In commenting on powers of expenditure the report noted that

The Housing Manager already has authority within the approved annual estimates to spend money on the sort of matters which the Area Housing Boards might be expected to consider. To give them a little more autonomy the Borough Treasurer and Director of Financial Services suggests that it might be possible to set aside an annual figure for each Board from the Housing Committee's approved annual estimates up to which amount the Housing Board could authorise the Housing Manager to incur expenditure on minor items.

This recommendation was approved in principle although the amount to be made available was left for further consideration.

Basically the committee accepted the other recommendations as well. The terms of reference and the boundaries of areas covered by each board were approved without change. It was decided that each board should comprise eight councillors and four co-opted tenant representatives. Two councillor places were filled ex officio by the Chairman and Vice Chairman of the Housing Services Committee. It was recommended that the Chairmen and Vice Chairmen of the Boards be drawn from that committee and noted that in filling other councillor places some allocation should be made on a ward basis. This provision was opposed by Conservative councillors on the grounds that opposition councillors were not necessarily assured of a seat on each of the four boards. As a result of opposition pressure a meeting of the Housing Services Committee in April 1972 decided to increase the councillor representation on two boards from eight to nine. This allowed for representation from each ward. However, in the other two areas where there are no opposition ward councillors Conservative and Liberal members continue to be excluded from board membership.

In regard to tenant members

In order that the Area Boards should begin to operate as soon as possible the committee indicated that tenants' representation should initially be invited from existing Tenants' Associations. In the long term it was hoped that new Tenants' Associations would be set up and representations would eventually be from Tenants' Associations whose areas would be co-terminous (sic) with those of the Area Boards.

The area board scheme has now been in operation for nearly four years and further comment with reference to this original framework can be made on the basis of their functioning in that time. Perhaps intentionally, the terms of reference of the boards were vaguely stated and matters considered within their competence were defined on an ad hoc basis. Thus, all board members appear to have accepted that issues concerning an individual tenant should not normally be taken up at board level. Matters of a general import were felt to be more appropriate. However, serious individual cases might be considered at the discretion of the chairman and of course outside the formal business of a meeting tenant representatives might raise particular questions with officers and councillors. Most issues taken up by the boards might be categorized as 'matters of management and maintenance relating to the dwellings under the control of the Housing Committee'. Matters concerning the 'welfare of tenants thereof' can and have been variously interpreted by different boards. The commitment and responsiveness of the individual chairman is probably important in this connection since the chairmen appear to be in a position to interpret and make a ruling on items put before the board.

At the time the boards were established two areas each had one active tenants' association and the remaining areas each had four associations. The description 'active' in this context apparently meant 'existing'. The committee's longer term aim was to foster area based tenants' associations. This seems never to have been followed up by officers or councillors and both have apparently opted to foster estate based organizations. At the same time it is not clear whether the development of the estate tenants' associations has been fostered specifically to create a grass roots platform for the area boards. Rather policy has been non interventionist; a stance exemplified by the procedures instituted to secure tenant representation.

Since the establishment of the first boards, annual elections for tenant representatives have been held. Shortly before an election all tenants in the area covered by the respective boards are circulated by means of an official letter and invited to attend a general meeting. Elections for the two boards in the north, and two in the south of the Borough take place at the same time in the same venue. Admission to these meetings is by production of a rent book. Nominations are called from the floor and there is no mechanism to ensure that representatives are members of estate tenants' associations even where these exist. Likewise, there are no provisions to ensure a fair geographical distribution of tenants representatives. It is therefore possible to have more than one representative drawn from the same estate. Officers and councillors are present at these general meetings and they suggest to the tenants that nominations and votes should be made with some regard to estate representation and in particular to ensure that the acquired property tenants are represented by a member. Nominees may be introduced to the meeting but they do not speak. Voting procedures have not been formally laid down. In practice, all tenants are issued with a slip of paper and instructed to record their votes for four nominees. Papers recording fewer names are held to be invalid. Counting is done on the spot by councillors and officers, with tenants called from the floor as scrutineers and the results are announced immediately.

When the establishment of the boards was being considered in committee the question as to whether they should have powers of expenditure was raised. In debate the sum of £500 per board was mentioned as a possible maximum sum allowed annually for minor items. In fact, as noted, the actual amount was left for further consideration and there is no evidence that the matter was taken up again. Indeed, as is hinted by the wording of the officers' report, White, then Housing Manager was opposed to granting any powers of expenditure to the boards. He considered that the powers which devolved on him were sufficient and that the boards should operate through him in regard to matters involving money. Effectively, this is how the boards have worked. And for issues involving larger amounts of money reference has, of course, to be made to the Housing Services Committee.

In its original recommendation, the committee instructed that the Chairman and Vice Chairman of housing be authorized 'to take all necessary steps to set up the Area Boards'. How this was to be done was not stated, nor was consideration given to an appropriate administrative set up. Rather the organization of the boards was modelled on that of other council committees. From the outset, meetings of the boards were arranged to fit in with the cycle of the Housing Services Committee so as to ensure that matters for reference to that committee might be submitted without lengthy delays. The Directorate of Operations services the boards more or less in the same way as it services all council committees. A formal agenda is prepared some two weeks prior to a meeting and items for inclusion should be submitted before then. Minutes are taken and circulated with agendas to all members. Issues raised for inclusion on the agenda are referred to the appropriate officers in the normal way and reports obtained prior to the committee meeting. Officers may also be called upon to report verbally at a meeting. The processing of committee business in between meetings was at first left largely to the administrative officer concerned. This was deemed to be inefficient and later the processing of board business was brought into line with other council committees. This meant that along with the minutes of particular board meetings action/decision sheets were written up for the attention of officers. These sheets itemize matters for action, designate the officers responsible and specify a target date.

Finally in looking at the overall context of the boards, some attention should be given to the rôles assigned to members of the boards. Again, no clear guide lines were given. Ostensibly officers were assigned a rôle similar to that they had on other council committees ie, to advise and report on matters for decision and to take action where appropriate. However, it has not been made clear whether the boards might instruct officers directly and the usual procedure appears to be for officers to refer matters as recommendations for decision to the Housing Services Committee and to take instructions on that basis. Councillors have been allowed to define their own rôle and most tend to try to minimize the part they play at meetings. The tenant representative for the acquired property tenants has a clearly defined rôle even if the distribution of properties makes his task especially difficult. Other representatives have it impressed upon them that they represent all tenants in the area covered by the board. It is assumed that they can function in this way by working through the tenants' associations.

The North Area Housing Board

The following account is an attempt to describe and assess the work of the boards by looking in detail at the operation of the North Board[55]. This board has as one of its constituent estates, the Parkview estate. It is thus one of the main formal mechanisms linking the council and the estate.

During the research period there were two elections and six North Board meetings. I attended both election meetings but did not vote. Initially I requested from area manager Black and Councillor Lawrence, as Chairman of the Board, permission to be present as an observer at board meetings. This was allowed and I attended two board meetings in that capacity. I was unable to attend the third meeting on account of a clash with a TA meeting and was later advised by the Secretary to the board that some of the tenants' representatives had raised queries about my presence and that therefore I had not received an agenda for a forthcoming meeting. The question of my attendance was then referred to Black, Councillor Mitchell, as Vice Chairman in the absence of the Chairman, Counouncillor Harty as Vice Chairman of the Housing Services Committee and a tenant representative, Mrs Ruble. The outcome of these informal consultations was that I should be excluded from further board meetings.[56] Consequently, the account given here is based on notes recorded at general meetings, verbatim accounts of two board meetings, and agendas and minutes for six.

Elections for the North and South boards in the Old Borough were held on 30 October 1974 and 10 June 1975. They took place in the Old Borough town hall some 10 minutes walk from Parkview. The October meeting was attended by about 150 people, approximately 100 from the North Board area. Most of these tenants came from the two largest estates in the area, Parkview and a nearby estate and they were predominantly middle-aged or elderly. Councillor Harty took the chair and was assisted by Black. Councillor Harty explained that the representatives elected would hold board membership only until April 1975. This was because the current boards had continued in office by special resolution of the council on account of an industrial dispute involving local authority officers. Councillor Harty then read a list of sitting members for the North; Mrs Ruble, Steed, Lloyd and Thompson. He stated the recommendation that there should be a fair spread of representation and also requested that tenants consider keeping one place for tenants in acquired properties. Nominations were called from the floor and five names were put forward, the sitting members plus the Parkview TA leader Mrs Field. It was impossible from the body of the hall to hear who nominated or seconded the candidates. Voters were directed to write four of the five names on a slip of paper. The results were announced as follows, Field 23, Lloyd 53, Ruble 63, Thompson 64, Steed 65. Ten papers were declared invalid. The meeting closed within half an hour of being opened.[57]

Elections were again held at a meeting in June. The process this time was less straightforward and the following account illustrates something of the kind of reaction which can be triggered off in public exchanges when officers and councillors find their position challenged in questioning from residents. On this occasion councillors and officers were well represented, with seven members and four officers present, the latter including Brown, the director of housing. Fewer residents were in attendance, 48 from the North and 43 from the South of the Old Borough. Eleven residents from Parkview were present, all except one connected with the TA committee. Councillor Harty opened the meeting by apologising for the fact that the time given for the meeting had been different on posters and on letters sent to tenants. He introduced himself and others on the platform and told all present they were there to elect four representatives. He thanked those who had worked as tenants representatives and said that since the boards had now been in operation for some years it was time to assess them and see how people felt they should be changed. Accordingly, each board would meet in a few months to decide how its work could be made more effective. He then asked Black to describe the functions of the boards. Black opened by saying that from looking around and seeing many familiar faces he doubted whether many people needed telling.

The boards have tenant representatives, council officers and councillors, one of whom was Chairman . . . The boards meet about every two months and their function is to bring to the notice of the council things which tenants are worried about, to bring about improvements on the estates and the acquired properties. You should try to elect three representatives from the estates and one from the acquired properties. More and more it is the case that the Housing Services committee want to know what the area boards think about a particular item on their agenda. It has all been a bit of a slog. We just got going and then Housing went through a process of reorganisation and then there were financial cutbacks. So we are back to square one but we must not despair; we are going to try and get it going and only you the tenants can do it. I must say it is a bit disheartening to send notices out and get so few people along to this meeting, but that's the way life is. As the Chairman pointed out the boards are in the process of change and the Director and councillors will be looking to see how their functions can be extended. You should keep this in mind when making nominations. What we want are people who will represent all tenants and not just their own estates. We would also like to see Tenants' Associations make more use of their area board representatives. TA's, their chairman and secretaries, should get onto the board representatives and bring up things which will otherwise not see the light of day.

Councillor Harty then called for nominations but was immediately interrupted by a Parkview resident Mrs Noakes who demanded time for questions and asked what the boards had actually achieved. Black replied that the boards brought matters to the attention of the housing committee and so made sure that committee members were aware of tenants' views. He cited as examples proposed changes to the tenancy agreement and the question of car parking on estates. Other Parkview residents followed Mrs Noakes' lead. Mrs Montgomery asked why board meetings were closed to the public and was told that they were officially sub-committees of the Housing Services Committee and Standing Orders did not allow for open meetings of sub-committees. Mrs Field requested that each board report back to the general meeting on its work over the past year. Mrs Biddle asked that TA's receive agendas and minutes of the board meetings and was assured that this could be arranged. Two tenants from other parts of the area asked about the proposed changes to the conditions of tenancy. Mrs Noakes, dissatisfied at the reply to an earlier question said she still could not see why the boards held their meetings in secret. By this stage it was evident that feeling, especially among the Parkview group, was running high and a few residents from the South were also becoming more outspoken in their questioning. Councillor Harty intervened and insisted on calling for nominations. The names put forward were Mrs Ruble, Mrs Clemmett, Mrs Field, Steed, Thompson, Lloyd and Dale. There were strong objections to the nomination of Lloyd from some Parkview residents on the grounds he was not present. These were overruled from the chair on an assurance from the proposer that Lloyd had consented to serve another term if elected. As previously voters were instructed to record four votes. The result was announced as follows; Dale 18, Mrs Ruble 21, Mrs Field 23, Mrs Clemmett 23, Lloyd 24, Steed 33, Thompson 35. A second ballot was held between Mrs Clemmett and Mrs Field and the former was elected 25 to 21 with one spoiled paper.

A number of features of these elections warrant further comment at this point. First, it appears that the pre-election publicity has very little impact.

There are approximately 6,000 households in the North and clearly the vast majority are not represented at the annual elections. One contributory factor may be the kind of letter sent to tenants to notify them of the board elections.[58] The format and language smack of officialdom and seem quite unrelated to any personal concern which a tenant might feel regarding his own flat or estate. Certainly such letters do little to overcome the general lack of awareness among tenants about the work of the boards. Interviews carried out on the estate at the time election letters were received still elicited negative response to queries about the boards. (When the letters were referred to in the course of interviews, typical responses were, 'Oh, I didn't bother to read that', 'I leave things like that to my husband', 'I don't understand things like that, you explain', 'Oh yes *that* it said caretakers won't fix tap washers and light bulbs anymore'. This last speaker referred to another item sent out with the June election letter and is an interesting comment on the point at which contact is made). However, when their purpose was outlined most respondents commented that area boards seemed like a good thing and asked why they hadn't heard more about them! It is hardly surprising then that most of those attending are TA committee members and their personal supporters. This is true especially of board members seeking re-election. There are also a few attenders from the acquired properties. At the same time it is difficult to account for the difference in attendance figures for the two elections.

The procedure adopted at the elections is also interesting. At the first election, no opportunity was given, nor was there a demand, for debate of any kind. At the second election it was clearly intended that the meeting should entail the business of nominations and voting only although an attempt was made beforehand to explain the purpose of the meeting and the functions of the board. The demand for question time came from the floor and was apparently a reaction against the cursory nature of the previous election. Following on from that election there had been among members of the Parkview TA and their supporters a good deal of discussion about what were considered to be unsatisfactory aspects of the elections and the boards. In part their dissatisfaction can be related to the disenchantment felt by members of that group to 'their representative' Lloyd. In part it would seem to reflect a more general feeling. 'Call that democratic–those elections are a proper farce!' 'I can't understand why you have to vote for four people – you might only like one or two ...' 'Those boards are just another talking shop as far as I can see'.

In fact, it is obvious that there is no set procedures for the election meetings. 'Problems' such as the nomination of a candidate in his absence or a tied vote are worked out at the time by the chairman with possible reference to an officer. This means of devising rules is a reflection of the various rôles adopted at the meeting. Basically, Councillor Harty is in control with Black as Old Borough Area Manager, acting as his adviser. Other councillors and officers play no part other than perhaps acting as scrutineers in the counting. Tenants, whether outgoing members, candidates or voters, are expected to play a minimal rôle.

Candidates are asked for no more than their name and place of residence. Questions from the floor are answered fairly shortly with no attempt to establish a dialogue between a resident and the chair to understand the underlying reasons for a question and to provide an answer satisfactory to the resident concerned. Even where a reply was apparently satisfactory as in the undertaking to send agendas and minutes of board meetings to TA secretaries the outcome was a failure to follow up with action.

Most estate residents attending appear to have some connection with an estate TA either through direct committee involvement or through support group ties to a committee member. Candidates nominated as estates representatives have all had TA experience. Thompson secures nomination as an experienced board member representing the acquired properties and an outsider like Dale was put forward as an unknown, 'the man in my road'.

The voting figures may be variously interpreted. At the October elections the highest returns were for Steed and Thompson. Neither takes a prominent rôle at board meetings nor are they particularly active in promoting board affairs by, say, attendance at TA committee meetings.[59] Lloyd and Mrs Ruble polled slightly lower and yet they have worked for many years with TA's on many estates in the area, have been the most vocal spokesmen at board meetings and have been prominent advocates of the boards since the inception of the scheme. Both undertake a good deal of constituency work. At the June election Thompson and Steed again polled highest. Lloyd, in the absence of his personal group of supporters, was re-elected with a smaller proportion of votes. Mrs Ruble was defeated and on a second ballot the fourth seat went to Mrs Clemmett a newcomer from another estate. Mrs Field was twice unsuccessfully nominated for the North Board; she has lived many years in the south, is fairly well known there, and served on the South Board, but in the north where she has recently taken up residence, is scarcely known outside the Parkview TA.

It is difficult to know on what basis votes are distributed. High returns go typically to those candidates least likely to be known to voters. This may be because those tenants present from the estates are likely to know several of the candidates and to be a firm supporter of at least one. They therefore cast at least one positive vote. However, they are also likely to make a negative judgment about one of the other candidates and will want to exclude him or her. The public activity of well-known candidates like Lloyd and Mrs Ruble tends to provoke a strong reaction among tenants who are themselves involved in tenant activity. This may be positive but there is also the risk that a negative reaction will develop. Since candidates are few this leaves a number of votes for candidates like Steed who may be labelled safe. Since tenants are strongly recommended to vote for a representative from the acquired properties an experienced member like Thompson is assured of a high poll. Other tenants not connected with a particular candidate and support group will most likely know very little about the candidates and have no way of becoming better informed. They are likely to cast a positive vote in favour of the candidate from their particular street or estate and their remaining votes will be distributed more or less by chance.

COMMITTEE WORK

Once elected the board meets about five or six times in the course of the municipal year. During the course of the research the North Board met six times. Background work to meetings is carried out by the officer who acts as secretary to the board. Most items for the board agendas come from officers, specifically housing management officers, and they are approached for this purpose some two weeks prior to a scheduled meeting. Generally officers respond with matters already before the board or with new matters referred on the instruction of council committees to the boards for comment. Individual councillors do not normally put forward items for inclusion on the agenda. Exceptions have been the tabling of petitions for consideration by the board. Tenants representatives may also request that particular items appear on the agenda but so far they have not done so, though of course representatives can and do raise items in the course of a meeting. Agendas are mailed to all members prior to the meeting.

The North Board has 14 councillors and resident members. Their record of attendance at meetings is shown in Table v. Some councillors are regular attenders at board meetings, others are more erratic. The most regular are the Vice Chairman, Councillor Mitchell, a Parkview ward councillor, and two councillors noted as b and l in Table v. These councillors have divergent views on the functioning of the boards and high attendance figures do not seem to be necessarily connected with a strong commitment to the boards as a form of tenant involvement in management. There may be a relationship between pressure of work on other council committees and lower attendance figures but again this is not always so. One councillor honestly admitted that most elected members regarded the boards as a duty and something of a bore and this attitude may account for at least some absences. On most occasions, three or four of the tenant representatives were present at board meetings. The full attendance of all members of the board would appear to be rare and it can be seen that on several occasions the chairman was in the position of having a casting vote. From the officer group, apart from the secretary, the area manager Black is required to attend. Officers from other sections and directorates are invited to appear before the board to discuss particular agenda items. The response to such an invitation is usually taken up at a high level. Thus, the borough architect and the controller of the DLBO appeared before the North Board during the study.

In the course of the six meetings monitored the North Board considered a total of 46 items. These items and the manner in which they were dealt with in committee are outlined in Appendix VI (p. 310). Most items were raised at more than one meeting and some were recurrent throughout the study period. The largest group of items may be categorized under a heading miscellaneous and comprises matters ranging from street signs and petitions to uniforms for

Table V;   Attendance at North Area Housing Board during the research period

	18 Sept 74	17 Dec 74	22 Jan 75	6 Mar 75	2 April 75	9 July 75	Total attend- ance
Cllor Lawrence† (Chairman) 2	X		X		X		3
Cllor Mitchell (V Chairman) (a)	X	X	X	X	X	X	6
b	X	X	X	X	X		5
o	X			X	X	X	4
l	X	X	X	X		X	5
Cllor Harty	X	X	X				3
Cllor Mackie (i)			X				1
p		X	X		X	X	4
Chairman of Housing Utilisation			X				1
Councillors attending	6	5	8	4	5	4	
Mrs Ruble	X	X	X	X	X		5*
Steed	X	X	X		X	X	5
Lloyd	X	X	X		X	X	5
Thompson	X	X		X		X	4
Tenants reps attending	4	4	3	2	3	3	
Totals	10	9	11	6	8	7	

Notes† Names of councillors are given only where they appear also in the text; otherwise the letters used to denote councillors in Table vi are used here also. See note to Table vi, p216.

There was an election between these last two meetings and Mrs Ruble was defeated, her place being taken on the board by Mrs Clemmett.

In addition to councillors and tenants representatives there are always present as secretary an officer from the Directorate of Operations and Black as Area Manager for the Old Borough. Other officers may also be called upon to report on particular agenda items.

caretakers. Other items fall under the headings repairs, planning or policy issues and administrative matters. Typically the policy and planning issues are referred to the board by other council committees for comment. They comprise either borough wide proposals or plans specific to a particular estate in the North Board area. Repairs, administrative matters and miscellaneous items are more likely to be raised by officers or tenant representatives. After deliberation most agenda items were referred to Black for further report. Repairs and administrative matters might be noted for action and this would involve Black in the issue of works orders or other administrative procedures. Other items were simply for noting by the board. The conduct of committee business thus entails a flow of information between the council, in particular the housing management section of the housing directorate and the North Board itself. At the same time it can be noted that both items for action and those on which further report is requested are the type of issues, often the same issues, taken up by individual TA's. There is thus a duplication of requests for action and information. Most time is taken up with minor trouble cases or with major issues over which the board has no control and there is little concern with policy matters affecting the North Board area.

The participants' viewpoint

In order to assess the work of the board it is necessary to consider the participants' understanding of the function of the board, their own rôle in serving on the board and their propensity to change both rôles and functions. Thus, as part of the research, tenants' representatives, councillors and officers were interviewed on these subjects and households in the Parkview residents sample were asked questions about the North Board and the issue of tenant participation.

I TENANTS' REPRESENTATIVES

At the time of the study all tenant members of the North Board had served on it from its establishment. As a result of this experience they had developed widely different views about their own rôle and that of the board and these will be discussed individually.[60] Lloyd, the representative resident on the Parkview estate, is 58 years old. He claims that since 1937 he has been active in trade union and TA affairs. He works for a brewery company and is a shop steward and branch chairman there. He was for several years chairman of the Parkview TA, took an active part in founding a federation of TA's in the Borough and is on the federation executive committee. He is a member of the ward branch of the Labour Party but stresses that he does not hold party political views on matters of concern to tenants.

According to Lloyd, the main aims in introducing the boards were to cut the costs of running estates and keep down the incidence of vandalism. In effect what they have meant is that tenants are able to take complaints first to their

TA, then to the North Board, and if that fails, to the federation. This organisation is considered to have more power because unlike the boards, it can consider questions like rates and rents.[61] Lloyd sees himself at board meetings as a tenant fighting for tenants rights and to this end he makes a contribution to most items on the board's agenda. Lloyd understands that representatives cannot instruct officers but if reports are considered to be unsatisfactory they can challenge them. They can also refer matters to other council committees. The board is thus like a miniature council. Similarly, the work of a board extends beyond meetings. As a board member, Lloyd feels he is able to get councillors onto an estate to investigate problems personally and this is seen as the real achievement of the system. 'Previously, you didn't see a councillor from one election to another.' Further, representatives act for councillors as well as tenants in that they have a councillor type rôle and take up some of a councillor's duties. Lloyd stressed, however, that while doing a councillor's job a representative should not get too involved with councillors or they risk losing tenant support. In Lloyd's estimation Mrs Ruble's election defeat was attributable to her close relationships with councillors. Representatives can also approach officers and there is a mutual and equal exchange of advice between the two parties. Lloyd considers that the work of the boards needs to be extended to allow discussion of matters like rates, rents and transfers. Trust in them needs to be developed and they should be given greater publicity. He suggested that participation might be extended by council calling meetings on issues like the setting of the rates to involve groups like ratepayers' associations, the trades council and the boards in open discussion. He feels that tenant control is an unworkable proposition and is opposed to the idea on that basis.

Mrs Ruble formerly lived on the Parkview estate and had experience of TA committee work there with Lloyd. She later moved to a newer neighbouring estate and was again active in TA affairs. Mrs Ruble is 39 years old and for the last seven years has worked as a home help in the Old Borough. She is a shop steward in her union and also serves on the management committees of one of the local schools and a community settlement. After her defeat in the last North Board elections Mrs Ruble was anxious to continue her involvement with council work and attempted, unsuccessfully, to secure nomination as a Labour Party candidate in a ward by-election.

Mrs Ruble, unlike Lloyd, considers that the board is not the place to take up complaints; rather it should consider the welfare of the whole North area and so should concern itself with issues like amenities, caretaker control and the general appearance and layout of estates. In board committee meetings Mrs Ruble adopts a forceful stance on most issues. In board work she feels herself cast in a rôle much like a councillor with a position somewhere between tenants and officers. She feels this has involved her appreciating more and more the viewpoint of officers and in turn this has left her open to attack from tenants. Mrs Ruble would like to extend membership of the boards to include representatives from all estates, representatives for gap sites and acquired properties, caretakers and surveyors from the Directorate of Housing and officers from all other directorates concerned. She would like to widen the province of the boards to include matters pertaining to Social Services, Finance and Leisure and Recreation. She considers their function should be to break down the conflict type situation where tenants oppose the council until a situation is reached where all accept responsibility for taking action. At the estate level Mrs Ruble feels this form of involvement can be attained by developing a TA organization based on block by block representation. This for her is the meaning of participation.

Thompson was nominated for board membership initially as the only person from the acquired properties to respond to the invitation to the first general meeting. He is 51 years old, a Jamaican resident in this country for 31 years and presently employed as an accountant with a government department. Formerly he was active on a municipal committee concerned with improving race relations in Birmingham and more recently he has worked with the then Community Relations Commission in London. Now the North Board is his only interest of this kind.

Thompson considers that as a representative it is his job to look after the general welfare of tenants in acquired properties and especially to see that all household services such as heating and plumbing, are functioning properly. He intervenes on behalf of tenants in dealing with officers and has some limited contacts with councillors. Thompson is opposed to any change in the work of the board, indeed he considers that in raising matters like traffic signs representatives are going outside their terms of reference and any such move should be resisted. Administratively it should be possible for the board to accede to requests for action more promptly but other than that no reforms are required. On participation generally Thompson considers the only possible change might come through some altered form of tenure which allowed a greater sense of individual home ownership and he would restrict the application of this kind of change to the acquired properties.

Steed, the fourth tenant representative was unavailable for interview. A resident on the same estate as Mrs Ruble he has some experience of TA work there. Steed, like Thompson, takes a less active rôle in board committee proceedings.

II COUNCILLORS

A total of 26 councillors, the ward councillors and those serving on the North Board, the Housing Services Committee, Housing Utilisation and Housing Services Provision review committees were approached for interview. Interviews were completed with 24.[62] Of course not all of these councillors have had direct experience of the North Board but as members of committees which refer items to the four boards and receive reports on their behalf they might be expected to have formed opinions about them. Moreover apart from the North Board councillors, seven members interviewed presently sit on other boards, one was formerly a board member and one is a member of all boards ex officio. Interviews were of an informal semi-structured kind. Councillors were asked to state their concept of participation, their views on the boards as at presently constituted and as they might be developed in future, and their definition of a member's rôle in the context of policies aiming to increase tenant involvement in housing management. It proved to be difficult to get specific answers on these questions. Several councillors commented that they had not personally thought out the issues clearly and that such matters had not been discussed in committee. It is not surprising therefore that the question on participation as a concept was seldom taken up at an abstract level.

Councillor views on the functions appropriate to the boards vary and are coloured by the opinion they have of the working of the present system.

... they are a glorified TA and they don't achieve much more. There needs to be a better complaints mechanism so that time is not diverted on those.
Area boards can be seen as advisory bodies concerned with minor matters.
The boards are back to being a talking shop. They are not representative enough to be an effective means of consultation or participation and you don't need boards to air grievances about repairs not being done.
Area housing boards are a good idea for feedback and the exchange of ideas.
Area boards are quite good. People can bring a list of outstanding complaints.

As with tenants there is a general agreement among members that the boards should present the tenant point of view, though some councillors are clearly more circumspect in their assessments of the extent to which this is achieved in practice. And like tenants, councillors are divided on the question of whether boards should have as a major function, the handling of complaints. Again like the tenant representatives some councillors would like to change the system and others consider either that change is undesirable or that there is little scope for it. In accord with the terms of the research brief most of the comments about changes to the board were related to the scope for involving tenants in housing management. The following statements can be said to reflect the range of views put forward.

The ultimate in tenant participation is to allocate the boards a budget.
Tenants should be running their own estates and by that means having control over their own environment. The difficulties come with the question of how to organize that—whether on a co-operative basis or what. Immediately we could consider handing over colour schemes, control over planting, checks to counter destruction as part of the planned maintenance scheme, and the running of tenant facilities with an auditor appointed on a honorary basis.
Housing boards might be better transformed into a consultative mechanism to discuss with tenant reps matters like say transfers and rents...
Ideally everybody would be interested at the grass roots level in taking responsibility, attending meetings and being informed, experienced and oriented towards taking part in the democratic process ... [the boards] can be seen as an attempt to head off any real demand. They have served a useful purpose to some degree in that they have put council in contact with some tenants but there is no structure for them to report back to the grass roots and this is a major weakness.
TA's and area boards foster an illusion of democracy—there is the possibility of raising grievances without the power to settle them.

214

Participation will take a very long time because on the whole people are very disinterested. It means membership of the TA and being prepared to help in the running of it, going on courses such as that offering now,[63] standing for elections and worrying about the kids pulling up the roses. A very few tenants toil away and the others just sit back and moan. The few do a tremendous job and all they get is kicked for it.

Hand the lot over except lettings and rent levels. They could have a pool of money for their own decorations, repairs, gardeners, caretakers and draw up their own conditions.

Tenant participation should go as far as tenants want it to go.

How much participation is enough 10%, 20%... what of the 70% who maybe just want to lead a quiet life and stay at home and watch the telly?

TA's should take over estates in liaison with council ... the first step is to get council tenants to accept more personal responsibility, for individuals to fix their own door knob instead of waiting for the council to do it, for parents to tell kids off for throwing rubbish around – to have more self respect and pride in the place where they may spend all their lives.

Boards should have a say on matters dealt with by Resident Services and Social Services. Maybe a ward basis would make better sense. And I see no reason why they shouldn't be open to all ratepayers and the general public.

The functions of the board might be extended in various ways – for instance voluntary help for childrens' supervised play might be organized through the area boards.

There is no need to change the present set up.... Eventually everything has got to come back to the council. A lot from the boards involves adjusting management and so it gets done. But if the boards were given more power well you can't have two people with authority over the spending of money.

Table VI gives a breakdown of councillor attitudes to the board according to age and party affiliation. From this it can be seen that 11 councillors consider that the boards as presently constituted work well although seven of these put forward suggestions for further improvement. The remaining 13 councillors expressed themselves dissatisfied in some way with the existing board system. The older councillors are more satisfied and least likely to want any radical change. Fourteen councillors were concerned to change the membership of the board in such a way that tenant representatives might be considered to be more representative of all tenants in the area.[64] Frequently this was related to ideas for alternatives to the area based board. Some suggested nighbourhood councils, estate or ward boards or tenants advisory committees with councillors co-opted onto them. The councillors who advocated wider terms of reference favoured the boards considering housing policy matters such as rents, allocations and transfers, and/or extending the boards province to areas like local bus service requirements, post office facilities and the lack of communication between different departments. Four councillors proposed the handing over of budgetary powers. As might be expected the suggestions for more radical change came from younger Labour Party councillors.

Few councillors felt they would need to change their rôle if more tenant participation was introduced in the Borough but some commented that they had not given the matter much thought anyway. As board members they are in agreement with Mrs Ruble and see themselves as bringing the council to the people, removing some of the mystique that surrounds public office. At meetings they listen and maybe prompt and subsequently may raise issues on

TABLE VI Councillor attitudes to Area Housing Boards*

| Age | Works well at present | Suggested modifications | | | | | |
		Change representation	Budgetary powers	Wider scope generally	More tenant participation than area boards allow	Full tenant control	Tenant Co-options to Housing Committee
35 and under	abg	adefgkl	adei	k	fhij	c	be
36–59	mpqs	mnpqrs		ns	mno		
60 and over	tuvw	t					
Totals	11	14	4	3	7	1	2
Party Affiliation							
Labour	ampqtuvw	aeflmnpqrt	aei	n	fhijmno	c	e
Liberal		d	d				
Conservative	bgs	gks		ks			b
Totals	11	14	4	3	7	1	2

*Note: These tables show a breakdown of the attitudes of 23 councillors. (One councillor Labour, 36–59, confessed to extreme cynicism at the whole idea, claimed to have had no dealing whatsoever with the boards and therefore declined to comment). I have adopted the convention of giving letters to each councillor in order to show the combination of viewpoints in individual cases. Thus councillor *a* is a Labour Party councillor under 35 years of age who considers that the boards would be improved by change in the form of representations and by the granting of some budgetary powers. There are 12 councillors in the 35 or under age group, 7 of them under 30. 8 are Labour councillors, 3 Conservative and 1 Liberal. There are 5 Labour and 1 Conservative councillor in the 36–59 age group. All 4 councillors in the 60 and over age group are Labour councillors.

behalf of tenants either in committee or with the officer concerned.

Councillors are there to take note of views.

Councillors listen to what is said and make sure cases are taken up by officers. They thus play a sort of vigilante rôle. They may also initiate proposals to go up to the Housing Committee.

The rôle of the councillor is to sit back and listen and spread the gospel. Not to dictate. A lot of the most important work gets done in the pub anyway – after the formal meeting is over.

Councillors on the boards should make tenants feel more at ease – previously tenants stood in awe of councillors – this is the main work of the boards.

One Labour councillor pointed to the possible conflict of rôles but minimized the extent to which this occurred.

The councillor is the representative of both the people in the area and the council – usually there is not much controversy. Basically members are on the side of the tenants and fight for what tenants want.

Another councillor commented that if altered rôles meant a reduction in the power of councillors that was probably all to the good. However, a fellow member took the opposite view.

There is a need to be very careful that the functions of the elected members are not handed over ... Councillors must remain in control.

III OFFICERS

The views of councillors while fairly diverse are at the same time in sum markedly different from the generally more conservative opinions put forward by officers. Many of the officers interviewed had no direct experience of the board system and so they were asked whether they felt there was any scope for tenant participation in housing management. Officers expressing positive viewpoints were asked about the extent and manner of involvement; officers in disagreement generally supported their stance with unsolicited arguments. In addition where an officer's duties did involve work with the North Board he or she was asked for an assessment of it.[65] Table VII gives a breakdown of views according to officer grades. This shows that at the senior level a wide range of views was expressed, at the middle officer level there is apparently little demand for reform and at the junior level there is almost no demand for change of any kind.

At the senior management level, the assistant director White is opposed as a matter of principle.

... it is copping out of providing an efficient service. You have the ordinary democratic processes and the way to change things is to see the vote goes differently next time round. You do not interfere once people have been elected. It is a good idea to consult with people and their views should be seriously considered by the appropriate committee but that's as far as it goes. Those committees have to take the general good into account and accept responsibility for the decision they take.

Paradoxically this argument is admitted by Brown, the director, the one advocate of tenant control.

I am interested in participation, not because of any commitment to the democratic process at all.

TABLE VII   Officer attitudes to Area Housing Boards

	No scope for tenant involvement in management	Works well as at present	Suggested modifications					
			Representation	Budget	Scope	More tenant participation	Tenant control	Co-options
Senior grade staff	e	ab	d	d	d	u	c	
Middle grade staff	f	hij			k	k		
Junior grade staff	mnopqrt	ls	m					
Totals	9	7	2	1	2	2	1	0

*Note: Interviews were conducted between July and December 1975 with 24 officers, most in the Directorate of Housing but some in the Directorate of Operations (1) The Direct Labour Building Organisation (2) and the Architect's Department (1). This table represents the views of 20 officers since 2 middle ranking officers declined to offer opinions both on the grounds of no knowledge of the issues involved. It should also be noted that 2 of the 8 estate caretakers refused to be interviewed on any issue. As in Table VI the convention of using letters for officers has been adopted though it can be seen that with few exceptions there is little qualifying of viewpoints. In addition a category signifying no scope for tenant involvement has been added. The grading of officers is in terms of the hierarchy within the Directorate of Housing and officers in other directorates of a comparable ranking. Thus senior denotes officers at the level of director, assistant director, and area manager, middle denotes estates manager, senior surveyor and comparable status, and junior denotes Parkview manager and comparable technical grades, clerical support staff and caretakers.

If I was doing a job supremely well I might not want to hand over but would be jealous of keeping it. Because I am not on top of the job I have to consider all possibilities—the only way to get there is to lessen the load by handing over part to tenants.

A senior officer in the DLBO who had appeared before the North Board saw it basically as a public relations exercise.

The area board does a lot of good in the sense that it gets the system across and people are better informed. Even so we cannot go too far in the public relations field or people would immediately think of ringing that nice man Mr B to work out a problem and we would be inundated.

He added that too often people went to the board to vent a personal grudge and commented 'We need to be careful there is not a tenant take-over'. The senior officer with most contact with the North Board is the area manager Black. He considers that the present framework should be modified increase its effectiveness. He would like to alter the election process so that tenant representatives are nominated by TA's. Black considers this would ensure a more effective feedback to the constituent estates and would avoid situation which arose, on Parkview when the tenant representative LI resigned from the TA committee. Black advocates allocating a small budget to the boards to increase the members' sense of responsibility and information or education sessions to increase the ability of tenant members to cope with the demands of board work. Aware of the problems involved Black cautioned against initiating changes to which the council may be unable to respond adequately.

At the middle grade staff level, one officer was opposed to any form of participation and three were in favour of boards as at present constituted. For these officers involvement meant tenant acceptance of limited responsibility. One officer, like Black, saw a danger in raising expectations which the local authority could not meet. Another commented.

Area boards are quite sufficient. Tenants should be involved in their own property more. This is on two levels. On the one hand they should accept responsibility for the behaviour of other tenants ... In private property people would come out and investigate if people were damaging their garden. Why not in council property? On the other hand they should take a greater interest in their own home.

One officer in this group viewed the boards as a not particularly effective public relations exercise and had formulated criticisms of the board and ideas for improvement. Area boards should be less formal and systematized; they should be open to the public; it should be possible for interested people to lobby members and their tenant representatives for, say, half an hour prior to the meeting; people should be taught how to assume responsibility say through their TA; the language used in meetings should be simpler and no jargon should be allowed.

Junior staff were very critical of any move to extend tenant involvement in management. All of these officers, especially the caretakers, have duties which bring them directly into contact with tenants and they may feel themselves threatened by any changes in the status quo. The following comments are typical.

They should be dealing with the welfare of the estate—the kids. So far as dealing with management is concerned no. Tenants would be on your back. Ideally it could work but practically no.

You'd get tenants spying and spreading ill feeling ... there should be a clear management structure which separates tenants from the supervison of the estate.

Tenants have too much say. They are inclined to take on too much and it would create further problems.

Tenants would only mess it all up. TA members are only in it for the glory.

At the same time it should be noted that three of the caretaking staff recommended that they be allowed to sit on committees such as the TA, and one advocated the appointment of a caretaker representative to the area board. Other junior staff members were prepared to be more accommodating so long as the areas of tenant involvement were clearly circumscribed.

It should be kept in the right context—not demanding. This idea of going and getting private surveys and asking for contracts etc that's not their concern.[66]

Area boards often deal with petty things now. They should be encouraged to carry out their own minor repairs and get an interest in their own property.

We need to know more of what tenants want but you can't have a tenant take over.

IV PARKVIEW RESIDENTS

Finally in this section attention should be given to the views of those whose interests the boards are meant to serve, the estate residents. Respondents were asked questions about the North Board, possible changes in management style and procedures, such as the formulation and enforcement of rules, which might be taken as indicators of a preparedness to become involved in management issues.

Three quarters of all respondents claimed not to have heard about the existence of the North Board, 8% knew the name of at least one of the tenant representatives to the board, fewer were aware of the work carried out by the board. At the same time when the composition and function of the board was outlined 79% considered the idea of consultative boards to be a good one.

The general lack of knowledge of the boards and the absence of any clear idea of the range of alternative management practices available for Parkview make it difficult to evaluate fully the responses to any further questioning. Nevertheless additional questions were asked and some important findings do emerge from a careful examination of the data on hand. Fifty one per cent of all respondents considered that residents should have some say in the way in which Parkview was managed. However, two thirds were unable to respond to a probing question on the form such a management system might take. One third of all respondents were quite definite and 90% of these favoured a joint management system involving both council and estate representatives. Even so, in discussion very few respondents were able to describe in what manner a joint scheme might be conducted and the most that respondents called for was 'more say' for residents. The demand is therefore for a consultative mechanism similar to a board but with presumably narrower geographical limits.

Respondents opposed to the idea of tenant involvement, in contrast to many of those in favour, often expressed in strong terms reasons for their views.

People don't want to know. Give people power and they think they rule the world. If there was a co-operative set up, one block would be going against other blocks and a keep off attitude would develop. Under one landlord at least we are all equal.

Tenant management is not a good idea—its simply taking on the council's work and reordering the firing line.

A good idea in theory but in practice murder.

Some people can't manage their own affairs and I wouldn't want them to manage mine.

One respondent indicated that tenant involvement could only be considered in relation to an altered tenure system, several suggested that the basic confidentiality preserved in dealings with officialdom was preferable to any form of shared responsibility with neighbours. It is of interest to note that all residents in the sample group with TA committee experience were opposed to any form of resident participation in management and other TA committee members interviewed in a different context concurred.

In answer to a question on whether, if management changes were introduced they themselves would be prepared to take part, respondents were fairly equally divided in their replies. Forty-two per cent of the sample expressed some degree of readiness, 46% rejected the notion of involvement and 12% remained undecided. Thus 42% of respondents may be labelled potential participators. However, a simple breakdown of this 42% may be construed in a misleading way. Figure VIII, for example, shows the breakdown of those in favour according to particular social characteristics. In this figure the total sum of percentages in each category will add up to 42% within round-off error. From Figure VIII it might be assumed that a typical participator would most likely be a white woman in the middle age group, married and with a family. She would have had limited educational experience and would regard other residents as socially similar to herself. Moreover, this is a likely pattern should a participation scheme be introduced.

FIGURE VIII   Number of potential participators by social categories expressed as a percentage of the total Parkview population

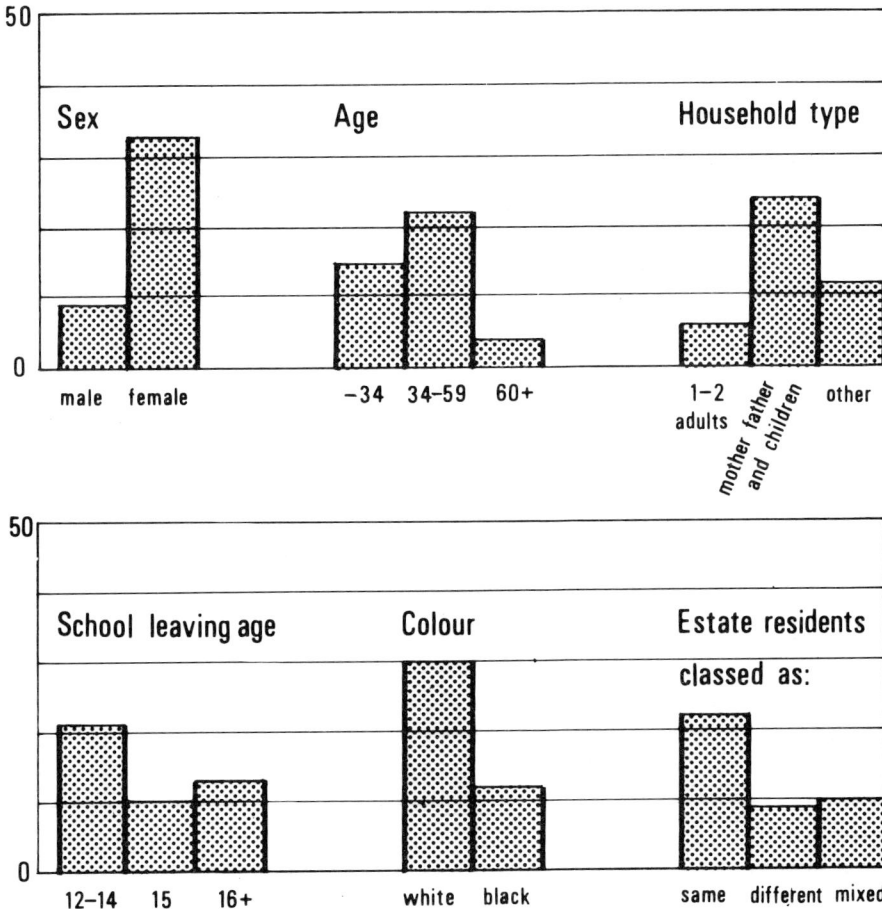

FIGURE IX   Potential participators as a percentage of each social category

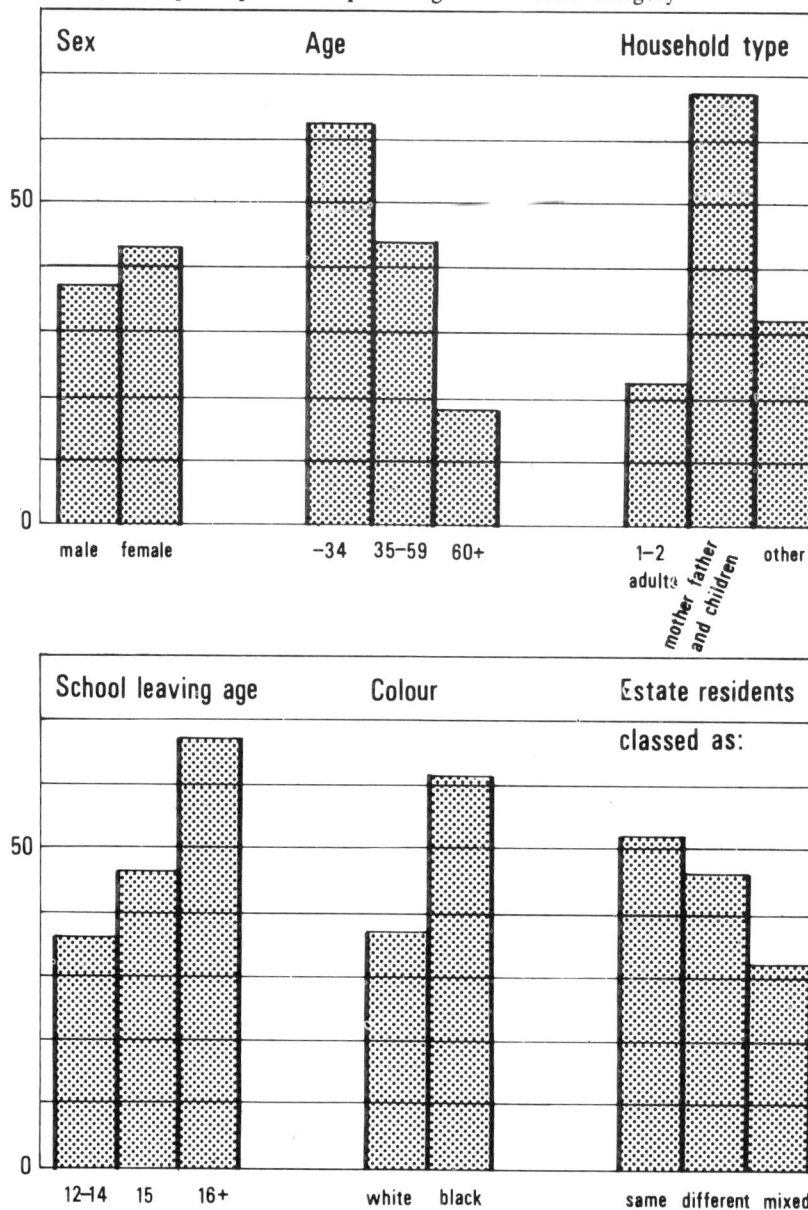

However, it should be recognized that this pattern does not accurately reflect the vaying degrees of commitment to participation within particular subgroups of the estate's population. This is evident from a closer analysis of the data. Figure IX shows potential participators as a percentage of each sub category. From this it can be seen that a high percentage of young respondents (62% of those under 34) were in favour. Respondents with a school leaving age of 16 or more also recorded a favourable response in high numbers (67%). Black respondents expressed a greater readiness to participate, (61% of all black respondents as compared to 37% of all whites). These peaks are not reflected in Figure VIII because their weighting factor within the total population is so small. These sub categories constitute minority social groups.

Other factors may further swamp these minority groups with high levels of potential commitment. It can be suggested for example, that while black residents may ideally wish to work together with their white neighbours in practice they have in the past eschewed any involvement with estate organizations, most often on grounds of assumed or feared discrimination from members of the majority groups.[67] Younger and more highly educated respondents often have family and other responsibilities and in real terms the amount of time they would be able to devote to meeting estate obligations might be quite small.

Together these figures point up the complexity of the tenant participation issue. First it would seem that the figure of 42% potential participators may in practice be unattainable. Secondly, it would seem desirable to consider schemes which would recognize that a high level of commitment is possible among minority groups whose interests might otherwise not be represented. The two factors are interconnected and there would appear to be considerable practical difficulties in devising and implementing a scheme which would effectively optimize resident commitments and representation.

Three further complicating factors need to be considered at this point. First this assessment cannot take into account the interaction between respondents drawn from different categories. Experience from the TA committee would suggest that categorizations such as male/female and others not included here such as place of residence on the estate may affect group dynamics to a considerable extent. Secondly, as noted in Part II the overall demography of Parkview is not reflected in the composition of particular blocks. Some blocks have a high proportion of households with children. Others of all adult, often elderly households. Black residents are concentrated in the garden flats and tower blocks. These factors together with those outlined suggest that potential participators would by no means be drawn evenly from all parts of Parkview. Thirdly, 77% of all respondents have never had any kind of committee experience. The experience of those who have served on a committee of some kind has generally been gained from trade union committees in the case of men, and single interest or social committees, for example parent teacher associations or pensioners groups, in the case of women. The committee experience on which potential participators could draw would therefore appear to be non-existent or fairly limited.

Similar analyses can be made of responses to questions about particular situations which might be considered as part of an estate management function. For example, respondents were asked whether or not there should be rules governing the behaviour of Parkview residents and who should be responsible for their formulation and enforcement. The majority (88%) favoured a body of rules. Forty seven per cent considered such rules should be drawn up jointly by the council and residents, 36% considered this task rested solely with the council and the remainder recorded a don't know or no opinion response. Contrariwise, the majority of respondents (52%) held the council responsible for the enforcement of rules, 23% placed responsibility on residents and 14% on caretakers. Younger respondents are most likely to advocate resident involvement in both the formulation and enforcement of rules. As already admitted, given the general lack of awareness of the management alternatives available for Parkview this information should be regarded with some caution. It does, however, clearly show the need both to look beyond the absolute figures recorded in such a survey and to understand the significance of a range of separate but related issues. Tentatively it can be concluded that there is on Parkview only scant knowledge of the existing procedures available for consultation with residents. On the whole resident demand for change in this regard is fairly minimal and would not extend beyond a more localised consultative mechanism. In this residents have more in common with the conservative officer group than the more radical Brown or the group of young Labour councillors who advocate moves towards tenant control. And as noted in Part II and elsewhere, recurring themes of more immediate concern to residents would appear to be less for an altered management system than for one judged more effective in meeting the most common resident demands, an efficient repairs and caretaking service, and more considerate in the manner of its delivery.

Parkview and the council; fragmented linkages

In politics we are concerned with the 'processes of alliance, challenge and compromise, trials of strength and allocation of rewards . . .'

(J Barnes in Mitchell (ed), p 51.)

The material presented in Part IV shows that the links between Parkview and the council tend to be discontinuous and easily broken. In part breakdowns result from the lack of communication within the officer group, between officers and councillors and between both groups and estate residents and their representatives. And in part breakdowns result from the weak nature of the organizations through which all parties work.

At the individual level encounters between estate households and officers are periodic and generally concerned either with the remedy of some grievance or with the imposition of sanctions against an infringement of rules.

The estate TA also has as one of its major concerns the remedying of resident grievances. In this work the committee relates primarily to the housing management section of the directorate and less frequently to individual councillors. The TA has found more difficulty in relating to Parkview residents. As an organization it has not developed roots within the estate neighbourhood and attracts temporary support from residents only for widespread complaints like the dampness in the garden flats or social events like the gala and children's Christmas party. Given the failure to attract ongoing resident support, committee members lack a real power base and have little means of building one either for themselves or for the committee as a whole.

As a consequence the TA committee has become inward looking and appears unable to control the factionalism which places under constant threat the survival of particular committee groups.

Other estate groups may develop on an ad hoc basis, as with the garden flats movement to secure private gardens and the tower block action group. Although surviving only so long as the attainment of the defined goal appears to be realizable, these groups do in that time find genuine support from residents because the goals themselves relate to immediate family domains. The officer and councillor response to such developments is to attempt to control them by incorporation within the one formal estate organization, the TA.

In many situations, whether involving individuals, informal groups or the TA committee, residents often have an experience of dealing with numerous representatives of the officer group. As exemplified in the case of dampness in the garden flats this multiplicity of contacts is itself confusing to residents. To the confusion can be added a sense of being put down. Many on going exchanges between officers and residents find expression in confrontations even when as over the management of the hall or Eshag residents attempt to initiate negotiations. The stance adopted by officers in these situations can be peremptory and dismissive. That adopted by councillors is in theory more conciliatory but in practice, as at the North Board elections, the meeting with Eshag and the meeting with the TA concerning management proposals for the community hall, there may be little difference. Indeed there would appear to be an effective albeit incongruent alliance of councillors and officers behind the more or less closed system of the council bureaucracy.

The single forum where officers, councillors and residents formally meet on a regular basis is the North Board. The predicament faced by TA committee members is more heightened for resident representatives on the board. Their support base is even more tenuous and in consequence the link is from the board to the council rather than back to estate residents.[68] In fact, the board may be more appropriately categorized as intermediate between the estate and the council and separate from both fields rather than as a key link.

Demand for reform of the present system comes mainly from within the councillor group and is expressed in terms of improving upon and developing further the mechanisms already instituted rather than in implementing new management policies within an innovatory framework. From the perspective of Parkview the preparedness to respond to such a modified consultative system appears to be constrained by a mix of factors related to the population structure of Parkview and the personal circumstances of those resident there.

These findings are not surprising given the household centred social life of Parkview residents on the one hand, and the bureaucratic and non professional nature of the housing management section on the other. The result is that in exchanges between councillors, officers and residents, there is an inequitable weighting of advantage in favour of the first two groups in the working out of '... alliance, challenge and compromise, trials of strength and allocation of resources ...'

Notes to Part IV

1   This is a subject which is being investigated in a study by SRD.

2   See for example *Housing Review*, Vol 23 No 3, May–June 1974.

3   DOE, *Final Report of the Working Party on Housing Co-operatives* HMSO, 1975.

4   DOE, Circular 8/76, Housing Co-operatives, Annex A, para 6.

5   Ann Richardson and A Wiles, *Getting Tenants Involved, A handbook on systems for tenant participation in housing management*, DOE, 1977.

6   See for example, C Ward, *Tenants Take Over*, London, 1974.

7   In this regard tenant participation can be seen as part of a wider movement which includes also moves to promote worker participation in industry.

8   For an account of schemes prior to 1971 see Julia Craddock, *Tenants Participation in Housing Management*, ALHE, 1975, pp 9–12.

9   Ann Richardson and Barbara Kendall, 'The Progress of Participation', *Housing Monthly*, September 1975.

10   In this and the earlier account of the TA as it relates to the estate (see above pp 89–92) I am indebted to Terry Simpson, a housing management trainee seconded to the project from the local authority. Terry carried out some preliminary analysis of fieldwork data on the TA and wrote a report on the development of the estate committee.

11   Macey and Baker, pp 364–8.

12   These may be compared with the more instrumental objectives of a TA in a private development in South London which are simply stated 'to promote the interests of its members and to deal with the landlords on behalf of its members'. Presumably the members of this association see no need to foster community spirit, good citizenship or self improvement.

13   These figures include a co-opted member from the sheltered housing unit. They do not include the informal and infrequent attendance by members of the youth group.

14   See above pp 95–100 and Case iii pp 189–191

15   See case IV below pp 191–195

16   See case II below pp 186–188

17   The same open attacks occur at general meetings when officers and councillors are present and when other tenants in attendance may be quite unaware of the internal politics of the committee and its rival groups.

18   For instance, when Lloyd drew on former members of his committee as helpers at a Christmas dinner for old age pensioners in the Old Borough this was construed as a piece of electioneering. The TA election was in fact much talked of but did not come off at that time so in April when individuals regarded as Lloyd supporters showed an interest in organizing an estate party for the children as a celebration of a local sporting event this was interpreted in the same way by some members of the Field committee. Given that the turn-out to general meetings is very low and made up largely of committed supporters it is difficult to see how such 'campaigning' could be very effective in securing votes even if that was the motive behind involvement. Nevertheless, beliefs of this kind persist and rumours of plots and intrigues start in all parties. And perhaps not surprisingly, after the elections had taken place a widely expressed view was that they had been 'rigged'. (I heard the same comments after both of the North Board elections as well).

19   In the period immediately following field work a rift in the Field committee was caused by what Mrs Montgomery and her supporters alleged was an intrusion of Labour Party politics into TA committee affairs. See Postcript p 238.

20   There have in fact been more than two building phases and I do not know to what extent the opening of, say, the two tower blocks affected committee politics. This was never mentioned as an issue and it may be that the scale of the garden flats extension and the area of the estate it covers is important in this regard.

21   See above p 90.

22   See case IV below pp 191–195

23   Section 99 of the Public Health Act 1936 gives a tenant the right to summons the landlord (private or Council), where a 'statutory nuisance' exists; ie any defect which interferes with personal comfort or is likely to be a danger to the mental or physical health of the occupier.

24   The contact with the Association of London Housing Estates was initially established as a result of a committee member approaching me for advice which I felt could better be provided from that agency. Other outsiders have approached the committee with offers to come and talk but these have not been taken up. These include the Old Borough Social Services area team leader and a representative from the ILEA youth service. At one time some committee members advocated purchasing pamphlets describing tenants rights particularly in regard to various health regulations. This recommendation was overruled on the grounds that the committee would be spending tenants money and would have nothing to show for it.

25   The petition read as follows: 'We the undersigned being residents of the Parkview estate wish to inform the council that they reached the limit of their tolerance over the heartless action or rather non-action to their legitimate complaints. The latest situation concerning fungus which gathers in the flats destroying the property and consequent costing of the ratepayers' money without a positive action by the council to rectify. We have been visited by various members of the Council, appropriate officers, and so called Housing Board. What we ask for is *Action*, no more promises or letters. Everyday it rains water pours down the stairs like a deluge, we paddle through inches of water on the footpaths, how much longer are we expected to put up with this?

The tenants in the older blocks have sought for years to get things done without success, some of them asked for a transfer to the new blocks, but found themselves lucky now they did not make the move'.

The councillor who objected to the wording considered that the words 'so called Housing Board' constituted a slight on the North Board.

26   A S York, 'Voluntary Associations and their Leaders in a Difficult Housing Estate', unpublished thesis, U of Leiecester, 1972, pp 116–19.

27   N Babchuk and A Booth, 'Voluntary Association Membership: A Longitudinal Analysis', *American Sociological Review*, XXXIV, 1969, cit York, p 120.

28   T Cauter and J S Downham, *The Communication of Ideas*, 1954, cit York, p 120.

29   Mrs Field is over seventy. A next door neighbour of Mrs Glenn's drawn into the committee only briefly, was in his twenties.

30   Mrs Noakes is a solo parent with a teenage son.

31   J M Simmie, 'Public Participation: a case study from Oxfordshire', *Journal of the Town Planning Institute*, April 1971, Vol 57, No 4, p 151f.

32   J Barnes, 'Class and Committees in a Norwegian Island Parish', *Human Relations*, vii, 1954, p 50.

33 R Frankenberg, 1957, pp 19, 111, 117, 129.

34 P D Wheeldon, 'The Operation of Voluntary Associations and Personal Networks in the Political Processes of an Inter-ethnic Community', in J C Mitchell (ed) *Social Networks in Urban Situations*, Manchester, 1969, p 140f.

35 Barnes, *op cit*, p 40f.

36 P M Blau, *Exchange and Power in Social Life*, New York, 1964, p 307.

37 Morris suggests a rather different class/culture-based explanation for this type of behaviour:

> Effective social controls … are largely external and formal and stem from outside the local community [ie the police and court system]. As a result the only kinds of anti-social behaviour which can be successfully limited are almost always illegal. Those delinquencies which are not illegal, and which would be kept in check by the informal pressure of public opinion in a middle class neighbourhood are integrated within a normative cultural pattern, the only control being exerted by an adaptation of the lex talionis. Feuds and reprisals, however, are essentially group activities and are confined therefore to those sections of the population which are organized on a group basis, the children and adolescents. For the rest, the principle of 'giving as good as you take' operates, so that abuse over the garden fence must be met by further abuse, slander, by counter-slanders and so on.

T Morris, in Carson and Wiles, 1971, p 89.

38 Letter dated 24 February 1975.

39 The notice of eviction should be preceded by two other standard forms. It is impossible from the files to comment on the merits of the claims and counter claims since not all relevant papers seen to be filed anyway.

40 Black retained the letter. Later Mrs Steel phoned and asked for it to be returned but this request was not met.

41 Part of this case covers the period immediately prior to my taking up residence on the estate. However, the use of council files and residents accounts has enabled what I am satisfied is a fair reconstruction of events.

42 White to Mrs Montgomery et al 6 June 1974.

43 White to Councillor Williams 27 June 1974.

44 White to Mrs Montgomery 25 June 1974.

45 Upper flats in these blocks have no balconies but flats at the end of a block have their own staircases. One of those was occupied by a middle aged couple who, prior to their move to the estate, had successfully entered the Borough's garden competition. They placed hanging baskets and planters up the stairs and expressed a desire to fix brackets to the walls for more baskets. They also wanted to tile the stairs and have a gate at the landing. My suggestions that a few paving stones alongside the stairs might be removed and a tree or creeper planted was received with enthusiasm. They did not however do any of those things because they said they would not be 'allowed'.

46 In a report on proposals for landscaping in a new development in the Borough the Housing Co-ordinator recommended that 'small private gardens should be supplied for the residents of the ground floor flats (and others perhaps). This provides a very important ingredient to the proper maintenance of the areas'. Late reports to the Housing Services Committee, 10 March 76, p 35.

47   See above pp 95–100

48   See plan p 244. Cf L Holman and E Barker. 'An Experiment with Tenant Involvement in the Planning and Design of Public Housing', "Living Places" 1975/76 p 16, where it was noted that even in a scheme involving direct participation, 'tenants still had difficulty understanding plans presented in diagram form. To be understood the plans had to have a realistic quality about them. If there were no such quality unintended qualities were attributed to the diagrams and faulty interpretations resulted.'

49   For example the committee expressed a preference for folding tables for ease of stacking and storage; those delivered are not collapsible, require heavy lifting and stack awkwardly.

50   I am at a loss to explain why the committee reacted in this way. It will be remembered that this was immediately prior to the resignation of Mandle, Lessor, Simpson and Davidson and the survival of the Field rump committee following the showdown with Lloyd. Undoubtedly the internal politics of the committee were very sensitive and some suspicion probably attached to my intervention at this point.

51   The other facilities referred to ranged from converted basements or laundries to purpose built halls. It should be noted that the Housing Committee at its meeting on 29 November 1972 received a report from the Borough Treasurer and the Director of Financial Services on the question of club room facilities on council estates. This paper set out guidelines 'for a policy applicable to the rents of clubrooms'.

> . . . In assessing a basis for a policy on rent charges, consideration needs to be given to the following factors:
> a. Nature of the user.
> b. Facilities provided and used.
> c. Cost of the facilities provided.
> d. Financial resources of the user.
> e. Indirect benefits to the council (eg reduction of vandalism).
> In almost all cases it would not be possible to charge a "realistic rent" in view of the limited resources of the organizations and it would, perhaps, be more appropriate, for the purposes of this report, to consider "rent" as a "contribution towards cost".
> Where possible and practicable, it is suggested that the user of the facilities be responsible for the cost of heating, lighting, cleaning, repairs (fair wear and tear excepted) and internal decorations.

With regard to the question of 'rent' the paper suggested that consideration be given to four possible methods; actual costs incurred; actual costs incurred abated as necessary; nominal rental and free use. The basis felt to be most appropriate was actual costs abated. 'The extent of abatement could be determined by the Housing Manager and the Borough Treasurer and Director of Financial Services and the position could be reported annually to the Committee'. Financial Appraisal No. 228, 23 November 1972. At the time I was not aware of this paper and I did not hear it referred to either by Black or any of the councillors subsequently involved in the Parkview discussions. However, I understand it did form the basis of the fixing of the rental.

52   20 January 1975. I was not present at this meeting. From accounts it would seem that Lloyd, Lessor and Mandle were the strongest supporters of a working man's club type facility; Mrs Field, Mrs Montgomery and Mrs Glenn opposed this and advocated a centre catering for all ages and interests.

53   The latter developments of this episode cover the period immediately following fieldwork but the details have been included here for convenience. An assessment of the impact of the hall is given in the Postscript below pp 243–253.

54   This advice was not accurate. Under the terms of the Local Government Act 1972 sub committees may be set up with either advisory or delegated decision making powers and without restriction on the number of tenants co-opted as members. Sec 101, 102. For a discussion of these provisions of the Act see Ann Richardson, 'Decision-making by non-elected members: an analysis of new provisions in the 1972 Local Government Act', *Journal of Social Policy*. 6, 2, 171–84.

55   I am well aware that each of the boards may operate somewhat differently though another study shows variations to be relatively minor. See Ann Richardson and Andrew Wiles, 'Tenant Participation in Council Housing...' unpublished report to 4 London boroughs, October 1975.

56   See above p10.

57   During this time elections were held for the South board as well but this was a simple matter since the positions were not contested. I am unable to explain the discrepancy between voting and attendance figures.

58   See Appendix v.

59   Such work is anyway inappropriate for Thompson; as an acquired property representative he visits on an individual house to house basis. Steed's job entails shifts with a lot of night work and he therefore has little time available for committee or constituency work.

60   Interviews were of a semi-structured kind and issues covered are outlined in Appendix II.

61   Federation membership comprises some of the Borough's TA's. As an organization it has no power but constitutes another pressure group. I am unable to comment on how influential it has been in this regard.

62   Two councillors, Councillor Harty and the chairman of the Housing Utilisation Review committee declined to be interviewed. One schedule was self completed at the request of a member. Interviews were carried out between August 75 and January 76. An outline of the schedule appears in Appendix II.

63   A course sponsored by the Institute of Housing and a local polytechnic with the support of the Borough was held shortly after the completion of field work. It was aimed at promoting resident awareness of management issues and was attended by tenant representatives from Boards and Associations throughout the Borough.

64   Membership of the boards was later increased. See below p 256.

65   Interview schedules appear in Appendix II.

66   These comments refer to committee action in regard to the Section 99 action in the garden flats affected by severe dampness.

67   As already noted Thompson, one of the resident representatives to the North Board is black. It may be significant in this context, however, that he is not an estate representative, and has no association with estate TA organisations.

68   This has been noted in other participation schemes also. Cf Craddock, 1975, p 89 ff

Part V

Postscript

Part v outlines events from the end of fieldwork to the time of writing (December 1976). Discussion centres on developments at Parkview, in particular an attempt to establish a community work project for the estate, TA committee politics and the management and use of the community hall. These developments are to some degree interconnected and in order to convey something of the complexity of this connectedness the account, with one exception, is given here in roughly chronological order. Most of the information was obtained during brief return visits to Parkview in the course of discussions with the main participants. The exception is the use of the community hall. This was the subject of two surveys and the activities of all user groups were monitored in the course of a weeklong study at Parkview. The results of these surveys and observations are discussed in a separate section. The Parkview developments are then assessed in more general terms in the context of the study as a whole. Finally and more briefly, changes in the housing directorate are noted.

Parkview politics; August 1975 to December 1976

Towards the end of fieldwork, the Social Research Division of the Department of the Environment mooted the idea of jointly funding the salary of an estate community worker with representatives of the local education authority and Borough officers from the Housing Directorate and the Community Development Unit (CDU). This action was prompted by an awareness of the extent to which there appeared to be a need for some continuing community work input on Parkview and the recognition of our indebtedness to estate residents. The TA committee was consulted and lent its support to the idea. The proposal was that an independent project committee should be set up to employ and direct a community worker for a period of one year. This committee would include representatives from the funding bodies but should have a resident majority. The project committee was to be responsible for defining the brief of the worker. Subsequently, these proposals were modified so that the CDU made a special appointment of a worker with responsibility for Parkview for a period of six months. It was intended that the worker appointed would 'investigate with the TA and other groups the need for long-term community work on the estate and . . . work with the TA to facilitate the full use of the community hall on the estate. It was clear that in looking at these two areas the aim was to produce proposals geared to long-term needs.'[1] In the course of this six months it was hoped to decide what form of continuing community work support might be most appropriate.

A community worker, John, was appointed from 1 September. Initially, TA committee members expressed themselves most impressed by him and they anticipated considerable assistance in promoting activities in the hall and in their dealings with the housing directorate. This mood of optimism was shortlived. John's brief was not made clear to him, and was certainly not explained to estate residents. The manner of his appointment[2] made it difficult to get equipment like a telephone for the office in the hall, other demands were made upon his time, and as a result he was not often to be seen at Parkview. Inevitably he became a target for suspicion–'Whose side is he on?' and attack– 'What is he doing?'.

Meanwhile, the TA committee had possession of the keys to the hall and little else. The secretary, Mrs Montgomery, assumed responsibility for the keys and had a hectic time opening and closing the hall for sundry contractors, inspectors and delivery men. The committee was, however, unable to finalise the terms of the agreement with the council and experienced considerable difficulty in obtaining insurance. Eventually the lease was signed in December. The terms for the first six months provided for payment to the council of a nominal rent of £5 per month. When a six months extension to this lease was being considered by the Housing Services Committee it was noted that 'The present policy in connection with rents for club rooms and community centres on housing estates is to establish an economic rent. However, if the financial resources of the users are small it has been the practice to gauge the rents in accordance with the Association's income'.[3] The TA committee also accepted liability for maintenance (excluding the structure of the building and breakages of windows), cleaning, electricity charges and insurance. This latter item was finalised in late January 1976.

These delays meant that the committee was uncertain what activities might be arranged in the hall. For a period of some five months the hall was completed but effectively untenable. Some adult activities took place during this time but understandably the committee felt unable to allow regular meetings of the youth group. Not surprisingly some of the early enthusiasm and impetus to foster hall-based activities were lost.

Within the TA committee management of the hall became a divisive issue even before opening and even although changes in committee membership appeared to result in the reformation of a one-party group. In November Mrs Field again became chairman when Mrs Dee effectively resigned.[4] Since the latter's Eshag supporters had already stepped down, this left mainly the members of the old Field/Montgomery group. At this point, however, Mrs Montgomery became the subject of criticism in allegations that she had assumed an organizing and controlling function in the management of the hall to the exclusion of all other committee members. This was most obvious in access to the hall. By early January Mrs Field was trying to organize a pensioners' club and a play group was in the early stages of development. On occasion both experienced difficulties in getting the keys.

Another contentious issue which threatened to divide the committee into factions was a policy of charges for hiring the hall. Some members felt that fees paid by user groups should be nominal and that the management should adopt a community service orientation, others that rents should be related to those charged commercially for comparable facilities elsewhere. In the event there was a compromise solution to this issue. An hourly rate of £2.50 was fixed for casual hiring of the main hall, £1.20 for the committee room. However, if the venture was non-profit making these charges were reduced to £2 and £1. In addition, reduced rentals, related to the capacity to pay were made available to those regular user groups which shortly became established. Thus, the play group was charged £5 weekly, the youth club £2, weightlifting and keep-fit classes £1 each per session[5]. The hall was made available on a daily basis for private lettings at a charge of £30 for Parkview residents and £40 for outsiders.

Other problems quickly became apparent. Mrs Montgomery and another committee member Mrs Glenn jointly organized an afternoon bingo session aimed at attracting pensioners. The prizes were groceries and the sociability aspect of the occasion was emphasized. In the course of these sessions they also ran a raffle to raise funds for an outing. The organizers wanted to keep these funds separate from TA funds, but Mrs Field, concerned at their lack of accountability, tried unsuccessfully to instigate some form of control over the pensioners' bingo activities.

Mrs Field was also concerned at the extent to which the organization of activities in the hall devolved on so few people. With John's help and more or less independently of her committee she decided to try and increase an awareness of estate affairs and thereby broaden the base of the TA by calling a series of block meetings in the hall. The immediate aim was to get block representatives who would act as collectors for TA subscriptions in their own building. Circulars were run off and delivered to each residence some two or three days prior to a meeting. The result was disappointing; from most blocks there was no response at all while from others only one or two residents attended.

The demands made upon the small and hardworking committee combined with John's failure to establish an image on Parkview contributed to the increasing disenchantment with his rôle. In February this came to a head when Mrs Montgomery, together with another committee member, Mrs Noakes, put forward the view that the estate community worker should be accountable to the Parkview TA committee. They claimed that they had on numerous occasions asked John to describe his job and explain the reasons for his absence from the estate but to no avail. John interpreted this move within the committee as an attempted 'kangaroo' court and advised the dissatisfied members to lodge an official complaint. Further, he refused to answer any charges of unsatisfactory conduct except in the presence of his senior officer and shop steward. Mrs Field supported John's stance. Mrs Montgomery then insisted on formally placing before the committee a motion to the effect that John's work be the subject of an official enquiry. The motion was lost on the casting vote of the chairman. Mrs Noakes and Mrs Montgomery resigned as a protest against the alleged intrusion of politics and trade union matters into committee business. Subsequently, these two women urged an enquiry through one of the ward councillors. They claim they were not satisfied with the verbal replies received and spoke of going to opposition members of the council and the press[6] but finally the matter was allowed to drop.

The following month, in March, the first TA annual general meeting to be held in the hall took place. Mrs Field was confirmed in the position of chairman. Mrs Glenn replaced Mrs Montgomery as secretary and a newcomer filled the position of treasurer. This committee was composed predominantly of newcomers to the estate politics, all volunteers rather than nominees from the meeting. Mrs Field had high hopes that this committee, free of all the dissension which had split previous committees, would mark a different phase in the TA's development. Nevertheless, problems soon appeared. Lettings of the hall continued to be made without reference to the committee. Sub-committees were set up and in a burst of enthusiasm the social entertainments committee went ahead and organized activities without reference to the main committee. This trend was firmly opposed by Mrs Field who maintained that sub-committees should first obtain the approval of the main committee and later report back to it.

John's term on the estate, by this time, was almost completed. On the basis of his work there and in view of the fact that neither the local education authority nor the Borough were now prepared to part-fund a worker, he proposed that the DOE's contribution be used to pay residents prepared to work to a project committee as Parkview community workers. Early in April 1976 I attended a meeting to discuss the proposal with the TA committee. Members were asked to approve the establishment of a project in principle. The committee would then be required to nominate four residents to sit on a special project committee. One of the ward councillors would be invited to join the committee, the DOE would nominate myself as their representative and John would have a place on the committee to service it and liaise with the CDU which would accept overall administrative responsibility. The grant of £1000 from DOE would be a once-and-for-all payment. The project committee would define a brief for the worker/s, make the appointments and generally oversee the work. It would be a condition of the terms of appointment that workers had a weekly session with John and that periodic reports be made available to myself for the purpose of completing the Parkview study. These arrangements were put to the committee as guidelines only and allowance was made for modifications to meet resident defined aims and priorities. Even so, consideration of the proposal was hesitant and non-committal apparently because of the feeling among some members that the committee had rather more responsibility than it could cope with. Accordingly, it was agreed to defer the matter to the next meeting.

Late in April the TA committee approved the setting up of a project in principle but again postponed action by leaving the selection of resident representatives to the project committee for consideration at the next meeting. By mid-May, four resident representatives including Mrs Field and Mrs Glenn were selected, [7] Councillor Mrs Ewing had accepted an invitation to sit on the project committee and the scheme could go ahead.

At its first meeting in June the project committtee decided to try to recruit workers to establish a good neighbour service on the estate. This was an acknowledgement of the need to provide various forms of assistance to estate residents as well as a recognition of the scope for working outside the hall. Moreover, while this kind of work was considered to be beyond the capabilities of the TA committee, once a register of those in need and those able to offer assistance had been set up the scheme could be sustained beyond the duration of the project. John agreed to write a circular, check the wording with committee members and arrange distribution to all estate households. In fact there was no checking and due to a misunderstanding the circular which went out left the definition of job function open and asked for suggestions from residents.

Perhaps not surprisingly the response was poor. There were four applicants including Mrs Montgomery. An application from the latter posed problems for the resident members of the committee. By this time it was evident that some TA committee members, dissatisfied with the leadership provided by Mrs Field, had approached Mrs Montgomery for advice and support. Mrs Field and Mrs Montgomery was adopting an activist rôle as the focus for a dissident faction. speaking terms, but Mrs Field and Mrs Glenn both assumed that Mrs Montgomery was adopting an activist rôle as the focus for a dissident faction. Even without interview it was agreed that Mrs Montgomery was the only candidate suitable for the job.[8] At the same time, however, it was felt that a single appointment of Mrs Montgomery would create a political situation which might well get out of hand. The committee resolved to distribute a second leaflet asking for applicants specifically for the establishment of a good neighbour service. These were never delivered. The committee met once more ostensibly to consider applications from both advertisements. I was not present at that meeting since it was felt that my previous identification with the Field/Montgomery group and my attempt to continue relations with both women, made it impossible for me to appear neutral. In the event, there was reportedly little discussion or debate. The committee had lost interest, the grant was turned down and the Parkview project ended without ever making a beginning. It is difficult to comment on the background to this decision without first-hand knowledge. From the outset, within the TA committee it seems that there was little enthusiasm for the idea of a project. Mrs Field and Mrs Glenn agreed to serve on the committee more or less by default. The other two resident nominees were both elderly and apparently influenced in their opinions by the two TA office holders. The ward councillor Mrs Ewing was committed to the idea of a project but while expressing disappointment at its demise, felt unable to exercise a leadership function in the context of a resident-controlled committee. John saw himself in a disinterested support rôle although as the project failed to develop he expressed the view privately that 'it would be better if the whole thing was just dropped.' Moreover, other committee members looked to him for information and guidance and he was always ready to give a personal opinion. At the same time John was planning to leave the CDU and Mrs Field was becoming increasingly disillusioned with the petty wrangles of estate politics. In these circumstances the distribution of wrongly worded leaflets and the poor response elicited simply eased the way for their withdrawal. John and Mrs Field were the dominant members of the committee; it was they who decided to disband the committee rather than continue.[9]

Meantime, the TA committee itself was in the process of forming factions. Since Mrs Montgomery's resignation Mrs Glenn had taken on the job of lettings officer with sole responsibility for the keys. Inevitably there were some difficulties. Access to the hall continued to pose problems and as a consequence the play group arranged to have their own set of keys cut. After taking this action the play group leader was invited to speak to the TA committee and won formal approval on a vote. Mrs Field opposed the motion and informed the committee that if keys were in the possession of any group apart from the main committee she would refuse to sign an extension to the lease. On another occasion a 'Keep Fit' class was unable to get into the hall and when criticized Mrs Glenn retaliated by closing an evening bingo session. Following this action a number of residents, of whom Mrs Montgomery was one, organized a petition requesting the calling of an emergency meeting to discuss the management of the hall.

Gradually the lines within the committee hardened with Mrs Field and Mrs Glenn becoming regarded as a controlling partnership able to keep everything from other participants. Older committee members were regarded as passive accomplices. Younger committee women formed a dissident group, sniping in between meetings and at times turning to Mrs Montgomery for support but for the most part lacking the confidence to raise issues directly in committee meetings.

There were other incidents. The emergency meeting took place but Mrs Field's control was apparently so tight as to disallow the full expression of resident grievances. At a dance sponsored by the North Board, when Mrs Field tried to close the hall at 11 pm a number of 'opposition' committee members together with Mrs Montgomery staged a protest in the form of a 'sit in'. Those at the dance included Labour party councillors and at the conclusion they and Mrs Field joined in the singing of a party political song. Thereafter attacks on Mrs Field strengthened. She took them personally and at the same time became less inclined to become further embroiled in estate politics as an application for a transfer to another estate seemed likely to be approved.

In July the political scene became potentially more complicated by the formation of a committee for the purpose of raising funds and organizing events for the Royal Jubilee celebrations.[10] The initiative was taken largely by Mrs Montgomery and the Jubilee committee could be seen as a counter group in much the same way as Eshag had been viewed. This was particularly so after leading members of the committee adopted a political stance and mounted an attack on some squatters who had taken up residence in several vacant Parkview flats. In fact this identification was prevented by other events. Mrs Field formally resigned in September; had she not done so it seems likely that there would have been a move to oust her from the position of chairman. At the elections held later that month all members of the Field committee stepped down. The incoming committee contained only a few members drawn from the former committee, the most prominent of whom was Mrs Glenn. Mrs Montgomery was back as secretary and the chair was taken by a newcomer to estate politics, Mrs Houlton. These two and others on the committee had been most active in the Jubilee committee; the latter was effectively incorporated within the TA.

This committee, like some of its predecessors had a predominance of women, but unlike others it incorporated an almost equal weighting of older established residents and more recent arrivals from the garden flats. Mrs Houlton had no prior experience of committee work. She claimed that it was her intention to allow for the open expression of conflict and debate within committtee meetings; outside that forum she expected a display of group solidarity and loyalty. It was soon made apparent to Mrs Houlton that the difficulties of committee management lay not so much in allowing or disallowing the expression of difference as in retaining the support of members holding minority opinions.

One of the first major issues facing the Houlton committee was the consideration of a new lease agreement for the hall. This was not a negotiated settlement; rather, council officers perused the association's books and on that basis advised the committee of an agreement incorporating a revised rent charge of £300 per six months. Rate charges were still to be assessed and other conditions remained unchanged. Mrs Montgomery opposed acceptance of these terms on the grounds that the rent had been assessed on the basis of all hall income and not only on private lettings. She further argued that the association had been building up funds for the purchase of much needed equipment and that under the new agreement these funds would be absorbed in rent payments. Mrs Montgomery maintained that in these circumstances it would be in the committee's best interests to charge only nominal rents to all user groups and to spend all funds from private lettings for equipment etc since otherwise they would simply be 'working for the council'. This was a minority view. The committee not only accepted the new terms but planned various fund raising activities in order to be able to meet the demand. Mrs Montgomery resigned in protest.

Another issue which threatened to divide the committee arose after a private letting when the hall was allegedly left in a bad state. The function had been hosted by a black resident and this led to a motion being put before the committee that henceforth no private lettings to black persons should be allowed. In the course of the debate one speaker pointed out that such committee action would be illegal and another committee member, herself married to a Jamaican, was firmly opposed to any discriminatory practices on the basis of colour. The effects of these divisions on committee politics were not fully apparent at the time of writing. Nevertheless, it was already clear that Mrs Houlton's chances of realizing her aims were doubtful.

Parkview community hall

As noted earlier, the architect saw Parkview as a community. It was intended that, in social terms, this community would most clearly find expression through activities organized by and for estate residents in a community hall. In a submission to the DOE for finance the architect noted that following requests from residents the housing committee '... considered that the provision of a community hall to serve the various age groups of the people living on the estate would be well justified. The building, therefore, has been designed to accommodate all the various uses and activities envisaged, and includes a portion of the existing car-park deck as a garden and sitting out space'.[11] It was not made clear exactly what uses and activities were considered and the hall appears to have been planned as a general multi-purpose one. (See Plan VII).

Towards the end of September 1976, after the hall had been in use for some nine months, I returned to the estate for one week to observe activities there and assess their impact on the estate generally. It was hypothesized that an assessment of the effect of the opening of the hall could only be made if information about use of the hall was supplemented by data about those residents who did not make use of the facilities offered. Accordingly, not only were those attending the hall asked to fill in a questionnaire but a postal questionnaire was sent to all residents in the project sample.[12] As in earlier sections the convention has been adopted of referring to the latter as respondents.

The range of activities and amount of use made of facilities in the hall are outlined in Table VII. A number of comments should be made about this table. Attenders at the pensioners' bingo formed themselves into an informal social club. Mrs Glenn, one of the main organizers, arranged a seaside outing for those attending and similar outings were planned for the future. Mrs Field deplored the emphasis on bingo and initiated an afternoon club for pensioners. It was hoped to introduce members to new hobbies and generally widen their range of interests. The club never attracted more than eight members and by the time of survey had folded. Other proposals, like whist-drives and a chess club, never got started for lack of support. The youth club initially attempted to cater for all ages in a single session. This was found to be unsatisfactory and later sessions were divided to cater separately for two age groups, 5–11 years and 12 and over. The youth club is a socially orientated one with a canteen, television set and record player much in demand. In addition there are opportunities for playing games like billiards, table tennis and draughts.

Outdoor sitting area over
car park

Tea bar

Sitting area

Meetings/
additional sitting

Underground
car park

chair/
store
under

up   up

stage
stored
under

ramp

Service
entry

Main activities hall

Demountable
stage

Store

Male
toilets

Cloaks

Lobby

Office

Female
toilets

Make up

0   5   10
feet

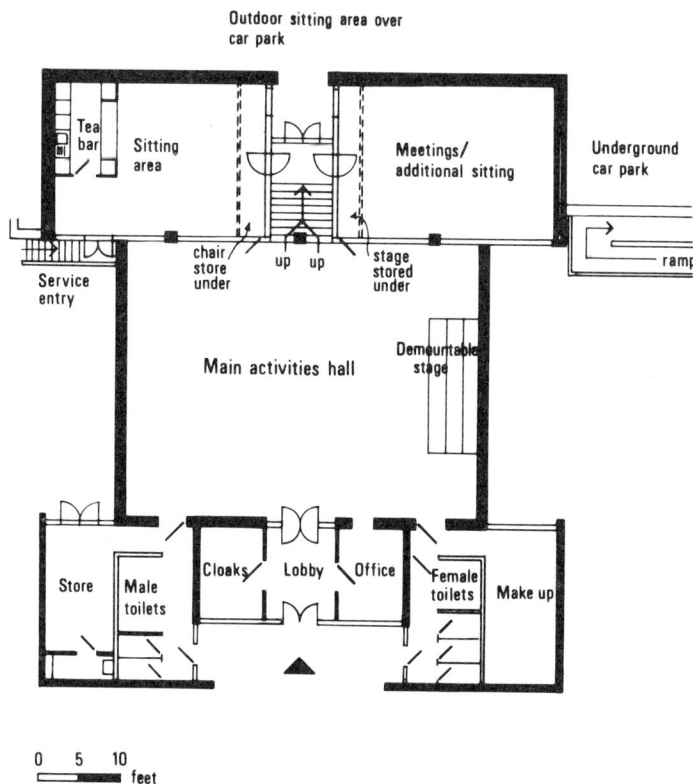

The occasional lettings organized by the TA have included discos and dances, a film show, jumble sales and Christmas parties. For the 12 months to December 1976, 30 private bookings had been made mostly for Saturday evenings. (Plates 42 and 43)

Three of the user groups are organized either entirely or with the assistance of paid helpers in the employ of outside agencies. The play group is conducted under the auspices of the Pre-school Playgroup Association and it provides the salary for one leader and one assistant. In addition there is a roster of volunteer mother helpers. The youth group has two youth leaders funded by the local education authority and one regular parent assistant, Glenn. The club also had the backing of an adult committee comprising three residents although the extent to which the committee was involved in the affairs of the club appeared to be very limited. The luncheon club staff comprised three women, one cleaner and two kitchen/servery staff, all in the employ of Social Services. The remaining activities were organized by residents, in some cases non TA committee members. Thus, the 'Keep Fit' and weightlifting classes are run by residents with a special interest in the activity and Mrs Montgomery continued to help organize the bingo sessions after she had relinquished committee work.

244

TABLE VIII   Parkview community hall, programme of activities, September 1976

Day	Morning Main hall	Morning Cttee rm/Kitchen	Main hall	Afternoon Cttee rm/Kitchen	Evening Main hall	Cttee rm/Kitchen	Less regular bookings
Mon	10–12 noon Pre-school play group+			12 noon–2 pm Luncheon club	7.30–8.45pm Ladies keep fit* 8.45–10 pm Men's weight-lifting		
Tues	10–12 noon Pre-school play group+		2.30–4.30 pm Pensioners' prize bingo*	12 noon–2 pm Luncheon club	7–8.15 pm Junior youth club* 8.15–10 pm Senior youth club+		
Wed	10–12 noon Pre-school play group+			12 noon–2 pm Luncheon club			TA cttee meetings approx 1 in 2 weeks
Thurs	10–12 noon Pre-school play group+			12 noon–2 pm Luncheon club	8–10 pm Prize bingo*		
Fri	10–12 noon Pre-school play group+			12 noon–2 pm Luncheon club	7–8.15 pm Junior youth club* 8.15–10 pm Senior youth club*		1 and 3 in month councillor surgery in office
Sat	Generally available for private functions such as wedding receptions etc.						Irregular TA organized social events fund raising activities
Sun							

+ excepting school holidays.

* user group makes use of the kitchen/servery for the making of tea and in the case of the youth club a canteen service.

245

The playgroup, youth club and pensioners' club each received grants for equipment and other materials from various sources. In addition groups themselves have raised funds by mobilizing the support of members in different ways and through activities like a jumble sale or dance.

In the course of the survey week some 220 members attended a group activity. Some 119 (54%) of these were resident on the estate. This represents 6% of the estate population. This figure is considerably lower than that recorded for Parkview generaly since 31% of all respondents belonged to some kind of club or organisation. It is, however, similar to that noted by other studies where 5% was found to be a typical level of involvement.[13]

A more detailed breakdown of these overall figures accentuates the distinction which can be made between externally sponsored and resident organized activities. The former cater to specific interests and needs and attract the greater part of their membership from beyond Parkview. The latter, although drawing more on the estate population, attract relatively limited categories of residents. The characteristics of the membership of each group will be considered here in turn. All figures are correct as at 27 September 1976.

The playgroup had a current membership of 19 and a capacity of 25 children. Fees of 25p per child were payable each session. Attendance of most children was very regular and the group enjoyed considerable parental support. The roster for help from mothers appeared to work smoothly and some fathers were involved to the extent of designing and building equipment such as a miniature carpenter's bench complete with tools. The group's committee was very active in raising funds and by the time of the survey the group had acquired a good range of interesting equipment and would face serious storage problems if more was obtained.

Four of the children attending the group were drawn from Parkview estate, four more from a large estate nearby. The small estate attendance is accounted for by several factors. Quite a number of pre-school children on Parkview are too young for the play group and mothers of those in the older age group appear to prefer the nearby Park nursery school. In addition the playgroup aims to involve both mothers and children; it is not intended, nor are the hours suitable, for working mothers. Many estate mothers are working and for that reason make use of nursery facilities or the services of child minders. As a consequence most of the children came from homes in nearby terrace streets, with a few from smaller estates in the locality. Many of the mothers[14] appeared to be most concerned to provide the best educational opportunities for their children. Those from the surrounding streets spoke of their horror of estate living; they preferred to struggle to convert a small terrace house into a modern home in the belief that in so doing they were creating a better social environment for their children.

The youth club had 90 junior and 130 senior members. Approximately 100, or less than half, lived on Parkview. This represents 24% of those in the 6–16 age range. However, on most nights, at both the junior and senior sections,

246

there was a core of 25–30 regular attenders. Most of these regulars came from the estate and the core of the senior club comprised members of the youth club formed with Don's help as part of the Parkview study.[15] Enrolment fees for the club were 25p with an entrance fee of 5p per session.

The effective drop-out rate from the club appears to be fairly high and aspects of its management and membership warrant further comment. The club leaders expressed themselves generally pleased with the way the club had developed. Some of the senior members complained that the leaders were 'too bossy'. On the other hand, the few parents spoken to claimed there was not enough discipline. Other residents agreed and referred to a fight on the estate between some estate youngsters and a rival gang and which ended in a stabbing and police patrols for several nights thereafter.

The sessions observed were trouble-free and obviously enjoyed by those present. However, in the senior club it was evident that the prominent rôles assumed by members of the old youth group and the relatively closed circle they formed might effectively exclude other members, especially those not members of similar informal groups and those with a more retiring personality. This situation is probably common to such clubs and doubtless the characteristics of the membership change fairly rapidly as members of the dominant group leave school and find a wider set of interests.

In July the luncheon club moved from its purpose built premises in Church Close[16] to the committee room of the hall (Plate 44). Little was changed except the premises[17] but both staff and clients were unhappy on that account. Initially, those attending had walked through the main hall thereby causing some disturbance to playgroup activities. Then a ramp was fitted to one side of the building enabling access through another entrance. Even so there were still complaints from the old people. Most expressions of discontent were probably related less to such minor inconveniences than to the widely expressed view that the hall was 'not the same'; it was not 'theirs' and felt less homely – 'in Church Close we were one happy family'. Staff complaints centred on the inadequate kitchen facilities, the inconvenience of having to store supplies in the freezer at Church Close and the disputes which inevitably arose over the cleaning of a kitchen used by so many different user groups as servery, bar and canteen (Plate 45). The opinions of the old people might over time incline to be more favourable. Already some regularly stayed on for the pensioners' bingo, they were advised of outings and social functions taking place on the estate and gradually at least some might come to have a wider range of hall based interests. However, it is more difficult to see how staff grievances could be remedied; indeed it might be expected that their conditions of work will deteriorate.

The resident organized groups, cash and prize bingo and the 'Keep Fit' class, were observed during the study week and those attending were also asked to complete a questionnaire. The weightlifting class was not attended but questionnaires were completed by all those attending. In the course of the survey week the estimated attendance figure for these groups was 120. It should be noted that the attendance figures given below for these groups do not add to this total because approximately 43% of all members attended more than one group. The most common combination was attendance at both the bingo and 'Keep Fit' sessions.

Both bingo sessions were run by Mrs Glenn and Mrs Montgomery with assistance from other residents in selling entrance tickets, books and raffle tickets, checking the cards of winners and in making tea and cleaning up afterwards. Entrance fee to the session was 5p and small charges were also made for refreshments and raffle tickets. Sales of books at cash bingo amounted to £82.10 all of it returned in prizes. At both the afternoon and evening sessions the break for tea and the short intervals between games were occasions for much chatter and it was clear that most tables attracted the same group of regulars each time. The combined attendance figure for the sessions was 160.

The 'Keep Fit' class had an attendance of about 40 women although only 8–10 took part in the exercises. The majority attended for the company, a gossip and a night out. The men's weightlifting was taken by one of the caretakers and it was hoped to attract a number of men from the estate. In fact only one other adult attended and the membership of 11 was drawn from the senior youth club.

Overall, the vast majority of hall patrons were women (84%). Most were married and the returns from the sample suggest that most of these would be from households with young dependents. Forty per cent of those attending bingo sessions were widowed.

Nearly one-third of all patrons were drawn from outside Parkview itself,[18] most attracted to bingo. Within the estate Parkview residents appeared to be drawn disproportionately from the different block types. Thus 13% of all garden flat households were represented at some hall activity, 12% of all balcony access and 9% of Y block while only 6% of tower block households were represented. This finding may be related to several factors. As noted in Part II the distribution of households with children and all adult households is not even across the estate as a whole and it might be expected that support would be drawn from particular household types. It was also noted that the tower blocks have fairly high concentrations of one parent family and black households. The findings of the postal survey indicated that neither of these groups had been attracted to the hall. Finally, personal networks may influence attendance figures. Thus Mrs Houlton, an Old Borough 'identity' of longstanding, had by then assumed a prominent rôle in the TA and in the management of the hall generally; she claimed to have 'roped in' a good many residents from her own block.

Older established residents were less likely to attend activities in the hall. Twelve per cent of those resident on Parkview for between 5–10 years and 12% of those resident for periods longer than that attended some activity. By contrast 20% of those resident on the estate for less than five years were members of some group. This may be related to the population structure of the most recently opened blocks and the desire of newcomers to establish more social contacts.

Patrons were most often attracted to an activity in the early stages of its establishment; new patrons were relatively fewer only 17% being attracted within the three months prior to the survey. Information on the drop-out rate was not available since these groups did not keep formal membership registers. However, according to the organizers very few patrons had stopped attending.

Once patrons had been attracted to a group it appeared that their attendance was very regular. Ninety one per cent claimed to attend once weekly. This need not, however, imply attendance of the same activity regularly since 43% of all patrons attended one or more other activities in the hall. Furthermore, 39% of all patrons claimed that at least one other member of their household also attended. The pattern of attendance would appear to be that of a solid core of supporters drawn from a relatively few households most of whose members were active patrons of a number of functions. This is probably due partly to the fact that those attending one function in the hall are more likely to learn from announcements or notice boards of other activities taking place. And partly it would seem to be a reflection of the fact that those attracted appear to be already committed 'joiners'. Thus 51% of all patrons had attended similar activities, clubs etc outside Parkview. Most of these (79%) retained membership of these outside organizations and most (74%) continued to attend. Since the most frequently cited outside activities were bingo, pensioners and social clubs, it seems that patrons of the hall are simply following at a more local venue the same or similar activities to those taken up elsewhere.

This localized setting appeared to make an important contribution to the social rewards looked for and enjoyed by those taking part in hall activities. This was evident both in the personal manner of recruitment and in the friendships formed or renewed. Just over half (51%) were introduced to an activity by an existing member or a friend. However, it is of interest to note that nearly half of the women attending 'Keep Fit' responded to an invitation outlined in a newsletter. This may be accounted for by the manner of presentation adopted in this particular letter; several women commented favourably on the fact that the class was described as 'a fun thing', 'good for a laugh' and 'a night off' from household chores. Most patrons cited social factors of a personal nature as their main reason for joining. Forty per cent instanced loneliness or a desire for company while 20% cited boredom. Only 15% claimed a liking for the activity as a major factor influencing their decision to join. The expectations of patrons appeared to be met. Very few (7%) made no new friendships and most claimed that not only had they made new friendships but that these friends were met also outside the hall itself.[19]

Eighteen patrons assisted in the running of a group. Somewhat surprisingly given the committee's claim that helpers were not forthcoming, another 17 (13% of all users) expressed their preparedness to help in some way. Most patrons expressed no desire for any further activities in the hall. Those who did suggest a greater variety proposed a fairly limited range, the most popular activities being discos/dances/social evenings, sports activities, art classes[20] and dressmaking. Most patrons expressed their satisfaction with the way the hall was managed. The suggestions of those who did advocate change can be categorized as follows: a separate luncheon club (3); a change in youth club leadership (4); more help from parents and children (4); a social committee separate from the TA (1); 'better' organization (1); representation of ethnic minority groups on the committee (1). Finally, and somewhat illogically, one user recommended that the hall be pulled down.

Some problems facing the user groups and the TA management committee have already been mentioned. Access to keys, co-ordination of lettings and responsibility for cleaning were all matters which had yet to be satisfactorily resolved. Other teething troubles were also evident. For instance, in those first nine months the committee received no bill for electricity, in spite of numerous visits to the local office. This situation apparently arose because the initial supply was to the contractor and thereafter the council was obliged to arrange a transfer to the name of the body liable for payments. All attempts to sort out this administrative tangle had failed to produce results, much to the consternation of the committee. Nevertheless, as management difficulties, all of these issues were amenable to solution.

Other problems appeared to be more intractable. The most serious was the lack of adequate storage space. That provided (see Plan VII) is not only awkward of access for regular use but is more or less useless on account of dampness. As a consequence the office was taken over as a chair store, tables when not in use were stacked against one wall, the make-up room was used as a store for play group equipment and the caretaker's store for the youth, 'Keep Fit' and weightlifting groups. The introduction of any other group activities involving the storage of equipment would pose considerable problems, particularly since the arrangement of a shared storeroom was proving unsatisfactory.

Furthermore, while from Table VIII it would appear that the hall was far from fully utilized, it has also to be kept in mind that it is generally not possible to schedule separate activities simultaneously for the main hall and the committee room on account of the noise nuisance felt in the upper room.

Vandalism has been another problem. Some damage resulting in flooding was caused through children climbing onto the roof and damage to the extensive glass panelling has been such that all panels at ground level were being replaced with solid panels and upper panels were being replaced with reinforced glass. Even the latter continued to be broken and the committee doubted that there was any remedy to this problem.

The management committee also claimed that particularly in organizing functions like a disco for young people, another design fault which posed problems was the large number of access doors into the hall. It was feared that in the event of 'trouble' youngsters could easily unlock doors from inside and so admit others whom those in charge might wish to exclude. These problems arise from design features of the hall and in most cases remedy would be difficult to effect. It should also be noted here that the sitting out area on the car park deck has not been developed or used for that purpose.

The account so far has concentrated on the hall as it is used and regarded by those residents enjoying the facilities it affords. The wider impact can be gauged from an analysis of the results of the postal survey. This was a self completion questionnaire sent to all 73 households in the sample group. Replies were received from 52 respondents. In addition three non-respondents were contacted and are known not to make use of the hall, a letter was received from another non-user and three respondents had moved from the estate. None of the other 14 respondents who failed to complete the forms were seen in the hall in the course of the hall study week.

Returns from respondent users of the hall confirm the analysis made on the basis of the hall users survey. The 14 respondents making use of the hall attended 24 activities on a very regular basis. Five respondents attended two activities, typically 'Keep Fit' and one or other of the bingo sessions, and two attended three or more activities. Ten respondents attended functions at least once weekly. Six respondents reported that other members of their household attended functions in the hall. In four instances membership involved children, in two other adults. Only one of the tower block households in the sample attended hall activities. Most respondent users comprised one person households (in three cases), typically widows attending bingo, or were drawn from households with young dependents (in nine cases).

Respondents who did not make use of the hall included residents in all kinds of block and household types. These respondents were asked to cite reasons for their decision not to take part. The replies are set out in Table IX.

TABLE IX   Respondents reasons for not using the community hall

Reasons cited	Number of respondents
Dislike joining any groups	5
Dislike activities offered	5
Dislike people attending	3
Feelings of shyness	3
Prefer to take part in activities off the estate	9
Just not interested	16

Several comments can be made about this breakdown. Firstly, the largest group of non-users are simply disinclined to take part in hall activities or preferred to take part in activities elsewhere. Secondly, the three respondents who cited their dislike of the people attending were Asian and all expanded on their answer in allegations of racial prejudice. One commented:

There are certain members in the TA who are racialist and practise discrimination ... so what I have to say is, these people do like our money, but they don't like us, because the moment they see a face of an Asian they believe we are Indians or Pakistanis. But they don't even bother to find out from which country we come or the way of life we lead. Furthermore, on the estate the tenants are being attacked by small kids and teenagers, so it is not safe for a non-white to be seen on the estate. Would you like to go anywhere where you are not wanted? I myself would not like to attend any such gathering where I would be an outcast.

In similar vein another claimed that 'An important reason for not usually participating in activities by minority groups, is not that they dislike the activities or feel shy, but they feel very much left out on their own'. The third respondent alleged that she and her family had been subjected to numerous acts of discrimination and the only way to cope was felt to be total withdrawal from the surrounding community.[21]

It is impossible to comment objectively on the validity of these claims. However, it can be noted that on my return visit there were reports of incidents of stone-throwing and daubed doorways. As during the field work period, the victims of such attacks were Asian families. It is also the case that very few residents of any racial minority group, black or white were seen in the hall and as noted above the committee was subsequently asked to consider barring lettings to black persons.

Finally, while not evident from Table IX, it should also be pointed out that a check on the names of both non-user respondents and those who failed to complete forms, shows that respondents who might be categorized as socially disadvantaged and those who were to some degree housebound and in need of assistance to get out, had not been involved in hall activities.

Most non-user respondents, like the users, made no suggestions for further activities. However, those suggestions which were made showed more variety and included sewing classes, cookery, crafts, flower arranging and art classes, yoga, social evenings, chess, music, darts, Sunday school classes and badminton. There is thus still some emphasis on social activities but more stress is placed on subjects with some educational content as well.

Other comments from non-user respondents concerned the management of the hall. One respondent recommended handing the management over to the council on account of the general disturbance and noise from activities there, another commented on the threatening behaviour of young people outside the hall and bullying behaviour on the part of older children towards younger ones. Unfavourable mention was also made of the bickering within the management committee.

Together with the results of the hall survey, these findings indicate that at that stage of its development the hall had attracted the support of a core of residents, their families and friends, the latter commonly resident outside Parkview. These residents made fairly extensive use of the limited range of activities offered. The non-users included those who are not interested or attracted to facilities elsewhere, those belonging to racial minority groups, and those who are in some way socially disadvantaged. This suggests that even if a wider range of activities were offered a sponsoring group might find it difficult to attract new supporters - and presumably the existing supporters would find their activities curtailed by personal considerations at some point.

The 'non-joiners' would not easily be attracted, black residents would need to feel genuinely welcome and might anyway prefer the familiarity of groups organized by and for blacks, while members of disadvantaged households would probably need the support of a personal introduction at least in the initial stages of joining. Thus as a community facility the hall allows for the expression of friendship ties between the estate's 'joiners' in a few limited contexts. It provides a service to a wider community than that defined by Parkview boundaries in the play group, luncheon club, and to a lesser extent the youth club. Other categories of potential estate users opt out by choice or feel themselves to be excluded by personal circumstance. This type of development may be inevitable but it is probably rather less than the results hoped for by those engaged in the planning and financing of the hall.

Commentary

Events on the estate in the 17 months following fieldwork indicate that the pattern of estate politics observed during fieldwork and described in Part IV is a remarkably consistent one. In 2½ years the estate TA has functioned through seven committees, each of which had an average life of just over four months. The pattern of committee development is one of breaks marked by a coup, election or mass resignations. This is followed by the formation or reformation of a new committee and the expression of high hopes regarding potential achievements. These are dashed by the appearance of factions and splits within the committee and the pattern then repeats itself.

Mechanisms which apparently have become built in to the Parkview political system to a large extent account for this cyclical pattern of events. In the Parkview setting there appears to be little tendency to acknowledge the legitimacy of opposing views so that members holding a diversity of opinions can still continue to work together. Rather, once disagreement on what is considered to be a major issue has been revealed, the defeated party generally feels obliged to resign or withdraw. The consequent instability of groups means that there is little continuity of personnel and hence a limited build-up of knowledge about estate issues and the means available to the committee for their solution. The potential of 'back bench' committee members is seldom realized and their commitment often remains half-hearted. The exceptions are those few leaders who provide some sort of continuity through their position in a series of committees. This situation perforce places a considerable reliance on the talents of a few key persons and at the same time their assumption of a dominant rôle contributes to their downfall.

Both factors, the political instability and the importance of a few leaders, may also account for the failure to implement the proposal for a Parkview community project. To my knowledge there were residents well able and interested to undertake work such as that envisaged. However, within the organizing group, the new committee members lacked confidence and by default the onus fell on Mrs Field. Once she felt unable to sustain the project committee other resident members accepted her judgement without question.

The opening of the hall added a new dimension to the work of the TA committee.[22] So far as the rest of the estate is concerned, apart from some 6% of the population, the impact on social life would appear to be limited. Such a judgement is difficult to substantiate and it is clearly a matter for debate as to how the impact of a hall is defined and how effectiveness is measured. Other studies have found that community halls have a unifying effect in housing areas by firmly cementing friendships between residents.[23] It has been claimed that where a hall has a 5% level of usage it nevertheless plays an important rôle in the process of community development. Indeed it has been suggested that the very existence of a hall and the knowledge that facilitates are available if required, has some influence on the resident's view of his environment.[24] I find it impossible to comment on such findings. My own assessment is based less on numbers than on the duplication of activities which are anyway available locally and on the apparent coincidence of membership within Parkview and other local groups. Exceptions to this criticism are the youth club, play group and luncheon club and estate residents constitute a minority of the membership of these. However, for all groups it may be that the description 'ours' considerably enhances the experience for the member.

Many of the faults found in the hall have been covered by a DOE bulletin published since the planning of the Parkview hall.[25] This study stressed the importance of providing adequate and lockable storage space sufficient for all user groups. It also emphasized the need for surveys and consultations prior to and during the planning stage and had these been carried out on Parkview at least some of the other design faults might have been overcome.

In dealings between the TA committee and the housing management section there was little evidence of improvement. The committee was still being presented with proposals for ratification rather than formulation and agreement. This is not surprising. Consultation on a level meaningful for the estate would require a considerable amount of officer time with officers who were not only themselves well briefed but were able and prepared to inform TA committee members fully and so allow open and more equal debate. The directorate continued to make claims for its policy of tenant participation, but outside the formal framework of the area boards, the practice belied the pronouncements.

Changes in housing management

Shortly after fieldwork, the ALHE and the Institute of Housing organized a course at a polytechnic in the area. The course, arranged with the active co-operation of the Borough's director of housing, Brown, was designed for residents to promote their awareness of the new policies of tenant participation. Two Parkview committee members Mrs Field and Mrs Montgomery attended this course. A second course devised largely by Brown attempted to relate the policy issues directly to conditions of the Borough. It is not known to what extent attendance at the course informed participants' subsequent contribution to committee work.

In March 1976 the Housing Utilisation Review Committee agreed to a number of changes in the composition and organization of the area boards. Resident representation was increased from four to six (later to eight) and representatives were to be elected for a term of two years. These changes had the support of two of the four boards. A discussion paper from the housing management section recommended that representation should also be based on sub-divisions within the area or on tenants' organizations. This proposal was rejected by the boards on the grounds that it would encourage the emergence of parochial attitudes. All four boards did, however, recommend that one representative should be allocated the responsibility for residents in acquired properties. The committee accepted the boards' recommendation on the basis of representation but decided that acquired property representation should be a matter for the discretion of particular boards.

On election procedures the committee decided that all nominees should consent to nomination and, except in special circumstances, this should be in person at the meeting. Residents should also be allowed to nominate themselves. Printed ballot papers would be distributed at the meeting, one per household, and returns and counting should be carried out immediately. It was not clear whether, as hithero, all electors would be required to vote for all (ie henceforth eight) representatives. The four boards recommended that an election meeting be chaired by the chairman of that particular board. This was overruled by the committee on the grounds that it was preferable for all meetings to be chaired by the same person, the chairman of housing or his nominee.

At about the same time, within the housing management section new officer posts were created intermediate between the position of area manager and estates manager. The rôle of this officer was specifically to foster tenant participation. Initially only one post was filled; in the Old Borough North team the estates manager Green was promoted to this position. This change was accompanied by the establishment of the four area teams. All teams continued to be based in the Community Housing Centre offices. Brown claimed that this arrangement allowed the advantages of decentralisation with personal contact on the estates without entailing the disadvantage of isolation. Nevertheless, this was regarded as a temporary arrangement and when the system was better established Brown intended that the area teams would be located in the areas served.

Early in 1976, as part of the corporate structure, various programme groups were set up to consider policy matters which affected more than one directorate. After an initial unfortunate experience in one such group, housing withdrew from any further involvement.

In March Councillor Mackie stepped down to become vice chairman of housing and the former vice chairman, Councillor Harty, assumed the leadership rôle. There were other minor shuffles in committee but it is not known what effect if any these had on the development of policies for public sector housing.

These changes are concerned basically with the formal structures of management. There is little evidence of altered processes, no indication of a move away from bureaucratic procedures, staff training schemes are still lacking. The description contained in Part III appears to need little modification on account of events in the interim period.

Notes to Part V

1   Anon, CDU report, nd, c Sept 1975.

2   John and other candidates for the Parkview position and another Borough community work vacancy visited Parkview estate. There they met with some of the TA committee and the views of these members on the prospective candidates were passed on to the appropriate officer. John was highly recommended. John's appointment was improved by a CD Programme group meeting without reference to committee. Administratively this apparently meant that he did not have a vote number and was unable to draw on funds for equipment etc.

3   Agenda item at a meeting 12 May 1976.

4   For some time afterwards Mrs Dee insisted that she had not resigned; she also failed to attend any committee meetings from this point onwards.

5   At the time of the hall survey the weightlifting group had made no payments and this was explained by reference to the small membership of the group. Frequency of payment varied; some groups paid by the session, others by the week or month.

6   There were oblique references in the local and metropolitan press to the project and the alleged involvement of CDU staff in Labour Party politics. These reports did not apparently originate from the estate but they did have the effect of increasing the suspicions of Mrs Montgomery and Mrs Noakes and their activity in relation to the ward councillors was for a time very intense.

7   The two remaining resident members were the TA representative from the sheltered housing unit and a newcomer to the TA committee, a woman resident in Ash Court. Both of these members and Mrs Field are pensioners. According to the latter when the matter was raised in committee only herself and Mrs Glenn expressed their willingness to take on the work.

8   The other applicants included two young people, one a man with a disturbed family background and a record of unemployment. He wanted to work with the youth club. The second was a young woman whose family came from Bangladesh. She was then at college studying biochemistry and proposed working with elderly people and giving advice on dietary problems. The third applicant was unknown to me personally. Mrs Field described her as an elderly woman in indifferent health. She proposed playing the piano for informal social gatherings in the hall. Mrs Montgomery proposed the type of house to house visiting that would be essential to the development of a good neighbour service. She had discussed the possibilities for this kind of work with me following on from the coffee mornings and before the project had been mooted.

9   This interpretation is derived from accounts from a number of participants. I myself was not on the scene at the time. Councillor Mrs Ewing reported that when she and her husband went to the estate to deliver the second batch of leaflets they were told then that it had been decided to call off the exercise. And applicants were advised before the meeting that there would be no interview that evening. It certainly seems that the decision was taken not by the committee as a whole but by its leading members.

10   Similar committees appear to have been formed in many parts of the Old Borough on a street basis as well as on other estates. The phenomenon is a very interesting one since the planning and organization need to be sustained over a period of almost one year, presumably quite large sums of money will be involved, (at the time of writing Parkview funds already totalled several hundred pounds), and all manner of events might be considered appropriate. There is probably a competitive element in this activity and coverage in the local press is no doubt sufficient to enhance the self image and status of the groups involved.

11 Director of Operations to the DOE, 13 April 1973.

12 These questionnaires are included in Appendix II. The forms were intended to be self-completed but at the afternoon bingo session Cathy Holland and Nell Leutchford, members of the SRD support staff, were on hand and assisted many of those present to complete the schedule. I am further indebted to both officers for their work on the analysis of the returns from this and the postal survey.

13 For example, a study carried out by the Washington Development Corporation in 1972 on village halls in the new town villages noted that 'From past experience, the average level of usage has been approximately 5.1% of the village population'. 'Village hall provision, A study of Blackfell', 1972, anon, unpublished paper, p 5'.

14 During the study week six of the women met at the home of one of the estate mothers for morning coffee. I was able to be present for part of this session and these comments draw on discussions there and in the hall with other mothers serving roster duty. The coffee mornings were an apparently more or less regular feature of the groups' activity.

15 See above pp 92–95. The core group represents approx 13% of potential Parkview members.

16 It was proposed to convert these premises into a kitchen from which meals would be distributed to several luncheon clubs in the vicinity.

17 For a note of membership see above p 103.

18 From observations and enquiry it appeared that most of these had some link, kinship or friendship ties, with a Parkview resident and had been invited to attend on that basis.

19 I was unable to follow up the manner in which friendships developed. However, from my knowledge of the activities of residents from the fieldwork period it was obvious that there was a remarkable overlap of attendance by the same women not only at bingo and 'Keep Fit' sessions in the hall, but at least formerly at commercial and boy's club bingo outside Parkview as well.

20 The popularity accorded this option was boosted largely by the fact that many women attending 'Keep Fit' filled in the forms around a table over a cup of tea. One woman was an enthusiastic supporter of the idea and after some general discussion others added art classes to their list.

21 See above p 65 f for comments on ethnicity as a factor affecting relations between residents.

22 Macey and Baker suggest that provision of a hall is a good means of diverting attacks on the council from the 'shoot the landlord' type of committee. I do not know whether this happened on Parkview. See Macey and Baker, p 363.

23 R Frankenberg, *Communities in Britain*, Pelican 1966 and Ruth Durant, *Watling a Social Survey*, London, 1939, p 98 are both cited in support of these arguments by the Washington Development Corporation Study, p 3.

24 ibid, pp 1 and 5.

25 DOE *Multi-purpose halls*, Design Bulletin 28, HMSO, London, 1973.

Part VI

Open Doors

... people do not only need to obtain things. I think they need, above all, the freedom to make things—things among which they can live. To give shape to them according to their own feelings, their own taste, their own imagination. . . .

(Ivan Illich, cit J F C Turner and R Fichter (eds) *Freedom to Build*, NY, 1972, plate I.)

Part VI comprises two sections: first, the main findings of this study are considered in terms of themes developed earlier under the headings, the estate, the council, and the links between the two. These findings are then related to the terms of the brief and an assessment made of the manner in which the brief might best be answered. Secondly, this assessment is translated into specific policy considerations. Both the findings and interpretation in policy terms relate to a case study. This by its nature imposes a narrow perspective and undoubtedly some significance should be attached to the peculiarities of local conditions. Nevertheless, the indications of a need to reorientate present policies are strong and relate to such basic issues as to have a significance far beyond Parkview and the Borough.

People, place and policy

Parkview estate constitutes a physical entity clearly demarcated by boundaries and set off from the surrounding streets by its markedly different architectural form and style. This unity of location and structure has not, however, been matched by a corresponding social cohesion. Residents relate to and identify with the neighbourhood of the Old Borough rather than to Parkview. The reasons for this are complex but certainly include as major factors the egocentric concerns of individual households, the significance of social ties outside the estate and the values attached to estate living.

The social life of most Parkview residents is home centred and kinship oriented. Many families have long associations with the Old Borough and it is common for residents to have close kin living in the locality or on the estate. The occurrence of kinship networks on Parkview is an incidental effect of slum clearance from areas with already established resident family groups. Contact with kin is generally regular and often includes assistance as well as sociability expressed through mutual visiting.

The neighbourhood in which Parkview is set is a familiar one, small in compass but extensively used for shopping, casual socializing, work and leisure. A family centred life style is complemented by the distinctive and humanly scaled environment of the market street. Some recent changes are pointed to (and decried), but there is still a large measure of continuity in the trader families manning the street stalls while the market shops provide a personalized shopping situation. Most leisure time is spent inside the home. Outside it the most popular venues are nearby bingo halls, pubs and clubs, all of which allow informal meetings between friends. Other leisure time facilities abound but few are patronized. Many women, and to a somewhat lesser extent, men, find work locally. Thus family ties and day-to-day activities build up personal associations with place, rich in variety and at times expressed through fierce loyalties.

The exception to this pattern of integration with the neighbourhood through personal ties is provided by the school situation. Pupils from Parkview travel widely to a remarkable range and number of schools. A corollary of that is that with few exceptions friendship groups at school and on the estate tend not to coincide. There are few contacts between the school and the home and little of the school experience that carries over into the child's environment.

Within Parkview, relations between neighbours may be characterized by casual friendliness expressed in chance meetings outside the home and by reserve expressed in the maintenance of social distance. There is reluctance to become 'too involved' in the affairs of neighbours and a premium is placed on 'keeping ourselves to ourselves'. This pattern has developed in spite of the fact that neighbours are often drawn from the same locality and share an experience of former place of residence and in spite of the ideal status accorded the close-knit neighbouring networks associated with terrace street living. An explanation of why these patterns of interaction were not transplanted to the estate would need to take into account a complex range of factors such as phase in the family life cycle, economic circumstances, the changing rôle of women, the presence or absence of semi-private spaces around the home and perceptions of other estate residents. The effects are easier to document. On Parkview there is a wide range of opinion regarding both expected and experienced behaviour between neighbours. There is a general absence of cohesive social networks between residents and hence of mechanisms for expressing group norms. For the individual resident the estate is not a significant entity in terms of personal social networks.

Perhaps inevitably, the importance attached to Old Borough loyalties and the egocentric kin-based form of social life means that some residents on Parkview are socially isolated. In some instances this isolation reflects a personal preference; more often constraints beyond personal control are at work. Thus, those housebound, those subject to depression, acute shyness or categorization as 'outsiders', may, without kin support, find themselves also lacking in significant social contacts with 'non kin.'

Within the estate residents are captive in an environment. It is a place designed to ready-made completeness regardless of the whims of the individual user. Yet few have the opportunity or the means to provide alternative housing for themselves. Moreover, freedom of action within the estate is constrained by the nature of the existing landlord-tenant relationship. Residents are discouraged from reshaping the interior of their own homes. Beyond the front door attempts to use a public lawn for personal purposes or to make private a patch of ground are liable to meet with official disapproval. A tenancy agreement couched in terms of prohibitions and injunctions has further contributed to the general belief among residents that most expressions of personal initiative will not be allowed by the council.

The artificiality of this environment has been recognized to some degree by both residents and planners. Certainly, the need consciously to create a community from an assortment of council houses has been accepted. The TA was set up to promote social activities for estate residents and to represent their interests to the council. The community hall was designed to allow for the ongoing expression of social ties in shared leisure activities. Other institutions, the library, luncheon club, nursery and sheltered housing unit, have been incorporated into the estate as integral features of the design. In fact, the importance of all of these organizations and institutions would appear to be minimal. The TA lacks a solid base of resident support and committee politics are marked by intense feuding between unstable factions.

On present evidence the hall attracts some of the estate's 'joiners' to a limited range of resident-organized activities and provides, through various outside organizations, services to client groups drawn largely from beyond Parkview. None of the other institutions placed on the estate have made any special attempt to make contact with estate dwellers; all are managed by various local government departments with scant regard for the implications of their situation.

Thus described, Parkview comprises a number of dwellings, residents, institutions and staff. This complex of buildings and people by its nature requires a sophisticated form of management. Overall responsibility rests with the Old Borough North team. This team carries out day-to-day management and also draws on the resources of other departments such as engineers, parks and recreation staff, DLBO and social services.

The stated aim of this housing management team is to provide a service that is 'efficient, expert and consumer-orientated' and dispensed by officers 'with intense social motivation'. The reality falls short of the ideal. There were frequent breakdowns in communication between all those variously involved. The housing management team is concerned with a few management tasks performed according to standard bureaucratic procedures. The staff often lacked housing management skills and had no opportunity to develop them. Economic cutbacks and the difficulties encountered in reorganizing the directorate under new leadership simply compounded these more basic problems.

Perhaps because the situation within the organization was so far from ideal, reforms were attempted outside it by making additions to the existing structure. Thus in order to initiate resident participation, the system of area housing boards was instituted. This change has done little more than grant some influence to a few residents. There is no evidence that this apparently more democratic process of decision-making is so in effect, nor does there appear to be any improvement in the situation of those supposed to benefit by the reform. There has been no sharing of responsibility for decision-making and the relative status and power positions of those involved remain unaltered. The North Board has not been incorporated into the management system as an integral part of it. Effectively all management functions can be carried out without recourse to the board with the result that it has simply become a complicating extra channel in an already cumbersome administrative machine.

The viewpoints which those involved bring to the board and other official duties, tend to be narrowly circumscribed and compensate little for the deficiencies of the organization itself. Resident representatives have no support base and the extent to which they can effectively report back to other residents is severely limited by the weakness of grassroots residents' organizations. Councillors and officers continue to have an approach to estate concerns that is not simply partial but extremely short-term in perspective. Councillors are called in to minister to individual crises or support the TA. Officers are involved

266

with 'problem cases', estate activists and applicants for benefits of one kind or another. Issues of longer-term planning and the development of a wider perspective are lost in this preoccupation with current incidents.

In part the brief of this study calls for an assessment of the scope for improving relations between local authority landlords and their tenants. Clearly the scope for improvement is considerable. However, formal tenant participation schemes, the means most commonly favoured for securing this improvement would appear to be unworkable at least in the short term. Some of the reasons for this contention should already be obvious.

First, it seems unlikely that the housing management section would be capable of sponsoring a truly participatory management scheme.[1] The sponsorship rôle carries heavy responsibilities. Moreover,

It seems to be a common experience that whenever existing organisations are used to sponsor indigenous social movements, the primary interests of the sponsoring organization tend to affect the selection of members, the form of organization, the specification of objectives, and determination and control of the implementing activities . . .[2].

Secondly, participation presupposes some form of the community organization through which the process of consultation can be affected. In applying a participation scheme to estates like Parkview, the administrator assumes that those who live near each other share a community of interest which can be expressed in a generalized social cohesion. On Parkview, the extent to which community organizations exist, whether expressed through formal organizations or informal social networks, is severely limited.

Thirdly, the question 'participation in what on whose terms?' has still to be satisfactorily answered. Resident demands are for a more efficient service in caretaking and maintenance functions, a more considerate manner of treatment and the reversal of trends considered undesirable – the influx of 'outsiders', the housing of 'problem' families, the lowering of social 'tone' on the estate. There is no evidence that residents wish to assume responsibility for cleaning and repairs. At least some residents however, might like to be involved in the ordering of priorities for maintenance and lettings. The findings of the study indicate that this form of involvement would be resisted by both officers and councillors.

Fourthly, the introduction of a scheme for more than token participation would demand a radical re-ordering of the rôles and relationships of those taking part. This form of social change is difficult to accommodate. It is difficult for a councillor to accept that campaigns organized by residents in opposition to the council are to be welcomed as expressions of democracy. It is difficult for an officer to accept residents in the rôle of colleague. And perhaps most of all it is difficult for a resident suddenly to re-order his relationships with both officers and councillors. Residents have an experience of officialdom that defines their position as subordinate. This is reinforced by the values of a society which accords little status to the label 'council tenant'. The dilemmas which accompany any attempt to alter these relative positions have been aptly described by Marris.

> When people formerly without influence were invited to participate in decisions, they lost their irresponsibility. All their familiar attitudes to authority were invalidated. They were now the colleagues of administrators, not merely the clients of their services. They could no longer regard established power as beyond their control, a given factor of their circumstances. They sacrificed the old freedom of apathy or dissent for an influence whose rewards were unpredictable. Yet if they were to act as authentic representatives of their people, they had still to be able to interpret life as those without power experienced it. Hence they were caught between the familiar irresponsible relationship to authority they had lost, and a rôle as responsible reformer, where they risked betraying both themselves and their constituency. Only a personality of exceptional integrity could contain such tension; only a politician of exceptional insight could have foreseen how to formulate a meaningful strategy in so untried a setting.[3]

On the present evidence, it is doubtful whether the existing organization could cope with the tensions and strains which would emerge in the process of establishing resident participation schemes.

On the basis of these findings the local authority itself should be the locus for reform. In the housing management field there are two interrelated key areas; the nature and performance of the management tasks and the quality of the staff assigned to them. In the present circumstances there is a downward spiral of service and resources. This needs to be broken at a number of points. The housing mangement section must be given a wider competence in all aspects of estate management. Innovatory approaches to problems and more flexible working systems should be encouraged. The bureaucratic structure of the organization should be reformed into teams in which hierarchic status is irrelevant. Regular and ongoing training programmes need to be set up and monitored. And in all this responses to and communication with the residents must be an essential part of the officer's brief.

In establishing and developing relations with residents both officers and councillors should relate more positively to individual households. In this it should be kept in mind that few residents have any experience of a participatory style of management and the concomitant acceptance of personal responsibility whether in contact with various official agencies, school or work. Ideally this total experience should be different. Nevertheless, housing is of vital importance for a general sense of personal comfort and security. If the provision of council housing was invested with a different set of values this in itself would greatly enhance the self-image of many residents. More consideration in lettings is called for. Residents should be assured that proposals to change or improve the inside or outside of the dwelling will meet with advice and assistance.

Officers and councillors should also accept and encourage the growth of self-help groups. On Parkview several have emerged. The garden petitions and the tower block action group both allowed the expression of issues which were of real concern to members. At the time these groups met with official rebuffs. Of course, not all resident demands can be met but, all can be accorded reasonable and open consideration. The idea of a single estate organization, the TA, to represent resident interests, manage a community hall, foster a sense of community through the organization of various social activities, etc, is undoubtedly convenient to management. The study has shown the inability of the TA to meet resident needs. It can be expected that other small groups with limited goals will from time to time arise or their development may be fostered by community work support. The life span of such groups may be short and their achievements limited. Residents may be attracted to various groups according to personal concerns and circumstances. A multiplicity of small groups allows for the gradual development of cross-cutting networks linking individuals and groups. These networks would provide the basis for a form of social cohesion which is at present lacking on Parkview. However, if given a climate favourable to the development of self help groups, these yet failed to emerge, then it would have to be accepted that the individualistic home-centred orientation was stronger and that management initiatives based on linkages with groups were inappropriate.

The second aspect of the brief calls for an assessment of the need for leisure time facilities. In answering this part of the brief two assumptions have been made. First, estate provisions need to be regarded as complementary to those in the area. Secondly, most estate resources should be made available to those whose need is potentially greatest; those who spend the major part of their time on the estate, the very young, the very old and non-working mothers, and those who are socially isolated by circumstance rather than choice and/or in need of social supports of various kinds.

Parkview has three designated play areas for children up to the age of about 12 and a fourth area is intended to cater for an older age group. The facilities these playgrounds provide tend either to be under utilized and/or abused, sometimes by those for whom they were not intended. The provision of play facilities for children has already been the subject of policy recommendations.[4] It is difficult to cater adequately for the leisure time needs of young people within an estate context. Some residents are likely to be critical of the noise and disturbance from children's play, others may prefer to overlook the play area. The children themselves may find sheds, basements and stairwells more attractive than landscaped hills and conventional equipment. Nevertheless, some general points can be made.

The whole estate will be used by children for play activities and estate design should take this into account. In addition, a variety of provisions should be made for both outdoor and indoor leisure activities. And both should be planned not simply in the context of the estate but in relation to the leisure and recreation programme for the neighbourhood. More attention should also be given to the need for supervised play. Supervision tends to allow a wider variety of activities and seems to be an important factor in attracting children from socially disadvantaged backgrounds. All this calls for more initial survey and planning work than is carried out at present. There is also a need for better follow-up services. Maintenance is often poor and replacement of equipment is seldom provided for. Subsequent use of equipment should be monitored and an allowance made for the possibility of changing facilities in accordance with, say, changes in the age structure of the school population.

Some indoor activities for youngsters, other residents and local groups take place in the Parkview community hall. These have attracted few people from the categories of special need cited above. This is due partly to the lack of planning and the failure to identify specific needs prior to the design stage. Groups like the playgroup and youth club require an open area which can withstand a good deal of boisterous activity and which allows the user group to personalize the space with children's drawings, posters etc. Other groups need smaller more intimate rooms as meeting places. The coffee mornings for isolated women would be one such example. Perhaps more importantly, the failure to meet hidden needs on the estate is due to the lack of staff input. Another project, aimed at fostering mutually supportive informal groups for estate residents who would normally not respond to overtures to join a formal organization, set up chat groups and street based education groups.[5] These groups met in residents' homes. In this instance, and generally, the provision of staff was more important than the availability of community meeting places, not to run the groups or provide courses but to assist with the ground work and the organization.

Thus, both in designing the facilities and determining the staff requirements it is essential first to decide the priorities and needs of estate residents. Once these issues have been settled, the physical and human resources required should be set in the context of other neighbourhood provision, some of which may well be under utilized. There should be more detailed planning, improved consultation with residents and better co-ordination with other departments and organizations. On Parkview these omissions have resulted in the establishment of a range of expensive facilities which yet fail to meet their intended objectives.

Policy considerations

What follows are policy changes which it is held would facilitate the realization of the objectives outlined so far. Some may be specific to Parkview and the Borough although in most instances analogous situations obtain elsewhere. Whenever possible similarities are drawn between recommendations and policies already in operation. Even so it is likely that housing management personnel will object to some proposals as being impracticable, too costly or too consuming of staff time. Certainly some difficulties, like possible trade union objections, can be expected and may impose constraints on implementation. It is also the case, however, that social cost benefit analyses in this area of policy-making have seldom been attempted. Even without such analysis it can be suggested that proposals which in the short term are economically justifiable, may in the longer term entail costly modifications.[6] Finally, it is intended that these proposals provide the basis for public debate between those involved; it is not intended that they provide a blue print for action.

Housing management functions

The competence of the area housing management team should be extended to include lettings, direct control over repairs and involvement in the formulation of a design brief for new projects as well as at present, arrears control, public relations with resident groups, the administration of transfer applications and other minor matters.

Lettings must be regarded as the first and key stage of good management practice. More attention should be given to some of the side effects of the present allocations policy. The findings of the study would suggest that a preference for housing in close proximity to kinsfolk should be recognized.

There should also be a greater awareness of and sensitivity to the longer-term effects of particular blocks being characterized by such features as high child densities, concentrations of black households or a predominance of those categorized as 'outsider' or 'problem' families. In part, these factors relate to the mix of unit size in specific blocks. However, this correlation is not a simple one as the reputation of certain blocks and the pattern of tower block lettings shows.

Lettings should also make some allowance for personal preferences in regard to the degree of privacy or sociability afforded by a particular housing situation. Some residents in the tower blocks value the privacy which they impose just as some residents around the green value the sense of intimacy and potential for contact with neighbours. Others are not so well suited. It is all quite fortuitous and the scope for individual choice is minimal. This situation should be altered so that the personal element in the choice of a home is extended as far as possible.

The organization of an efficient repairs service is also essential and would remove a major source of resident dissatisfaction. Repairs should be carried out by a small team of tradesmen located on site and responsible to a surveyor. Tradesmen and surveyor would be part of the area management team. This repairs service team could become a point of co-operation with residents rather than a cause of friction. Not only are residents loud in their complaints about a poor service but they do have a good local knowledge of work outstanding. This knowledge is of value and should be used to order the priorites of work. Under the existing set-up it would appear that certain categories of repairs are not being carried out. Where the local authority is unable to meet the demand this should be openly acknowledged and the type of repairs to be excluded from the service should be determined on the estate by agreement with residents. The repairs service team should also have a function in providing advice to residents wishing to carry out their own home improvement plans.

Arrears control is undoubtedly the most intractable and complicated problem facing housing management. The reasons for arrears and the possible ways of dealing with them is the subject of other studies.[7] On the basis of the present findings it is contended that a single procedure relying on the completion of a series of standard forms, each containing more severe threats, is singularly ineffective. There should be a more flexible approach with practical assistance available to a resident at the earliest stage of financial difficulty. This would involve more personal and intensive contact than at present and would necessitate co-operation between housing management staff and other agencies able to offer specialist help and advice.

Public relations between housing management teams, residents and resident groups shoud be accorded higher priority. Encounters should not take place in predominantly confrontation type situations. More meetings should take place informally on the estate. There need to be more open exchanges of information and where appropriate the initiative should be taken by the housing management team.

The organization of housing management
The area housing board system of tenant participation places considerable demands on officer and councillor time and resources with apparently little return for residents generally. The system should be abolished and more attention given to developing contacts between officers and residents in less formal contexts. (See below under housing management and estate residents.) In time, a demand may arise for a formalized scheme tailored to meet resident rather than management requirements.

The management function should be carried out by area teams.[8] These teams should be decentralized to a conveniently placed location and each area team manager should be responsible for the administration of all the management functions outlined above. There is no reason why this devolution of powers should not be accompanied by the allocation of a budget for the area.

Similar views have been put forward in the Inner Area Study for Liverpool, while in North Tyneside a scheme is currently underway to decentralize all housing management functions to local offices, each with responsibility for some 5,000 households. It is intended that these offices should shortly assume budgetary powers and are competent to handle most lettings.

Within the area team, the style of management should be participatory rather than bureaucratic. Personal initiatives are to be encouraged rather than stultified. All members must be equally involved in working as a team towards the achievement of common goals as defined by council policy. These goals should be clearly stated to officers and residents. There should be a regular review of team policy, and mechanisms for monitoring the effectiveness of group performance should be developed. These in turn provide a feedback for further policy-making by the council's elected members.

Within the housing directorate some tasks should be organized through a project or task force management team. These teams should be assembled to solve short term problems. Officer mobility through assignment to a variety of projects would be assured. As a rule, project teams would involve personnel temporarily assigned from several directorates and from all levels of the administrative and/or professional hierarchy. They may also involve persons drawn from outside the council. Resident interests should be represented on all teams where the task was of concern to residents.

This form of management is common in industry, particularly those where the co-ordination of many segments is necessary for the realization of a specific one-time proposition.[9] Some local government tasks which traditionally have been classified as routine should, given the accelerated rate of social change, be redefined as non-routine and more appropriately tackled by project management teams.[10] This approach would also inject a greater capacity to adapt into an organization otherwise resistant to change. Once a team has been set up, the project leader, to be effective, must be given full responsibility for meeting the prescribed goals and allowed access to any resources needed to accomplish the task. Examples of housing management tasks suitable for this approach are the various stages in planning for community facilities and the handover of a new block of flats. In the first task a team would be assembled to assess the demand for and feasibility of providing community facilities of various kinds on an estate. Other stages in the process, the commissioning of the design, design development and construction, and the formulation of a management policy might involve different teams depending on the special skills required at each stage. In this and other tasks survey work would be necessary to provide the team with basic background information. Whenever this concerned estate residents the commission for such work should first be offered to resident groups. In the second task a representative of the project team might best be located on site in a flat left vacant for, say, the first six months.

The advantages of this system include the directed input of staff time for the solution of a specific problem, the assembly of a small team incorporating the skills most appropriate to the task, the clear definition of areas of responsibility and the improved co-ordination of staff and functions. Officers assigned to project teams would benefit from working in a multi-disciplinary team and after serving on several teams would become expert at handling new and changing situations.

In addition to this form of linkage between personnel from different backgrounds, relations between the area team and other council departments in the working out of day-to-day management functions should be improved. Housing management would benefit from closer links with Social Services, Leisure and Recreation and the Community Development Unit in particular. This may necessitate formal meetings between senior officers to establish common ground for co-operation but unscheduled communication at all levels should also be actively encouraged.

The organization of the repairs service has already been commented on. The site team might comprise a site supervisor, carpenter and plumber. The area management office would also need to incorporate a works depôt to provide other specialist tradesmen on request and to arrange for the purchase and supply of materials.

Housing management rôles

It should be evident that the combination of area teams to carry out comprehensive housing management functions and task force management teams allocated to specific problems would mean extending the brief of all management officers. The change would, however, be most apparent at the more junior level, and the rôle of the housing management assistant can be noted in more detail.

The housing management assistant would continue to be the member of the area team with most ongoing contacts with residents. Hitherto, the duties of the housing management assistant have been defined in negative terms, the preliminary follow-up of arrears cases, dealing with other 'problem' families, the processing of applications for transfers ultimately handled by another section and other minor management matters. This officer should be encouraged to develop a wider working knowledge of his patch – an area defined less in terms of numbers of dwellings than the intensity of contact required for good management.[11] The knowledge acquired through day-to-day contact should be considered essential in lettings, public relations work, responses to resident initiatives and in some project management issues. In all of these functions the estates management assistant should be actively involved.

There is also a case for re-evaluating the rôle of resident caretakers. The cleaning and servicing function carried out by them might be better undertaken by employees without resident status and directly under the control of the area manager. Resident posts might be created for, say, a caretaker/playleader for the playgrounds, a night caretaker and a community worker. This kind of arrangement would mean the employment of, say, three and a half resident workers on Parkview in place of the existing eight.

Staff training

At all levels staff training would be required on a continuing basis to ensure that officers were able to cope with the job tasks allocated to them. Even so, it may need to be acknowledged that some of those staff members at present occupying management positions are basically unsuited for the work. If the service is to be effective it is essential that officers with the appropriate educational background and personal resources for the development of management skills are attracted and retained by local authority housing directorates. The content of training programmes needs to be carefully considered and this is the subject of another study currently being sponsored by the department.[12] On the basis of the present study the following points can be made. Of key significance is the need for attitudinal training and instruction in basic communication skills such as interview techniques, speaking to public meetings and letter writing. Some special attention should be given to possible communication difficulties with clients from racial minority groups, especially those for whom English is not a first language. Moreover, it needs to be kept in mind that for most residents the written word is not the easiest form of communication.

Officers should also know something of the policies which underpin their work. They should be able to give advice on the form of government aid available to clients. This kind of information is probably best obtained through regular briefing sessions.

Staffing requirements

Some of these changes will require extra staff. For example, there should be an officer with sole responsibility for staff training. However, some staff could be redeployed from other sections and/or funds obtained from the reduction of the number of staff now employed in specific capacities.

Since the completion of field work, an additional tier in the management hierarchy has been created, with the appointment at a senior level of officers responsible specifically for the promotion of tenant participation. This seems to be not only an unnecessary complication of functions and posts but also an exercise in itself quite inappropriate at this stage.

The introduction of project management should not involve an increase in staff levels. In industry under normal conditions it has been found that staff can cope with both day-to-day management and project management assignments because the latter are typically part time and temporary by design.

More generally, attention might be given to attracting women to the service and training and working hours should be arranged to meet the needs of women with families. At present few women are employed in the housing management service yet in many cases officers have dealings with women whether at home or in part or full time employment. Furthermore, the fact that women more often have dealings with officials reflects not simply a lower earning capacity or more flexible working routine but the view that most household matters are primarily the concern of the housewife. Many women and elderly residents of both sexes expressed a preference for dealing with a woman especially where the subject of enquiry included such personal matters as financial difficulties.[13]

Housing management and estate residents
The area team officers should be easily accessible to residents. In addition to a convenient geographical location, more flexible office hours are desirable. Both within the office and on the estate the service provided should be client-centred. At one level this would involve the introduction of very simple changes. Thus, there should be a receptionist able initially to handle all visitors and telephone enquiries and to make appointments for residents wanting to see particular officers. There should be adequate facilities for private interviews and the taking of notes and monitoring the outcome of such meetings should be routine. Residents should be kept informed of progress. Where communication by letter is necessary these should be written in a clear, direct style. These are elementary practices; nevertheless, they are noticeably lacking in the Borough offices.

On the estate area team officers should indicate their preparedness to be responsive to various resident groups. The past record of attempting to stifle all attempts at resident action outside an 'official' TA in community development terms can only be seen as negative. Resident groups formed to improve estate amenities should be accepted and assisted rather than opposed.

Perhaps most importantly, contact between officers and residents in all types of situations need to be informed by altered officer attitudes. These must be based on respect. Changed attitudes towards residents could be expressed also through different kinds of contacts. At present, most public exchanges between officers and residents concern complaints with residents on the attack and officers on the defensive. There should be more ongoing contact with officers giving unsolicited information using not simply meetings but posters, local newspapers or area office newsletters. At the same time expectations should not be raised unless the prospects for meeting them are real, and shortcomings in the services offered should be honestly admitted.

Estate provision
On the estate the planners attempt to draw demarcation lines between grassed areas and planted gardens for visual attractiveness, parking and access ways for cars, playgrounds for children etc, will, in terms of actual use, be largely ignored. The estate should be laid out in such a way that recognizes this multiplicity of uses.

Within this general framework developments should be carried out so that areas adjacent to particular blocks relate to them with small playgrounds, sheltered sitting out areas, etc., planned in association with the residents themselves. Where private gardens are not practicable it should still be possible for residents—including children—to be encouraged to take part in tree planting, care of gardens, choice and painting of play equipment and so on. Larger and more elaborate play provision should be related to neighbourhood need and provision. In this regard there is considerable potential for making use of existing provisions in school buildings and playgrounds and on the estate itself. Underground car parks, unsuitable or unacceptable for their intended purpose may well convert to youth centres, workshops, craft studios or sports facilities.

Alternative approaches to meeting social needs should be explored. At present, the needs of those who are socially isolated, notably some mothers of young children, especially those heading a single parent family, and some elderly residents, are not being met either by the facilities on Parkview or by those external agencies working there. Staff allocations rather than buildings are more important in this aspect of community development.

Other facilities located on the estate should relate more to it in physical and in management terms. The library should have an entrance from the estate. It could function as a homework centre in term time and a story reading group in school holidays or, given the limited space available, library staff could sponsor these activities elsewhere. The staff and voluntary helpers of the playgroup would benefit from some contacts with the Ash Court nursery. The sheltered housing facilities could to some extent be opened to other elderly residents on the estate.

Finally, there should be many more opportunities for residents to do more for themselves. The resident who would like to remove a few paving stones, plant and tend a tree and a creeper on the outside wall of his flat and fronting onto a main pedestrian path has not done so because 'it would not be allowed'. An application to rent a garage for a play room was discouraged. The use of a grass area for family play was stopped. Residents are constantly made aware of possible or actual prohibitions on behaviour in areas which they might but do not regard as part of their home. There has to be a balance between group interests and individual concerns, but council policy should go as far as possible towards meeting and encouraging these individual initiatives. On new developments planners and architects should allow as much scope as possible for a resident input. Lifeless houses are transformed by this process into homes by those who live there. On Parkview there is limited scope for resident-controlled alterations and it may well be too late to change overall perceptions of public space as no man's place. However, at the least, small piecemeal developments may to some degree remedy the faults of a physical and social environment which intrinsically is far from ideal.[14]

Notes to Part VI

1 A similar view has already been put forward. H Wilson and L Womersley suggest that '. . . successful tenant participation in the Study Area could not be achieved without a change in the system of local estate management which must be considered a pre-requisite of any viable scheme.' Inner Areas Study; Liverpool, paper on Housing Management, February 1975 p 1. For more general reservations on tenant participation see B Randall, 'Doubts thrown on value of tenant participation,' *Municipal Engineering*, 30 April 1976, p 669f.

2 L Ohlin, cit Marris and Rein, p 217.

3 Marris, p 99.

4 See DOE, *Children at Play*, Design Bulletin 27, HMSO, 1973; DOE Circular 79/72, Children's Playspace. My own findings accord closely with those of the bulletin.

5 The New Communities Project on Leigh Park Estate near Portsmouth under the auspices of research fellows from Southampton University. See the *Guardian*, 2 December 1975.

6 An instance of this is provided by a move in the GLC to demolish tower blocks on the grounds that 'they create more social stresses than the housing difficulties they solve'. The report made no mention of how social stress was measured. *The Times*, 15 March 1977.

7 This research is being undertaken by the National Consumer Council, the Association of London Borough Housing Officers and the Department of the Environment.

8 The areas for which the teams should be responsible can be variously determined. Manchester area officers are responsible for 7500 dwellings, and as noted, North Tyneside for 5000. On these figures the Borough might be split into 2 teams, one for each of the former metropolitan borough areas.

9 W J Taylor and T F Watling, *Successful Project Management*, Business Books, London, 1970 and D L Cook, *Educational Project Management*, Charles E Merrill, Ohio, 1971.

10 The method has been used in studies of local government undertaken by outside consultants but to my knowledge has not been adopted as a management strategy within any local government organization.

11 Some areas will require more intensive care than others. The needs of an area in this regard are related to past management practice. Thus, there often tends to be a concentration of 'problem' families on particular estates which then become a difficult patch. Five hundred dwellings is probably an upper maximum. Gray at present has responsibility for approximately twice this number although according to Brown each estate's management assistant had approximately 750 dwellings in his care. This figure is average for most London boroughs.

12 The Education and Training for Housing Work project is being carried out by a team working under Charles Legg at City University.

13 It should be noted, however, that this whole question of appropriate male/female rôles is a complex one; for example, it may be the case that residents would see the adoption of 'most important' or authoritative management functions as male prerogatives.

14 A good example of how residents and architects view this process from different perspectives is provided by Le Corbusier's Pessac. Many architects consider it a failure. Residents regard it as a success. The changes which have taken place in many homes amount to a complete transformation. See P Boudon, *Lived-in Architecture*, London, 1972.

Appendices

I *Selection and characteristics of Parkview sample households*

Data for all 726 estate households was obtained from council files and transferred to edge punch cards. These cards incorporated information on family size and composition, previous housing history and present housing situation. In addition information on colour was coded on the basis of the door knock campaigns; the white category was therefore white or unseen. A sample of 100 households was drawn from a set of 673 cards. (Information on the remaining 53 households was then unobtainable owing to the fact that the file was in use or the flat was on offer). The sample was a random selection within stratified groups defined in terms of size of household; type of block; length of residence on Parkview; and colour.

Interview schedules were completed for 73 households. There were 12 refusals to requests for interview. Of these two were very elderly and the refusal was made on their behalf by sons or daughters visiting at the time of contact, one was mentally subnormal and another, while refusing a formal interview, consented to a long discussion which was later written up in the form of field notes. In 11 cases it was impossible to make any contact despite numerous attempts. Three households moved and one elderly householder in the sample died during the field work period. It is worth noting that there were no refusals from the garden flats; the highest number of refusals and non–contacts were in the tower blocks. All black households consented to interviews.

Comparisons between the sample and estate populations in terms of some basic characteristics are given below:

I   Households by block type

	Sample %	Estate %
Balcony	25	24
Y blocks	34	35
Tower	14	19
Garden	27	22
	100	100

II   Households by floor level

	Sample %	Estate %
Ground	20	15
1/2	23	33
3/4/5	37	24
6/7/8/9	11	19
10 and above	8	9
	99	100

III Household size

	Sample %	Estate %
1 person	15	18
2 person	18	21
3 person	25	25
4 person	25	21
5 or more	18	14
	101	99

IV All adult households

Sample %	Estate %
51	54

V Length of residence on Parkview

	Sample %*	Estate %
less than 3 years	34	40
3 and less than 5	11	7
5–10	18	22
10 years or more	29	30
	92	99

*information lacking for 8% households

VI Place of residence prior to rehousing

	Sample %	Estate %
Old Borough	68	73
Borough	30	24
Elsewhere	1	2
	99	99

VII Black households

Sample %	Estate %
15	8

VIII Age structure

	Sample %	Estate %
0–5	7	9
6–8	9	7
9–12	7	7
13–16	6	6
17–19	1	4
20–29	21	15
30–39	11	11
40–49 } 50–59 }	23	24
60+	15	17
	100	100

II *Interview schedules*

1 *Interviews with sample households*

This schedule was not completed as a formal questionnaire and many of the questions provoked general discussion. The schedule comprised four parts; A, basic household data and housing experience; B, reactions to the estate and neighbourhood, personal social networks; C, attitudes towards the estate and its amenities; D, leisure activities, estate involvement and dealings with the council. These sections might be completed in any order in the course of one or more sessions.

The schedules were framed to allow for subsequent coding and computer analysis.

The schedule is reproduced here in a compressed form.

PART A

Name of head of household

Flat No: Block: Floor: Type:

Who interviewed session 1:   Date: etc

Name, sex, age, school of all dependent children together with relationship to head of household.

Name, sex, age, place of work all other members of household including relationship to head of household.

Where household includes children:

1. What level of education would you like your children to reach?

2. Would you like your children to have the same kind of job as yourself? Why do you say that?

If no

3. Do you have any ideas about the sort of job you would like for your children?

4. How old were you when you left school?

5. Did you want to leave school at that point?

6. Did you have any further training after leaving school? Where respondent is working:

7. Including overtime how many hours do you work in a week?

8. In your job how much say do you have over the way you use your time at work?

9. In your job do you supervise the work of others?

10. What do you like/dislike about your present job?

11. How long have you been in your present job?

12. What do you think you get most satisfaction from? work, leisure, both equally.

Part B

1. Where did you live before coming here?

2. What kind of accommodation did you have there?

3. What was the tenure of the property?

4. Why did you move?

5. How many flats etc were offered by the council before you accepted this? Where? Why did you turn them down?

6. What made you decide to accept this flat?

7. Did you have any choice about blocks? floor?

8. Do you prefer living here to living where you were before?

9. How did you feel when you were offered this flat? How do you feel now?

10. Looking at the estate as a whole is there any other part of it in which you would prefer to live? Where? Why?

11. Given what you can afford do you feel Parkview is a good place to live? If no then what?

12. If you were given a completely free choice where would you like to live? What sort of accommodation would you like?

13. Do you know the names of your neighbours on either side of you?

14. Do you know the names of any other neighbours on your balcony/landing?

15. Do you know any other persons on the estate?

16. What sort of neighbours do you have?

17. What do you think makes a good neighbour?

18. Do you think people on Parkview are good neighbours to each other?

19. If you are in any kind of trouble, say sickness, is there anyone on the estate you could go to for help? If yes – details. If no – is there anyone else?

20. Looking back now how do you feel about life in the streets of terrace housing in the Old Borough?

21. Do you think Parkview is this kind of neighbourhood.

22. Where do you go shopping for daily needs? Do you do much shopping elsewhere? Where?

23. Do you use any local pubs? Which? Elsewhere?

24. Do you make use of any parks in the Borough? Elsewhere?

25. Do you go to the cinema/theatre/bingo? Where? How often?

26. Do you have any relatives living on the estate? If yes details.

27. Do you have any relatives living nearby? If yes details of categories and visiting patterns.

28. Do you have any friends living nearby?　　　Friends from work? If yes details of visiting/meeting.

29. Do you think that by and large people living on Parkview are the same sort of people as yourself?

30. What sort of people are you thinking about when we talk about people like yourself?

31. Do you think there are any groups of people on the estate who are different to the people you are familiar with?

PART C

1. Do you like the general appearance of the buildings on Parkview? Why? Why not?

2. Which blocks do you find most attractive and which least? (Photographs used for ranking order).

3. Do you think the entrance/this block is generally well maintained? If not why? Similarly where applicable lifts/stairs.

4. Sometimes these areas of the block are damaged. Who do you think is responsible for the damage? How do you think they should be dealt with?

5. Do you think it is a good idea to have shared open spaces like the green between the garden flats? What do you think these spaces should be used for?

In households with children

6. Finding places for children to play is a major problem in towns and cities. Where do your children play?

All households

7. What kind of facilities do you think should be provided for very young children? Where should they be? Likewise for older children.

8. What do you think about the new playgrounds on Parkview?

9. What do you think about the boys' club?

10. If the council could spend more money here what would you like it spent on?

11. What if any particularly bad features are there about living here as it is now? Good features?

PART D

1. What do you like to do in your leisure time?

2. When you moved to Parkview did it make any difference to your social life?

3. Do you think there are enough facilities on the estate for leisure activities? I do not mean just for yourself but for all ages. If no details.

4. As you may know a community centre is being built on Parkview. Do you think there is any need for this? What do you think the centre should be used for?

5. Who do you think should be in charge of the centre?

6. Do you use the Parkview library? If yes, how often?

For pensioners:

7. Do you make use of the Church Close luncheon club? If no, would you like to?

For mothers with pre-school children:

8. Do you make use of Ash Road nursery/play centre/play group eleswhere?

If no, would you like to?

9. Are there any other facilities which you think should be provided on the estate?

10. Are you an active member of any of the following kinds of organisation or clubs? If yes are you an officer or committee member, now,—in the past?

11. Are you a member of the Parkview TA? If no, have you been in the past?

12. Do you know any present committee members? If yes, in what way?

13. Have you ever been a committee member of the TA? Would you like to take on committee work?

14. Is there any point in having a TA.? If yes, what do you think the work of the TA should be? Do you think the Parkview TA does this?

15. Do you know there is an area housing board for the Old Borough North? If yes, do you know what work the board does? Do you know your representative? If no, explain then.

16. Do you think this is a good idea?

17. Do you think tenants should have a say in the management of their own estate? if yes, what things should tenants/council control? How should this be done?

18. When you took up the tenancy of this flat you signed an agreement of council rules. Do you know what these rules are? Do you think these rules are sensible? Do you think there should be rules? If no reason. If yes, who should be responsible for deciding the rules? Who should be responsible for seeing that people keep the rules?

19. If tenants were given more say in how the estate was run would you be prepared to take part? If yes, How?

20. Are you satisfied with your dealings with council?

21. If you felt there was something on the estate needing attention, would you try to do something about it? What would you do? What result would you expect to get?

22. How much do you trust officials in council to do what is right?

23. Have you had any contact with council officials in the last year? If yes, What? What happened? Likewise re councillors.

24. How do you find that people who deal with complaints, repairs, lettings etc, treat people like yourself?

25. How do you feel if you have to have dealings with officials?

2   Interviews with officers

These and the interviews with councillors were structured interviews conducted in an informal way. Sections might be filled in in any order and during sessions, particularly those with councillors, questions might be put and answered in the context of a wider ranging discussion.

Name

Section

Job description

Work with the Borough

Previous job/training experience

Officer to whom immediately responsible

Officer/s supervised if any, in what way

In the course of your work do you have any contact with:

    other sections of housing
    other directorates
    outside agencies of any kind
    TA's

If yes in what way and for what reason? Do you have contact with councillors?

If yes who?

    what topics come up most frequently?

What does your job entail in detail?

(This question was made more specific to cover procedures for applications, rents, rebates, repairs, complaints, arrears etc depending on the job description given).

Do you feel there should be any kind of facilities/services provided on council estates? If so what?

Do you feel there is any scope for tenant participation in housing management? If so what? How might this be arranged?

Have you had any contact with Parkview estate? How do you rate that estate compared to others in the Borough?

Would you like to see any change in your job description? In the work of the directorate generally?

3   Councillors

Name

Age

Occupation

Party

Years resident in Borough

Experience of council committee work
    current—   major—   minor—
    previously

Do you have any contact with officers? If yes at what level?

How do you see the rôles of councillors as compared to officers?

Do you feel there should be any kind of facilities/services provided on council estates? If so what?

How would you define the concept of tenant participation?

Do you feel there is any scope for tenant participation in the Borough?

How would you assess the work of the Area Boards? Do you want to see any changes made to their membership/functions?

What is the rôle of a councillor on an Area Board?

Have you had any contact with Parkview estate?

How do you rate that estate compared to others in the Borough?

Do you want to see any changes in the scope of work, procedures etc, of the committees in which you are at present involved?

Other organizations in which involved.

Other comments.

4 *Interviews with resident representatives on the North Board.*
These were semi–structured interviews covering personal background; experience of TA's and the Area Housing Board; views on the work considered appropriate to each; the roles appropriate to the various participants on the board; the scope for change; attitudes towards tenant participation; involvement in other organizations.

5 *Interviews with committee members of the Parkview TA.*
These were semi–structured interviews covering personal background; experience of TA work; views on the work considered appropriate to TA's; the form of organization considered most suitable; views on the North Board; the scope for tenant participation in housing management; involvement in other organizations.

6 *Parkview community hall–Users survey, September 1976.*
These survey forms were completed by the users in the course of some particular hall activity. At all sessions I was on hand to answer any queries and at the afternoon bingo session two other members of Social Research Division staff assisted those attending with the forms.

Activity
1. Sex   Tick a box   ☐ Male

                                       ☐ Female

2. Marital status   Tick a box   ☐ Single

                                       ☐ Married

                                       ☐ Widowed

                                       ☐ Divorced/separated

3. Where do you live?   Tick a box

☐ Church Close

☐ Ash Court

☐ Goodson Road

☐ Chestnut Road

☐ Red block

☐ Green block

☐ Blue block

☐ Tower blocks

☐ Garden flats

☐ Sheltered Housing

☐ anywhere off the estate

4. How long have you lived on Parkview?
   Tick a box

☐ Less than one year

☐ 1–5

☐ 5–10

☐ more than 10

5. How often do you come to this group?
   Tick a box

☐ twice weekly

☐ once weekly

☐ every 2 weeks

☐ less often than that

6. What were your main reasons for joining?
Please write down in this space.

7. How did you hear about this group?
   Tick a box

☐ from a friend who is a member

☐ from a friend who is not a member

☐ another member

☐ a TA committee member

☐ a newsletter

☐ a poster

☐ other – please write down

8. How long have you been coming to this group?
Tick a box

☐ less than 3 months

☐ 3 to 6 months

☐ more than 6 months

9. Since coming to the hall have you made new friends?
Tick a box

☐ Yes   ☐ No

If you answered YES please say how many
Tick a box

☐ one new friend

☐ a few new friends

☐ lots of new friends

Do you meet any of these new friends outside the hall?
Tick a box

☐ Yes   ☐ No

10. Do you belong to any other Parkview group?
Tick a box

☐ Yes   ☐ No

If YES tick to show which they are*

☐ Playgroup

☐ Ladies keep fit

☐ Men's keep fit

☐ Pensioners bingo

☐ Evening bingo

☐ Youth club

☐ Luncheon club

*Tick more than one box if you need to.

11. Do other members of your family attend any groups?
Tick a box

☐ Yes   ☐ No

If YES tick to show which they are*

☐ Playgroup

☐ Ladies' keep fit

☐ Mens' keep fit

☐ Pensioners' bingo

☐ Evening bingo

☐ Luncheon club

☐ Youth club

*Tick more than one box if you need to.

290

12. Do you help to run any of these groups?

Tick a box ☐ Yes ☐ No

If your answer is NO would you like to help run any activities in the hall?

Tick a box ☐ Yes ☐ No

13. Before you came to the hall did you belong to any other groups, or clubs, or activities?

Tick a box ☐ Yes ☐ No

If YES tick to show what they are:*

☐ Bingo

☐ Sports club

☐ Pensioners club

☐ Adult education classes

☐ Social clubs eg British Legion

☐ Youth clubs

☐ Other—please write down details in this place

*Tick more than one box if you need to.

14. Do you still belong?   Tick a box   ☐ Yes   ☐ No
    Do you still go?   Tick a box   ☐ Yes   ☐ No

15. Would you like to see any other activities in the Parkview hall?

Tick a box ☐ Yes ☐ No

If your answer is YES please write down details in this space:

16. Would you like to see any changes made in how the hall is run?

Tick a box ☐ Yes ☐ No

If your answer is YES please write down details in this space.

17. Any other comments?
Thank you for your help.

7   *Parkview community hall—Sample residents survey, September 1976.*

This schedule was posted to all 73 respondents from the sample survey group. The schedule was accompanied by the following letter:

Dear

Last year you kindly helped me in the work for the Parkview study. When I was on the estate the community hall had not been opened. I am now carrying out a short survey to learn more about how the hall works. I would appreciate it if you would please help once again by filling in this form and posting it to me by Friday 24 September. Please add extra comments if you would like to. There is no need to put your name on the form, the number in the top left hand corner is the computer code for your interview.

I will be on the estate working in the hall from Monday 27 September until Friday 1st October. I expect to be there for all sessions. If you have any difficulties with the form do pop in and see me. *However, it would be most helpful if you would post the form back to me before then.* I would of course still like to see you so if you have a chance stop by for a chat sometime. Looking forward to seeing you soon.

This letter was on official paper and a stamped addressed envelope was also included. In most cases I added a personal note to the standard letter.

Parkview community hall–Sample residents survey schedule.

CODE NO.

1. Do you go to any activities in the hall?

Tick a box ☐ Yes ☐ No

If YES tick to show which they are:*

☐ Playgroup

☐ Ladies' keep fit

☐ Mens' keep fit

☐ Pensioners' bingo

☐ Evening bingo

☐ Youth Club

☐ Luncheon Club

*Tick more than one box if you need to.

2. How often do you attend?

☐ More than once weekly

☐ once weekly

☐ every 2 weeks

☐ once monthly

☐ less often than that

3. Do other members of your family go to any activities in the hall?

Tick a box ☐ Yes ☐ No

If YES tick to show which they are:*

☐ Playgroup

☐ Ladies' keep fit

☐ Mens' keep fit

☐ Pensioners' bingo

☐ Evening bingo

☐ Youth Club

☐ Luncheon Club

*Tick more than one box if you need to.

292

4. If your answer to question 1 was NO please say why*

Tick a box

☐	Dislike joining any groups
☐	Dislike activities offered
☐	Dislike the people there
☐	Feel too shy
☐	Prefer to take part in activities off the estate
☐	Just not interested

*Tick more than one box if you want to.

Are there any other reasons why you do not use the hall?

Please write down in this space:

5. Do you have any other comments about the hall?

For example: How should it be run?

What would you like to have there?

Please write down in this space:

III *Estate statistics**

TABLE AI   Households with children by floor level

Level	Hh with pre school children	%	Hh with Children 5–9	%	Hh with Children 10–13	%
Ground	14	11	18	16	20	17
1/2	62	47	29	27	41	35
3/4/5	28	21	35	32	33	28
6/7/8/9	15	11	14	13	16	13
10 and above	13	10	13	12	8	7
Total	132	100	109	100	118	100

TABLE AII   Households with elderly persons by floor level

Level	Households	%
Ground	66	25
1/2	74	28
3/4/5	64	24
6/7/8/9	49	18
10 and above	15	5
	268	100

*Note: The base date for all tables is 1 June 1974.

294

TABLE AIII Children and elderly persons per unit

Block	1 Pre school child per x unit/s	1 child under 13 per x unit/s	1 person aged 60 or over per x unit/s
Chestnut Road	4.8	1.4	3.0
Goodson Road	4.3	1.25	1.7
Ash Court	16.0	8.0	0.9
Market Street	0	4.0	2.7
Church Close	3.8	0.8	7.6
Blue ⎤	9.1	2.1	1.5
Red ⎬ Y blocks	6.8	2.6	1.6
Green ⎦	9.8	3.5	1.5
Tower block 1	4.9	1.4	2.1
Tower block 2	3.6	1.3	2.7
Garden flats	1.8	0.94	3.1

TABLE AIV Households with no children under 13

Block	Count	Type	Count	% of units in each block type
Chestnut Road	40 ⎤			
Goodson Road	22 ⎥			
Ash Court	44 ⎬ Balcony	119	69	
Market Street	7 ⎥			
Church Close	6 ⎦			
Blue	59 ⎤			
Red	65 ⎬ Y blocks	196	76	
Green	72 ⎦			
Tower 1	36 ⎤ Tower blocks	77	57	
Tower 2	41 ⎦			
Garden flats	62		62	39
Total			454	62

TABLE AV   Households with all adult residents*

Block	Count	Type	Count	% of units in each block type
Chestnut Road	30	Balcony blocks	96	56
Goodson Road	16			
Ash Court	44			
Market Street	4			
Church Close	2			
Blue	53	Y blocks	184	71
Red	63			
Green	68			
Tower 1	32	Tower blocks	63	46
Tower 2	31			
Garden flats	51		51	32
Total			394	54

*ie all residents aged 17 or over.

TABLE AVI   Black or mixed marriage households* by block type

Type	Count	% in each block type
Balcony	11†	6
Y blocks	9	3
Tower blocks	14	11
Garden flats	26	16
Total	60	8

*The Borough does not keep records of ethnic origins. In some few cases the information was noted on file; in other instances information was recorded in the course of introductory visits on the estate. The white group is therefore white or unseen and the black category may be understated.
† 8 in Chestnut Road.

TABLE AVII Black population by block type

Type	Count	% of total block population
Balcony Blocks	46	8
Y blocks	30	5
Tower Blocks	44	11
Garden Flats	108	20
Total	228	11*

*Note: 18 households or 30% of all black households comprise 5 or more persons. This may be compared with a figure of 12% for all white households of 5 persons or more.

TABLE AVIII Residence of black households prior to rehousing

Place	Count	% of all black households
Old Borough	26	43
Borough	33	55
Outside Borough	2	3
Total	60	101

TABLE AIX Applications for transfer by block

Block	Count	Type	Count	% of units in block	% of total units	% of total transfer applications
Chestnut Road	11					
Goodson Road	10	Balcony blocks	33	19	5	28
Ash Court	4					
Market Street	1					
Church Close	7					
Blue	10	Y blocks	45	17	6	39
Red	22					
Green	13					
Tower 1	20	Tower blocks	36	26	5	31
Tower 2	16					
Garden Flats	2		2	1		2
Totals			116		16	100

TABLE AX   Length of residence in the Old Borough

Period	Old estate	Col %	Garden flats	Col %	Total	%
less than 5 years	96	17	77	48	173	24
5 years and less than 10	69	12	15	9	84	11
10–20	141	25	20	13	161	22
20 years or more	238	42	38	24	276	38
not known	22	4	10	6	32	5
Totals	566	100	160	100	726	100

TABLE AXI   Place of residence prior to rehousing

Place	Old estate	Col %	Garden flats	Col %	Total	%
Old Borough	435	77	94	59	529	73
Borough	109	19	64	40	173	24
Outside Borough	17	3	1 ⎱	1	18	2
Not known	5	1	1 ⎰		6	1
Totals	566	100	160	100	726	100

TABLE AXII   Length of residence on Parkview

Period	No of households	%
less than one year	209	29
one year and less than 3	82	11
3–5	53	7
5–10	161	22
10 years or more	221	31
Total	726	100

TABLE AXIII   Reasons for rehousing

Reasons	Count	%
Overcrowding/poor conditions	241	33
Redevelopment/slum clearance	160	22
Homelessness	32	4
Exchange	11	2
Medical grounds	87	12
Unit size	132	18
Not known	63	9
Total	726	100

TABLE AXIV   Time lag between date of application and rehousing by length of residence on the estate.

Time lag; years		Length of residence on Parkview; years					
		<1	1–3	3–5	5–10	>10	Totals
<1	Count	85	32	22	46	65	250
	Row %	34	13	9	18	26	
	Col %	41	39	41	29	29	
1–3		50	23	12	28	53	166
		30	14	7	17	32	
		24	28	23	17	24	
3–5		25	10	5	25	16	81
		31	12	6	31	20	
		12	12	9	15	7	
5–10		17	8	3	10	34	72
		24	11	4	14	47	
		8	10	6	6	21	
>10		8	6	6	15	19	54
		15	11	11	28	35	
		4	8	11	9	12	
Not known		24	3	5	37	34	103
		22	4	5	36	33	
		11	5	9	23	21	
Totals		209	82	53	161	221	726

TABLE AXV   Time lag between date of application and rehousing by reasons for rehousing

Time lag; years		Over crowding	Redev	Homeless -ness	Exchange	Medical	Unit Size	NK	Total
<1	Count	71	81	23	2	19	40	14	250
	Col %	30	51	72	18	22	30	22	35
1–3		64	35	7	2	24	27	7	166
		27	22	22	18	27	20	11	23
3–5		38	13	2	0	7	18	3	81
		16	8	6	0	8	14	5	11
5–10		27	6	0	1	10	22	6	72
		10	3	0	9	12	17	11	10
10 or more		28	8	0	1	7	8	2	54
		12	5	0	9	8	6	3	7
Not known		13	17	0	5	20	17	31	103
		5	11	0	46	23	13	48	14
Totals		241	160	32	11	87	132	63	726
		100	100	100	100	100	100	100	100

TABLE AXVI   One parent families by block type

Type	Count	% of units in block type
Balcony	10	6
Y blocks	19	7
Tower	18	13
Garden	15	9
Total	62*	12

*19% of all households with dependent children.

TABLE AXVII   Non nuclear family households by block type

Type	Count	% of units in block type
Balcony	13	8
Y blocks	14	5
Tower	16	12
Garden	4	2
Total	47	6

300

TABLE AXVIII Reasons for rehousing of households with pre-school children at or above the third floor

Reasons	Floor level		
	3/4/5	6 and above	Totals
Overcrowding/ poor conditions	14	13	27*
Redevelopment/ slum clearance	1	2	3
Homelessness	7	10	17†
Exchange	0	0	0
Unit size	1	1	2
Medical	2	1	3
Not known	3	1	4
Totals	28	28	56

*Including 6 black families and 4 one parent families.
†Of 21 such families.

TABLE AX IX   Block by household size

Block	No of persons					
	1	2	3	4	5 or more	Totals
Chestnut Road	0	8	18	18	18	62
Goodson Road	11	2	0	8	9	30
Church Close	0	0	4	11	8	23
Market Street	0	1	3	2	2	8
Ash Court	24	16	6	3	0	49
Blue	21	24	9	12	16	82
Green	24	20	24	15	3	86
Red	22	28	27	10	3	90
Tower 1	1	19	22	19	7	68
Tower 2	9	10	29	13	7	68
Garden	18	24	43	43	32	160

SUMMARY

		1	2	3	4	5 or more	Totals
Balcony	Count	35	27	31	42	37	172
	Row %	20	16	18	24	21	
	Col %	27	18	17	27	35	
Y blocks		67	72	60	37	22	258
		26	28	23	14	8	
		51	47	32	24	21	
Tower		10	29	51	32	14	136
		7	21	37	23	10	
		8	19	27	21	13	
Garden		18	24	43	43	32	160
		11	15	27	27	20	
		14	16	23	28	30	
Totals		130	152	185	154	104	726
as % of 726		18	21	26	21	14	100

IV *Conditions of tenancy*

Conditions of tenancy for council dwellings in the Borough

1. The Tenancy shall be from week to week.

2. Four weeks' notice in writing to expire on Monday shall be given by either party to the other to terminate the Tenancy, and the keys of the premises must be surrendered to the Council on the expiry of the notice.

3. The Tenant shall:

1. Pay the weekly rent (which is inclusive of General and Water Rate) in advance on Monday in each week in such manner or at such place as the Council may from time to time direct.

2. Keep all internal fixtures and fittings upon and belonging to the premises in good repair.

3. Immediately replace or repay to the Council the cost of replacing all windows cracked or broken during the Tenancy.

4. Keep the premises at all times in a thoroughly clean and sanitary condition to the entire satisfaction of the Council

5. Keep the windows of the premises clean.

6. Have all chimneys in use swept whenever neccessary.

7. Deposit dry refuse and ashes only in the dust bin or chute, pour liquid refuse into the water closet or sink, according to the nature of the fluid, and in all respects observe the arrangements made by the Council from time to time for the disposal and collection of refuse. Use the Garchey waste disposal system where installed and follow the makers' instructions.

8. Repay to the Council the cost of repairing any damage done to the premises or to the Council's electric light fittings and fixtures (other than that resulting from reasonable wear and tear), of replacing keys and of clearing stoppages, due to carelessness, in water closets and drains.

9. Observe and keep the Regulations from time to time made by the Council relating to the use of common open spaces, and generally for ensuring the comfort and convenience of the tenants and for preserving and maintaining the amenities of the Estate.

10. At all reasonable times permit the Council, their officers or servants, or other persons authorised by the Council, to enter and view the premises and the state and condition thereof, to take inventories of the fixtures, to see that the Conditions of Tenancy are being observed, and to do any necessary repairs to their property.

11. Deliver up the premises in good repair order and condition at the end of the Tenancy (reasonable wear and tear only excepted) and shall pay the cost of removal and disposal of any rubbish or chattels left therein.

12. Be responsible for mischief, damage or breach of any of these conditions by his/her children, and restrain them from disfiguring the premises by marking them with chalk, pencil or otherwise.

13. Produce all rent cards or similar documents in his/her possession whenever required, for the inspection of the District Auditor of the Department of the Environment, or any authorised officer of the Council.

14. Be responsible in his/her turn, as directed by the Council, for the cleansing of the common stairs, landing and balconies (if any) which are to be swept daily and washed weekly by the Tenants in turn.

15. Observe and keep the Regulations made from time to time by the Council relating to the use of lifts, laundries, drying rooms, perambulator and cycle sheds.

16. Cultivate the garden ground (if any) of the premises and maintain the same, including hedges, in a good state of cultivation to the satisfaction of the Council, and give the Council's staff reasonable facilities for maintaining and cutting any hedges abutting on the roads or common passages.

17. Be responsible for the orderly conduct of all persons (including his/her children) who occupy the premises, his/her and their visitors, on any part of the Estate, indemnify the Council against all claims in respect of any damage, nuisance or annoyance they may cause to other persons and repay to the Council the cost of making good any damage or defacement they may cause to any building, wall, fence, gate, tree or any other property of the Council.

18. Be entitled at the discretion of the Council to use in the manner prescribed any facility provided for clothes washing and drying.

19. Use any supply of heat and/or hot water for domestic purposes only, confined to the needs of the Tenants' own household.

20. Preserve all existing trees, shrubs and plants on Council property.

21. Himself/herself occupy the premises comprising his/her tenancy.

4. The Tenant shall not:

1. Erect or permit to be erected on any portion of the Council's Estate, any shed or structure of any kind or make any alteration whatsoever to the structure of the dwellings, or to external colour schemes, or to the fences or affix any article, television or wireless aerial or apparatus without the written consent of the Council.

2. a. In a flat keep any dog or keep any livestock of any kind which in the opinion of the Council might be dangerous or a nuisance.
   b. In a house, keep any dog or other livestock of any kind which in the opinion of the Council might be a nuisance.

3. At any time, without the prior written consent of the Council, take in lodgers, let apartments or assign, underlet or part with possession of the premises, or any part thereof.

4. Use or permit the premises to be used for wholesale or retail trade, or as a workshop or business premises or any purpose other than as a private dwelling, or fix or permit to be affixed to the premises, any nameplate, bill, advertisement or placard of any description whatsoever.

5. Misuse or improperly occupy or allow disorderly or intemperate conduct, or do or suffer to be done any act or thing likely to be a nuisance or cause annoyance, discomfort or inconvenience to other residents on the Estate or to the owners or occupiers of neighbouring properties, or play musical instruments, radio or television to the annoyance of others.

6. Permit any mats, rugs or carpets, to be shaken or beaten on the landings or in the corridors or on the common open spaces or permit any rubbish or other articles to be thrown on or over such landings, corridors or open spaces or anything to be placed or deposited thereon which may cause a nuisance or obstruction.

7. Permit any washing to be hung out of the windows, corridors or in the common open spaces.

8. Permit children to play on the landings, staircases, or common open spaces in such manner as to be a nuisance or a danger.

9. Permit any creepers or other plants to cling to exterior walls.

10. Park vehicles in or on courtyards, service roads, greens or gardens except as permitted by the Council in writing.

11. Waste or misuse any supply of heat and/or hot water.

12. Allow anything to be done or brought on to the premises which might invalidate any policy of insurance against fire in respect of the premises.

13. Deposit any liquid or offensive matter in lifts, or on landings.

14. Leave milk bottles in such places as to constitute a nuisance.

5. On breach by the Tenant of any of these conditions the Tenancy may be terminated by the Council forthwith.

6. The said weekly rent and other sums as shown on the front cover of the rent card may be increased or decreased on notice being given by the Council.

7. Any written notice required to be served on the Council shall be sent to the Housing Manager. Any notice required to be served on the Tenant (other than a notice to terminate the Tenancy) shall be sufficiently served if sent to the Tenant by ordinary prepaid post or left for the Tenant at the premises.

8. The Council reserves the right to add to or vary these conditions and in that event the Council will furnish the Tenant with the revised condition/s.

9. Any supply of heat and/or hot water shall be given at such time and to such standard and temperature as the Council shall from time to time determine. The Council shall not be under any liability whatsoever for, and no rebate of the total rent will be allowed in respect of, the failure of such supply from any cause.

10. The Tenant shall be responsible, in addition, for ensuring that members of his/her family, his/her visitors and other persons who occupy the premises or any part thereof comply with Condition 4 (1–14) hereof and accordingly any infringement of such conditions by such persons will be treated as an infringement thereof by the Tenant.

11. The Council will not be held liable for any damage or loss to property or inconvenience a Tenant suffers arising out of the negligence of another Tenant or his/her family or his/her visitors.

12. Entry into possession shall be deemed consent on the part of the Tenant to be bound by the above terms.

This document was signed by the incoming tenant and returned to the housing directorate. As noted above, p 133f, under Brown's direction the Borough considered changes to these terms. Brown advocated an alternative agreement whereby the tenant agreed to look after the property, make regular rent payments, cause no annoyance to neighbours and, except where permission was sought and granted to use the premises solely for the use of his family. In return the council gave an undertaking to maintain the property in good repair and subject to the tenant meeting his responsibilities, to ensure his uninterrupted enjoyment of the tenancy. The tenancy would be subject to four weeks notice by either party. Provision was made for extra conditions to be set by tenants associations.

The simplified agreement was circulated to the area boards and tenants' association committees for comment. Four associations and four boards responded. All accepted that conditions of tenancy should remain and comments concerned revisions of the existing agreement. None considered the alternative proposal acceptable. In these circumstances Brown put forward the following.

1. The tenancy shall be a weekly one, expiring by four weeks notice in writing by either side. The rent (and other sums due) and these Conditions of Tenancy may be varied on notice being given by the Council.

2. The tenant agrees

i. to pay the full rent (including rates and other charges) due on Mondays each week;
ii. to occupy the whole of the premises him/herself solely as a private residence and not to assign or sublet the tenancy or take in others to live there without prior consent in writing;
iii. to maintain the premises and environs in a tenant-like manner and to inform the Council of any defects likely to cause personal injury;
iv. not to commit or allow conduct which causes a nuisance to others;
v. to repay to the Council the costs of any damage to the premises or its fittings as a consequence of his/her misuse, neglect or carelessness;
vi. to allow Council officers access to premises and to inspect tenant's rent payment records when necessary;
vii. to allow the Council to dispose of any items left in the premises on termination of tenancy;
viii. not to keep animals on the premises which in the opinion of the Council causes a nuisance to others (dogs are not permitted in flats);
ix. to conform with any Council regulations issued in the interests of good estate management.

In return the Council agrees

i. to maintain the structure and supplies in good order, to carry out reasonable repairs to landlord's fittings, and to repaint the exterior every 5 years;
ii. to allow the tenant quiet enjoyment of this tenancy; any action for possession of the premises will be through the courts after due notice to the tenant.

V *Official letters to residents*

Borough Directorate of Housing
Housing Centre
Borough Road
LONDON   October 1974

Dear Sir/Madam

AREA HOUSING BOARDS
ELECTION OF TENANT REPRESENTATIVES

The period of office of tenant representatives on the Area Housing Boards expires in October and it will be necessary to obtain further representation for the coming year.

The election of new representatives or the re-election of those existing will take place at public meetings of Council tenants to be held as follows:–

Borough North	Public House Borough Road Monday 28 October 1974 at 7.30 pm.
Borough South	Church Hall Garden Square Monday 28 October 1974 at 8.30 pm.
Old Borough North and South	Old Borough town hall Market Street Wednesday 30 October 1974 at 8.00 pm.

Adequate representation can only be achieved if tenants vote at these elections and I trust you will make every effort to attend.

Admission to the Meeting will be given only on production of a rent book.

This letter was signed by White and sent to all Borough tenants.
A similar letter was sent on the occasion of elections held in May 1975. However, in this instance the wording of the paragraphs following the announcement of the meetings was altered.

Councillor Harty, Vice-chairman of the Housing Services Committee and other council members will be present.

The Council is most anxious that tenants should participate fully in Estate Management, and each Area Housing Board includes four tenant representatives. It is therefore, in *your* interest to attend your Area Meeting to ensure the election of the tenants you want to represent *you*. Admission to the Meeting will be given only on production of a rent book.

It is very much hoped that you will be able to attend the Meeting.

Other letters concerning housing matters may go out under the signature of the chief executive. One such example is given below.

Mrs J Cliffe
XYZ Blue Block
Parkview Estate   Borough Offices
Old Borough North   15 August 1975

NOTICE OF INCREASE IN RENTS

The Council has decided to renew the basis on which rents of its dwellings are charged, and on the revised basis of 1.15 times the gross value the maximum rent on you dwelling will be £7.53. As a first step towards this maximum rent, rents will be increased initially by up to 50p per week.

I hereby give you notice that with effect on and after the 6th day of October, 1975 the rent payable to the Council under your tenancy of the dwelling described in the panel above will be increased by 50 pence per week. Accordingly the weekly amount payable by you in respect of rent for the dwelling (excluding rates and other charges) on and after 6 October next will be £6.47.

Under the Prices and Incomes Act 1968 you have the right to terminate your tenancy in accordance with the provisions of Section 12(2) of that Act which reads as follows:—

"Where a local authority gives notice of increase under subsection (1) above for the beginning of a rental period and the tenancy continues into that period, the notice shall nevertheless not have effect if the tenancy is terminated by notice to quit given by the tenant in accordance with the provisions express or implied of the tenancy, and—

a. the notice to quit is given before the end of the period of 2 weeks following the date on which the notice of increase is given, or such longer period as may be allowed by the notice of increase; and

b. the date on which the tenancy is made to terminate is not later than the earliest day on which the tenancy could be terminated by a notice to quit given by the tenant on the last day of that period."

If you wish to terminate the tenancy you must give the Council a notice to quit which should be given not less than 4 weeks before the date on which it is to take effect. Furthermore, if the above increase in rent is not to be effective the notice to quit must be received by the Council not later than 8 September 1975 to terminate the tenancy on or before 6 October 1975.

Any notice given by you may be addressed to the Director of Housing, Housing Centre, Borough Road, London.

Under the signature of the chief executive the following proviso was added.

OCCUPIERS ALREADY UNDER NOTICE TO QUIT

For the information of any occupier who has received a notice to quit this letter and/or the acceptance of any charges by the Council after its despatch is not to be taken to indicate the creation of a new tenancy or to be regarded as evidence thereof.

This letter was accompanied by a more general one to all tenants, again under the signature of the chief executive, of same date and with the proviso for those under notice to quit appended.

Dear Tenant

HOUSING RENTS AND SUBSIDIES ACT 1975

The Council is required by the above Act to charge reasonable rents for its dwellings and to review these rents from time to time. The last increase in rents was in October, 1973 and since then the costs of the Housing service have risen sharply. Therefore, in order to maintain a reasonable balance between the rent payer and the rate payer in meeting housing expenditure, it is necessary to increase rents this autumn. To achieve comparability between one Council tenant and another, the Council has decided to fix maximum rents on the basis of 1.15 times the gross value.

A leaflet describing the Council's Rent Rebate Scheme is also enclosed with this letter and, if after reading this, you feel that you may be entitled to a rebate you may obtain an application form at any of the offices mentioned in the leaflet. The Council is anxious to ensure that no tenant fails to take advantage of the rebate scheme which is his by right and if you have any difficulty in understanding the Scheme, please call at the Director of Finance's Rent Rebate Office (address and telephone number given).

If you now receive a Rent Rebate which expires on 6 October 1975, you will have already been sent an application form which should be returned not later than 1 September 1975.

Rebates which expire after 6 October will be automatically adjusted to take account of the new rent without any action on your part.

If you receive Supplementary Benefit you need take no action as your case will be dealt with by the Department of Health and Social Security.

It should be noted that partly as a result of the research findings, attempts have recently been made to simplify letters from the housing directorate to residents.

VI   *The work of the North Board*

In the course of the six meetings held during the study period the North Board considered a total of 119 items or on average about 19 items per meeting. These items can be variously categorized but the following headings seem appropriate and are given with listings of the items raised.

A. *Planning or Policy Issues*
   the development of play areas
   plans for new estate development
   club rooms for a new estate
   changes to the conditions of tenancy
   the introduction of planned maintenance
   the introduction of a new policy on redecoration
   the use of derelict land adjoining an estate
   management of sheltered housing

B. *Major repairs*
   faulty floors in a new estate development
   dampness and other faults in new flats

C. *General repairs and day to day maintenance*
   bins and bin doors
   garchey repairs
   trimming of hedges
   loose paving stones
   fencing for flats
   exposed cable
   delays to individual repairs
   estate gates
   rubbish collection
   gates to underground garage

D. *Administrative matters*
   arrangements for access to property
   arrangements for visit to a new estate
   ID cards for members
   the preparation of lists of acquired property

nominations for a training course for tenants
the setting of election dates
a refund to tenant

E. *Miscellaneous items*
  car parking
  status of estate roads
  film of TA's
  street signs
  notice boards for estates
  estate names
  laundry facilities for sheltered housing
  the installation of a kidney machine in a tenant's flat
  a dispute within a constituent TA
  uniforms for caretakers
  seats in Market Street
  warning system for a block of flats
  petitions
  issue of supplies to caretakers
  sheds/basements
  a pigeon nuisance
  a problem family
  lifts
  a leaflet for tenants

These listings and the count of total items exclude procedural matters like the acceptance of minutes. The list shows eight items under planning/policy, two major repairs, 10 general repairs, seven administrative matters and 19 miscellaneous, a total of 46 items. The discrepancy between this and the total number of items raised at all six meetings is accounted for by the fact that all except 16 items were raised at more than one meeting. In addition, some headings such as playground development incorporate a number of estate schemes which are counted separately in the overall figure. (It should also be kept in mind that the cut-off points are quite arbitrary. Thus, some of the issues raised in meeting one were undoubtedly carried over from previous meetings and some items under consideration during the study period would recur after meeting 6).

These items can be dealt with by the board in a number of ways. The policy and planning issues are generally referred to the board for comment by other council committees. Where the board's recommendations involve expenditure as in the case of one of the playground items, reference has to be made to the appropriate committee. Other recommendations are of a more general type and may or may not be taken into account. Indeed whether the views of the board are put forward on a particular matter would seem to depend fairly much on councillors reporting back to other committees and forcefully or otherwise presenting the case of tenant board members, or on the preparedness of chairmen of committees to follow up items referred to the board for comment. Two items under this heading, the introduction of a system of planned maintenance and a change in policy on the internal redecoration of council dwellings, concern policy decisions already made and were in this case only for noting by the board. The general repairs and day to day maintenance can be dealt with by Black, either by investigation as in the case of alleged non-collection of rubbish, delays to individual repairs, and danger from exposed cable, or by the issue of works orders. In dealing with this category of items, and most of those listed under the miscellaneous heading, Black can use his own initiative. Such matters need not be referred to any committee but can, if Black decides action is warranted, be passed directly for implementation by the officer concerned. The administrative matters can normally be dealt with by the board except where committee approval is required, as is the case of the issue of ID cards, or where an officer response outside the meeting is necessary, as with the preparation of lists of acquired properties.

The manner in which items were dealt with in practice may be discussed by reference to the number of times items appeared before the board and by noting the kind of decisions actually taken. The most frequently raised items were major repairs; the faulty floors issue was raised at all six meetings and the dampness issue at five. Discussion of these issues took up a good deal of the board's time. The board did obtain reports from the Architect's Department on action being taken and in the case of the floors was able to press for explanatory letters to be sent to all tenants and to the TA. As a potential pressure group the board had to rely on councillors and since other groups and individuals were actively lobbying the same people it is difficult to assess its effectiveness in this instance.

The question of issuing a leaflet to tenants outlining basic information on household services like central heating systems and waste disposal units was discussed on four occasions at which point it was said to be in the course of preparation for general distribution. Sixteen items were dealt with at one meeting. Three of these, a petition, the resiting of a public telephone and a request for club rooms, were referred back to the TA's concerned and presumably nothing further was heard. Seven items were noted 'for report'. In fact five of these involved minor investigations and only two, the proposal for the installation of a warning system and planned new estate developments seem to warrant further formal report. For all items, there is no evidence that reports were received during this period. The date for an election was announced, an item concerning the installation of estate gates was actioned, a request to make a film on TA's was turned down, the estates manager was asked to leave an estate name on a notice board, a date was set for a visit to estates, and a request that tenants be informed about the reasons for delays in attending to repairs was passed for consideration to the Housing Utilisation Committee. All other items, ie many of those listed under the general repairs and miscellaneous categories above, were raised at two or three meetings.

Another way of analysing the work of the board is to look at the way in which items were dealt with. Items may be classified for noting, for report or for action. In addition, one item, the proposal to change the conditions of tenancy was for discussion. (See Appendix IV). The largest group of items, 21 was for report. Tenants representatives were asked to report on two items, a councillor on one and officers on 18. Seventeen items were for action. These were as follows; arrangements for a visit to a TA run community centre; the fixing of gates to an underground garage; repairs to bin doors; the provision of bins; investigation into the faulty floors; the installation of estate gates; arrangements for a visit to new estate developments; repairs to waste disposal units; the preparation of lists of acquired properties; the supply of notice boards; inquiring into delays to individual cases of outstanding repairs; the issue of ID passes; the preparation of information leaflets; the upgrading of play facilities; the implementation of car parking regulations; the referral of a dispute within a TA committee to the appropriate committee; the trimming of hedges and shrubs. Most of the items involved the issue of works orders or other administrative procedures. Most could be carried out directly by Black; few involved reference to other directorates or committees.

Finally, in order to give further insight into the working of the board, the rôles adopted by participants in the course of the two meetings observed may be described. The first meeting was attended by councillors Lawrence, Mitchell, Harty, b, o, and 1, the four tenant representatives Lloyd, Steed, Thompson and Mrs Ruble, Black, and as secretary, an officer from the Directorate of Operations. (See Table v). Essentially there were three active participants at the meeting, Lloyd, Mrs Ruble and Black. Cllors Lawrence and Mitchell and Thompson took a more minor role in the proceedings and others in attendance were passive participants.

Lloyd commented how impressed he had been by the visit to an estate in another borough which had been arranged to enable members to see how community facilities there were organized. He advocated further visits for more councillors and tenants. Lloyd raised as queries: the fixing of the gates; the issue of tower block lighting; the supply to caretakers of replacement parts for garchey units; the clearing of the garchey tanks; all with reference to the Parkview estate; the fixing of a gas hot water system; play equipment; cycle sheds; a notice board and plans for a community centre on another estate in the borough. In addition Lloyd commented at length on a matter raised by Councillor Mitchell, namely, the nuisance caused by pigeons nesting on the balcony of a flat at Parkview. Mrs Ruble asked that the following matters be attended to: the defective floors at the estate where she lives; a problem family causing distress to neighbouring residents on the same estate; outside lighting and repairs to the doors of a club room on another estate. She also raised the question of whether the sheltered housing block on Parkview was to be regarded as part of the estate since the warden appeared to be running it as a separate institution. Black replied that basically the warden was in charge but suggested that a diplomatic approach might secure her support. Lloyd undertook to take the initiative in trying to establish easier relations between the sheltered housing residents and those on the estate. Thompson complained about the rubbish collection on his own estate and put forward an individual complaint from the same estate. The councillors who spoke at the meeting also raised complaints. Councillor Mitchell took up the question of bin sheds, the repair of gates to the underground car park, the pigeon nuisance mentioned above and maintenance work to the new extension. All of these issues concerned the Parkview estate. Councillor Lawrence followed up Lloyd's query about the garchey with a similar query about the system on another estate.

Thus at this meeting a series of complaints was raised directly with Black, the officer most concerned in remedying them. Throughout he was able to give assurances that all matters raised were either already in hand or would be actioned. There were no matters put forward from councillors or officers for general discussion and no requests from tenants for policy issues to be raised in committee.

The second meeting was chaired by Councillor Mitchell in the absence of Councillor Lawrence. Others present were Councillors Harty, b, 1 and p, the four tenants' representatives, Black, a secretary, and the Borough Architect. For the most part this meeting followed a pattern similar to the previous meeting. However, in addition to the raising of various complaints there were lengthy and somewhat heated exchanges involving officers, tenants and councillors on two agenda items, the defective flooring and the defects in the new extensions at Parkview. The Borough Architect was present particularly to discuss the plans for club rooms on another estate and to report on action being taken in regard to the floors. He apologized for having overlooked the agenda item on the garden flats at Parkview. Nevertheless, in response to questions, he outlined the normal procedure adopted by the council to ensure that any contractor fulfilled all his obligations to the local authority within the six-month maintenance period. This entailed an initial inspection and subsequent check by a council surveyor. Lloyd objected that those surveys had not been carried out and Black explained how desperate the staffing shortage had been at the time. The Borough Architect countered that inspections were indeed carried out by a council surveyor for every council house built and he said he could provide the board with reports. Councillor Mitchell asked Lloyd if he could supply lists of properties where it was alleged that no such survey had been carried out. Mrs Ruble asked if the board could have copies of the reports held by the architects' department. Her request was not taken up and Councillor Mitchell asked instead that a further report be made to the next board meeting. There was more discussion over the action to be taken regarding the defective flooring on another estate. Throughout the meeting the main participants were again Black, Lloyd, and Mrs Ruble. Councillor Mitchell in the chair assumed a more prominent role in the proceedings and the Borough Architect made substantial contributions wherever the interests of his department were involved. Steed raised a complaint about his building. Councillor Harty took part in the discussion concerning the floors and pressed for immediate action. He also asked that matters of lift replacement and inspection of the exposed cable at Parkview be 'chased up'. Other board members made no contribution.

Tenants tend to raise matters concerning their own estates but issues from elsewhere are also considered. One or two representatives, particularly Mrs Ruble, are prepared to press hard for agenda items considered important but it would seem to be difficult for them to secure a strong position in instituting an inquiry. In part this is due to the structure and terms of reference of the board. Tenants cannot instruct officers; there is therefore no point to working within such a system unless some form of dialogue with officers can be sustained. This has a moderating effect on demands. Further, tenants representatives have a limited knowledge of the council system and at that time no attempt had been made to better inform tenant members. In part however, this weakness can be explained by reference to the rôle adopted by councillors and officers. Thus Mrs Ruble's request that the board have copies of the surveyors' reports was not supported by councillors and Councillor Mitchell instead asked a tenant representative Lloyd to provide lists of properties where it was alleged no inspections had been carried out. The councillor thus placed the onus on the tenant representative rather than the officer though in a different context the same councillor may well be prepared to press the same officer rather harder. Officers appear to be open about mistakes made and adopt a conciliatory tone in undertaking to amend them. Thus on the inspection issue Black commented that properties '. . . should still be inspected by our surveyor to decide whether it is our responsibility or the contractors and the problem is that we just haven't been getting around to it. Its a hopeless situation but I take your point that it seems wrong that faults on site become the responsibility of the council and that we face the charge.' During the meeting on several occasions Black answered the Board that 'as always' he would do all he could to sort out problems and where possible get action. He emphasized that some matters were beyond his control especially in regard to building maintenance. The Borough Architect was also sympathetic and told board members that he was interested in learning from tenants and meeting with them so that his department would have useful information for their next planning exercise. All these mechanisms, the minimal role of the councillors, the helpful attitude of officers, and the restricted content of meetings, have the effect of defusing the potential conflict between participants. This is accentuated further by the common practice of following the formal meeting with an informal session in a nearby pub. All board members excepting Thompson, the Conservative councillor and visiting officers generally join these gatherings. They provide an opportunity to go over aspects of the meeting, bring up issues of common interest for informal discussion and allow for the affirmation of a group identity.

From this account it can be seen that in regard to the formal processes of board meetings the North Board has provided a forum for the consideration of general management issues, mostly concerning day to day maintenance. Within the board contributions come predominantly from Black and two of the tenant representatives, Lloyd and Mrs Ruble. Black is in a position to filter items raised; fairly straight forward issues which meet with his approval can be dealt with directly and instructions issued; more contentious issues or those necessitating a budget allocation are more likely to be referred to committee; other items may simply be dropped and at least some of these never appear on the agenda or minutes. Where instructions are subsequently issued by Black there is, even so, likely to be some delay since the implementation would in most instances be the responsibility of the DLBO. This at once gives Black a scape-goat mechanism and explains why so much board business is repetitive. Councillors seldom intervene at the board meeting, though outside it in a more informal situation they may become more involved, and in committee they may draw on their board experience. Tenants' representatives ascribe to councillor members a generally supportive rôle; none are critical of the stance adopted by councillors or officers.

Items before the North Board are typically the subject of discussion with officers responding to tenant enquiries. Potentially the chairman has a key rôle in directing discussion. In fact both the chairman and vice chairman on the board tend to adopt a non-directive rôle and the effective chairman is often Black. There is little debate or formulation of motions and consequently no voting takes place. Tenant representatives reach a consensus of opinion on issues and the officers are conciliatory in their public response.

Most of the items referred to the North Board are fairly predictable. A few are interesting in the terms of the status of the board. Thus one petition referred to the board requested fencing around the playground at Parkview. This was unfavourably received by the board and the tenants were advised accordingly. Other petitions have been referred to council committees or to the full council. It is not clear on what basis it is decided to refer petitions to the various committees or the board, nor is it clear whether in such a case the tenants could appeal and ask for their petition to be resubmitted elsewhere. Similarly, a request from a local settlement for permission to make a film on TA's was refused by the board but it was doubtful if the decision would be considered binding on the council as a whole or on individual TAs. At the same time tenant representatives like Mrs Ruble and Lloyd complain that the board does not consider all matters which they feel are relevant to it. In particular they have referred to the commencement of the study and the follow-up appointment of a community worker on Parkview. Questions may be asked of them about such projects; representatives are loathe to admit a lack of knowledge and feel they should be fully briefed. Further, they may feel that the tenant representatives or the board should exert some real influence on such local developments. This may result in conflict. Thus, whatever the stance of

316

the board, Lloyd and Mrs Ruble felt strongly that they had a right to be involved in the affairs of a constituent TA on the Parkview estate and their position was tacitly accepted by the other estates representative Steed. Their concern was construed as unwarranted interference by members of the estate committee. Certainly there would seem to be a somewhat arbitrary process in deciding both on the range of items placed before the board and then on the manner of their despatch. This can be seen as a reflection of the way in which the rôle and the functions of the boards and board members have developed. None of the participants knows clearly what is expected nor what the limits are. The board does not have any power to act as an effective clearing house for the complaints which take up so much of its time and denied that executive function it does not have the skills to act as an advisory body on policy matters.

Bibliography

ABRAMS, M, 'This Britain: A contented nation?' *New Society,* Vol 27, No 594, 21 February 1974, pp 439–40.

—'Owners and Tenants', *New Society,* Vol 33, No 672, 21 August 1975, pp 417–19.

ADAMS, B and CONWAY, J, 'The Social Effects of Living Off the Ground', HDD Occasional Paper 1/75, Department of the Environment, 1975.

ASSOCIATION OF LONDON HOUSING ESTATES, (ALHE), 'Tenant participation in Housing Management', Information Paper, 1973.

ALHE and Housing Department, London Borough of Southwark, 'Tenant Participation in Housing Management and beyond', unpublished paper, November 1975.

AMICK, D J and KVIZ, F J, 'Social Alienation in Public Housing–The Effects of Density and Building Types', *Ekistics,* Vol 39, No 231, February 1975, pp 118–120.

Anon, 'Adolescent Violence', *New Society,* Vol 26, No 584, 13 December 1973, pp 664–65.

—'Old People's Clubs', *New Society,* Vol 31, No 647, 27 February 1975, p 527.

—'Youth Work', *New Society,* Vol 31, No 647, 27 February 1975, p 527.

—Action Report on Housing Associations, *Community Action,* No 17, December/January 1975, pp 15–27.

—'Alternative to Fear', *Progressive Architecture,* October 1972, pp 92–105.

—'Building Study, Housing at Palace Fields, Runcorn'. *AJ,* 9 October 1974, pp 845–62.

ARNSTEIN, S R, 'A Ladder of Citizen Participation in the USA', *Journal of the Town Planning Institute,* Vol 57, No 4, April 1971, pp 176–182.

ARMSTRONG, G and WILSON, M, 'Social Problems, Social Control and the case of Easterhouse', Paper to the British Sociological Assoc. Annual Conference, London, 1971.

BAGLEY, C, 'The Built Environment as an Influence on Personality and Social Behaviour', in D Canter and T Lee (eds), *Psychology and the Built Environment,* Architectural Press, London, 1974.

BALDWIN, J, 'Problem Housing Estates', unpublished paper, np, 1973.

BANHAM, R, 'The Parkhill Victory', *New Society,* Vol 26, No 576, 18 October 1973, pp 154–56.

BARLOW, K, 'The Peckham Experiment', *Ecologist,* Vol 4, No 10, December 1974, pp 382–84.

BARNES, J A, 'Class and Committees in a Norwegian Island Parish', *Human Relations,* Vol VII, 1954, pp 39–58.

BECKER, H S, 'Inference and Proof in Participant Observation', *American Sociological Review,* Vol 23, No 6, December 1958, pp 652–660.

BERTHOUD, R and JOWELL, R, *Creating A Community: a study of Runcorn New Town,* SCPR, London, 1972.

BIRD, H and WHITBREAD, M, 'Council house transfers and exchanges', *New Society,* Vol 33, No 671, 14 August 1975, pp 359–61.

BIRKSTED, I K, 'School Performance Viewed from the Boys', *Sociological Review,* Vol 24, No 1, New Series, February 1976, pp 63–77.

BLAU, P M, *Exchange and Power in Social Life,* New York, 1967.

BOOTH, A and CAMP, H, 'Housing Relocation and Family Social Integration Patterns', *Journal of the American Institute of Planners,* Vol 40, No 2, March 1974, pp 124–28.

BOTT, E, *Family and Social Networks,* London, 2nd ed, 1971.

BOUDON, P, *Lived-in Architecture,* London, 1972.

BRACEY, H E, *Neighbours: On New Estates and Subdivisions in England and the USA,* London, 1964.

BRITISH ASSOCIATION OF SETTLEMENTS, *A Right to Fuel,* London, June 1975.

BROWN, G et al, *The Red Paper on Scotland,* Edinburgh, 1975.

BROWN, G W, BHROLCHAIN, M N and HARRIS, T, 'Social Class and Psychiatric Disturbance among Women in an Urban Population', *Sociology,* Vol 9, No 2, May 1975, pp 225–254.

BROWNLEA, A, 'The Offensive Community', *Ekistics,* Vol 39, No 231, February 1975, pp 84–88.

BRYANT, D and Knowles, D, 'Social Contacts on the Hyde Park Estate, Sheffield', *Town Planning Review,* Vol 45, No 2, April 1974, pp 207–214.

BUCHANAN, C, 'Why every man must have a shed', *The Countryman,* Summer 1975, pp 20–26.

BURAK, M J, 'You mean there is more to it than collecting rents?', *Housing Monthly,* November 1975, pp 8–15.

BURBIDGE, M, 'A Constructive Approach to Vandalism', *Building,* Vol 225, No 6808, 23 November 1973, pp 120–24.

—'Design and Management for Better Maintenance', unpublished paper to the Welsh Office/Welsh School of Architecture Symposia, April 1975.

BYNNER, J, 'Deprived Parents', *New Society,* Vol 27, No 594, 21 February 1974, pp 448–9.

CAMPBELL K, 'Public Architects and the end of Innocence', *Riba J,* Vol 80, No 10, October 1973, pp 492–3.

CARSON, W G and WILES, P, *Crime and Delinquency in Britain,* London, 1971

CATHOLIC HOUSING AID SOCIETY, *What Chance a Home,* London, 1974.

CDP, *Whatever happened to Council Housing?* Co-operative Press Ltd, London, 1976.

CHERMAYEFF, S and ALEXANDER, C, *Community and Privacy,* London, 1963.

CHILD, J, 'Participation, Organization and Social Cohesion', *Human Relations,* Vol 29, No 5, 1976, pp 429–51.

CLARK, D B, 'The Concept of Community, A Re-examination', *The Sociological Review,* Vol 21, No 3, New Series, August 1973, pp 397–416.

COHEN, A, *Two Dimensional Man,* University of California Press, 1974.

COOK, D L, *Educational Project Management,* Charles E Merrill, Ohio, 1971.

COUPER, M and BRINDLEY, T, 'Housing Classes and Housing Values', *The Sociological Review,* Vol 23, No 3, New Series, August 1975, pp 563–76.

322

CRADDOCK, J, *Tenants Participation in Housing Management*, ALHE, London, 1975.

CULLINGWORTH, J B, 'Who Needs Housing?', unpublished paper to conference of Housing Centre Trust, July 1971.

—'The Shifting Sands of British Housing Policy' *Riba J*, Vol 80, No 10, October 1973, pp 488–91.

DAMER, S and MADIGAN, R, 'The Housing Investigator', *New Society*, Vol 29, No 616, 25 July 1974, pp 226–27.

DAMER, S, 'Wine Alley, the Sociology of a Reputation', unpublished paper to the British Sociological Association, at the Annual Conference, University of Leeds, September 1972.

DAVIES, J G, *The Evangelistic Bureaucrat*, London, 1972.

DEMERATH, N J, 'St Louis Public Housing Study Sets Off . . .', *The Journal of Housing*, Vol 19, No 8, October 1962, pp 472–8.

DENNIS, N and REX, J, 'Whose is the "Good City"?', *New Society*, Vol 26, No 585, 20 December 1973, pp 719–20.

DENNIS, N, 'Changes in Function and Leadership Renewal', *Sociological Review*, New Series 9, March 1961, pp 55–84.

DEPARTMENT OF THE ENVIRONMENT, [*MHLG*] *The Deeplish Study*, HMSO, 1966.

—[MHLG], *Council Housing Purposes, Procedures and Priorities*, HMSO, 1969.

—*Living in a Slum*, Design Bulletin 19, HMSO, 1970.

—*Moving out of a Slum*, Design Bulletin 20, HMSO, 1970.

—*Families Living at High Density*, Design Bulletin 21, HMSO, 1970.

—*Children at Play*, Design Bulletin 27, HMSO, 1973.

—*Multi-purpose Halls*, Design Bulletin 28, HMSO, 1973.

—'Neighbourhood Councils in England', Consultation papers, July 1974.

—*Final Report of the Working Party on Housing Co-operatives*, HMSO, 1975.

DIXEY, M G D, Local Recreation Centres, London, 1974.

DOBSON, F, 'Tenant Involvement in Practice', *Housing Review*, Vol 23, No 3, May–June 1974, pp 69–70.

DOMBECK, B and WINTERSON, B, 'Freeway Detached Youth and Community Project', Workers Report, unpublished paper, October 1973.

DONNISON, D, 'What is the "Good City"?', *New Society*, Vol 26, No 584, 13 December 1973, pp 647–9.

DONNISON, D and EVERSLEY, D, (eds) *London: Urban Patterns, Problems and Policies*, London, 1973.

DOUGLAS, M and NICOD, M, 'Taking the biscuit; the structure of British meals', *New Society*, Vol 30, No 637, 19 December 1974, pp 744–70.

DUGMORE, K, 'Social Characteristics of the Tenants of 72 GLC Housing Estates', GLC Research Memorandum, 1975.

EGGLESTON, J, 'Values of Youth', *New Society*, Vol 31, No 641, 16 January 1975, pp 129–30.

ELIAS, N and SCOTSON, J L, *The Established and the Outsiders*, London, 1965.

ELLIS, P, 'Letterbox living: making friends on housing estates', *New Society*, Vol 34, No 678, 2 October 1975, pp 10–12.

EVERSLEY, D, 'Landlords Slow Goodbye', *New Society* Vol 31, No 641, 16 January 1975, pp 119–21.

FAIR HOUSING GROUP (NOTTINGHAM), 'Report on coloured families in council housing', September 1971.

FAIR HOUSING GROUP (MANCHESTER COUNCIL FOR COMMUNITY RELATIONS), 'Report on coloured families in council housing', January 1971.

FESTINGER, L et al, *Social Pressures in Informal Groups*, London, 1959.

FIRTH, R, Hubert, J, and Forge, A, *Families and their Relatives*, London, 1969.

FORESTER, T, 'Out of the library,' *New Society*, Vol 33, No 672, 21 August 1975, p 425.

FOX, D, 'Tenant Participation – a new task for housing management?' *Housing*, Vol 10, No 1, July 1974, pp 18–23.

—'Council Housing: Performance, Problems and Promises', *Housing Review*, Vol 24, No 4, July–August 1975, pp 107–108.

—'A Case of Stunted Growth', Housing Management Supplement, *Municipal Journal/Muncipal Engineering*, Vol 83, No 44, 31 October 1975, pp 56–7.

—'D O E Con-trick – An Adviser on Housing Management', *Municipal Engineering*, Vol 152, No 45, November 1975, p 2113.

FRANCESCATO, G et al, 'Residents' satisfaction with low and high rise housing', *Journal of Architectural Research*, Vol 4, No 3, December 1975, pp 4–9.

FRANKENBERG, R, *Village on the Border*, London, 1957.

FYVEL, T R, *The Insecure Offenders: Rebellious Youth in the Welfare State*, London, 1961.

GAULDIE, E, *Cruel Habitations*, London, 1974.

GILMORE, A, 'Oslo's Tenant Co-operatives – the lessons', *Housing Review*, Vol 23, No 3, May–June 1974, pp 66–9.

GILMORE, A and MUSGRAVE, S, 'Alternative Patterns of Housing Tenure within the Public Sector', unpublished paper, September 1974.

GOETSCHIUS, G W, *Working with Community Groups*, London, 1969.

GOLDSTEIN, B, 'Participation workshops', *AD*, Vol XLIX, 4/1974, pp 207–212.

GOLDTHORPE, J H and LOCKWOOD, D, 'Affluence and the British Class Structure', *Sociological Review*, Vol II, No 2, NS 1963, pp 133–63.

GOODCHILD, B, 'Class Differences in Environmental Perception: An exploratory study', *Urban Studies*, Vol 11, No 2, June 1974, pp 157–69.

GOODEY, B et al, *City Scene: an exploration into the Image of Central Birmingham as seen by Area Residents*, Univ of Birmingham, Centre for Urban and Regional Studies, Research Memorandum No 10, October 1971.

GOULDNER, A W (ed), *Studies in Leadership*, New York, 1950.

HABRAKEN, N J, *Supports, an alternative to mass housing*, London, 1972.

HALL, E T, *The Hidden Dimension*, New York, 1966.

HALOE, M, ISSACHAROFF, R, and MINNS, R, *The Organization of Housing*, London, 1974.

HAMPTON, W, *Democracy and Community*, Oxford University Press, 1970.

—'Little Men in Big Societies', *Journal of the Town Planning Institute*, Vol 57, No 4, April 1971, pp 168–70.

HANDS, J, *Housing Co-operatives*, London, 1975.

HARDMAN, C, 'Fact and Fantasy in the Playground', *New Society*, Vol 29, No 625, 26 September 1974, pp 801–03.

HARRINGTON, M, 'Co-operation and Collusion in a Group of Young Housewives', *Sociological Review*, Vol 12, No 3, November 1964, pp 255–82.

HARRINGTON, R, 'Inflation and the Inequities of Housing Finance', *Riba J*, Vol 80, No 10, October 1973, pp 494–97.

HARRIS, P, 'Community Work and Local Government', *The Planner*, No 8, Vol 59, September-October 1973, pp 357–60.

HARRISON, P, 'The Young Criminals', *New Society*, Vol 32, No 655, 24 April 1975, pp 197–9.

—'The Gambling Class', *New Society*, Vol 31, No 650, 20 March 1975, pp 720–2.

HAWKES, D, 'Are Floors and Ceilings Really Necessary', *Riba J*, Vol 80, No 10, October 1973, pp 498–502.

HESPE, G and WALL, T, 'The Demand for Participation among Employees', *Human Relations*, Vol 29, No 5, 1976, pp 411–28.

HILL, D M, 'Democracy in Local Government; A Study in Participation', Thesis submitted for the degree of PhD, U of Leeds, June 1966.

HOINVILLE, G, 'Evaluating Community Preferences', *Journal of the Market Research Society*, 15/1, 1973, pp 1–23.

HOLMAN, R, 'Why Community Action', *Municipal and Public Services Journal*, 5 April 1974, pp 397–99.

HOLMEN, L and BARKER, E, 'An Experiment with Tenant Involvement in the Planning and Design of Public Housing', In Living Places 1975/76.

HOWES, J, 'Co-operative Tenancies Pay Dividends', *Local Government Chronicle*, 18 July 1975, p 687.

JAMESON, C, 'Architects' error', *New Society*, Vol 32, No 657, 8 May 1975, pp 351–3.

JEPHCOTT, P, *Homes in High Flats*, London, 1971.

JOHNSON, M, 'Old Age and the Gift Relationship', *New Society*, Vol 31, No 649, 13 March 1975, pp 639–41.

JURALEWICZ, R S, 'An Experiment of Participation in a Latin American Factory', *Human Relations*, Vol 27, No 7, September 1974, pp 627–37.

KARPF, A, 'Tenants Own Up', *New Statesmen*, Vol 91, No 2338, 9 January 1976, pp 31–2.

KERR, M, *The People of Ship Street*, London, 1958.

KESSLER, N, et al, 'Wohnungen fur Alleinstehende', *Bauwalt*, 18 October 1971, pp 1682–6.

KLOOS, P, 'Role Conflicts in Social Fieldwork', *Current Anthropology*, Vol 10, No 5, December 1969, pp 509–12.

KNIGHT, L, 'A Tenants' Co-operative', *New Society,* Vol 29, No 619, 15 August 1974, p 420.

KONYA, A and HENK, K A, 'Danish Community Housing' *AJ,* Vol 161, No 14, 2 April 1975, pp 717–32.

KUPER, L (ed), *Living in Towns,* London, 1953.

LAMBETH INNER AREA STUDY, Local Housing management, report to the working group and steering committee, March 1976.

LEACH, E, 'Social Anthropology in search of system', *New Society,* Vol 28, No 606, 16 May 1974, pp 371–3.

LEE, T, 'Psychology and Architectural Determinism', *The Architects Journal,* Vol 154, No 31, 4 August 1971, pp 253–62; Vol 154, No 35, 1 September 1971, pp 475–83; Vol 154, No 38, 22 September 1971, pp 651–59.

—'Psychology and living Space', in Downs, R M and Stea, D, *Image and Environment,* Chicago, 1973.

LEES, R and SMITH, G, *Action-Research in Community Development,* London, 1975.

LEWIS, O, 'An Anthropological Approach to Family Studies', *American Journal of Sociology,* Vol 55, No 5, pp 468–75.

LISCHERON, J and WALL, T D, Attitudes Towards Participation among Local Authority Employees, *Human Relations,* Vol 28, No 6, pp 499–517.

—'Worker Participation Works', *Municipal and Public Services Journal,* 10 May 1974, pp 563–5.

LOIZOS, P, *The Greek Gift: Politics in a Cypriot Village,* London, 1975.

LYNCH, K and BANERJEE, T, 'Growing up in cities', *New Society,* Vol 37, No 722, 5 August 1976, pp 281–4.

MACEWEN, M, 'Our National Housing Crisis', and 'Housing and Politics – time to liberate the public sector', *Riba J,* February 1975, pp 14–21.

McGRATH, M P, 'Feedback', *AD,* Vol XLV, 2/75, pp 69–70.

McKEAN, C, SPRING M and PRICE, C, 'Planning and Transportation–Who are the Vandals?' *AD,* Vol XLIX, 4/1974, pp 249–54.

McMAHON, J T, 'Participative and Power Equalised Organizational Systems', *Human Relations,* Vol 29, No 3, 1976, pp 203–214.

MACEY, J P and BAKER, C V, *Housing Management,* London, 2nd ed, 1973.

MALPASS, P, 'Professionalism and the role of architects in local authority housing', *Riba J,* June 1975, pp 6–29.

MAMMEN, H, 'The Decline of Self Determination in Housing', *The Planner,* No 6, Vol 61, June 1975, pp 222–4.

MARRETT, C B et al, 'Communication and Satisfaction in Organizations', *Human Relations,* Vol 28, No 7, pp 611–26.

MARRIS, P, 'Planning for People: The docklands Example', *New Society,* Vol 31, No 646, 20 February 1975, pp 447–49.
Loss and Change, London 1974.

MARRIS, P and REIN, M, *Dilemmas of Social Reform,* London, 2nd ed 1972.

MARSHALL, T F, 'Vandalism The Seeds of Destruction: Research in the Home Office', *New Society*, Vol 36, No 715, 17 June 1976, pp 625–7.

MENZIES, W S, 'The Space Between', *AD*, Vol XLV, 1/1975, pp 26–30.

MILIEU W B, 'Lower Class Culture as a Generating Mileu of Gang Delinquency', *Journal of Social Issues*, Vol 14 part 3, 1958, pp 5–19.

—'The Corner Gang Boys Get Married', *Transaction*, November 1963, pp 10–12.

MITCHELL, G D et al, *Neighbourhood and Community*, University Press, Liverpool, 1954.

MITCHELL, J C (ed), *Social Networks in Urban Situations*, Univ of Manchester Press, 1969.

MONTGOMERY, R, 'Comment on "Fear and the House-as-Haven in the Lower Class"', *Journal of the American Institute of Planners*, Vol 32, No 1, January 1966, pp 31–7.

MOORE, R, 'Patterns of Activity in Time and Space: The Ecology of a Neighbourhood Playground', in D Canter and T Lee (eds), *Psychology and the Built Environment*, Architectural Press, 1974.

MORRIS, B, 'Deck Access . . .', *New Society*, Vol 32, No 661, 5 June 1975, p 589.

MORRIS, R N and MOGEY, J, *The Sociology of Housing; Studies at Berinsfield*, London, 1965.

MORTON, J, 'Society at Work: In Defence of ATAAC', *New Society*, Vol 17, No 441, 11 March 1971, pp 396–7.

—'Beyond Housing', *New Society*, Vol 30, No 638, 26 December 1974, p 831.

—'Tenants into Owners', *New Society*, Vol 33, No 670, 7 August 1975, pp 295–6.

NATIONAL ASSOCIATION FOR THE CARE AND REHABILITATION OF OFFENDERS, *Housing Management and the Prevention of Crime*, London, 1975.

NAPPER, J, 'The Long Weekend,' *Riba J*, 11/12 November–December 1975, pp 26–32.

NATIONAL COMMUNITY DEVELOPMENT PROJECT, *Inter Project Report*, 1973, London, 1974.

NATIONAL COUNCIL OF WOMEN, 'Guidelines for Happier Living in High Blocks', unpublished paper, np, October 1969.

NEWMAN O, *Defensible Space*, London, 1972.

OLIVEGREN, J, 'Better Sociopsychological climates for housing estates', *Ekistics*, Vol 41, No 245, April 1976, pp 216–23.

PAHL, R E (ed), *Readings in Urban Sociology*, Pergamon Press, 1968.

PARKER, H J, 'The Joys of Joy Riding', *New Society*, 3 January 1974.

—*View from the Boys*, Sociology of Downtown Adolescence, "People, Plans and Problems" 6/74.

PARKER, S R, 'Professional Life and Leisure', *New Society*, Vol 30, No 627, 10 October 1974, pp 77–8.

PARKINSON, G N, *Parkinson's Law*, London, 1958.

PAWLEY, M, *Architecture Versus Housing*, Praeger, New York, 1971.

PITTMAN, S, 'Vandalism under Control', *Municipal and Public Services Journal*, 10 September 1971, pp 1244–8.

PRENDERGAST, M, 'Scandinavian Report: A study of day care and leisure time facilities for young children in Denmark, Norway, Sweden and Finland with reference to their possible application by the Save the Children Fund in the U.K.', nd, np.

PRINGLE, M K, *The Roots of Violence and Vandalism*, NCB, 1973.

QUANTRIL, M, 'I like it here', *Riba J*, February 1975, pp 22–35.

RAINWATER, L, 'Fear and the House-as-Haven in the Lower Class', *Journal of the American Institute of Planners*, Vol 32, No 1, January 1966, pp 23–31.

—*Behind Ghetto Walls; Black Families in a Federal Slum*, Chicago, 1970.

RANDALL, B, 'Doubts thrown on value of tenant participation', *Municipal Engineering*, 30 April 1976, pp 669–70.

RAPOPORT, A, *House Form and Culture*, Prentice Hall, 1969.

RAVETZ, A, 'The History of A Housing Estate', *New Society*, 27 May 1971, pp 907–10.

—'What is Vandalism', *Riba J*, December 1973, pp 620–28.

—*Model Estate*, London, 1974.

—'Housing for the Poor', *New Society*, Vol 32, No 653, 10 April 1975, pp 71–3.

—'Housing at Byker, Newcastle-upon-Tyne' *AJ*, 14 April 1976, pp 731–42.

RAY, J J, 'Do Authoritarians Hold Authoritarian Attitudes?' *Human Relations*, Vol 29, No 4, 1976, pp 307–325.

REDCLIFFE–MAUD, *Royal Commission on Local Government in England*, Vol III, Research Appendices, HMSO, London, 1969.

REDPATH, R, 'The Hard Case for Community', *New Society*, Vol 30, No 634, 28 November 1974, pp 541–2.

REDPATH, R U and CHILVERS, D J, 'Swinbrook: a community study applied' *Greater London Intelligence Quarterly*, No 26, March 1974, pp 5–17.

RESEARCH SERVICES LTD, 'Living on Wates Estates; An Attitude Study', Report J4818, December 1965.

REYNOLDS, I et al, 'The Quality of Local Authority Housing Schemes', *AJ*, Vol 159, No 9, 27 February 1974, pp 451–60.

RICHARDSON, A, 'The Participation of Council Tenants in Housing Management, – Some Recent Developments in London Boroughs', unpublished paper, London School of Economics, July 1972.

RICHARDSON, A and WILES, A, 'Tenant Participation in Council Housing in the London Borough of Hammersmith', October 1975.

RICHARDSON, A and KENDALL, B, 'The Progress of Participation', *Housing Monthly*, Vol 11, No 9, September 1975, pp 20–24.

RICHMAN, N, 'The Effects of Housing on Pre-School Children and their Mothers'. *Developmental Medicine and Child Neurology*, Vol 16, No 1, February 1974, pp 53–8.

ROCHE, F L, 'A Place to Live', *Riba J*, Vol 82, No 3, March 1975, pp 18–22.

ROGALY, J, 'Putting Pride Back into City Living', *Financial Times,* 10 April 1974.

ROSE, A, 'Voluntary Associations under Conditions of Competition and Conflict', *Social Forces,* XXXIV, 1955, pp 159–63.

ROSENTHAL, S J, 'Turf Reclamation, An Approach to Neighbourhood Security', *Ekistics,* Vol 39, No 231, February 1975, pp 89–90.

ROWNTREE, D, 'Byker', *AD,* No 6, 1975.

SAVILL, D, 'Tenants' Participation in Management', *Housing Review,* January–February 1972, pp 12–16.

SCHUTTER, B L, 'It Works', *Public Management,* Vol 57, No 12, December 1975, pp 13–15.

SEGAL, W, 'Home Sweet Home? 85 years of LCC/GLC housing', *Riba J,* Vol 80, No 10, October 1973, pp 477–80.

SHEARER, A, 'An Ark for Survival', *New Society,* Vol 31, No 649, 13 March 1975, pp 650–1.

SIMKINS, A, 'Spreading the Information', *Municipal and Public Services Journal,* 16 August 1974, p 993.

SIMMIE, J M, 'Public Participation; a case study from Oxfordshire', *Journal of the Town Planning Institute,* Vol 57, No 4, April 1971, pp 161–2.

SMITHSON, A, 'The Violent Consumer or Waiting for the Goodies'. *AD,* Vol XLIV, 5, 1974, pp 274–8.

SUMMER, R, *Personal Space,* New Jersey, 1969.

SPENCER, J et al, *Stress and Release in an Urban Estate,* London, 1964.

SPITTLES, B, 'Black is English', *New Society,* Vol 30, No 627, 10 October 1974, p 93.

STACEY, M et al, *Power Persistence and Change,* London, 1975.

STANION, R O, 'Expanding to meet demand', *Municipal and Public Services Journal,* 10 September 1971, pp 1233–7.

STEVENSON, A et al, *High living; a study of family life in flats,* Melbourne University Press, 1967.

STRINGER, P and TAYLOR, M, 'Attitudes and Information in Public Participation. A case study', CES Research Paper, April 1974.

STYLES, B J, 'Public participation – a reconsideration', *Journal of the Town Planning Institute,* Vol 57, No 4, April 1971, pp 163–7.

TAYLOR, W J and WATLING T F, *Successful Project Management,* Business Books, London, 1970.

THURLEY, K and RICHARDSON, A, 'Organizational Problems in Housing Maintenance', *Housing Review,* Vol 21, No 3, May–June 1972, pp 81–4.

TOWERS, G, 'Swinbrook: Testbed for Participation', *AJ,* Vol 161, No 11, 12 March 1975, pp 547–50.

TRANTER, R A F, 'People: Partners in Problem Solving', *Public Management,* Vol 57, No 12, December 1975, pp 10–12.

TURNER, J B (ed), *Neighbourhood Organization for Community Action,* New York, 1968.

TURNER, J F C, 'Housing by People—from the bottom up or from the top down?' *AD,* Vol XLV, September 1975, pp 527–33.

TURNER, J F C and FICHTER, R, *Freedom to Build,* New York, 1972.

VICKERY, R L, *Anthrophysical Form: Two Families and Their Neighbourhood Environments,* University Press of Virginia, 1972.

VINCENT, J, 'A flat is not enough', *New Society,* Vol 27, No 596, 7 March 1974, pp 580–1.

WALKER, S and RIGBY, A S, 'Public Participation in the Rhondda Valleys', *Journal of the Town Planning Institute,* Vol 57, No 4, April 1971, pp 157–60.

WALKER, I J, 'Housing Management: Old Concepts Revised', *Housing Monthly,* July 1975, pp 20–21.

WALLIS, H F, 'Towards Tenant Control', *Municipal and Public Services Journal,* Vol 82, No 13, 29 March 1974, p 362.

—'Running estates with the aid of tenants', *Local Government Chronicle,* 9 February 1973, pp 157–158.

WARD, C (ed), *Vandalism,* London, 1973.

—'Let Tenants Take Over', *Riba J,* 6, 1974, p 3.

—'First Tenant Co-operative Housing', *AJ,* Vol 160, No 49, 4 December 1974, pp 1312–3.

—*Tenants Take Over,* Architectural Press, 1974.

—'It won't work without dweller control', *Town and Country Planning,* June 1974, pp 300–301.

WASHINGTON DEVELOPMENT CORPORATION, 'Village hall provision, a study of Blackfell, 1972', unpublished paper, Social Development Office, Washington, 1972.

WASHNIS, G T, 'Community Involvement . . .', *Public Management,* Vol 57, No 12, December 1975, pp 2–6.

WEIGHTMAN, G, 'Ronan Point Observed', *New Society,* Vol 29, No 614, 11 July 1974, pp 69–70.

—'Behind with the rent', *New Society,* Vol 32, No 654, 17 April 1975, pp 139–40.

—'Council Homes', *New Society,* Vol 32, No 664, 26 June 1975, p 779.

WEST, D J, *Present Conduct and Future Delinquency,* London, 1969

WILKINSON, R K and Sigsworth, E, 'Attitudes to the Housing Environment; An Analysis on Private and local authority households in Batley, Leeds and York' Urban Studies, June 1972.

WILLIS, R, 'Is the Anthropologist Human?' *New Society,* Vol 31, No 651, 27 March 1975, pp 778–9.

WILLMOTT, P, *The Evolution of a Community,* London, 1963.

—*Adolescent Boys of East London,* London, 1966.

WILSON, H and WOMERSLEY, L, Inner Areas Study: Liverpool Housing Management', report, February, 1975.

WILSON, P J, 'Filcher of good names: an enquiry into anthropology and gossip', *Man,* Vol 9, No 1, March 1974, pp 93–102.

WILSON, R, *Difficult Housing Estates,* Tavistock Pamphlet No 5, London, 1963.

WILSON, S and STURMAN, A, 'Vandalism research aimed at specific remedies', *Municipal Engineering,* Vol 153, No 19, 7 May 1976, p 705, 709, 713.

WOOLLEY T, 'Housing' *AD,* Vol XLV, October 1975, pp 636–7.

'Tenant Control in Housing', *Riba J,* January 1974, pp 5–8.

WYATT, J F, 'Residential Stability in an Inner Urban Housing Block; a restudy after 18 years', *Sociological Review,* Vol 24, No 3, NS, August 1976, pp 559–77.

YATES, D, 'Landlord and Tenant – Evicting Council House Tenants?', *New Law Journal,* Vol 125, No 5715, September 4 1975, pp 873–6.

YORK, Y, 'Voluntary Associations and their Leaders in a "Difficult Housing Estate,"' Thesis for the Degree of MA in Social Work, Univ of Leicester, June 1972.

YOUNG, M and WILLMOTT, P, *The Symmetrical Family,* London, 1973.

—*Family and Kinship in East London,* London, 1957.

YOUNG, R, *The Politics of Change in Local Government,* LGRU, Occasional Paper No 6, December 1974.

Index

Index

Administration
North Board, work of, 310–311
Adult
households with all adult residents,
296
Adventure playground
provision, 82
Age
distribution, 35
structure of households, 282
Architects
Directorate of Housing attitude
towards, 140
Architecture
development, 14 *et seq.*
Area housing boards
changes in, 256
election of tenant representatives,
202–203, 307–308
election procedures, 256
geographical boundaries, 200–201
matters considered, 202
meetings, 203–204
membership, 201–202
North *see* North Area Housing
Board
powers of expenditure, 201, 203
reconstitution, 200
rôles assigned to members, 204
South, 205–209
tenant participation, as means to
encourage, 266
tenant representation, 201, 202, 256
tenants' associations encouragement
for, 201
terms of reference, 200
Ash Court
building, 17
contact between neighbours, 57
Ash Court Road nursery
allocation of places, 104–105
boundaries, 104
location, 104, 105
parental involvement, 105
responsibility for, 89
Asians
prejudice against, 251–252

Assistance
difficulty, when in, 59
Association of London Housing
Estates
Parkview Tenants Association,
model constitution for, 163
relations with, 177
tenant participation, course on, 256
Balcony blocks
accommodation, distribution, 34
Bedsitter
accommodation, 17
distribution, 34
Bibliography, 319–330
Bingo
community hall, at, 243, 244
organization, 248
provision, 79
Block types
ranking by residents, 46, 47
situation, 46, 47
visual attractiveness, 46, 47
Borough
population breakdown, 36
Boys
schools. *see* Schools
Boys club
provision, 81
use, 84
Car parks
provision, 20
use, 25, 29
Caretakers
changes in work, 138
duties, 131
opinions of Parkview, 138–139
re-evaluation of rôle, 274–275
residents perceptions of, 86
rôle, 198
supervision, 131
Caretaking
criticism of standards, 46
Charitable trusts
housing development, 13
Children
elderly persons and, per unit, 295
environment, perception of, 6

Children (*contd.*)
floor levels, 37
households with, by floor level, 294
households with none under 13, 295
impressions of Parkview, 50–52
knowledge of neighbours, 58
leisure activities, 81–85
leisure activities away from estate, 84
leisure facilities, 3, 81–85
planned child bedspaces, 112
population density, 35–36
pre-school, reason for rehousing
households with, 301
schools influence on, 6
Chiropody clinic
responsibility for, 89
service provided by, 104
situation, 103
Chestnut Road
building, 17
Church Close
building, 18
luncheon club *see* Luncheon club
Cinemas
use, 78
Class
neighbours, used to define, 55
Club
boys', 81, 84
membership, 80
young people's social, 82
youth *see* Youth club
Coffee mornings
attendance, 101
barbecue organised after, 101
conversation topics, 102
establishment, 89, 100
mothers, for, 89, 100–103
social significance, 102–103
types of women attending, 101–102
Coloureds
black households, 282
black or mixed marriage households, 296
black population by block type, 297
community hall, non-use, 253
group categorization, as, 55–56

Coloureds (*contd.*)
  officers response to individual
      problem case, 184–186
  residence prior to rehousing, 297
Community Development Unit
  community worker, appointment, 236
Community education
  place in curriculum, 6
Community facilities
  management, 193
Community hall
  activities,
      externally sponsored, 246
      programme, 245
      resident organized, 246
  activities organised, 243–253
  attitudes towards, 80–81
  design, 191–192
  design faults, 250–251
  environment, effect on, 265–266
  facilities, reasons for non-use, 243
  faults, 255
  furnishing, 192–193
  hiring, 237
  impact on community, 254–255
  insurance, 195
  lease, 242
  lettings, 244
  level of involvement, 246
  maintenance, 237
  management, 166, 193–195
  older established residents, use by,
      248
  patrons as helpers, 249
  place of residence of patrons, 248
  plan, 244
  plans for, 191
  problems for users, 250
  provision, 22
  purpose of provision, 243
  race discrimination, 242, 251–252
  rates, 242
  reasons for non-use, 251–253
  regularity of attendance, 249
  rent, 193, 194–195, 237, 242
  sample residents survey, 291–293
  satisfaction with management, 250
  social expectations of users, 249
  status, 194
  tenant management, 3
  user group, 193–194
      assistance given to, 244
  users survey, 288–291
  vandalism, 250
  women using, 248
Community Housing Centre
  effect of opening, 154

Community service
  school curriculum, in, 74–75
Community services
  housing estate, 3
Community spirit
  inspired by Tenants Association, 92
Community worker
  appointment, 236
  brief, 236
  circular, 239–240
  disenchantment with, 238
  good neighbour service, 240
  grant from DOE, 239
  need for, 236
  Parkview project, 239–240, 254
  residents as, 239
  special project committee, 239
Conflict
  inter racial tension, 65–66
  residents, between, 64–65
Concert
  provision, 79
Constituents
  councillors relations with, 150–151
Corporal punishment
  school, at, 73, 74
Council *see* Local authority
Cycle track
  provision, 81
Decision making
  appearance of harmony, 181–182
  cross-cutting ties, existence of, 182
  informal, 146
  process, 147–150
  scapegoat mechanism, 182
  unofficial, 148
Direct Labour Building Organization
  bonus system, 139, 157
  Directorate of Housing, relations
      with, 99, 139–140
Discipline
  school, at, 73
Dwelling size
  distribution by block type, 34–35
Education
  discrepancy between aspiration and
      achievement, 72
  parents and children's experience, 71
      et seq.
  parents aspirations, 71 *et seq.*
  school age population, 72
Elections
  area housing boards 202–203
  North Area Housing Board, 204,
      205–209
  South Area Housing Board, 205–
      209

Employment
  estates interaction with surrounding
      area, 76–78
  experience of, 110
  hours of work, 76
  job dislikes, 76
  job likes, 76
  mobility, 76, 77
  Old Borough, 24
  parents' expectations for children,
      71 *et seq.*
  predominant types, 76
  stability, 76, 77
  status of adults, 77
  upward mobility, 77
  women, 76, 77
  workmates, relations with, 68
Entertainment
  Old Borough, 24
Environment
  child's perception of, 6
  housing estate, 3
Eshag
  complaints by residents, 95 *et seq.*
  conflicts aroused by, 189–191
  councillors, response to factions and
      feuds, 189–191
  development of tower block, 96
  establishment, 89
  local authority,
      relations with, 98 *et seq.*
  officers' response to factions and
      feuds 189–191
  Parkview Tenants Association and,
      98 *et seq.*, 166 *et seq.*, 189–191
  planning exercise, 96 *et seq.*
Estate politics
  community hall, involving, 236 *et
      seq.*
  community worker, involving, 236 *et
      seq.*
  factionalism, 10
  instability, 254
  Parkview Tenants Association,
      involving, 236 *et seq.*
Ethnic minorities
  figures for, 37, 38
  relatives living nearby, 53
Extended families
  figures for, 37
Facilities
  construction of, 20
Families
  effect of better amenities, 107
  extended networks, 54
  knowledge of neighbours, 58
  non nuclear, by block type, 300

Families (*contd.*)
  one parent, by block type, 300
  problem, officers, response to, 184–186
  slum clearance effects on, 54
  working class, visiting between neighbours, 114
Fencing
  illegal, 186–188
Flats
  design, 14
Floor level
  influence on residents, reactions, 44
Football
  support for, 85
Friends
  contacts on the estate, 67
  contacts outside the estate, 67–68
Gambling
  attitude to, 79
Garden flats
  accommodation, distribution, 34
  contact between neighbours, 66–67
  defects in, 178–179
  neighbourliness, 58
  requests for transfers, 41
  residents activities to achieve, 186–188
  residents reactions to, 43, 44
Girls
  schools, *See* Schools
Good neighbour service
  establishment, 240
Goodson Road
  building, 17
Greater London Council
  population breakdown, 36
Group categorization
  coloureds, 55
  Irish families, 55
  problem families, 55
  residents, by, 55 *et seq.*
Hawkers
  Old Borough, 24
High rise blocks
  advantages, 18
  development, 17
  doubts about, 18
  public reaction against, 28
History
  Old Borough, 23–24
  Parkview, 13 *et seq.*
Home
  school, link between, 6
Homelessness
  rehousing, as reason for, 39–40

Households
  adult, 36–37, 282, 296
  age structure, 282
  black, 282, 296
    population by block type, 297
    residence prior to rehousing, 297
  block type, by, 281
  children and elderly persons per unit, 295
  children, with, by floor level, 294
  elderly, with, by floor level, 294
  ethnic minorities, 37, 38
  floor level, by, 281
  length of residence in Old Borough, 298
  length of residence on Parkview, 282, 298
  mixed marriage, 296
  no children under 13, 295
  non-nuclear family, 37–38
    by block type, 300
  one parent families by block type, 300
  place of residence prior to rehousing, 282, 298
  pre-school children, with, reasons for rehousing, 301
  reasons for rehousing, 298
  researcher's informal links with, 8
  sample,
    characteristics, 281–282
    choice of, 7
    detailed interview sessions, 7
    interview schedules, 283–286
    population, 34
    quality of findings, 7
    selection, 281–282
    size, 35, 282, 302
    time lap between date of application and rehousing, 299–300
Housing
  Action Group, 95–100
  allocation process, 37
  applications for transfer by block, 297
  area housing boards, *see* Area housing boards
  Borough Housing Department prior to reorganisation, 124
  conditions of tenancy, 303–306
  co-operatives, 161
  council, history, 13 *et seq.*
  Eshag *see* Eshag
  government policies, 3
  history, 39
  length of residence in Old Borough, 298

Housing (*contd.*)
  length of residence on Parkview, 298
  length of stay, 41
  movement, 41
  notice to quit, 130
  occupiers under notice to quit, 308
  offer of accommodation, acceptance, 41
  'outsiders', 39
  personal preferences, 271–272
  previous accommodation, 40
  proceedings for possession, 130, 131
  rehousing *see* Rehousing
  Rents and Subsidies Act 1975, 309
  rents, notice of increase, 308
  repairs service, 272
  standards, 13
  stock, 121–122
  transfers, 41
    priority, 136, 157
  Utilisation Committee, 312
  waiting list, 40
Housing, Directorate of
  accusations of 'fiddling', 87
  architects, attitude towards, 140
  changes, 137–138, 152
  development and administration sections, 125
  Direct Labour Building Organization,
    relations with, 99, 139–140
  estates management, 125
  government cutbacks, effect of, 125
  Housing Aid staff training programme, 156
  housing management section,
    Parkview Tenants Association, relations with, 176–177
    relations with other sections, 176–177
  officers' opinions of Parkview, 138
  organization, 122–127
  Parkview management team, 128 *et seq.*
  Parkview Tenants Association, dealings with, 255
  policies, 122–127
  practice, 127 *et seq.*
  premises, 122
  prime objectives, 123
  problems facing 121
  procedures, 127 *et seq.*
  proposed structure, 124
  rent arrears cases, 130–131, 134–135
  reorganization,
    aims achieved, 126–127

Housing Directorate of (*contd.*)
 constraints on, 125–126
 prior to, 124
 resistance to, 126
 residents, contacts with, 86–87
 responsibility for specific localities, 123
 social services, attitude towards, 140–141
 staff, 123, 127 *et seq.*
 status, 122
 tenant participation, efforts to foster, 256
Housing estate
 community services, 3
 environment, 3
 high-density, 3
 scale, 18
Housing management
 area housing boards, 6
 changes in, 256–257
 concepts of, 152
 co-operatives, 161
 decentralization, 272–273
 Directorate of Housing *see* Housing, Directorate of
 estate residents, accessibility to, 276
 functions, 271–272
 local authority, 3
 local authority officers, by, 121–141
 organization, 272–274
 participation scheme, 162
 policy considerations, 271–277
 participators,
  as percentage of each social category, 222
  by social categories, 221
 practice, 127 *et seq.*
 procedures, 127 *et seq.*
 public relations, 272
 reforms in local authority, 268
 repairs service, 272
 rôles, 274–275
 staff, 123, 127 *et seq.*
  previous experience, 133, 134
  requirements, 275–276
  training, 132, 133, 275
 style of, 273–274
 surveyor's responsibilities, 131–132
 tenant oriented, 122
 tenant participation, 161–162, 200–224
 tenants, by, 3
 visits to tenants, 136–137
Housing Provision Review Committee
 meetings, 143
 membership, 144

Housing Provision Review Committee (*contd.*)
 standing orders, 143
 subjects covered by, 143
Housing Services Committee
 consideration of TA petition, 178–179
 delegated powers, 142
 meetings, 143
 membership, 144
 review committees, 143
 terms of reference, 142
Housing Utilisation Review Committee
 agendas, 149–150
 area boards, changes in, 256
 delegated powers, 143
 meetings, 143
 membership, 144
 standing orders, 143
 structure, 150
 subjects covered by, 142
Hyde Park estate
 phase/stage hypothesis, 58
Institute of Housing
 tenant participation, course on, 256
Institutions
 provision, 89–106
Interview schedules
 community hall,
  sample residents survey, 291–293
  users survey, 288–291
 councillors, 287–288
 officers, 286–287
 Parkview Tenants Association
  committee members, 288
 resident representatives on North Board, 288
 sample housholds, 283–286
Irish families
 group categorization, as, 55
Job careers
 parents' expectations for children, 71 *et seq.*
Keep fit
 attendance at, 248
 classes, 244
Kickabout area
 provision, 81
Kinship
 black residents, 53
 categories, 54
 extended family networks, 54
 metropolitan situation, in, 53
 networks as effect of slum clearance, 264
 Parkview estate, on, 53–55
 relatives living nearby, 53
 visiting, 54–55

Landscaped areas
 use, 80
Legal Advice Centre
 use by Parkview Tenants Association, 177
Leisure activities
 children, 81–85
 organized for children away from estate, 84
 provision for, 78–85
Leisure facilities
 adequacy, 82
 assessment of need, 269–270
 availability, 3
 children, 3, 81–85
 construction, 20
 limited use by young people, 83–85
 maintenance, 269–270
 parents, views on provision, 82
 planning, 269
 provision, 78–85
 staff requirements, 270
 supervision, 83
 teenagers, 3, 81–85
 young people's needs, 6
Library
 building, 17
 proposals for, 277
 provision, 80
 responsibility for, 89
 service, 104
Local Authority
 change, 152–154
 chief executive, power, 150
 committee chairmen, briefing, 145
 conservatism, 152–154
 councillors,
  concept of rôle, 152–153
  consituency work, 150–151
  election of, 142
  intervention in disputes, 198, 199
  interview schedules, 287–288
  North Area Housing Board, attitudes towards, 213–217
  officers, relations with, 144–147
  Parkview, contacts with, 153
  Parkview Tenants Association, relations with, 177–179
  personalisation of relations with, 88, 199
  policy maker, as, 145
  relations with tenants, 197, 198
  residents contacts with, 87–88
  response to conflict between groups, 189–191
  rôle, 149

Local authority (*contd.*)
  decision making,
    informal, 146
    process, 147–150
  elected member structure, 142–144
  Eshag, relations with, 98 *et seq.*
  gardens, attitude towards, 186–188
  landlord, as, 161, 267
  links with Parkview, improvement
    of, 225–226
  officers,
    abuse of power, 145
    councillors, relations with, 144–
     147
    duplication of functions, 196
    failure to carry out planned
     actions, 196
    housing management activities,
     121–141
    intervention in disputes, 198, 199
    interview schedules, 286–287
    North Area Housing Board,
     attitudes towards, 217–220
    relations with tenants, 197–198
    response to conflict between
     groups 189–191
    response to individual problem
     case, 184–186
    Parkview, contacts with, 153
    personalisation of relations with,
     88
    policy maker, as, 145
    residents contacts with, 86–87, 88
    visiting slips, 136, 157
  official letters to residents, 307–309
  organization, complexities of, 53
    attitude to, 153–154
    relations with, 195–199, 225–226
    care studies, 184–195
  Parkview Tenants Association,
    complaints from, 175
    links with residents through, 163
    model constitution for, 163
    relations with, 88
    support for, 179–180
  problem families and, 88
  reforms, 268
  residents relations with, 86–88
  state of parties, 142
  tenants relations with, 3, 161–162
Local political forums *see*
  Parkview Tenants Association
Luncheon club
  community hall, use of, 247
  complaints about premises, 247
  premises, 104
  responsibility for, 89

Luncheon club (*contd.*)
  service provided by, 103–104
  staff, 244
  use of, 70
Maintenance
  North Board, work of, 310 *et seq.*
  surveyor's responsibilities, 131–132
Maisonette
  Y block layout, 22
Market
  Old Borough, 24
Market Street
  building, 17
  shopping facilities, 69
Medical grounds
  rehousing, as reason for, 39
Mothers
  coffee mornings, 100–103
Neighbourhood
  estate's interaction with, 69–85
Neighbours
  assistance from, 59
  casual friendliness between, 264–
   265
  characteristics of relationships, 108
  class distinctions, 55
  conflict between, 64–65
  expected neighbourliness, 60
  experienced neighbourliness, 60
  group categorizations, 55–56
  inter racial tension, 65–66
  knowledge of, 57 *et seq.*
  patterns of interaction, 55 *et seq.*
  rating of qualities, 56–57
  social isolation of, 57
  status characteristics, 55
  Y block, 60–64
Noise
  conflict over, 65
North Board *see* North Area
  Housing Board
North Area Housing Board
  aim, 266
  attitudes towards,
    councillors, of, 213–217
    officers, of, 217–220
    residents, of, 220–224
    tenants' representatives, of, 211–
     213
  changes to, 214–215
  councillors' contacts through, 151
  councillors' rôles on, 215, 217
  dance sponsored by, 241
  deficiencies, 266
  elections, 204, 205–209
    procedure, 207–208
    voting figures, 208–209

North Area Housing Board (*contd.*)
  functions, 205–206, 214
  interviews with resident
    representatives, 288
    meetings
    agenda, 209
    attendance figures, 209, 210
    categories of items dealt with,
     209, 211
    frequency, 209
    researcher's attendance, 204
    rôles adopted by participants, 313
     et seq.
    way in which items are dealt with,
     313
    work of, 311 *et seq.*
  Parkview Tenants Association,
    relations with, 177
  participants' view point, 211
  pre-election publicity, 206–207
  researcher's coverage of, 10
  researcher's links with, 5–6
  work of, 310–317
Old Borough
  architects' aims, 23
  employment, 24
  entertainment, 24
  hawkers, 24
  history, 23–24
  length of residence in, 298
  market, 24
  neighbourliness between ex-
    residents, 56
  Parkview integration with, 109–110
  rehousing from, 39
  social interaction, 23–25
  social life, 23 *et seq.*
Old people
  population density, 37
One parent families
  figures for, 37
Opera
  provision, 79
Organizations
  membership, 80
  provision, 89–106
Overcrowding
  rehousing, as reason for, 39, 40
Parents
  educational aspirations, 71 *et seq.*
  involvement in schools, 75, 76
  working class, 72
Parks
  use, 78
Parkview estate
  architect's aims, 23
  artificiality of environment, 265

Parkview estate (*contd.*)
children's impressions, 50–52
decline in standards, 25
design, 14, 108–109
development, 14
freedom of action on, 265
housing management team, 128 *et seq.*
isometric drawings, 21
layout, 19
local authority,
    officers' opinions, 138
    relations with, 195–199, 225–226
    care studies, 184–195
    improvement, 225–226
management, 110–111
neighbourhood, 264
Old Borough, integration with, 109–110
organizations and institutions, 89–106
'outsiders', 25
planning, 276–277
plans, modification, 18
politics. *see* Estate politics
population breakdown, 36
ranking in relation to other estates, 48
resident perceptions, 41–52
responsibility for, 236 *et seq.*
sample households,
    characteristics, 281–282
    selection, 281–282
self-help groups, 268
social cohesion, lack of, 264
statistics, 294–302
surrounding area, contacts with, 69–85
variation of circumstances, 111
wear and tear, 25
Parkview Gazette
publication, 95
Parkview study
aims and methods, 3 *et seq.*
    notes, 26–27
approval of project, 5
arrangement of material, 11–12
choice of estate, 4
circular,
    introductory, 5
    purpose of study, on, 7
commencement, 4
council decisions on, 148
historical perspective, 13 *et seq.*
    notes, 27–29
reports on, 9
researcher,

Parkview study (*contd.*)
introductory visits, 5
residence on estate, 4–5
rôle, 9–11
sponsorship, 9
tension between researchers, 11
terms of brief, 3–4
Parkview Tenants Association
ability to meet residents' needs, 268–269
analysis, 179–183
Association of London Housing Estates, relations with, 177
attitude to assistance, 59–60
chairmanship, 164 *et seq.*
committee,
    annual elections, 164
    back bench members, 254
    compared with others, 181–182
    continuity of personnel, 254
    co-options, 164
    crisis in, 164 *et seq.*
    cross-cutting ties, 183
    decisions, implementation, 171–172
    difficulties of management, 242
    diversity of views, problems, 254
    factionalism in, 169–170
    housing management section, dealings with, 255
    imbalance of sexes, 171
    informal groups impingeing on, 168–169
    meetings, 164, 169
    membership, 164 *et seq.*, 180–181
    old/new categorization, 170
    one party, 171
    politics, 164–172
    scapegoats, 183
    work,
        categorization, 172–175
        complaints to council, 175
        effectiveness, 175
        involving outside agencies, 175
        status attached to, 197
community hall, management of, 166, 193
community spirit inspired by, 92
community worker and, 236 *et seq.*
complaints taken up by, 89, 90, 163, 164
constitution, 163 *et seq.*
councillors,
    contacts through, 151
    relations with, 177–179
criticism of, 91–92
difficulties of, 92

Parkview Tenants Association (*contd.*)
Eshag, relations with, 98 *et seq.*, 166 *et seq.*, 189–191
estate politics, 10
faction forming, 181, 240–242
'good citizenship' fostered by, 163, 164
'good fellowship' fostered by, 163
housing management section, relations with, 176–177
interviews with committee members, 288
Jubilee celebrations, 241
Legal Advice Centre, relations with, 177
local authority,
    as link with, 163
    relations with, 88
    support for, 179–180
membership, 89
North Board, relations with, 177
old/new categorization as cause of stress, 170
organizational structure, 90
outside agencies, relations with, 175, 176–179
pattern of relationships as factor, 167–168
petition organized by, 178–179
researcher's links with, 5
resources, 166
social activities, 89 *et seq.*
social organization and, 109
sponsorship, 89
sub-committees, establishment of, 164–165
suggested activities, 90
welfare function, 91
work of, 89–92
Youth group, links with, 94–95
Pensioners
activities of, 69–71
afternoon club, 243
children and, per unit, 295
community service in schools, 75
households with, by floor level, 294
North Board, work of, 310 *et seq.*
Play
place of, 82
Play areas
provision, 22, 80, 81
use, 269
Play group
community hall, use of 244
membership, 246
Playgrounds
adventure, 82

Playgrounds (*cont.*)
   provision, 81
   rubbish bins for, 176–177
   use, 84
Police
   residents unwillingness to be
     involved, 86
Policy
   decision making, *see* Decision
     making
Policy issues
   North Board, work of, 310 *et seq.*
Politics *see* Estate politics
Poor conditions
   rehousing, as reason for, 39, 40
Population
   breakdown, 36
   change in, 13
   overall density, 34
   planned density, 34
   sample households, 34
   structure, 35
   total, 34
   variations between blocks, 35
Pre-school Playgroups Association
   community hall use, 244
Pressure groups
   informal, 186–188
   residents as, 88
Problem families
   group categorization, as, 55
   local authority, relations with,
     88
Property developers
   housing, 13
Public areas
   criticism of, 45–46
Public houses
   use, 78
Race discrimination
   community hall, in use of, 242, 251–
     252
Race relations
   inter racial tension, 65–66
   social interaction, 65–66
Railway
   extension, 13
Rates
   community hall, 242
Redevelopment
   rehousing, as reason for, 39
Rehousing
   households with pre-school children,
     301
   place of residence prior to, 298
   reactions after, 42 *et seq.*
   reasons for, 39–40, 298

Rehousing (*cont.*)
   residence of black households prior
     to, 297
   time lag between date of application
     and, 299–300
Rents
   arrears cases, procedure for, 130–
     131, 134–135
   arrears control, 272
   collectors, adjustment to new work,
     134–135, 156
   community hall, 193, 194–195, 237,
     242
   Housing Rents and Subsidies Act
     1975, 309
   notice of increase, 308
Repairs
   North Board, work of, 310 *et seq.*
   service, 272
   surveyor's responsibilities, 131–132
Residents
   councillors, contacts with, 87–88
   floor level, reactions to, 44
   hostility towards officialdom, 196
   local authority, relations with, 86–
     88, 154
   North Area Housing Board,
     attitudes towards, 220–224
   officials, contacts with, 86–87, 88
   perceptions of Parkview, 41–52
   pressure group, as, 88
     reactions,
      after residence, 43
      before residence, 43
      on taking up residence, 41 *et seq.*
   relatives living nearby, 53
   rôle in dealings with officialdom, 196
   self-help, encouragement to, 277
   surrounding area, contacts with, 69–
     85
   unwillingness to become involved,
     86
Schools
   boys, 73–74
   boys' attitude to, 74
   child, influence on, 6
   community service in, 74–75
   corporal punishment, 73, 74
   council, 74
   discipline, 73
   estate's relations with, 71
   experience at, 110
   girls, 74
   home, link between, 6
   infant, 73
   junior, 73
   limitation of research study, 76

Schools (*cont.*)
   parental involvement, 75, 76
   primary, 73
   provision, 72
   school age population, 72
   secondary, 73
   single sex, 73
   truanting from, 74
Self-help groups
   encouragement of, 268
Sheltered housing unit
   allocations, 105–106
   boundaries, 106
   building, 106
   estate, relations with, 106
   exclusiveness of, 106
   responsibility for, 89, 105
   size, 105
Shopping
   facilities for, 69–71
   outside estate, 69
Slum clearance
   extended family networks, effect on,
     54
   kinship networks effected by, 264
   rehousing, as reason for, 39
   tenure of properties, 112
   values attached to, 107
Social activities
   Tenants Association, organized by,
     89 *et seq.*
Social interaction
   children, effect of, 58
   friends, 67–68
   groups involved with, 109
   influx of outsiders, 25
   kinship, 53–55
   neighbours, *see* Neighbours
   Old Borough, 23–25
   Parkview Tenants Association, 109
   patterns of, 8
   personalized locality, advantage of,
     69–71
   race as factor, 65–66
   workmates, 68
   Y block, 60–64
Social life
   effect of move to estate on, 59
Social services
   Directorate of Housing attitude
     towards, 140–141
   facilities, 103–104
Sound installation
   lack of, 45
South Area Housing Board
   elections, 205–209
   functions, 205–206

341

Squatters
  attack on, 241
Status characteristics
  neighbours, used to define, 55
Steel family
  radio aerial problems, 184–186
Surveyor
  maintenance responsibilites, 131–132
Swimming pool
  provision, 81
Teenagers
  leisure facilities, 3, 81–85
Tenancy
  conditions of, 303–306
    amendments to, 134
    enforcement, 134
Tenants
  community hall management, 3
  election to area housing boards, 200, 307–308
  housing management by, 3
  landlords, relations with, 267
  local authority, relations with, 3, 161–162
  North Area Housing Board
    representatives, 211–213
  participation,
    area housing boards as means of encourage, 266
    community organization and, 267
    course on, 256
    efforts to foster, 256
    housing management, in, 161–162, 200–224
    official policy and practice, 200–204
    order of priorities, 267
    rôles of participants, 267
    scheme, background to, 200–204
Tenants Associations
  active encouragement for, 201
Terrace
  house layout, 16
  street layout, 15
Theatre
  use, 78
Tower blocks
  accommodation, distribution, 34
  neighbourliness, 58
  proposed development, 96
  public areas, 6
  residents reactions to, 44
  residents transfers, 41
  socially disadvantaged, use for, 38
Truanting
  school, from, 74

Urban renewal
  process of, 107 et seq.
Vandalism
  boredom, as diversion from, 84
  community hall, 250
  concern for, 3
  levels, 112
  reduction in, 161
  responsibility for, 46
Vegetables
  growing of, 188
Visiting
  kinship ties, as expression of 54–55
  Y block, 62 et seq.
Visual
  contact, 45
  overlooking, 45
Voluntary associations
  membership of, 180
War
  damage to property, 14
Weightlifting
  classes, 244, 248
Welfare
  Tenants Association, as function of, 91
Women
  coffee mornings, 100–103
  employment, 76, 77
  feeling of inadequacy, 8
  loneliness, 8, 100–103
Work see Employment
Workmates
  contact with, 68
Y block
  blue block, layout of fifth floor balcony, 61
  casual contact, 114
  dwelling size, 34–35
  maisonette layout, 22
  neighbourliness, 60–64
  residents reactions to, 44
Young people
  leisure facilities, 6
Youth
  club see Youth club
  leisure facilities, limited use of, 83–85
Youth club
  activities, 94, 95
  committee, 93
  establishment, 89, 93
  financial resources, 94, 95
  functions, 92
  leaders, 244
  management, 247
  meeting place, 93–94

Youth club (cont.)
  membership, 246–247
  organization, 243
  social, 82
  Tenants Association, links with, 94–95